The publication of this
book was made possible
by the generosity of the
HENRY REGNERY
LEGACY FUND
at the
Intercollegiate
Studies Institute.

THE
MAN
WHO
INVENTED
CONSERVATISM

THE
MAN
WHO
INVENTED
CONSERVATISM

The Unlikely Life of Frank S. Meyer

DANIEL J. FLYNN

Encounter
BOOKS

INTERCOLLEGIATE
STUDIES INSTITUTE

New York ◆ London

First American edition published in 2025 by Encounter Books,
an activity of Encounter for Culture and Education, Inc.,
a nonprofit, tax exempt corporation.
Encounter Books website address: www.encounterbooks.com

Manufactured in the United States and printed on
acid-free paper. The paper used in this publication meets
the minimum requirements of ANSI/NISO Z39.48–1992 (R 1997)
(*Permanence of Paper*).

FIRST AMERICAN EDITION

LIBRARY OF CONGRESS CATALOGING-IN-
PUBLICATION DATA IS AVAILABLE

Information for this title can be found at the
Library of Congress website under the following
ISBN 978-1-64177-449-9 and LCCN 2025020661.

Table of Contents

To Karen Myers and David Zincavage,

two who saved history

◄ ◆ ►

Introduction

Two British Communists spoke over the telephone in
1949 about a former comrade turned enemy.

"Who is listening in?" Phillis asked upon hearing a click.

James Jeffreys, a party historian, reassured her that he had
merely switched from one extension to the other.

"Oh, I see," the caller responded. "I thought it was possibly
the other people."

"No, they probably are," Jeffreys conceded. "But you
wouldn't hear them that way."

Indeed, the authorities *had* tapped the phone and were
taking notes on the conversation. The reason for the call involved a figure revered among British Communists during
the early 1930s who generated headlines across the Atlantic
that distressed former comrades during the late 1940s.

"PHILLIS mentioned a man named FRANK," those notes
explain. She recalled, in retrospect, his "faults" and so "spoke
of not being surprised at news of him."[1]

The previous month Frank Meyer, the American credited
as the founder of the Communist student movement in the
United Kingdom, had emerged on the side of the "other people" as a surprise witness during the longest, most expensive
trial to date in United States history.[2]

I

The public fixated upon Joseph Stalin's American lackeys as they stood trial. The case, which came in the aftermath of the Soviet Union's subjugation of eleven European nations, and right before the fall of China to Communism and the Soviet Union's successful test of an atomic bomb, validated the public disquiet. Meyer, too, was disturbed.

He had come to believe that his former political faith posed an existential threat to civilization. After much anguish, he joined the fray. He told the truth under oath about comrades alongside whom he had served for more than a decade.

"JAMES said they would now have to re-write their history," the eavesdropper's notes conveyed. "He talked of the history written on the Students Movement which was going to be brought up to date."[3]

Thus did Frank Meyer vanish, like the fallen-from-grace commissars in that famous picture of Stalin, from the history of Communism. "Who controls the past," George Orwell wrote regarding lies becoming established history, "controls the future."[4] In a textbook case of this, the Communists redacted Frank Meyer as though he were an obscenity.

The document British intelligence marked "secret" chronicling Meyer's deletion languished unnoticed in papers-prison for decades. And for decades Meyer wondered whether the Communists who had erased his place in their history would move to erase him from existence.

◆ ◆ ◆

INCREDIBLY, the man who Johnny Appleseeded Communism in one country reprised the role for conservatism in another. Yes, a fervent Communist became the man who invented conservatism.

The New Deal's revolutionary transformation of American politics forced a shell-shocked right to define not merely what it opposed but what it believed. Domestically,

President Franklin Roosevelt advanced a managed economy that seemed a milder version of the statism fashionable
throughout much of Europe; in international affairs, his recognition of and then alliance with the Soviet Union befud-
dled observers until the revelation that there were Communist agents working inside the U.S. government suggested
to critics why the administration behaved as it did. Beleaguered conservatives searched feverishly for an answer to
the assault on their values.

Enter Frank Meyer, a commissar of sorts in the Communist
Party who brashly sought to identify principles and heresies
as a conservative. Previously marinating in a stew of systems,
the ex-Marxist initially tried to *invent* conservatism. The
would-be Marx of the right came to understand this effort as
an oxymoron. He instead *developed* a philosophy grounded
in the native soil.

An American conservatism, he argued, must conserve the
American tradition, which is the ordered freedom inherent
in the American Founding. Thus, he fused two disparate
camps—traditionalists and libertarians—into one. This fusionism was his Big Idea. As shown in these pages, it remarkably first came to him as a Stalinist in his attempt to reform
the Communist Party.

Ultimately, the Big Idea united the right. The competing
partisans, of freedom and individualism on the one hand
and of order and virtue on the other, saw in fusionism compelling reasons to reconcile their interests. Meyer shows up
everywhere on the right. Along with popularizer William
F. Buckley Jr., politician Barry Goldwater, fundraiser Marvin Liebman, and a few others, idea-man Meyer constructed
the skeletal structure of the burgeoning conservative movement that eventually elected one of the most consequential presidents of the twentieth century in Ronald Reagan,
transformed American politics, and altered the trajectory
of world history by bringing a peaceful triumph to end the
Cold War.

When discussion turns to Meyer's 1962 book *In Defense of Freedom*, one thinks of what Brian Eno famously said of the meagerly selling *Velvet Underground & Nico*: "I think everyone who bought one of those 30,000 copies started a band."[5] Meyer's book did not appear on the bestsellers list. Everyone who read one of the three thousand copies of the initial printing seemingly later ran for office or started a political club or founded a magazine.

One discovers the book's influence not among the conservatives who read it but among the ones who never did. The political philosophy articulated in its pages, the fusing of tradition and freedom, became the default position of the American right from Barry Goldwater to Ronald Reagan and beyond. Fusionism presented conservatism in a form well suited for capturing electoral majorities. Millions of Americans adopted it as their political creed knowing neither the name Frank Meyer nor the word fusionism. The few who knew both did not know that the light bulb for conservatism's guiding idea first illuminated above Meyer's head during his years in the Communist Party.

Meyer was present at the creation of the biggest little magazine of the twentieth century. In the pages of *National Review*, as in so many compartments of his complicated life, he played a schizophrenic role. On the one hand, he used his "Principles and Heresies" column to act as the ideologist of the postwar right. On the other hand, he created one of the greatest book sections of any magazine by attracting and cultivating talents, without much reference to politics or name recognition, to include Joan Didion, John Gregory Dunne, Garry Wills, Hugh Kenner, Arlene Croce, Guy Davenport, and Theodore Sturgeon. Repeatedly, Meyer showed himself a study in contradictions and an exploder of stereotypes.

The big changes he effectuated required small-scale organizing. He left his mark on the founding of Young Americans for Freedom, which supplied the shock troops of Goldwater's presidential run. He took an official role in the Conservative Party of New York that elevated William F. Buckley Jr. to megacelebrity in his Big Apple mayoral run and elected his brother James to the U.S. Senate. He helped launch the Philadelphia Society, in whose gatherings he conscripted Irving Kristol, Harry Jaffa, and others into arguments over the meaning of conservatism. He acted as a founding father of the American Conservative Union, which eventually sponsored a Conservative Political Action Conference strongly resembling the forum Meyer had first urged upon it during the 1960s.

Writers invoke such words as "forgotten" and "underappreciated," and offer such assessments as "his name is little remembered nowadays," on the rare mention of Frank Meyer.[6] William F. Buckley Jr., James Burnham, Willmoore Kendall, William Rusher, and L. Brent Bozell—his core colleagues during *National Review*'s golden era—all lent their lives to in-depth biographies. To the extent that Meyer receives attention in lengthier treatments, they fixate on the ideas he espoused during his last seventeen years, as though the subject were not so much a person as a set of beliefs with a name. How did the story of one of the conservative movement's founding fathers disappear?

✦ ✦ ✦

REMARKABLY, evidence of Meyer's second act became a disappearing act as well. The documented details of his adventures and accomplishments sat hidden from the world in a warehouse in Altoona, Pennsylvania, a place which held no connection to him. There the lost papers of the conservative movement collected dust and the attention of insects.

Far away in Stanford, California, the Hoover Institution Library & Archives detailed a Frank Meyer collection comprised in large part of issue files: folders kept by writers on subjects to give context should the writer revisit them in preparing a future article. To the biographer, the articles a writer clipped from the newspaper ranks at the bottom of the list in terms of value. It made no sense to anyone with archival experience that the boxes at Hoover, which stored material on the papal encyclical *Pacem in terris* but not his correspondence with his wife, parents, or *National Review* colleagues, represented the sum of his papers.

So began a multi-year search to locate the papers of Frank Meyer. It initially yielded scant results and inspired thoughts that of course Communists did not chronicle their activities and of course a guy known during his conservative phase for talking on the telephone just did not correspond much. Jameson Campaigne Jr., who wrote for Meyer in *NR* and edited him at Regnery, turned over correspondence mainly pertaining to *In Defense of Freedom*. My Freedom of Information Act request for Federal Bureau of Investigation files on Meyer seemed like a way to get around the absence of his papers. The response from the National Archives the year after the request indicated that it had just then processed requests made eight years earlier but because of COVID-19 the one on Meyer possibly faced greater delays.[7] In other words, check with us in a decade or so. The prospect of a worthy biography seemed doomed.

In October 2021, in one of several conversations with Meyer's eldest son John over a period of eighteen months, he casually noted that David Zincavage and his wife, Karen Myers, fellow members of Yale's Party of the Right, had purchased the Meyer home and all of its contents. When I phoned David, who had long since sold the farmhouse, he insisted that the couple had transferred Meyer's papers to the Hoover Institution. I insisted that they had inadvertently kept some boxes. David speculated that possibly Hoover librarians had failed to process all the donated papers. I insisted he and Karen had inadvertently kept some boxes. It continued in this manner. David later revealed the existence of a warehouse with as much nonchalance as John Meyer had revealed Karen and David's purchase of the house and everything in it.

Warehouse? What warehouse?

It contained a thousand or so of their boxes, according to David. Why bother? If it held any material on Meyer, then it consisted of duplicates of whatever Hoover possessed—and nobody could move all those boxes, open them, and put them back anyhow. I insisted I could. They granted me access and warmed to the idea that the warehouse sheltered something of value.

I traveled to Altoona, Pennsylvania. There, in the back of a dimly lit warehouse, sat 663 boxes on dozens of pallets in two long rows spanning nearly half the width of the cavernous building. A search of all of them over the course of three days revealed that fifteen contained Meyer's papers. Rather than junk the documents as most people would have done, David and Karen had saved history.

The uncovered material necessarily reorients what one thinks one knows about the formation of the conservative movement in America. The Frank Meyer papers include expected materials such as his birth certificate, passport, diplomas, dance cards, contracts, pictures of girlfriends, and tax returns. Tens of thousands of letters, starting prior to the First World War and ending during the Richard Nixon presidency, occupy most of the real estate within the collection. These include correspondence, much of it heretofore hidden, between Meyer and William F. Buckley Jr., L. Brent Bozell, Barry Goldwater, and others who created the conservative movement. Clashes more than confluence characterize many of these relationships. The most colorful and voluminous material from a single correspondent came from the green pen of the brilliant but combustible Willmoore Kendall. Here their friendship and estrangement play out in dramatic detail in a thousand letters.

So long as the material in that building remained buried under that mountain of boxes, Meyer's story would remain suppressed. Its liberation necessarily compelled the telling of the tale.

◆ ◆ ◆

THE opened boxes unleashed amazing stories from an amazing century. Connected to puzzle pieces found at Yale's Sterling Memorial Library, the Hoover Institution Library & Archives, the Wren Library at Trinity College, Cambridge, and dozens of other repositories, as well as close to one hundred interviews, the warehouse discovery rescued a mislaid, vibrant history destined for something greater than the landfill or incinerator.

Meyer operated in technicolor among the black-and-white militants of left and right. Here his penchant for contradiction—*interesting ideologue* would seem an oxymoron—shined. A nocturnal creature known for his ideas, he lived not in his mind but in the world and with *abbondanza*.

The Man Who Invented Conservatism's protagonist travels from communist to conservative, peace activist to soldier, Jew to Catholic, rhapsodist of Satan to cheerleader for Ronald Reagan, and free-love enthusiast to family man. Readers who take that journey of great change alongside Frank will also meet the prime minister's daughter clandestinely enjoying his romantic attentions, one of the twentieth century's most notorious dictators employing Meyer as a lieutenant, America's most acclaimed playwright, a late-night host turned Meyer pen pal, the pop star living next door, and so many other eclectic characters drawn into this magnetic man's orbit.

The man who invented conservatism conducted himself in ways, at least prior to the penitential second act of his story, offensive to those who embrace that label. He navigated a labyrinth of sex, secret agents, suicide, and Satan. His close encounters, in ways peripheral and profound, with the giants of his age in literature, music, science, art, and politics follow that pattern of intersecting with the main players when it mattered. He knew everybody. Everybody knew his charisma. Famous women wanted (and got) him, and famous men wanted to become his friend.

Suppressed by the Communist Party and abandoned in an old soda warehouse by conservatives, Frank Meyer's biography needs no more delay by way of a lengthy introduction.

◄ I ►

Newark

Frank Straus Meyer entered the world on May 9, 1909, in his parents' home on 28 Central Avenue in Newark.[1] His first name, not an abbreviation of Francis but just plain Frank, came from the maiden name of his paternal grandmother. The etymology of his last name, which means "enlightener" in Hebrew, foreshadowed his role as a teacher. His mother, Helene Straus Meyer, gifted her maiden name as his middle name.

The boy joined a family that helped him in becoming the man. At nine months old, the youngster elicited the first extant maternal comment that describes him as "certainly getting cuter" and "full of mischief."[2] The latter remained true. So did another of mother's observations to father: "Mrs. Hertz and Mrs. Foster came in for a few minutes to see the Baby— He certainly seems to enjoy admiration."[3] It amplified their doting that he arrived as their first and only as his mother approached age forty and his father entered fatherhood in his fifth decade. The prospect of leaving the world without leaving offspring seemed real. The son transformed that.

Meyer's German-Jewish maternal great-grandfather had graduated from Denmark street peddler to owner of a Newark store, which stood where the Prudential Building now does. His forebears enjoyed greater success in the dry-goods business. The Straus Department Store, from which the family derived much of its wealth, had long boomed before it busted.[4]

Fellow Newarkers described his mother as "a person held in high regard by both the Jewish and non-Jewish community" and "one of the most devoted workers in charitable and welfare enterprises in this city."[5] Her picture, indicating that her genes heavily dictated her son's look, appeared as one of the "outstanding men and women" of Newark in its Jewish "blue book" of 1926.[6] Prior to marrying, Helene had served as vice president of the Hebrew Ladies Orphan Aid Society, which her sister Amelia later led.[7] She volunteered for the Council of Jewish Women. A mélange of pressure group, well-to-do do-gooders, and progressive moralizers, it listed "Mrs. Jack F. Meyer" as one of four voting delegates from Newark to its 1923 convention in St. Louis, where the group petitioned Funk and Wagnalls to drop recognition of "the slang definition of the word 'Jew,'" promoted a World Court, and advocated for universal kindergarten.[8] Back home, while she was chapter president, the section became the first to hold Americanization classes for coreligionist newcomers and provided religious instruction for deaf-mutes.[9]

Jacob Meyer, known as Jack, joined his wife's charitable interests. They donated, for instance, $400 toward a new Beth Israel Hospital.[10] Frank later explained, "I was raised by an old-time strict-constructionist, tariff-for-revenue-only Democratic father."[11] Elsewhere he said that his father struck fellow businessmen as "radical."[12] His membership in the Progress Club, an exclusive collection of Jewish city fathers, indicated status.[13] He married money. He made money. This influenced his free-market outlook.

The birth certificate lists the father's occupation as "manufacturer."[14] In 1913, he founded, alongside two partners, the Peerless Company with $25,000 in authorized capital.[15] It sold raincoats to the army during the Great War, and then mass marketed its wares for $13.50 per men's long coat and $12 for a comparable women's garment. "With the signing of the armistice and termination of our Government contracts, we found ourselves stocked with a large supply of material and, having lost our civilian patronage, we decided to sell direct from the factory to you," a Peerless Company ad touting raincoats as a "sensible, inexpensive" Christmas gift explained in *Popular Science Monthly*.[16] Local directories until at least 1922 listed Meyer as company president.[17] The 1924 directory omits his affiliation.[18] Around this time, Frank's school forms list his father as "retired."[19]

Jack Meyer's son, obsessed with the glacial shifts of ideas rather than quick cash exchanges, paid little attention to money because of its omnipresence. Unearned wealth enabled the pursuit of ideas.

◆ ◆ ◆

THE TIMES did not immunize the nine-year-old from its triumphs and turmoil. "You probably got more military education drilling this summer than I have," a pen pal stationed in France writes days before the armistice. "All I ever learned was the wig-wag you taught me in the summer of '17, and I've forgotten that long ago." The soldier, a lawyer who performed legal work for the family, disabuses his admirer of notions of wartime heroism by confessing an innocence to the sound of gunshots and the sight of trenches. "Hope you've dodged the 'flu in great shape," the correspondent scrawls. "I think more people I know have died at home from that than over here from the war."[20]

The changing times and fortunes impacted their ancient faith. The family belonged to B'nai Jeshurun, a Reform congregation that had long spoken English in the temple and dispensed with mandatory head coverings therein.[21] The maternal line's great-grandfather, Abraham Newman, two years after his 1846 migration, was one of thirteen founders of the temple (later Polish Jews felt so grateful for his help that they named *their* temple partly in his honor).[22] B'nai Jeshurun attracted wealthier, native-born Jews of German extraction. Brick, big, and byzantine, the temple on High and Waverly Streets seating 1,600 in its cavernous auditorium opened around when Frank turned six. The congregation had hosted Woodrow Wilson in its previous building and broadcast its rabbi's sermon during radio's infancy.[23] Frank attended its Hebrew school, for whose newsletter he wrote on Sukkot, the Feast of the Tabernacles.

"For those who say that religion is dying out among our people," the fourteen-year-old concluded, "let the crowds in the temples on these holy days be a complete answer to their claims."[24] A few months later, he resigned his position as lieutenant of the safety patrol to devote himself more fully to the newspaper.[25] As he emerged from boyhood, he joined the temple's junior alumni association.[26]

He absorbed his parents' political allegiances as well as their religious beliefs. New Jersey's governor became president. The boy hung a Woodrow Wilson poster on his door.[27]

❖ ❖ ❖

DURING that age of "abnormalcy" between the sinking of the *Titanic* and the election of Warren Harding, the Meyers prospered. Their wealth allowed the family to move into the Hotel Riviera around its 1922 opening and the only son to matriculate at Newark Academy. Their twenties roared.

Wealthy Jews of German extraction occasionally sent their children to the predominantly Christian preparatory school whose atmosphere did not particularly incubate antisemitism.[28] The headmaster regarded Frank as a well-mannered, timid, trustworthy, feeble boy. "There used to be constant complaint that his classmates were annoying and treating him unfairly," Newark Academy's Wilson Farrand noted. "In many cases it turned out that he had started the affair and complained when the tables were turned on him. He also aroused feeling by the fact that he excelled the other boys in scholarship and was distinctly conscious of that fact." Farrand explained that Meyer's troubles dissipated and he gained popularity.[29] Six peers still voted him "class baby" in 1926. He placed a distant runner-up.[30]

He surged toward the head of his class early but settled as a B student. He ranked in the first quarter in a graduating class of forty-one. The headmaster described him as an "unusually good" student.[31] About a month after turning sixteen, he won admission to the Cum Laude Society and graduated on June 10, 1925.[32] Rejected by his choice of colleges ostensibly because of his youth, he continued for an additional year at Newark Academy.[33]

He spent the better part of a decade at the tony school. He managed the tennis team and played right guard on his class's intramural football team. His extracurricular focus veered toward intellectual matters.[34] He won the student oratory contest in his sophomore year, or, as the Anglophilic prep school called it, "third form." He won the fifth form essay contest. He sat on the board of the school publication *The Polymnian* for four years.[35] In an arrangement he experienced not for the last time, he served under an editor-in-chief in a troika of assistant editors.[36]

His face appears blurred in a photograph in which he looks among the shortest of the Class of 1926 despite graduating just after his sixteenth birthday the year prior. A clearer visual comes via the yearbook photo, in which the teenager still sports baby fat. The pudgy boy wears a mop of ink-black hair invading his forehead and parted starboard. He neither frowns nor smiles but sits expressionless save for his eyes, which stare in a penetrating manner as if to indicate the activity in the brain behind them.[37]

His peers repeatedly joked, in a student publication overflowing with bad humor, about his height.[38] His growth spurt arrived late.

Meyer's hometown grew with him. By his departure, the city boasted more than two thousand factories, a small subway, around one hundred theaters, and a population approaching half a million people. Marshes combined with pollution and poor sanitation to saturate the air with a smell distinctive to all but those marinating in it. Market and Broad, dubbed the world's busiest intersection, featured a famous bronze-and-stone traffic signal housing a policeman who manually changed the "stop" and "go" indicators.[39] In emulation of nearby New York's 92nd Street Y, Newark's Jews, in 1924, opened a Young Men's Hebrew Association.[40] An orchestra formed in 1922, and a symphony hall followed. Newark Museum, born the same year as Frank, soon played a pivotal role as a rite of passage from boy to man. Its cultural ambitions, like its young patron, ran ahead of its host city. Newark looked on its way even if its destination perpetually appeared further away.

The city's son looked on his way to becoming Frank Meyer. The class will bequeathed a Maxim silencer, and the class prophecy sarcastically predicted his success with a novel called *Silence*.[41] In the 1925 yearbook, two *Merchant of Venice* quotes mashed together captured him: "Young in limbs, in judgment old" and "I never knew so young a body with so old a head."[42] A similar cento from James Beattie attached to his 1926 yearbook read, "He thought as a sage, though he felt as a child."[43] Peers knew him here as protégés knew him later.

Meyer emerged from high school as a deracinated, agnostic Jew drifting from the parents to whom he provided meaning.[44] Many German Jews, to include perhaps Frank, felt greater kinship with German Christians than with their Eastern European coreligionists. He embodied the phenomenon he had abjured in his Hebrew school newsletter.

In his award-winning school essay "Our Debt to the Puritans," the sixteen-year-old credited his subject with gifting liberty, a religious spirit, and stick-to-itiveness to the nation. Then he cited blue laws, prohibition, Anthony Comstock, and Boston's Watch and Ward Society as part of the Puritan legacy, too. He wrote that "as always in a rich, luxurious civilization, men with leisure have begun to question everything from God to the proper manufacture of rubber, but especially God and the economic-political scheme of the world. Whether one agrees with these men or not, they should be allowed a free expression of their views; but in comes our Puritanical heritage, shocked, indignant, interfering with those researches by which progress can only come to a bewildered world. 'You are a Bolshevik,' it says; or 'You are an atheist,' and proceeds to clap you into prison, fine you, deport you, or ostracize you."[45] The essay faintly signaled its author's rebellion against his mother's Judaism and his father's capitalism.

Newark felt constraining, too. Frank sought escape. The family settled for periodic furloughs. The trio ventured forth to enjoy water decidedly cleaner than the Passaic and skies ornamented by trees instead of smokestacks.

◆ ◆ ◆

IN A STORE in rural Maine, Meyer met Eugene O'Neill Jr. through the introduction of a Horace Mann School classmate.[46] His name, changed after the initial desertion of the paterfamilias, reverted to Eugene O'Neill upon learning of his father's identity after his sudden fame as a playwright.[47] He became fast friends with Meyer at Belgrade Lakes, the inspiration for E. B. White's essay "Once More to the Lake" and Ernest Thompson's play *On Golden Pond*.[48] Gene, an honors student at the posh Bronx school, and his new friend bonded.

Amid fishing and swimming and canoeing, the teenagers discovered a decidedly adult admiration for Hector Charles Bywater's *Great Pacific War*, which inspired a Marco Polo–meets-*Risk* game in the lake that witnessed the players, including the playwright, become countries.[49] O'Neill Sr. lent Meyer books, including *Tristram Shandy*.[50]

"I found him very kind and gentle," Meyer said of his friend's funereal father. "What I especially liked was that he talked to you as an equal, none of that talking down because you were a kid. The three of us, including young Gene, discussed Bywater's prophecy of war between the United States and Japan in the 1930s, and we agreed that it was very likely to come true. Another time we talked about Freud. I remember in particular our discussing puns and slips of the tongue in connection with the unconscious."[51]

Discussing highbrow topics with one of America's leading men of letters opened up a new world. Already confident in his intelligence, the encounter validated him. The time with the son meant even more than brief back-and-forths with his father. Meyer encountered someone also captivated by books, debate, thinking, and so much so often shunned by youngsters. In an idyllic setting, he made a best friend.

Gene marinated in the happy days in ways more profound than those of his sudden confidante. While his friend established a longed-for connection to the outside world, he enjoyed an elusive closeness with an aloof father increasingly impressed with his intellect. And when senior daily replayed, in microcosm, the disappearing act from fifteen years earlier by writing in seclusion, junior could play with his younger half-siblings Shane and Oona as well as his new pal. A neglected son felt grateful rather than resentful for some family time at last. Eugene Sr. labored, at great difficulty given the thin walls of Loon Lodge, writing *Strange Interlude* during mornings. The play nevertheless awarded him his third Pulitzer when no other dramatist owned two. His second wife Agnes, two sons, toddler Oona, a stepdaughter, and interested visitors all laid claims on the withdrawn man's attention.

So did a woman whom senior came to see as his savior and junior came to see as his tormenter. The self-named, thrice-divorced succubus Carlotta Monterey parlayed a Miss California title into acting roles that owed to her beauty and not her stagecraft. She left behind the New York apartment bankrolled by the investor James Speyer to travel to Maine with a lesbian benefactor twice her age. There she started inserting herself, slowly but deliberately, into O'Neill's life. The failed actress saw in the celebrated playwright a patron who validated her. Her influence eventually would close off his contact from others in his inner circle. But in 1926 young Gene, delighted to finally spend quality time with his dad, knew her only as a strange woman who sometimes took rowboat rides with his father.[52]

✦ ✦ ✦

THE WORLD looked wider in the summer of 1926. On the college boards, which Newark Academy founded along with fourteen other institutions, Meyer scored above the 60 percent threshold, with 70s in English, 93s and an 85 in mathematics, 83s in physics and American history, an 80 and 87 in Latin, and a 73 and 64 in French.[53] The headmaster gushed, "With the stiff marking of the Board your record is excellent."[54]

Presumably a future in letters rather than the numbers that dominated his father's life awaited Frank. By his midteens, he wished to discard the tethers of family, religion, and values. Newark, suffering from an inferiority complex situated between New York and Philadelphia, held few charms, despite the striver city's aspirations, for the intellectually self-assured teen. He hoped to create himself anew.

"He probably became an atheist by the time he turned sixteen," his son John said. "He didn't have much Jewish identification."[55]

He soon discovered that others strongly identified him as a Jew.

◀ 2 ▶

Princeton

---

rinceton University rejected Frank Meyer in 1925. It
came as but the first rejection from the Ivy League
school.

The school's director of admission, Radcliffe Heermance,
cited the boy's age to Jack Meyer in justifying the exclusion.[1]
He offered another reason to Newark Academy's headmaster.

"Here is this boy Frank S. Meyer coming up again for admission," Heermance wrote Meyer's headmaster Wilson Farrand. "I frankly do not want to take him, but of course he has
very excellent grades on the Board examinations. Is there any
possibility of steering him to another college? There will be
plenty of fine clean cut Christian Americans who can make
up our next year's class, and taking the Meyer boy simply
means turning down some other chap to whom we could
probably give more and who would add more to our college
life. . . . We have some fine young Jews applying, and of course
we will take them, but it does not seem to me that Frank S.
Meyer measures up even to the best Hebrew type."[2]

Though Farrand appears to be very much his student's
booster, he had invoked Meyer's religion in describing a
fifteen- or sixteen-year-old as "an able little Hebrew of the better type" in the first sentence of his recommendation letter

to Heermance's committee. While volunteering that Meyer's "racial characteristics are unmistakable," the Princeton grad assured his audience that the youngster would "prove an inoffensive member of the college community."[3]

Heermance, who scrutinized the religious and ethnic backgrounds of applicants the way others in his spot might scrutinize grades and college boards, found Meyer anything but inoffensive. Meyer's intellect—and will—ultimately overpowered Heermance's bigotry, and he won admission upon a second try. He had set his heart on Princeton. As he stated in his application, he wished to attend a school not far from home and the Princeton men he knew impressed him. He hoped to possibly make a career of the law, meet new friends, and develop a "stronger body and a finer mind from Princeton."[4]

He found the school of his dreams to be a nightmare. The bigotry invisible in his prolonged admissions process materialized during his abbreviated attendance there. A student body handpicked by Heermance inevitably reflected its creator's biases.

◆ ◆ ◆

MEYER later reflected on the "essential Anglo-Saxonism of Princeton" in a manner almost suggestive of post-traumatic stress disorder.[5] The quintessential Princeton Man as the seventeen-year-old walked onto campus was James Burnham, who towered over Frank in social standing, academic standing, and, especially, standing standing. Decades later, when the two reunited at *National Review*, Meyer challenged his fellow Princetonian's place on the totem pole. Here, he could only look up. The senior golfed, drove about Princeton in his car, and graduated first in the Class of 1927.[6] If the short freshman with racoonish eyes appeared as the physical embodiment of all that Radcliffe Heermance did not want, Burnham looked the poster child for the "fine clean cut Christian Americans" he wished to populate campus. Not for the last time did Burnham possess what Meyer craved.

But Meyer rejected them, too. He rebelled against the clean-cut Christians by taking up the cause of an earlier rebel against their cause.

Professor Albert Elsasser called Frank's paper on *Paradise Lost* "an admirable essay, both in substance and style" and awarded him the highest grade possible. "What is this but an exposition of some of the noblest qualities known to man?" the freshman asked. "For this Satan is nothing more nor less than another of the company of men of heroic proportion and unhuman humanity whom the great poets have always created as a type of all their longings, ever since the first shepherd sang of Prometheus."[7] As a synopsis of *Paradise Lost*, it rings true. Yet the paper-writer's enthusiasm for the epic poem's main character went beyond textual summary.

Meyer, an aspiring poet himself, appears to have internalized Milton's casting of Satan in a heroic light. More so did he fetishize Lucifer's rebellion and alternative deities to the Judeo-Christian God. For another course, he wrote,

> God who bares himself to Hell,
> God of sensual, maddening joy,
> God of love, God of passion
> Great Dionysius—Hail, Hail, Hail.
> Thee we salute, thee we embrace forever through the ages,
> Whate'er thy name be, what thy fashion,
> For thee our love, for thee our lust.
> Pan or Beauty, Love or Satan, Lucifer hailed or radiant Lyaeus,
> To thee we bow, to thee we offer up our flesh.[8]

Frank did not merely disbelieve in God. He despised God.

In a poem scribbled in pencil exuding positive literary qualities if fueled by negative sentiments, he wrote:

> If there should be a god of prattling preachers, pale and
> thin, covering all beauty with their hideous filth, their

ugly words of right and wrong, of this thou shalt and
this thou shalt not;

If there should be a god of vulgar, flabby, fat good-
fellows scratching for gold with never a single thought
of where or why or how of all the world holds before
their fat pig-eyes. . . . If such a god should reign now or
ever, some day in wrath unthinkable, awful earth will
rise and tear him from his throne.[9]

An armchair psychologist might see Frank's embrace of the
Christian symbol of evil as a response to Christians rejecting
him. His poetry lashed out, perhaps subconsciously, against
those excluding him. Antisemitism to this degree represented a culture shock. He returned the disfavor.

Frank crafted an identity. It involved a divorce from the
ancient faith even as others married him to it. Next came separating himself from the man of his house and convincing a
woman to guide him to manhood.

◆ ◆ ◆

HIS PASSION for poetry mixed with a passion for women,
and violating social restrictions on sexual behavior played
into this rebellion. An admirer of Satan predictably succumbed to his temptations.

"What is this thing that is a woman's body!" he asked. "I
do not know it—I search for it everywhere." He divulged,
"I know hands, lips, hair, breasts, the deep mysterious cunt."
But most of what he believes he knows about women's bod-
ies, he confesses, arrives through dreams and masturbation.
"I have kissed breasts," he noted, "and lain thigh to thigh."[10]

His ardor focused on a sophisticated woman five years his
senior working under John Cotton Dana at the Newark Museum, which struck many visitors as too good for New Jersey's largest city. The museum attracted Frank's mother as a

benefactor and Frank as a visitor. Its star employee, Dorothy Canning Miller, attracted Frank.

Later famously the Museum of Modern Art's curator, Miller here inspired not paintings but poetry.

"You are coolness in the heat of city, / A fragile touch of Attic grace / Beside the synthesis that is our life," Meyer rhapsodized.[11] Elsewhere he wrote of her as "Beauty Incarnate."[12] In one poem, Meyer lamented the suicide of a rival suitor, presumably of Miller.[13] A mutual friend described a poem by the enraptured student about the older woman as "too many words for a much too delicate subject."[14]

The columns of photo-booth pictures retained by her not-so-secret admirer reveal a lissome woman sporting angular features, light eyes, hair pulled back to make it look like the cropped style popular among flappers, and a face that physiognomists would certainly find radiating intelligence. She occasionally smiles and occasionally shows teeth when she does. Rarer still come those moments when she looks at the camera. A lack of makeup, slightly messy hair, and drab dress suggest someone far more Greenwich Village than Hollywood. Her outward-arching eyebrows combined with a sharp visage provoke curiosity in the starer. She looks more interesting than beautiful, though she looks both.

Her culture, intelligence, and Nordic appearance made her the perfect woman for Heermance's Princeton Man—just not for this Princeton man.

When Carrington Cabell Tutwiler, scion of an aristocratic Virginia family that included the science fiction writer James Branch Cabell, asked Frank in February 1929, "Are you (I blush) still a virgin?," the answer likely came back in the affirmative. Within two months, though, Frank knew Miller in a carnal sense. "I don't think your making love to her has touched her initially," a mutual Newark friend wrote Frank. "She is certainly the same as ever." Though he had ventured through this passage rite, it undoubtedly struck him as bittersweet. He lusted for women. He loved this woman. In return, she enjoyed his company. The mutual friend described pursuing her as "futile," advice which seemed just that. The friend wrote the besotted nineteen-year-old, "I can't bear to have you living on illusions."[15]

Frank maintained a close, albeit asymmetrical, relationship with Miller. His love life indulged these illusions, and it seems Miller occasionally indulged them, too. His lust life, on the other hand, eventually dispensed with the romanticism she provoked.

♦ ♦ ♦

TUTWILER knew Frank as well as anyone at Princeton. Frank, peers, and posterity knew him as Tut. A letter Tut wrote that spelled out "Frank S. Meyer" and then its author's initials in each line's first letter began, "Frienzied youth, so mad beyond your years / Recall'st thou not the words of Jung and Freud? / Away with wretched Eros, much employed."

Poetry, a gateway for friendship, served as Meyer's primary avocation, and women served as his primary preoccupation. He scribbled verse in notebooks, on the backs of envelopes, on scraps of paper. Some satisfied course assignments.

"Cross-Section" wound up in the school's literary magazine. It began, "New York, Little Rock, Omaha, Chicago / Too busy, too busy / Sorry, can't help you / In a hurry / Time is money."[16]

Meyer increasingly railed against men like his father. The teenager resented the capitalism that paid his tuition. The alienation did not prevent freshman Frank from joining his father at Palmer Stadium to watch Princeton suffer its only loss of the football season against undefeated Navy.[17] And he kept a picture of his mother as a young woman during his travels.[18] But he left home when he left home.

Princeton never became home. His grades, solid at Newark Academy, appeared middling and worse in college. The *mens sana in corpore sano* zeitgeist put the undersized boy at a disadvantage in such courses as Artillery 101 and Physical Education. He struggled in Greek and French, scoring a 7 on Greek 101 and a 5 in the retry and a 4 and two 5s in French.[19] On the school's 1–7 grading scale, higher numbers meant lower grades.

Did they grade his work or his Jewishness? The question seems impossible to answer. That the director of admission took such an interest in his background makes it plausible that others might have as well.

Frank scored a single 1 in Latin 203 and decent grades in English and philosophy. But against peers—Burnham's transcript consists almost entirely of 1s—Frank did not measure up.[20] After three terms, the dean of students and Joseph Raycroft, a former football and basketball coach who inexplicably held great power over the academic future of students, forced his withdrawal.[21]

The dean characterized the separation as "requested to withdraw for medical reasons" rather than "under discipline" for academics. The possibility exists that grades, which appear mediocre rather than failing, came as a symptom of his "unhappy state of mind" causing his departure (and his Luciferian enthusiasms) rather than the cause themselves. "The event occurred when Mr. Meyer was laboring under unusually severe emotional strain," Dean Christian Gauss wrote, "and he has since undergone, successfully I understand, a course of treatment under Dr. Lambert of New York."[22]

Frank Meyer left no mark on Princeton. It left a mark on him.

◀ 3 ▶

England

Y ou come in from god blasted joint Joisy," Eugene
O'Neill Jr. wrote. "You must write me cause I don't
know what part of MY New York you pull into. You
write me or Damn you you won't go."[1]

While O'Neill visited Meyer prior to his dropping out, a
lemonade-from-lemons aspect of the withdrawal became apparent. The friends now more easily met to review one another's literary output, joke, and discuss romantic prospects.
O'Neill referred to his slightly older pal as "laudship" and
himself as "servant."[2]

For one Friday night gathering, they meet in Midtown at
the Hotel Pennsylvania, which opened less than a decade earlier as the world's largest auberge.[3] Presumably, the conclaves
involved violating the Eighteenth Amendment. Prohibition
vexed Frank, but he looked forward to New York's wet governor Al Smith's election to the presidency in a "landslide"
that fall. Whatever happens "they'll never enforce the law in
New York."[4]

Atop rebelling against the drys, he prioritized women. "I
am glad to hear that you are a slave to passion again, as it will
probably be productive of some good poetry," Tut writes in
March. "Poor Clarice! Or was it poor you? I give this poor

girl about a month—whatever happens don't forget that you are a PRINCETON MAN."[5]

He *was* a Princeton man.

"Total abstinence is merely one expression of an attitude toward life that is definitely disgusting, dangerous and indecent," he wrote. "For want of a better name this attitude can be called the Judaeo-Christian moral code." He blamed the denial of life's pleasures on the likes of the "leper-licking" St. Francis and such "sublimated nymphomaniacs" as St. Teresa.[6]

One earthly force stood athwart these villains of heaven yelling stop: the Soviet Union. Even the alphabet hints at the short distance between Satan and Stalin. The teenager drifting between these dark forces discounted stories of religious persecution in Russia even as he applauded them. Before his twentieth birthday, he denounced private property, religion, the Western refusal to disarm, and prevailing sexual mores. Yet, he believed in natural inequality and did not know whether Communism, which he regarded as treating religion with a correct hostility, would improve society more than other systems. As an ideologue and a student, he remained in flux.[7]

Enticed by his close friend Peter Nehemkis, and more so by his friend's girlfriend Natalie Brody (who briefly became Frank's love interest), he considered attending Alexander Meiklejohn's new University of Wisconsin Experimental College.[8] Downtrading amounted to the rational choice. It did not amount to the characteristic choice. Rather than matriculate at a less competitive institution, the college dropout elected to pursue his education at a more prestigious school.

◆ ◆ ◆

MEYER sailed for England in 1928 with a dream.

"Cambridge is much more beautiful than Oxford—I shouldn't regret coming here at all," he wrote his parents, adding, "But the chances are strongly against my getting in at all."[9] To bolster those chances, he traveled to Bacton on the North Sea to live at the Cliff Holm resort and study for the Caius College entrance examination under Major T. H. Russell.[10] There, the nineteen-year-old studied, shrimped with a befriended Indian national, and swam.[11] But in failing admittance, he departed for London near the end of September with nothing to show for Bacton save for a pleasant month on the ocean.[12] He received rejections from St. John's, St. Catherine's, and Emmanuel colleges as well, which ended the Cambridge dream.[13]

Another dream took its place.

Charles Morris, overseeing admissions at Oxford's Balliol College, suggested Meyer study under a well-known tutor to bolster his chances of admission.[14] He worked under Martin Gilkes in an old Birmingham vicarage. "I know nothing of Birmingham," he admitted, "except that people say it is the best of the provincial cities, even though it is a sort of Pittsburgh."[15] The industrial scenery and smells reminiscent of Newark offered something less than Bacton. The lack of distraction provided the silver lining on the smog cloud.

"I'm really at work at last," he reported. "I'm taking two courses at the University [of Birmingham], Greek & Latin— and I'm taking some private tutoring with Mr. Gilkes."[15] He found the Japanese boy and English girl studying alongside him uninteresting, which, like the industrial setting, nudged his nose further into books.[17] He fell in love with the Gilkes's library but later concluded that his hosts "bore[d]" him.[18] Inevitably, he conjured up a romance with an Oxford student he described as "frightfully brilliant" and "not one of these damned girls that let you know it." They walked fifteen miles together during the Christmas season, which served as a highlight for three months in Birmingham.[19]

In December, he prepared to take Responsions, the test to gain entry to Oxford, by studying Latin, French, math, and English.[20] For a test for Balliol administered in early 1925, he focused his Birmingham study on literature and philosophy, worried about whether his acumen in foreign languages met the English standard, and selected John Donne as a special author on whom to concentrate.[21] With study and tests behind him, a wonderful waiting began.

◆ ◆ ◆

THE AMERICAN journeyed from the provincial city to the capital in January. He wrote home expressing delight to see the *Winnie-the-Pooh* creator A. A. Milne's *Fourth Wall*, less because of the "clever" performance onstage than because of the royals in the seats. "King George is extremely handsome," he explained. "Queen Mary is rather dried up."[22] He told his parents of attending the ballet, participating in a regatta, joining a sports club, subscribing to *The New York Times* to stay abreast of the 1928 elections, visiting galleries, and traveling to Paris.[23]

Simultaneously, he described himself as "penniless" and a step away from "debtor's prison" lest he receive a letter of credit.[24] "I hate to talk about money again," one letter stated.[25] The subject's ubiquity in correspondence indicated otherwise. "Got father's letter. You misunderstand. I wasn't complaining," he defensively responded.[26]

If it struck him that his extravagances resulted in his recurring shortages, he expressed it in neither correspondence nor behavioral alteration. His allowance amounted to just over $45 a week.[27] This far exceeded the weekly take of the average United Kingdom worker. Their conditions he predictably found substandard. In taking this view, he shuffled further down the path he started with that award-winning anti-capitalist essay and trudged further still through his iconoclastic poetry.

"The unemployment is hideous. I've gotten into a lot of corners, and talked to all sorts of people," Meyer observed more than a year before the Great Depression washed up on

British shores. "If it wasn't England, there would have been a revolution years ago."[28]

If only they could receive allowances, too.

The nineteen-year-old felt no compulsion to sacrifice alongside them.

"If the King dies, I shall certainly go to France," he reacted to rumors of the sovereign's ill health. "All England goes into mourning for six weeks. All theatres, etc. are closed."[29]

King George V survived his health scare; the visitor traveled to Paris anyway.

✦ ✦ ✦

HE HAD come to England on a mission. He found himself no closer to achieving it than upon his arrival. The teenager with his parents' fortune to burn decided he needed a pick-me-up in the form of a trip to Paris. Perhaps French, which dragged his grades at Princeton, would come easier from such jaunts. And if it did not, women and booze surely would. He left England for France in April.

With rejection from Cambridge and uncertainty from Oxford, he enjoyed himself on what amounted to an extended holiday. The anxious applicant reasoned that "it's almost impossible for any American but a Rhodes scholar to get in to Oxford."[30] He tried, but five months after consulting with Morris as to the best route to gain admission, Meyer remained without a college. The silence sparked thoughts of applying to schools in France, Germany, or Italy.[31] For someone who graduated high school a month after turning sixteen, facing his twentieth birthday with neither degree nor even acceptance from a college was humbling.

Then, nine months after arriving in England, he learned his fate. He telegrammed home: "ADMITTED BALLIOL STOP THANKS PRESENT STOP SEND FARE PARIS STOP SIXTY-FIVE DOLLARS ABOUT RIGHT ALL LOVE."[32]

◄ 4 ►

Oxford

F rank Meyer parlayed a forced withdrawal from one of the best schools in the United States into admission at the most prestigious university in the world. When your great-grandfather founds the temple, you live in a fancy hotel, and your middle name appears on one of your city's main department stores, audacity comes naturally.

The social handicaps for a Jew at Princeton did not quite exist for Frank at Oxford. The extrovert merrily dived into social life.

He joined both the Labour *and* Conservative clubs as means of attending members-only events, became an Oxford Union lifetime member, and characteristically used his mouth rather than his body to help a Balliol boat to victory as coxswain in the Morrison Fours in November 1929.[1] He played lacrosse, tennis, and cricket.[2] "I've also played goal-keeper for my college second hockey team," he informed his mother. "It's a pretty good game here though in America it's only played by girls except on the ice of which there is of course none here."[3]

One Englishman signed the American's boat-club program "Abe Lincoln." Such clever doggerel as "Beer women, women beer / intercourse and plenty of cheer" and "Buggery, buggery fuck / The man ran up the clock" appeared.[4] A classmate summed him up: "Grand organiser, wizard, successful cox."[5] The famed medievalist R. W. Southern described Frank as "responsible" for his and Jack Dunman's "education" at Balliol.[6] Herbert Squire awarded him the epithet "The life and soul of the college."[7]

Venturing miles from Balliol to The Trout on the Thames with friends for "one of the best binges I've ever been on," he drank "large quantities of beer" to celebrate his birthday "in the traditional Oxford way for a 21ster."[8]

The hangover soon came.

◆ ◆ ◆

"IS YOUR FATHER BETTER?" Fred Bartlett asked.[9] Unwell for several years, the family breadwinner had declined precipitously in 1930. "I hope nothing serious is the matter," Frank responded from Paris to his mother. "I wish you had been able to wire me more of what was wrong—but I know you're awfully worried."[10] The wayward though not estranged son sailed home on the state-of-the-art, one-year-old SS Bremen.[11] Its speed likely enabled him to arrive with days to spare before Jack Meyer died of cancer short of his sixty-fifth birthday. He had lived a full life by the standards of his time.

At 11:30 a.m. on Thursday, August 14, the family held a no-frills memorial with a prayer and little else at the Hotel Riviera.[12] On his American sojourn, Frank comforted his mother and found comfort in friends old and new.

Through Peter Nehemkis, who handled his mistress's aborting their child with glee as his friend mourned losing his father, Frank met a bookish prep school teacher caught in the whirlwind of his intellectual prowess and certitude.[13] The Hill School instructor found a deeper appreciation of T. S. Eliot through his poet friend, read The Death of the Gods by Dmitry Merezhkovsky upon Frank's recommendation, and described himself "impressed" by the Oxford student's interpretation of the story of Jesus instructing those without sin to cast the first stone as written into the Bible centuries afterward.

That teacher, James A. Michener, wrote Meyer that "I would like to take a Cook's Tour of this particular part of the world with you, for there is something about your not being able to sympathise with, or understand this sort of view that is refreshing. Very nearly every one else falls into that utterly rotten crowd: the group that can see both sides of every question. I long for a few good round oaths that have a clinging favor about them. Yours are such, at times, when you feel strongly, or are drunk. I prefer you in the latter mood."

Not yet the Pulitzer Prize–winner whose book served as the basis for *South Pacific*, Michener likened Meyer to the jewel thief in Frederick Lonsdale's play *The Last of Mrs. Cheyney*. He qualified the assessment by noting he did not think Frank a crook "but it does infer that you have the same tendencies, and I suppose that those are the very ones about which you are most proud."

Michener felt nostalgic for their skull sessions. "I'm living on an intellectual desert, here, and it seems all the more arid in view of the fact that I can remember the scintillating conversations which took place shortly before I came here in the fall," he explained. "They are very poignant, now."

He petitioned Frank to write, "for I know your letters will be as uneven, interesting, and provocative as your conversation."[14] Frank though, received the letter furthest from an intellectual desert. Back at Oxford, he did not need to petition friends a continent away for "scintillating conversations." They happened daily.

◆ ◆ ◆

THE CERTAINTY and charisma rooted in Meyer's intelligence that so captivated Michener also seduced women. His pursuit of the fairer sex, rarely fair and always sexual, received an assist from his ideology in its contempt for social norms.

"You promised me a boat letter, you Oxon," his Princeton pal Tut wrote in the fall of 1929. "But I haven't seen the papers for some time so perhaps the cuckold shot you."[15]

Dating partners at Oxford included Joan Waldo, the heiress to the largest supplier of construction materials in New England; Shiela Grant Duff, who later as an anti-appeasement journalist championed Czechs against Hitler's aggression; and her friend Diana Hubback, who told Frank, "You are too young to know so much!! And what you don't know, you think you do!"[16]

The dates usually involved walks, teas, or concerts. If the relationship were serious or the paramour were not, she would come over to his "digs."

One dating partner became as much a debating partner.

"I can come next Friday for a walk—I cannot go very far but that will not matter," responded Sheila MacDonald, a student at Oxford's Somerville College, to a date request. "It is possible to remove the fact of class-warfare."[17]

Meyer became accustomed to that refrain. As he became intensely Marxist at Balliol, others came to view him as a revolutionary. He certainly regarded himself, despite subsisting off an allowance and living in a high-hat hotel back home (or perhaps because of all the social insulation), as a revolutionary. And, as such, conversations between the pair inevitably turned to world events and political philosophy.

MacDonald challenged him and embraced a brother's-keeper government that rejected the brother's-jailkeeper approach favored by totalitarians. In MacDonald, the American met his match. Fit, attractive, and intelligent, the Scotswoman knew politics better than did her walking and tea partner. Whereas Frank's late father made his name in Newark making money, Sheila's father made his name in London as prime minister. For most of Meyer's time in Great Britain, the handsome, mustachioed widower Ramsay MacDonald lived at 10 Downing Street. And for most of that time, Meyer dated the prime minister's youngest daughter.

This did not stop him from dating others. What felt good fit the philosophy. He believed in Marxism and not the antiquated institutions of marriage and monogamy it sought to overrun.

He wrote to Winifred Gillett, his girlfriend in France, of longing for "your brain, your body, your lips, the whiteness of your thighs."[18] Alas, he explained, his longtime love from America, Dorothy Miller, would soon travel to England. He insisted to Gillett that he did not want Miller to come but he especially did not want the two in the same place at the same time. "[W]hen I touched your hand in the cab it was as if a magnetic force was holding me to you," he explained. "[T]here was a strange pull not wholly pleasant but as full of life as manure in spring[.] I have never felt for you the emotional haze I call love but something else impossible to define[,] something I have felt for no one ever before."[19]

Not wholly pleasant? As manure in spring? The emotional haze I call love?

It all sounded like a young man cartoonishly devoid of romance attempting to alchemize his deception into truth. He wanted his girlfriend on the continent, his girlfriend in the States, and his girlfriends at Oxford. He wanted them especially not to object to the outré arrangement.

"Thanks for sundry compliments etc.," one Oxonian Juliet wrote her Romeo. "Who was the stunning looking girl you had with you in the parks last week?"[20]

If they did not know initially, the revolutionist eventually told them. His conscience commanded confession even if some other region commanded the pursuit of multiple women simultaneously.

"I am not a monogamist—even at one time—I think of you lots now—even when I'm with Dorothy," he wrote Gillett. He added, "We had such fun—and we will again—if you can possibly accept me as I am."[21]

The letters ceased. One assumes she could not overcome her hang-ups.

◆ ◆ ◆

HE LIVED the lifestyle many young men fantasize about but few experience. College did not sit in the background, but neither did it occupy the foreground. The wine, women, and song he enjoyed at Oxford he enjoyed more during breaks between terms, which allowed for travel.

In Capri, he found a place immune, save for the worthlessness of his German friend's money, from the world's problems.[22] "I've seen a good deal of [E]urope in the last few years," he wrote home. "[B]ut this is the first place I've ever felt I'd want to live in more or less permanently if I ever get the chance."[23] The beauty of the island, with its grotto, ancient architecture, and stunning cliffs rising above the harbor, floored Frank.[24] He put daydream to paper and suggested that maybe he, Aunt Ida, and his mother could open a Capri villa and live off rents.[25]

The summer of 1931's travels, which included stops in Vienna, Genoa, Rome, and Florence—where he visited a three-hundred-year-old synagogue—sparked thoughts of taking a gap year. As his final year at Oxford approached, he volunteered that "passing examinations is not the aim of my life."[26] He soon discovered said aim.

Francis Fortescue "Sligger" Urquhart, the first Catholic to act as an Oxford tutor since the sixteenth-century purge, initially oversaw Meyer's work in Balliol's philosophy, politics, and economics program. Other tutors guiding the American included Alexander Bankier Rodger, Charles Richard Morris, Kenneth Norman Bell, and Benedict Humphrey Sumner.[27] Meyer described the position as a "glorified crammer."[28] Still, the eschewal of the lecture-hall style for this close-knit tutorial system inflated Urquhart's influence. The student wondered about adopting the teacher's religion. He felt that the demanding—and opposing—faiths of Catholicism and

Communism stood as the only two that made sense to him.[29] The lectures of Father Martin D'Arcy, too, caused him to consider Catholicism.[30] Urquhart, allegedly a partial basis for Mr. Samgrass in *Brideshead Revisited* and the entire reason for the famous Oxford reading gatherings at Switzerland's Mont Blanc, grew ill during Meyer's time, so another tutor, John Scott Fulton, took over his duties prior to Meyer's embrace of a faith.[31]

Near the end of 1931's Michaelmas term, Meyer and Richard Freeman founded the October Club, an explicitly Marxist organization. Impatience with the Labour Party and frustrations with its student offshoot motivated the former; work on a collective farm in the Soviet Union fueled the latter. The party lacked a student presence at Oxford and recorded three or four members each at Cambridge and the London School of Economics. Meyer recalled Emile Burns and other members of the Communist Party of Great Britain (CPGB) being "rather taken aback" by the Oxford Communists upon their first interaction.[32] The young people they envisioned someday walking through the door had just walked through the door. Frank Meyer led them there.

The pop received by Communism in the aftermath of the October Revolution merely crackled in the following years. From the perspective of Oxford in the late 1920s, Communism looked like a fad from a decade earlier or the preoccupation of droolers. The onset of the Great Depression opened minds to alternatives. If propagandists could effectively blame capitalism for the suffering, then perhaps they could win supporters to an ideology opposing the free market. Meyer's crusade benefited from the times. But the crusade benefitted from someone as uniquely suited to convert others as this dark-eyed personification of surety, magnetism, and intellect. For the same reasons friends and lovers wanted to be with Frank, strangers wanted to join his movement.

✦ ✦ ✦

OTHER strangers looked at his movement with a jaundiced eye. Some wore badges.

The October Club aroused the interest of the local police within a month of its founding. It started with a January 1932 letter regarding "COMMUNIST ACTIVITIES IN OXFORD" sent from Oxford city police chief constable Charles Fox to MI5. He included literature on the club, which laid out a schedule of meetings and noted its president: F. S. Meyer.[33]

By January's end, MI5 wanted more information on Meyer from the chief constable.[34] The authorities intercepted a letter from Meyer to the CPGB honcho Emile Burns. They collected information about him from Oxford's student magazine *Isis*.[35] As Meyer's impact grew, so did the tactics used to watch him.

For now, the conspicuous Communist's exuberance allowed for a passive approach. The voyeurs counted themselves lucky to surveil an exhibitionist. Meyer did their job for them by emerging from the chrysalis of campus character to become campus caricature.

The October Club took on its flamboyant founder's behavior. A student critic, talking about the American specifically and his English followers generally, found that "the manners of some of its members are nothing short of disgusting," decrying "the cheap and boring succession of unenlightened insults which is hurled with much laughter and gusto every Friday night."[36]

At an Oxford Union debate, participants considered whether the Conservative Party offered the superior fiscal policy, which resulted in a student scribe observing, "Mr. F. S. Meyer (Balliol) said as usual that this was an issue between Fascism and Communism. Then, as usual, he proceeded to choke himself."[37] The student magazine continued to lampoon him when a debate considered the question of whether to welcome a socialist electoral victory: "Mr. F. S. M. (B[alliol]) was too bitter to be very coherent, but he quoted Karl Marx magnificently." *Isis* noted that the Labour Club forcibly ejected the campus bad boy, despite his putting up a struggle, from the hall when Member of Parliament George Lansbury addressed the group.[38] On a mock Christmas list, the magazine gave the energetic ideologue the present of "a long rest."[39]

When students returned after Christmas, the October Club's leadership hoped for and received assistance with lectures from the CPGB. Speakers during 1932's Hilary term included CPGB General Secretary Harry Pollitt on "The Revolutionary Situation of the World To-Day," the Sri Lankan Communist Philip Gunawardena on "Imperialism," the future Soviet spy and Lenin Peace Prize–winner Ivor Montagu on "The Film as a Revolutionary Weapon," and, on "Lenin," Prince Mirsky.

Mirsky, who died in an Eastern Siberian gulag later in the decade, had encouraged a reticent Meyer and about ten of his fellow club members to join the Communist Party.[40]

Two consequences of officially joining followed. First, the October Club became from this point forward ostensibly an instrument of the CPGB, which acted as an instrument of the Soviet Union. Second, Meyer earned appointment as secretary of the student bureau of the CPGB. For the next two years, an American ran this youth wing of Great Britain's Russian-directed Communist Party. He also became a CPGB board member.[41] A reality emerged: The tail wagged the dog. The student movement, in terms of energy and much else, overshadowed the long-floundering party. The children, to some degree, held power over the adults.

◆ ◆ ◆

FRANK spent the time between the Michaelmas and Hilary term in America, where his revolutionary ardor again justified scortatory designs. He could now bed men's wives with the imprimatur of his social religion rather than the stern judgment of his old faith.

"I never dreamed that one could fall in love so utterly and completely in so short a time," a New York correspondent wrote Frank after his departure for his final months at Oxford. "I still can't believe it though I know it to be true."[42]

The besotted woman told in a series of lust letters, "I wish I knew how to make love to you in words," "My breasts are still very restless for you," and "You have certainly done drastic things to my body."[43]

This fantasy scenario for many twenty-two-year-old men naturally contained complications.

The teacher at the Professional Children's School in Manhattan enthralled by Frank arrived at her obsession after less than two weeks of dating. She wrote of needing to see a psychiatrist, and her out-of-control life and attention seeking indicated the wisdom of such a course.[44]

A false-alarm pregnancy scare occurred. "Tell me why my breasts hurt, darling," the Bryn Mawr graduate wondered. "They are simply torturing me. It feels as it did after my abortion, when they secreted milk."[45]

Worst of all, Eleanor Woolley Fowler, the older woman sexually awakened by Frank, remained married to another in their social circle. Cedric Fowler, a Columbia graduate and son of a former Canadian member of parliament, doted on her only to find rejection and a wife flaunting infidelity. When the jilted husband bought her nice clothing, she offered to model them for her boyfriend.[46] "What you can make me feel with a touch of your hand, Seedy can't at all with his whole body," she wrote. "He's being just awfully nice to me, though."[47]

The budding revolutionary and his contempt for bourgeois conventions excited the progressive teacher from a family of prominent education reformers.

"I explained my perfect nonchalance about [curse words]," she boasted about a conversation with her family. "I think they were rather horrified at the idea that any decent people really used such a word as 'fuck' in ordinary conversation. I couldn't help laughing up my sleeve at the horror [they] would probably feel at your vocabulary."[48]

Husband and wife moved into separate dwellings Mrs. Fowler spoke of the three-year marriage in the past tense.[49] Mr. Fowler, perhaps in gamesmanship, found a girlfriend though he clearly still loved his wife.

"For God's sake, take up boxing or jiu jitsu," Eleanor petitioned Frank. "Seedy says he'll kill you the next time he sees you."[50]

Numerous others, including Mrs. Fowler's own family, came to despise a man they did not know. Some warned Eleanor that, should Frank boast of his conquest, he may ruin her.[51]

"I have been to see the family," she wrote, "and they hate you with a really amazing hate."[52]

The affair divided the social circle. And why not? Mrs. Fowler doubted that anyone could love her as much as her husband did. Rather than respond in kind, the bride found the doting groom "pathetic."[53]

The drama engulfed Dorothy Canning Miller, moved on, mostly, from her former boyfriend. Eleanor and Dorothy shared awkward silences at a Manhattan gathering when the Victrola needle ran out of grooves. Eventually, they discussed the man in their middle, whom the love of Frank's life to this point bad-mouthed.[54]

"I suppose that every woman hates to lose the absolute devotion of a man even when she does not really want him and I think that Dorothy feels that way about you," Eleanor explained. "She says that you are perfectly delightful but nothing to build on. I don't think she was trying to put monkey-wrenches in the works, but simply felt that she had known you for so long that she ought to warn me about your defects."[55]

Other friends saw defects in Frank's affair partner. Fred Bartlett, caught in the middle, offered a clear-headed diagnosis of the situation:

As for what she feels and thinks, God himself knows. I don't think she herself does. At the moment she evidently won't admit to herself that Seedy has ever, can ever, or will ever mean anything to her. Of course, that's all the bunk. She's a quite normal young girl and Seedy must be a normal young man. What the outcome of this defensive attitude will be I don't know. There may come a time of terrific stress when she will rush back to her old conceptions of life much more strongly than if she had never left them. At the moment she undoubtedly does not know where the stable values in life lie. She evidently found something in those ten days in Greenwich Village and Brooklyn which have left an impersonal, but a very strong hankering after something. She does not want to shut herself off from the possibility of that impersonal something by going back to Seedy.[56]

Within days of a discussion of summering with Frank in Paris where judgment did not come down so heavily, the mercurial Mrs. Fowler proclaimed her love for Mr. Fowler, who gave her three kids and remained her husband until death they did part. Frank, as Fred Bartlett correctly identified, served as but "an excuse for something that does not concern you."[57]

His own behavior concerned him but not enough to change it. In a will prompted by his father's death, the son wrote his mother, "I'm sorry I've been such a mess for you." He asked for his body to go to medical science or into a crematory and, in a sign of hubris, named his friends Dorothy Miller and Peter Nehemkis his literary executors, with the former enjoying final say. He gave his belongings to his mother and all that she did not care to keep he bequeathed to Dorothy and Peter. "p.s. to Dorothy," he wrote, "I adore you."

Yes, he pursued the lust life over his love life. But he did so after giving his heart to a woman who, although enjoying his company and affections, ultimately did not respond in kind.

"Please remember," he pleaded, a special concert they attended in 1928, "the Royal Hotel," "the pain of this year—1930-1931," and "all the nice things you said to me on request."[58]

The will did not precipitate his demise. It did acknowledge the death knell struck on his first love. And the end of the first love can depress more than death, at least in the minds of twentysomethings experiencing the former and not quite fathoming the latter.

❖ ❖ ❖

THE OXFORD experience, too, reached its coda. The twenty-three-year-old suddenly experienced close encounters with the brilliant and famous. "He is very Jewish—smokes a fat cigar—magnificent sense of humor—had English breaking into German," he reported to his mother of Albert Einstein, who, he said, "reminded me a little of father." He talked with the philosopher Bertrand Russell for half an hour on a train platform. He received an invitation to supper with the former prime minister David Lloyd George. Harold Laski, the British left's leading intellectual spokesman, conspired with Frank on postgraduate plans.[59] He showed his poetry to T. S. Eliot, who provided favorable comment.[60] *Isis* noted his "little success" at a Labour Club event, presumably during a give-and-take with George Bernard Shaw.[61]

The "handshaking notes" that monitor progress in Balliol's tutorial system require that the student and tutors come before the master for discussion. John Scott Fulton evaluated Frank as a "good mind" during his first term. But tutors soon included such phrases as "silly fool," "last essay was dreadfully disjointed," "not as good as it ought to be," and "unsatisfactory" though "not hopeless." Frank pulled it together. Observations in 1932 included "good," "high quality," and, from Charles Richard Morris, his first real contact at the school, "absolutely first rate."[62]

In the summer of 1932, after three happy years at Balliol following the tumult of half that time at Princeton, Frank received his bachelor of arts in philosophy, politics, and economics.

The college graduate spent part of his summer watched by British intelligence.

MI6 noted that he departed Great Britain without notifying the authorities, for which he received an official caution, and then spent eleven days in Amsterdam. There, the World Congress Against War inspired further stealth. MI6 reported that he appeared on a list of attendees under "S. S. Meyer" and that he did not sign his name.[63] Like hundreds of others, he sailed to the continent to capture the group for Communism. Upon its capture, Communists renamed it the World Committee Against War and Fascism. Significantly, he attended the congress as a delegate not from the U.S. but the U.K.[64]

In September, he left Holland for home—England.

◄ 5 ►

London

F rank Meyer entered the London School of Economics to study anthropology in 1932 with an eager assist
from fellow traveler Harold Laski, a Marxist though
not a Communist Party member who taught at the school.[1]
The subject matter marked a reorientation of Meyer's academic interests. It coincided with a reordering in his economic status.

The days of summering in Capri or taking in the opera
as royalty sat nearby existed now as memories. In late 1931,
Helene Meyer had designated more than a dozen local charities to receive $5,000 between them upon her death. By
early 1932, taxes in arrears compelled her to withdraw that
amount. Months later she noted, "I find my funds very low"
in a second will addendum. "So it is impossible to meet my
requests at this time, especially as to charities."[2] For a woman
who served in leadership in many of those nonprofits, the
inability to fulfill promises to herself undoubtedly stung and
underscored the change in fortune.

Her son had lived a life on scholarship through his first
two decades. Now his father's death and the collapse of the
stock market compelled him to scrounge for actual scholar-
ships. He successfully pursued the War Memorial Scholarship,

49

which paid £50, an amount possessing present-day purchasing power sixty times that, from Oxford that helped bankroll him at LSE.[3] In spring 1933, he worked for remuneration perhaps for the first time for the Royal Anthropological Institute, assisting the New Zealander Raymond Firth at the British Museum. The Rockefeller Foundation underwrote the LSE position, from which Meyer earned £79 over the course of about ten months.[4] The financial setbacks neither evicted Mrs. Meyer from the Hotel Riviera nor spurred her son to withdraw from graduate school. They did compel both to sacrifice.

Atop sudden dearness of money, Meyer's landing perhaps the most coveted mentor in his field heightened the importance of his studies. Bronisław Malinowski, the Polish ethnographer whose fieldwork in Oceania elevated his name to global recognition during this time of almost faddish public interest in anthropology, advised the young American. He oversaw his Ph.D. student's doctoral dissertation, "The Correlation of Various Aspects of Culture in Primitive Societies," which focused on Mexicans and Pueblo Indians. For the new LSE hire Firth, he worked on "Polynesian Kinship and Social Structure."[5] Meyer held research responsibilities assisting Malinowski in an academic sense and Firth in a paid, professional sense. LSE presented its new graduate student with an opportunity dreamt by many but experienced by few.

He blew it.

✦ ✦ ✦

"I have not seen you doing one single stroke of honest work since you started to work with me," Malinowski wrote Meyer immediately after a conversation between the two about the student's lax effort. "I understand on the other hand that in assisting Dr. Firth you have really been effectively and constructively at work. About that I feel envious, but also resent being discriminated against. Is it that as a good communist you can only work when you are paid?"[6]

The young intellectual who had hired private tutors to obtain entry to one of the world's great universities, specially shipped a trunk of books to England, and traveled Europe in part to improve his fluency in modern languages became a rigid ideologue who regarded the academic life as secondary to the political one. He behaved as though his ever-present brilliance coupled with these newfound political associations, which placed him "in" with the academic in crowd, guaranteed advancement and accolades. One senses an entitlement from him that regarded degrees as awards for his ideological correctness rather than certifications obtained by applying intelligence through hard work.

Malinowski certainly came to see it that way. He periodically joked about Meyer's tardiness and truancy. His student did not take the hint.[7] He attended lectures in seven of his ten courses half of the time or less in his first year and in his second regressed into going to lectures 35 percent of the time in his best-attended course.[8] Malinowski privately expressed his concerns. The graduate student continued to regard classes as impediments to activism. So Malinowski wrote the firm letter that praised his intellectual strengths but criticized the shirking.

"Your activities in several seminars, both of Dr. Firth and myself, I would describe frankly as nihilistic: that is, you raise half formulated objections, you stop the discussion without being able to shunt it on any definite lines and then you construct nothing out of it. Yesterday was a good example of that, as you remember, yesterday I was fully in sympathy not only with your criticism as such, but also with some of its details. But it is no good having the best ideas if you cannot either formulate them or convince other people of them," the powerful mentor explained.[9]

Malinowski urged him to concentrate on academics, apply himself to an upcoming paper, and show up to seminars and on time. He warned that if his student did not dramatically change his approach then he would not remain his student.[10]

To a true believer under party discipline, the advice did not, *could not*, persuade. Activism won out over scholarship.

◆ ◆ ◆

MEYER worked extremely hard, just not for his professor. Malinowski could not possibly see all the hours his student labored for the cause. Others did.

On December 2, 1932, a Special Branch sergeant characterized Meyer to MI5 as "obviously a suitable subject for further police observation" as his inspector suggested he become "the subject of a Special Branch periodical report."[11]

They watched often, intensely, discreetly.

An informant called his flat at 12 Morningside Crescent a "hot-bed of Communists."[12] The founder of MI5 described him as the "moving spirit in the foundation of the Student Vanguard," a publication important to young English Communists in general but in a more profound sense to Meyer in particular.[13]

Starting around the end of 1932, Meyer and his colleagues began producing the well-edited though dogmatic student magazine *The Student Vanguard*, which was distributed throughout the U.K. British authorities adduced Meyer's importance to the project after encountering an unfamiliar spelling indicating sibilance: "It will be noted that Meyer's influence has caused 'defense' to be spelt in the American style."[14]

The publication advertised summer tours of the U.S.S.R. and featured such articles as "The Universities Under the Soviets" and "All Out on May Day."[15] Under his own name, John Cornford, himself a poet and short story writer since early childhood, criticized T. S. Eliot, Wyndham Lewis, James Joyce, Ezra Pound, and others for not using their art as a weapon to

wage class war.[16] In extant issues, Meyer likely appears pseudonymously. For instance, the moniker "F. J." attached to the
review of *Memoirs of a Bolshevik* by Osip Piatnitsky, later executed in the Great Purge, likely belonged to Meyer as he used
that initialism at other times as a Communist.[17]

Among scores of comrades, no friendship became more
meaningful than that with the great-grandson of Charles
Darwin. Under Meyer's tutelage, Cornford, who had attended LSE briefly just after turning seventeen before heading to
Cambridge, became secretary of the Federation of Student
Societies, an editor of *The Student Vanguard*, and a participant in a host of other groups also largely controlled by his
older schoolmate.[18] In summer 1933, Cornford camped with
his girlfriend Ray at Horsey, Norfolk. "An American student
leader at L.S.E. and his girl came with them," the authors Peter
Stansky and William Abrahams note.[19] John's brother Christopher, then sixteen, later described this camping excursion
with Meyer in the dunes as exuding a "mythical radiance in
my memory."[20]

"I first knew John Cornford as a young student at LSE,
who became a close personal friend, and in a sense protégé
of mine, and was associated with our whole group there,"
Meyer later recalled.[21] Others saw it similarly. A fellow October Club member, in the words of his British debriefers,
pointed out that the older American "exercised a powerful
influence on John CORNFORD," who soon became "the idol
of left-wing undergraduates."[22]

Meyer played this idol role before Cornford assumed it. He
did so as a traveling act speaking, whether by the host's invitation or his own, at campuses, meetings, and demonstrations.

On campus, Meyer's group hosted such speakers as the British Communists Wal Hannington, Allen Hutt, and Bert Williams. A weekend commemoration in March 1933 of the fiftieth
anniversary of Karl Marx's death culminated in a procession to
his grave in Highgate Cemetery.[23] The next month, Meyer oversaw a conference that attracted students from sixteen different

universities to form the Federation of Student Societies, a collection of student organizations of varied left-wing outlooks nevertheless controlled by the Communists.[24]

◆ ◆ ◆

MEYER'S LSE classmates, particularly the ones stuffing ballot boxes, elected him president of the student union. The powerful man aiding his ascent soon became the most powerful man in India next to Jawaharlal Nehru. And whether four thousand miles away and twenty years later or in this student election, the "nonaligned" V. K. Krishna Menon aligned with Communists.

"I was defeated by, I think, 8 or 10 votes, whereupon Krishna Menon discovered there had been fraud in the election," Meyer noted. "It did turn out that the fraud was somebody on our side, but at least it was fraud, and the election was canceled at his demand and after constitutional discussions in the union the election was held again, and this time I was elected by 35 votes. So that, in this case, the Indian students and their leader played a rather big part in my election, in the election of the Communist candidate."[25]

The Whitney family heir Michael Straight, a seventeen-year-old who got caught up in espionage a few years after getting caught up in Frank Meyer, gazed amazed upon his fellow countryman presiding over the student union high in a chair that resembled a throne. "He looked like an Aztec priest, with his high cheekbones, his arched, sensual lips, and his long, narrow nose," the future publisher of *The New Republic* observed. A fellow awestruck onlooker informed him in a whisper that the president was a "revolutionary."[26]

LSE's student union predictably served as an instrument for the young Communists to promote their ideology. Marxist activism initially did little to raise the administration's ire. After all, Beatrice and Sidney Webb had founded the school just four decades earlier with a bequest from a fellow Fabian Society member who wished for an institution of higher learning to advance their ideas. While the exponent of Austrian economics Friedrich Hayek taught at LSE and received Rockefeller money as Meyer did, the identity of the school, particularly in its early bestowal of degrees in *social* sciences, evoked *socialism*. Frank and his friends initially perhaps appeared as Fabians in a hurry to the more mainstream leftists who ran the institution. To Frank and his friends, the leftish gradualists overseeing the school appeared as obsolescent naïfs to stampede when they were not ridiculing them.

This attitude soon became obvious. Meyer harbored contempt for William Beveridge, and the LSE director reciprocated. When Raymond Firth brought Meyer's name before the board overseeing the Rockefeller money in spring 1933, Beveridge resisted the anthropologist's choice to such a degree as to require a private meeting to discuss whether Meyer amounted to a "suitable" candidate.[27] Firth successfully advocated for Meyer as his aide, but the mere fact that he needed to when approval came almost in a perfunctory manner for other faculty requests suggested trouble.

In early 1934, the university offered lectures on Marxism delivered by speakers deemed insufficiently Marxist by Meyer. The Marxist Society attempted to offer an alternative series that, because of resistance from the administration, ultimately took place off campus.[28] Further, a censure attempt against Meyer in student government failed, and caused cheering onlookers to toss papers in the air in celebration. The director reacted to all this and more by seeking limitations on the body, such as the abolition of lifetime membership and of rules that ensured that undergraduates primarily held power.[29]

His position and notoriety meant that at the school's annual commemoration dinner the twenty-four-year-old Bolshevik, after attendees surreally toasted the king and ate a seven-course meal, delivered the night's main remarks with Philip

Kerr, the Marquess of Lothian and soon ambassador to the United States, offering a reply.[30] The spectacle of an extremist representing the school did not ingratiate Meyer with the administration. It surely raised his profile with the agents thickening their files.

◆ ◆ ◆

HE did not cease to embarrass Oxford simply because he now attended school elsewhere.

The alumnus's October Club hired a gymnasium to host H. G. Wells in the fall of 1932. This followed his infamous "liberal fascism" speech at Oxford that summer. Wells warned his autumn hosts, and the largely non-Communist audience, of the folly of importing ideas prevalent in Russia to the West and endorsed violence only against violent extremists. Taunts and a "burst of indignation" unwitnessed anywhere else, an astonished American Rhodes Scholar insisted to his father, greeted the *Time Machine* author, who could not predict his immediate dystopian future:

> One lad made a ringing speech to the effect that Mr. Wells had spent his life in a bed of roses and could therefore scarcely be expected to have any sympathy with the struggling, suffering masses of humanity. He had never seen any hard times and therefore didn't believe there were any. Mr. Wells didn't think there were any classes, or that if there were there were only two? Well, there were two, but not the two that Mr. Wells had described. There were those that own property and bleed the rest of humanity. That, the second group, whether Mr. Wells liked it or not, was the proletariat, and an inability to recognize the great surge of effort and violence that it is at this moment directing against the strongholds of capitalism was, to put it very simply, only the result of Mr. Wells' pur-blind stupidity.[31]

That Rhodes Scholar was Willmoore Kendall, who, likely without ever realizing it, described Meyer. Decades later, this "lad" would become one of his closest friends and intellectual sounding boards. But Kendall's formal introduction to Meyer would not come until the 1950s. Here, events introduced him to a nameless force of nature. Meyer exerted a more substantial, though indirect, influence on his future colleague's outlook. Revilo Oliver, who met Kendall in 1929, partly pinned his friend's adoption of Communism to Oxford's "atmosphere," already terraformed for Marxism by Meyer.[32]

Others issued a harsher take on the son of American privilege's lambast of a son of the British working class.

"People like Mr. F. Meyer, bred in the lap of American luxury, should think twice before they taunt Mr. H. G. Wells with never having known what poverty is," lectured *Isis*.[33]

The spectacle of disrupting the speech of a world-famous author again raised Meyer's profile for the secretive brotherhood profiling him. That the club he founded invited that world-famous figure whom he so forcefully upbraided only further piqued the interest of government agents.

Who was this young malapert?

✦ ✦ ✦

A SPECIAL BRANCH UNIT noted during the 1932 holiday season that Meyer would run a stall at *The Daily Worker*'s upcoming Bazaar & Fun Fair at the Hoxton Baths.[34] He received an assist from his understudy John Cornford, his girlfriend Ray, and his brother Christopher.[35] The following month, the Special Branch informed MI5 that the American took a phone call at a British Anti-War Council meeting at the Pindar of Wakefield, a socialist halidom whose significance as a watering hole once patronized by Karl Marx and Friedrich Engels went unnoted by authorities.[36]

Meyer's letters, reflecting caution or obliviousness, do not exhibit awareness that powerful people, including those holding the highest positions in the British security apparatus, monitored him.

In April 1933, a clean-shaven man with a sallow complexion wearing a light brown tweed jacket, gray flannel trousers, and a blue pullover emerged from a Young Communist League meeting in Aldgate. The police followed him to his home.[37] Ten days later, the Special Branch police identified the subject of the surveillance as Frank S. Meyer, the same person who had elicited notice months earlier.[38] Ten days after that, the Special Branch requested a mail cover lasting less than a month, which revealed innocuous letters from his aunts, mother, and Dorothy Canning Miller but also one from the British Anti-War Movement, the U.K. equivalent of the American League Against War and Fascism—both outgrowths of the World Congress Against War attended by Frank the previous year.[39]

That last missive helped the spies paint a more accurate picture of Meyer, whom they noted a few months later as "reported to be in charge of the anti-war propaganda, especially among the students."[40]

At the new Bermondsey Town Hall in London, Meyer served as one of more than one hundred delegates from twenty schools to the Anti-War Congress.[41] He robotically mouthed the party line in an address to the gathering: "The students want to impress the Congress with our determination to fight against War. By passive individual resistance we cannot stop War. We realise it is only by mass action that we can prevent War. We pledge ourselves to work for the stoppage of the manufacture and transport of munitions. We pledge ourselves to work against scabbing by students, and by strikes and other action to stop war."[42]

The Communist line then called for peace in response to Nazism and Japanese bellicosity, which Stalin perceived as threatening. In pursuit of this line, the Communists organized more massive popular-front events of an international nature, such as the World Congress Against War in Amsterdam in August 1932, the European Anti-Fascist Workers' Congress in June 1933 at the Salle Pleyel in Paris, and the International Youth Congress months later again in Paris, all of which Meyer attended.[43]

The young American fostered international connections. He held cachet with the forces above the forces above him. The action of the party concentrated on the youth. So power drifted toward Meyer's generation. When the Communist Party of Great Britain clashed with its student bureau, Frank visited Brussels for favorable adjudication from Comintern member and fellow Balliol man Palme Dutt.[44]

◆ ◆ ◆

THE CULMINATION of his antiwar efforts led Meyer back to Oxford as well.

Sir Reginald Craddock wondered on the floor of the House of Commons whether the three hundred October Club members might do themselves a favor by taking up rowing and other vigorous exercise in place of Marxism.[45] When Meyer entered Oxford, no Communist presence existed among students.[46] Now the oldest university in the world overflowed with Communists to a degree that caused notice in Parliament.

The infamous King-and-Country pledge, introduced by a socialist, passed the Oxford Union in February 1933. The Communist in charge of student antiwar agitation throughout Great Britain just happened to be the same one who took Communism from nothing to three hundred members of the Communist student organization that he cofounded at Oxford. Though the October Club held its own event the night the Oxford Union motion passed, widespread public sentiment, summed up by the pseudonymously placed "Disloyalty at Oxford: Gesture Towards the Reds" by an aging

Oxford alumnus in *The Daily Telegraph*, blamed the Communists, not without reason.⁴⁷ The oath scandalized Craddock and others, including the mayor of Oxford, who pointed to the disruption of an Armistice Day remembrance, perpetrated by the October Club, as a precursor: "I say that, as Mayor of the city that fathers a university of such foreign Communist sentiments, I am ashamed." The Anti-Socialist and Anti-Communist Union cited the October Club, *Student Vanguard*, and the Students' Anti-War Council—all groups Meyer founded or led—as proof of the "Communist inspiration" of the university antiwar movement behind the Oxford Pledge.⁴⁸

The lifelong member of the Oxford Union, though he had graduated more than six months prior to the Oxford Pledge's passage, prepared the ground for its victory. He naturally set about creating upheaval inspired by the Oxford Pledge at the London School of Economics. By a 10-1 margin the motion "This House will in no circumstances fight for King and Country but will do all in its power to prevent transfer of arms to belligerent countries" carried at LSE.⁴⁹ His more directly ensuring that the motion triumphed by such preposterous margins at LSE illustrated the seizure of campus politics by his Marxist clique. The Oxford Pledge occurred around the time Adolf Hitler became chancellor and the Enabling Act of 1933 transformed Germany into Nazi Germany. So rather than encouraging peace as many of those pushing it had intended, it instead sent a message to warmongers that the soldier generation of one of the world's great powers lacked an appetite to fight.

♦ ♦ ♦

MEYER possessed a gluttonous appetite to fight. What an ex-girlfriend wrote to explain her alienation from Meyer's understudy applied to him as well: "He has got to fight—I know that—and lead an abnormal life fighting."⁵⁰ Meyer, like

Cornford, needed conflict the way others need air. This made their demands for peace disingenuous. They aggressively pushed for disarmament and the like because it aided the object of their devotion. When some more violent course aided the Soviet Union, both men followed it.

This performance, as performances do, brought spectators. The foreign actor and his mostly British-born fellow players took clandestine measures to avoid detection. They did this not as a game or merely under external instruction but because to some degree they understood that others watched. They sought the violent overthrow of not just the government but the entire societal structure. Presumably, they believed the dark forces they hoped to squash took them as seriously as they did themselves. Of course, the guardians of the old order did spy on the revolutionaries.

"Communications between the Student Bureau and the university units was on a strictly conspiratorial basis, with mail drops, coded references to individuals, etc.," Meyer recalled nearly two decades later. "The Bureau itself functioned conspiratorially, maintaining a secret headquarters in a private apartment with its records concealed there but nevertheless in code. The student conferences were conspiratorially organized under the cover of being some harmless organization and with guards, security measures, etc."[51]

Their countermeasures could not always ensure escape from the state's eye of providence.

A watcher ultimately "considers it possible that [Meyer] is connected with the more secret side of the Students' activities."[52] His conspicuousness as a campus presence undermines this theory. But on September 4, 1933, in a discussion of the "potential usefulness" of the German Communist Ernst Jablonski, who became Ernest Jouhy in the French Resistance, Meyer nourished the theory. He suggested, to the objection of a fellow member of the Students' Anti-War Council, that their comrade go underground.[53] After Meyer's permanent exit from his residence, the authorities, tipped off to a special wireless contraption, found a garden-variety radio, albeit one registered to the spouse of a German anti-Nazi activist.[54] They also discovered an Adana Press used to create innocuous company labels to evade detection for Communist materials sent to China and India; "they kept this machine at M[e]yer's place, but after the latter's departure, it was transferred to the Minority Movement office," a document labeled "very secret" explained.[55]

Meyer's off-campus rabble-rousing aroused MI5's interest. At LSE, it ultimately resulted in attention from the press. The government then moved against him.

Newhaven

M eyer's insolence, not his politics, damaged him at LSE. The bold president of the student union's scoffing at the edicts of the school's director pro-voked action against him that cascaded action of an even less welcome sort. The student leader's conspicuous presence as an activist and a playboy, and his conspicuous absence from the classroom, added to the disdain administrators felt for him. His antics increasingly attracted more powerful masters.

The first months of 1934 were the crescendo leading to the frenzied climax of the American's years in England. Future Nobel Prize–winners and a prime minister, members of Parliament and leading philosophers, and novelists, clerics, and student hordes banged the timpani, rang chimes, and blew trumpets for Frank Meyer. His brashness attracted the wrong kind of attention from spies, bureaucrats, and dons. He defied the counsel of a celebrity academic, pursued Britain's most dangerous bachelorette, and inspired the soon-to-be superstar of the U.K. left. His activities generated too much controversy. The chaos culminated in an "1812 Overture" of an exclamation point to his six years in England.

The ostensible catalyst occurred during 1934's Hilary term. *The Student Vanguard* published a passage smearing a faculty member.[1] It followed an article, written anonymously, like all of the pieces that surrounded it but unlike most of the articles in an issue the previous year, that alleged that the advisors to Indian students at Cambridge and Oxford spied on them for the British government.

"The above statement, coming from a reliable source, adds considerable weight to a thesis we have been led to hold, namely, that a well-organised system exists for spying on colonial students," the *Vanguard*'s italicized addendum informed. "It is not restricted to Oxford and Cambridge; in the London School of Economics a retired Indian policeman fulfills the same function."[2]

Professor Harold Laski, who had been instrumental in Meyer's matriculation at LSE, catalyzed his demise. He alerted John Coatman, the only retired policeman who had served in India on the small faculty. Coatman expressed outrage to LSE's director, William Beveridge, and contacted a barrister with an aim to extract a retraction and apology. Beveridge issued an order, delivered in writing and verbally to Meyer and a few others, prohibiting the distribution of the magazine on campus. He cited not only its libelous content but the fact that the periodical "does not bear any clear indication of who is responsible for its publication."[3]

At least six students, led by the perceived ringleaders Meyer and Jack Simons of South Africa, brazenly hocked the magazine mainly in and around the refectory. W. J. Blyth Crotch and university porter George Panormo confronted the students, who provided their names but otherwise sassed them.[4]

Meyer owed the Indian nationalists who had fraudulently elected him president; whether he pushed the charge out of indebtedness to his anti-colonialist allies or out of general sympathy seems unclear. If *The Student Vanguard* erred in specifics, then it did not err in a general sense. The police indeed spied on Meyer and his comrades. They felt this and became concerned enough to levy accusations. Beveridge, the director of the school, ordered on February 27 that students henceforth receive permission before distributing literature on campus and banned the issue in question. The student union president, despite receiving notice of this, balked. He continued distributing *The Student Vanguard* in a very public way.[5] He wrote Beveridge that his orders constituted "censorship," "a complete break with tradition," and "another addition to the series of restrictions on freedom of speech and assembly which you have been attempting to impose on the students."[6]

Beveridge, a Liberal Party stalwart who had helped design the British welfare state, reacted in dudgeon. He suspended Meyer and four others. He excluded a South African student from punishment because of her youth, ignorance of the offending passage, and contrition.[7] Two days after openly violating the order, the defiant ones wrote the director a chastened apology acknowledging the disobedience as "deliberate" but concluding that it represented, "after mature consideration," a "grave error in judgment."[8] Two days after that, Frank, understanding his precarious spot, wrote an apology.[9]

The groveling appeared anomalous not just for the brash graduate student but for Communists. Perhaps realizing the threat to their organizing, some of the students likely abased themselves more for the good of their cause than to avert expulsion. They sensed danger. Still, Frank, reverting to characteristic arrogance, deemed it "unnecessary" when asked by Beveridge to provide a written statement to the emergency committee.[10]

The involved members of the student union, including its president, also apologized to the student governing body for cavalierly taking action without consulting it.[11] The offenders appeared on March 5 before an unfriendly committee that included Beveridge, the Bank of England director Josiah Stamp, and the Conservative Party politician Arthur Steel-Maitland. Meyer's comrades alleged the panel did not permit him to make his case "fully," possibly indicating that he had tested their patience before they hushed him.[12] A swaggering young foreigner arguing against his impertinence likely showcased it.

The committee allowed two undergraduates, whom they reasoned "had acted under the influence of elders," to resume their studies. They regarded the Canadian Phyllis Freeman's as a more difficult case but withdrew her penalty, too, in part because she never received a direct warning from the director to stop disseminating the libel. The expulsions of Meyer and Simons remained.[13] A few weeks later, after Simons indicated Meyer had misled him into action by mischaracterizing the director's words to him, the committee modified its punishment by allowing for his conditional return after the term.[14]

The school ordered Meyer to vacate the premises, fired him from his Rockefeller-funded research job, withdrew recognition of him as student union president, and informed the Home Office that he remained in the country in violation of the Alien Registration Act.[15] Very quickly, the head of the U.K.'s domestic security and counterintelligence agency saw this as an opportunity to expel a foreign menace surveilled for more than two years.

"We understand that Meyer is in receipt of an ample allowance, for his mother is a wealthy woman, and as his studies here have been forcibly terminated, there would seem to be no reason why he should not return to the United States," the MI5 founder and director Vernon Kell, relying on a somewhat dated sense of Meyer's finances, wrote the Home Office. "I should be glad if you would let me know what action it is proposed to take."[16]

◆ ◆ ◆

THE DISCIPLINE case reveled in the attention, at least the attention of a public and not secret sort. His standing as the secretary of the student bureau of the Communist Party of Great Britain gave importance to the cause that gave

self-importance to Frank. In a movement of levelers, he enjoyed this moment as first among equals. Others wished he
would bury his head in books.

"I feel that I still must urge you once again to consider seriously my advice & to declare to the Director that you will
give up your political activities at the School and turn seriously to Anthropology," Bronisław Malinowski wrote in April.
He repeated complaints about his student not applying himself. Here, though, he included new arguments, based more
on utility than truth, claiming, for instance, that by scoffing
at the director's edict and then apologizing for doing so he
managed to alienate moderates *and* radicals. He surely could
no longer command the allegiance of students in their governing body. "Be wise & honest, pocket your pride & resign,"
he wrote.[17]

Again, he balked in response to a Malinowski plea. He also
balked at another who knew his best interests better than
he did.

He had continued the relationship, the intention and intensity of which posterity can only venture an educated
guess, with the daughter of Prime Minister Ramsay MacDonald. After saying she could not fit a Thursday tea date into her
schedule, Sheila invited him for supper that night.

"Come here at 7.0—or if you don't like the idea of Downing Street—even though I am the sole occupant at the moment—fix any other place you like," she wrote Frank.[18] Like
her guest, the youngest daughter of the prime minister found
herself single, in her mid-twenties, attractive, and occupying
a political space left of center.

In more than 150 pages of declassified material on Meyer,
the authorities curiously express no notice of the relationship between the Communist they surveilled and the daughter of the leader of the government for which they toiled.
They knew Helene Meyer sent her son funds through Lloyd's
Bank, that his late father had worked in manufacturing, that
their subject had once roomed in a former Birmingham

vicarage, and that he "used to at one time to be frequently in the company of Phyllis Freeman."[19] But they knew nothing, or at least memorialized nothing of what they knew, of the daughter of the big boss dating the "very dirty and unshaven" Communist with "thick black unruly hair which is always untidy," a "thin Jewish face," and "thick lips" whom they sought to deport.[20]

The U.K. Home Office, despite Meyer's five years in England, his Oxford degree, and his gainful employment at the British Museum, ordered him to leave the country should the LSE not revoke his expulsion. This order, like the expulsion, looked for a time subject to change.

Deportation seemed harsh. But the foreign leader of a foreign movement courting the youngest daughter of the prime minister also courted disaster. If allowing a revolutionary to remain on a student visa even as he played hooky on graduate school struck authorities as a bad idea, then permitting that same person to stay as he made calls upon Ramsay MacDonald's fetching daughter probably struck any authorities who knew of this embarrassing dalliance as a terrible one.

The letters from Sheila MacDonald exude a warm, familiar tone even as they exhibit deep separation in the correspondents' worldviews. The corrective guidance proffered by Malinowski to Meyer regarding his studies MacDonald concomitantly provided on his politics. But Meyer inhabited an ideological hallucination, which worked as an antidote to doses of reality from both.

Responding generally to their conversations and specifically to an unspecified book Meyer gave her, MacDonald wrote in late May,

> What strikes me most, when reading Communist literature, is the, as I think, wrong notion of human nature on which it is founded. I am all for alleviating economic oppression, and any contribution Communism has to

make to the solution to that problem—excellent. But where I think you are mistaken is in assuming that, given economic justice, a la Communism, the world will be a pleasant place. What should be aimed at is not so much "rights for everyone" as a friendliness amongst everyone, and Communism is the unlikely method to bring that about. That is why I dislike class-war—it only accentuates the disease of hatred.

Of course, Communists will presumably exterminate everyone they hate! You are so lucky to be so fully convinced that what you aim at is the most desirable end to achieve. And therefore you can muster strong and determined forces. We Social Democrats have not so much faith in our own judgments, and so not wish to establish dictatorship but to encourage individual freedom. Marx himself writes about individual freedom approvingly—somewhere in Vol. III I believe. And we fully agree with him that people cannot be fully free when trammeled by economic limitations. But they are more free when they aren't sat on by fascists and Communists.[21]

The sober and sensible letter, like Malinowski's, left the fanatic unpersuaded. His devotion made him unpersuadable. So, too, likely, did the euphoria felt as a whole movement coalesced around him. Powerful people wanted him deported. Popular people celebrated him. Either way, the spotlight shone.

◆ ◆ ◆

THUS, through actions of foes and friends, Meyer became a cause célèbre. Off campus, he morphed into the second coming of Margaret Mead denied a chance to make his mark on anthropology by a vengeful male schoolmarm. In London lingo, bedlam broke out around the Communist organizer posing as an anthropology student.

Plaints for tolerance yielded to a pressure campaign involving some of the most famous Englishmen of the twentieth century. A prime minister, Nobel Prize–winning scientist, and one of Edwardian England's most celebrated novelists took up his cause. The initial interest came from trade unions and, especially, campus groups.

Sundry demonstrations and demands arose. Sheffield University's student government passed a resolution demanding reinstatement, socialists elsewhere at London University organized a dance fundraiser, and Cambridge students protested. Meyer's comrades brought grievances to Parliament and the Home Office.[22] Michael Straight recalled marching around the streets of London with a passel of students chanting "Free Frank Meyer."[23] *The Times, The Daily Telegraph, The Manchester Guardian,* and other large circulation dailies covered the controversy.[24]

The LSE student union launched an investigation, the results of which they sent to the press and the powerful.[25] The innocuously named National Student League (NSL), a Communist front, telegraphed its objections to Beveridge from the United States and announced plans to send a delegation to the British consulate in New York.[26] The Soviet Union's TASS received a situation report via telegram.[27] The Federation of Student Societies framed the suspensions as part of a campaign by school authorities to further restrict the rights of student groups.[28] Very quickly a Reinstatement Committee was formed, which falsely claimed no association between Meyer and *The Student Vanguard.* In reality, Meyer oversaw the publication. As a matter of conspiratorial policy, he initially put names of people not really involved in the magazine and kept names of those involved largely off it.[29] By the release of the issue in question, the publication featured no full names but initials, unsigned articles, and pseudonyms.[30]

Meyer enjoyed the support of powerful well-wishers.

"Is the right hon. gentleman aware that this gentleman is pursuing a course of study at the British Museum, and is there any reason why, even if he ceases to study at the School of Economics, he should not be allowed to continue his research work at the museum?" asked Labour Party Deputy Leader Clement Attlee from the well of the House of Commons.[31]

Others in Parliament wished him gone.

The dashing flying ace Alec Cunningham-Reid, a Conservative MP described as England's handsomest man, inquired of Sir John Gilmour, the home secretary, at whose request "he issued and subsequently withdrew instructions for an American student—Frank Meyer—to leave this country in connection with subversive political activities; and if he will consider renewing them." Gilmour answered by describing his involvement, to the disbelief of many, as merely routine.[32]

"The expulsion has had far-reaching consequences—reaching to the House of Commons itself—and has had an effect on the life and career of Mr. Meyer," read a petition to reinstate the expelled student signed by scores of figures of import.[33]

Signatories included the future prime minister Attlee, the philosopher Bertrand Russell, the author of the novels *Howards End* and *Passage to India* E. M. Forster, Dean of Canterbury Hewlett Johnson, the publisher Victor Gollancz, the future Nobel Prize–winning physicist Cecil Frank Powell, the wife of a former prime minister Margot Asquith, the Labour Party leader George Lansbury, and the Cambridge classics professor F. M. Cornford, the father of Meyer's protégé John.

"The fact that Mr. Meyer's left-wing political views appear to have influenced the Home Office in taking this serious step," the petition charged, "has increased the apprehensions of many, that this consideration also influenced the Director in discriminating against Meyer, and we feel that if this discrimination was now ended and Mr. Meyer was treated in the same way as Mr. Simons, these apprehensions would clearly prove groundless."[34]

Political allies attempted to persuade Malinowski to inflate Meyer's importance to the anthropology department. Malinowski, whose own student secretary according to his

troubled student belonged to the party, informed Meyer that
he had rebuffed these backdoor entreaties.[35]

Without Malinowski's backing, the movement para-
phrased Firth's description of Frank, from long before his
activities overwhelmed his anthropology, as "probably the
student best fitted in the world to give his assistance with his
work on Polynesian kinship." This assertion was a means of
rebutting the LSE director's claim that he took into account
his "whole past record in the School" in expelling him but
granting leniency to the others.[36] Malinowski saw through
this as tommyrot. Whatever the Balliol graduate's potential
a year or so prior, by early 1934 he stuck out academically as
a deadbeat.

Beveridge refused to budge. The LSE director remained
gobsmacked decades later by "six or seven students, led by
a very red politician from America" distributing a publication in defiance of his order. This shows the degree to which
Meyer invaded his headspace. "It is a curious fact that the
American leader of the revolt, whom the Emergency Committee after full consideration felt to be better suited to the
United States than to the School, had been not only President
of our Students Union, but a paid research assistant to one of
our teachers," Beveridge wrote.[37]

Then and later, Beveridge surely wondered why fellow
men of the left treated him so. He took it as a personal af-
front, which guaranteed consequences for the most flagrant
of the rebels.

Malinowski, "astonished" over a reconsideration in the
Home Office as well as at LSE, advised Beveridge to feel free to
describe Meyer's scientific work as "completely terminated"
should the authorities inquire. He wrote the school's director:

> I hear, though I have not seen it myself, that the Home
> Office has been asked, to postpone the end of his Brit-
> ish permit, because his scientific work had not been
> finished. I think I can take it for granted that you have

not countenanced any of these moves, that you are not prepared to suggest to the Governors that they should reconsider their decision. In case there were any question of that sort, I think it would be quite as well for me to make it quite clear that I should not accept Meyer as a research student under my supervision. I have had a conservation with Dr. R. W. Firth on this matter, and he is fully in agreement with me to the extent that he also would refuse to undertake Meyer's supervision. My decision is based on the fact that previously to his first expulsion, I have had several times to admonish Meyer for neglect in work, irregularity of attendance and other purely technical matters. After his suspension I told him that I might intercede on his behalf if he gave me the full assurance that he will completely subordinate his other activities to the work on Anthropology. Such a request I made twice verbally and once in writing; three times Meyer failed to give me this assurance.[38]

In April, Meyer received notification that foreign students finished with their studies must leave the country. His plea that he still conducted research fell on deaf ears. Three weeks into April, the Home Office refused to allow him to prolong his stay.[39]

◆ ◆ ◆

"I HEAR YOU are having a contre temps with the Home Office," the prime minister's daughter wrote. "I do not suppose I can do anything by interfering, but if you think that there is any thing I may able to do, I am at your service."[40]

Even the prime minister's daughter could not save him from deportation. Perhaps especially the prime minister's daughter could not save him from deportation. Whether Beveridge further encouraged the Home Office to rid him of a campus menace or the Home Office used the expulsion to rid the country of a foreign agitator whose social network now extended into the prime minister's family mattered little. The chess enthusiast knew checkmate.

The center of attention prepared to depart the first weekend in June. His understudy John Cornford prepared to replace him as the leader of Great Britain's Communist student movement, a phenomenon that had not existed upon the American's arrival.[41]

"Following on the expulsion of Frank Meyer from L.S.E. for his political activities, he is being forced to leave the country," a notice galvanizing demonstrators read. "He is taking the 8.10 Newhaven Boat train from Victoria. Rally to protest. The agitation for permission for him to return at once must be begun NOW."[42]

Frank Meyer never returned.

He moved on. His comrades in England soon did, too.

◄ 7 ►

Student

M eyer did not go home, at least not immediately. He spent about a month in Paris enjoying one of his favorite cities and working directly under Walter Ulbricht, the future leader of a country, East Germany, that did not then exist. He prepared a World Student and Youth Congress Against War and Fascism.[1] The contrast between gay Paris and stern Ulbricht summed up his lifestyle as hard to sum up.

"This class struggle sure plays hell with your poetry," Jack Reed famously noted.[2] What this earlier playboy-poet revolutionary had observed Meyer soon experienced. In a matter of days, he had traveled from the embrace of the prime minister's delightful daughter to the clutches of the grim German who later built the Berlin Wall. Meyer did not die in Europe as Reed did. But his poetry did. His gaiety in large part did. The life of the party spent the next decade giving his life to the party.

"MEYER signed a letter from the COMITE MONDIAL DES ETUDIANTS CONTRA LE GUERRE ET LE FASCISM, Paris, to the Students Anti-War Movement at 53 Grays Inn Road, W.C.1.," the British Embassy in Paris reported. "Enclosed with this letter was copy of another letter addressed to the

75

adult movement by Secretariat of the International Anti-War Movement, and signed ULRICH," by which the writer possibly meant Ulbricht, or possibly Ulbricht used a *nom de guerre*.[3]

Meyer provided instruction from the continent to British comrades on how to prepare for the upcoming peace conference and cited the Communist activism at Cambridge, already involving John Cornford and future espionage agents Guy Burgess and Donald Maclean, as an example to emulate.[4] His impact on the older British university seemed more profound. The Oxford Pledge endorsed the year after Meyer's graduation by the Oxford Union sent global reverberations that led to press coverage in Nazi Germany and a mention by Benito Mussolini.[5]

"You may be interested to know that MEYER is now in Paris working on behalf of the Initiative Committee for the World Youth Congress which is to take place on 28–30 September in Geneva or Paris. The Committee is a subsidiary of the Youth Anti-War Movement," MI5's head Vernon Kell pointed out. "MEYER is pressing for the better organization of a student opinion against what he calls 'the present drive towards war', and advocates intensive anti-war and anti-fascist propaganda among the Universities in England, particularly among the [Officers' Training Corps]."[6]

✦ ✦ ✦

HELENE MEYER'S son finally returned to the States on July 4, 1934.[7] Armed with a letter of introduction from Harry Pollitt, the general secretary of the Communist Party of Great Britain, Meyer soon entered the Greenwich Village offices of the Communist Party of the United States of America (CPUSA). Pollitt's note acted, in Meyer's words, as a "transfer."[8] In the CPUSA headquarters, party goon Jack Stachel referred him to Gil Green, national secretary of the Young Communist League.[9]

On the ninth floor of the East Twelfth Street headquarters, he informed Green of his activities in Great Britain. They talked on at least two occasions. "At the end of this series of conversations I was assigned to go to Chicago to work in the preparation and organization of the Second United States Congress against War and Fascism then about to be held," Meyer remembered.[10] This represented a continuity with his most recent work under Ulbricht, which technically continued.

There, at the September event, he again met Green. The newcomer became the secretary of the Illinois Youth Section of the Second United States Congress against War and Fascism.[11] On orders from Ulbricht's World Committee Against War and Fascism and not his new American masters, he attended the first conference of the Congress of the Canadian League Against War and Fascism, held on October 6 and 7 in Toronto.[12] During this northern sojourn with the Americans Green and Max Weiss, he also attended conferences of the Canadian Student League and Canada's Young Communist League.[13] With international obligations fulfilled, he went to work for the American party by going to school. As Meyer reflected to an old friend years later, "I was formally a graduate student but mainly a party functionary."[14]

♦ ♦ ♦

MEYER'S effectiveness as a campus organizer in Great Britain practically assured some task organizing young people. Green's assigning Meyer to Chicago likely stemmed from his knowledge that a spot in one of the nation's most important universities awaited the younger man.

Bronisław Malinowski exported his problem child. He left Meyer's predicament with the Home Office and LSE vague but requested in a recommendation letter to Fay-Cooper Cole of Scopes Monkey Trial fame that the student's focus take on "an exclusively anthropological and scientific character."[15] The

University of Chicago's anthropology department could muster but a half scholarship given the lateness of the inquiry.[16]

Meyer looked forward to again using the cover of academia to recruit party members, promote Marxism, and capture institutions for Stalinism. The twenty-five-year-old graduate student matriculated on October 3.[17] Less than a week later, the student newspaper carried a page-one item promoting a campus lecture by him.[18] He spoke on "The University Student," detailing the experiences that led to his deportation.[19] The following month he again spoke on behalf of the NSL, a Communist-directed front group, against charges that the group amounted to a Communist-directed front.[20]

Edward Shils, a sociology research assistant, observed the new campus phenomenon as "a demonic figure with flashing black eyes, a mop of black hair before mops on the head became the fashion, shabby in dress, eloquent, voluble, excitable." He judged Meyer "by nature a mischief maker."[21]

The extracurriculars left little time for the curriculars. He enrolled in Introduction to Anthropology, Comparative Science of Culture, and Ethnography of Malaysia. He received grades in none of them. Cole and his colleague Robert Redfield discovered in one academic quarter what took Malinowski nearly two years. Perhaps Malinowski forewarned them. Maybe they just lacked his patience. Possibly they boasted more advanced anthropological insights into the campus subculture of Stalinists. The department dumped Meyer.[22] Strangely, the school allowed the graduate student without grades to remain. Meyer shifted to political science. Shils, who assisted Professor Lewis Wirth, recalled that Meyer frequently interrupted sociology lectures "with Marxist corrections, supplements, and reinterpretations."[23] During the winter quarter he received an A in Recent Political Thought. But that remained the sole grade awarded to him by a professor during his first fifteen classes over six quarters at the University of Chicago.[24] His real grades came from outside the university.

◆ ◆ ◆

"HOW LONG, Martin, how long?"²⁵

The party's campus recruiter asked the question to a younger fellow traveler who, like so many before him, felt the pull of his galvanic personality. Martin Gardner wanted Frank Meyer as a friend. Meyer wanted Gardner to join the Communist Party. Years later Gardner became one of America's most famous popular science and math writers, magicians, puzzle aficionados, and, especially, skeptics of pseudoscience. During the mid-1930s, he supported his education working as a waiter and soda jerk at the Fifty-Seventh Street Maid-Rite Grill, where in the back booth Meyer took part in evening bull sessions on Marxism with a crowd that included Gardner and the future *Chicago Sun-Times* columnist Sydney J. Harris. A reticent Gardner never quite succumbed to the older man's pressure. He chalked up refusing Meyer's commanding invitation to cowardice.²⁶ But it took courage to rebuff the party's tenacious talent scout. More likely Gardner's inherent skepticism, which later made him the scourge of spoon-bender Uri Geller, prevented him from falling for the miracle idea touted as sure to bring heaven on earth.

So many could not escape his magnetism. Campus political groups proved a boon for him. The Oxford Union lifetime member helped organize a similar organization.²⁷ Ominously, the student newspaper listed him as one of the University of Chicago Political Union's vote counters.²⁸ It also noted the election of Paul Goodman, later of *Growing Up Absurd* fame, and other decidedly left-wing campus characters on the "Conservative" line.²⁹ Whether rigging involved creative mathematics or Manchurian candidates, the election resulted in Meyer's becoming the body's vice president and dominating the group.³⁰

"One of his jobs every year as a party guy was to make sure that the editor of the University of Chicago student newspaper, the *Maroon*, was a young Communist," explained his friend and editor Jameson Campaigne Jr. "He said, 'I performed that task pretty easily every year. But one year, the student that I made the editor of the *Chicago Maroon* died the day before school opened.' He was very proud of the fact he was able to get another young Communist from New York City admitted to the University of Chicago and made editor of the *Chicago Maroon*, so that the following day, Saturday, the young Communist was on the Broadway Limited on the way to the University of Chicago to become a student there."[31]

Communism, as it did at the London School of Economics, permeated even his accommodations. For a good part of his stay in Hyde Park, he lived in the International House. Party members from around the world converged on the newly built residence hall. This eased their ability to partake in conspiratorial and merely organizational activities.[32] His free time at the Maid-Rite Grill, his largely nonexistent class time, his extracurricular activities in the Political Union and National Student League, and his home life all centered on Communism. He could not escape Communism for a few hours even if he wanted to. He did not want to. He did his best to ensure that others could not escape, either.

◆ ◆ ◆

THE GENERATION born during the First World War did not want a Second World War. Over 80 percent of American students polled by *Literary Digest* in 1935 said that they would not fight for their country if the United States invaded another nation. About 17 percent said they would refuse to fight even if another country invaded the United States.[33] The Communists capitalized on the zeitgeist by glomming on to a peace movement spearheaded by the Fellowship of Reconciliation and other groups that despised spearheads. Their interests during the Popular Front period called for alliances with non-Communists to defend the Soviet Union from fascism, Nazism, and other rival ideologies. Joseph Stalin feared encirclement. So pushing for peace made sense.

The idea of a group touting expropriation, revolution, and other acts of violence posing as peace advocates proved too rich for many. That the American League Against War and Fascism's monthly publication, *Fight Against War and Fascism*, emphasized the first word in exponentially larger font than the rest of the name on its cover told many pacifists all they needed to know. Frank's and his comrades' methods became so notorious that in Chicago the Young People's Socialist League specified the exclusion of the NSL, American League Against War and Fascism, and other Communist fronts from their protests against the Reserve Officers' Training Corps.[34] Not all antiwar activists shunned Communists.

The Second United States Congress Against War and Fascism met September 28–30, 1934, in Chicago. The Communists claimed an attendance of fourteen thousand. Meyer, in the weeks prior to starting classes in his new graduate school, helped ensure that young people (sixteen- to twenty-five-year-olds) neared one in four of the 3,332 delegates.[35] When Chairman Harry F. Ward in his opening remarks described the group as a "united front," he spoke more to the wishes of the Communists than to reality. By the time the new Chicago graduate student immersed himself in the American League Against War and Fascism, the National Association for the Advancement of Colored People and the League for Industrial Democracy had pulled their associations. The Fellowship of Reconciliation, suspicious of the Communists, refused involvement.[36] One speaker, Corliss Lamont, affirming to many on the non-Communist left why they had stayed home, described the Soviet Union at the event as "a whole country organized against war" and "the greatest single factor in the world today toward keeping international peace."[37]

Meyer organized an antimilitarism march within a larger peace event that resulted in opponents tossing eggs at the Communists in 1935. The following year, he led scores of marshals in white armbands in again serving as the grand marshal of the parade. The wider event aimed "to inform the world students will not fight a second great war" by imposing an 11 a.m. to noon classroom strike.[38] To the tune of the school's fight song, the demonstrators sang: "March our students from the classrooms / Raise our slogans high / Strike for peace and let the world know / For profits we won't die / Students of the world stand with us / Determined war must cease / March on, students of Chicago / And we'll win our strike for PEACE." Sixteen hundred people convened in the school's fieldhouse to hear antiwar speeches. Not until Meyer staged banners for photographers and repeated a talk for the press did a not-so conscientious objector throw a half dozen eggs at him and his comrades.[39]

◆ ◆ ◆

THE CAMPUS'S reputation as a hotbed of radical activity drew the interest of the state legislature.

The Communist Club sought to affiliate with the Young Communist League, but the school administration, worried about lawmakers in Springfield, blocked the move. In keeping with the ethos of the Popular Front period and in the spirit of keeping away anti-Communist politicians, the Communists increasingly held open meetings—open to all but Trotskyists.[40] Even if they still engaged in machinations and conspiracy, they wished to give the appearance of working with non-Communists and operating in the sunlight. Doing this also helped their Popular Front aims, so it pertained to more than mere appearances.

They engaged in, according to the student newspaper, "misbehavior" at a socialist meeting to the degree that they posted guards to prevent reciprocation.[41] When newsman Garrick Utley's newsman father Clifton spoke on the Spanish

Civil War, *The Daily Maroon* reported the high point "came when Frank Meyer arose shouting 'A matter of procedure,' and proceeded to turn the meeting from a question and answer session to a discussion of the neutrality policy of the United States."[42] The Communists did not play by the rules that they insisted others follow.

To stave off legislators citing state sedition laws, Communists found the campus liberals useful. Meyer rejected a report indicating that he had ordered his comrades to "moderate" activities in response to outside scrutiny. Instead, he characterized his outlook: "That at the present moment in my opinion the NSL should work with the whole university against the legislative enquiry and the Red-baiting of Mr. [William Randolph] Hearst and Mr. [Charles] Walgreen."[43]

Whether Hearst or Walgreen took interest in the campus Communists, campus Communists took an interest in them. In early 1936, putting action to his pledge not to moderate in the wake of the legislative inquiry, Frank mounted a pressure campaign that compelled the Midway Theatre to drop Hearst Metrotone News. The confirmed anti-Communism and alleged militarism of the media magnate suddenly anathematized his newsreel service.[44]

The external attack helped him engineer the united front he desired. The broader left circled the wagons around the extremists targeted by the legislature. In an era when Communists privately mocked non-Communist leftists as dupes rather than publicly denigrating them as fascists, the Hyde Park Stalinists welcomed the support. They did not reflexively reciprocate.

The lapdog in the united front continued to play the role of pit bull when circumstances, or his natural disposition, demanded. In the student newspaper and at a campus forum, he attacked University of Chicago President Robert Maynard Hutchins's attempts to reform the school.

A Hutchins-era joke described the University of Chicago as a Baptist school where Presbyterians sent their children to be converted to Catholicism by a Jew.[45] Under the influence of his gnomish friend Mortimer Adler, the towering Hutchins sought to transform the university into a Great Books school. He instituted a program focusing on the classics for those so inclined and sidelined the school's famous football team on the grounds that a gridiron corresponded with the mission of a university about as much as a pool hall or a bowling alley did.[46] But most of his educational ideas found a receptive audience outside the campus walls. In his book *The Higher Learning in America*, Hutchins called for the abolition of academic departments, the institution of a common core composed of Great Books courses, the banishment of professional education to trade schools or the professions themselves, and the careful design of a curriculum by educators rather than a course of electives randomly chosen by the uneducated.[47]

The Communist student leader described this philosophy as expounding "totalitarian education, a return to the philosophy of St. Thomas Aquinas and reactionary Catholicism."[48] He countered with education relativistic rather than absolutist regarding first principles and democratic in allowing professors and students to determine curriculum.[49]

When Meyer "jumped" up to question the guest speaker at the *Daily Maroon*'s annual banquet in 1937, Hutchins said a thousand words in two by mumbling, "Oh, God."[50]

Meyer's reputation preceded him. He again became a campus celebrity. A student poet wrote of the relationship between Marx and Meyer, "If the soapbox battalion expounded Karl / Frank Meyer would run to Albemarle."[51] A columnist in the student newspaper recounted, or perhaps fantasized, about a debate between Meyer and Gertrude Stein, who had visited Chicago months prior, with the former answering the latter's criticisms of Marxist jargon with "but . . . but . . . but . . . yes, but . . ."[52] When students informed the twelve-year-old sister of an undergraduate that she had just shared a lunch table with "the campus #1 Communist," she responded, "Pooh, he's no communist, he's just a boy."[53]

✦ ✦ ✦

AT THE END of April 1937, that boy wrote his mother that "in case you were worried that I am not devoting enough time to study, you will probably be pleased to know that from now till my prelims are over I am going to concentrate much more on my academic work. I have made the necessary arrangements as far as my political work is concerned."[54]

That spring he received two incompletes and a C.[55] He submitted that year a "preliminary sketch" for a dissertation on African American advancement that emphasized such party-infused themes as the emergence of the "Negro proletariat" from the Great Migration and the idea of a separate black nation carved out of the American South.[56] It led to nothing concrete. Yet, his letter to his mother represented less deception than aspiration. The flailing student, thinking of himself and thinking a Communist with a Ph.D. made for a more useful Communist than one without one, convinced party bosses to grant him a sabbatical to "knuckle down" on academic work. This lasted a few months, but inevitably party needs trumped student work.[57]

Despite enrolling in four additional quarters after pledging more studiousness to his mother, that spring C—one of six actual grades he received from thirty-six total courses—came as his last lettered grade at the school. He withdrew in the spring of 1938. "Not permitted to reregister," the angry red ink stamped on his transcript announced by the summer. "By action of the dean of students and university examiner."[58]

Membership had its privileges. These did not include immunity to that red ink. The academic bouncers tossed even party people when they made a mockery of the institution's purpose. Meyer brazenly did that. Academics, including such luminaries as Bronisław Malinowski and Charles Merriam, charmed by his personality, seduced by his intellect, and vaguely sympathetic to his politics, allowed him to essentially play hooky on graduate school. Their tolerance eventually expired. Everyone's tolerance expired by 1938.

He wasted their time. More so did he waste his own. The graduate student enjoyed access to some of the best minds at two of the world's great educational institutions during their heydays. Instead of learning from them, the student arrogantly acted as teacher. That he did this during the Great Depression made the sin more egregious—and more understandable. The terrible times fostered the delusion that the revolution just around the corner assuredly obliterated grades and other vestiges of the soon-defunct hierarchal society. So why bother?

In the thirteen years since his high school graduation, he had attended six different institutions and attained just one degree. The euphoria of his front-row seat on the movement's ascent during its halcyon decade obscured in real time the opportunities discarded. That realization arrived much later. Sooner came the movement's decline.

◄ 8 ►

Husband

T he University of Chicago expelled Frank Meyer from its graduate school in 1938. The Chicago Workers School (CWS) promptly named him its director.

Though John D. Rockefeller founded the accredited university and Earl Browder served as the founding director of the makeshift school, the change likely did not feel much like one. He wrote "Section Schools in Chicago" for the national Communist publication *Party Organizer* in October 1936, so his involvement predated the appointment.[1] His responsibilities still very much involved education and organizing young people. The twentysomething who behaved like a stern teacher when a student now acted like a sybarite student as a teacher. If an audacity marked his upgrading from Princeton dropout to Oxford graduate, then going from expelled pupil to principal radiated a preposterous quality.

The CWS, like similar institutions elsewhere, attracted non-Communists as it imparted undiluted Marxist theory to the initiated. It operated a layered system. Meyer taught doctrine within the deepest layers.

Main courses were split between Marxist theory and the left's history. The political scientist James Farr noted additional classes on "party organization, public speaking, parliamentary procedure, mimeograph technique, labor journalism, social insurance, fundamentals of political education, and 'Training for Children's Work.' To this last should be added language courses: English for the foreign-born cadres and new members in Chicago, as well as Russian for those who aspired to read Soviet literature."[2]

Meyer ran the CWS. He also taught a series of courses within it, and outside of it, on Marxism. As Meyer assumed responsibility, the Illinois party secretary Morris Childs described the school as underused in the report to the state convention and insisted that every Communist must set aside a few hours a week for taking classes.[3] Meyer used *The History of the Communist Party of the Soviet Union*, as directed by the Kremlin, as the primary text for students in his advanced courses once it became available in the United States after its publication there in 1939. Class discussions focused on that textbook, written by Joseph Stalin's advisors and revised by them whenever a line changed or a Communist fell from favor.[4] Both occurred often when Meyer served as director from 1938 to 1941.

◆ ◆ ◆

APART from CWS, he launched, as part of a much broader push by the Communists, a Science and Society group at the University of Chicago after his departure. It depicted Karl Marx as a scientist no different from Isaac Newton or Charles Darwin and his "science" as deserving of classroom study.[5] It sought to attract scientists to what Marx described as scientific socialism.

The group's name derived from a journal launched in 1936 by the CPUSA, which eventually enlisted Meyer to critique it for the party press and directly for V. J. Jerome, head of its Cultural Commission. *Science & Society* answered the question of whether the publication directed its loyalty to science or the strange, small society from which it sprang by refusing a $25,000 donation, an enormous sum during the late 1930s, because of the string attached that the party must relinquish veto power over contributors to allow it to operate more like a normal academic journal.[6]

The cause demanded service beyond the job description; the circumstances demanded that the peace activist morph into a military recruiter. The party tasked Meyer with convincing Americans to fight against Francisco Franco's forces in Spain. Meyer gauged that fellow Communists accounted for close to 90 percent of American volunteers as a result of party-imposed quotas on recruiters and pressure on members to fight.

"This meant, so far as disciplined cadre Communists were concerned, something very close to actual assignment to volunteer, and so far as rank-and-file members were concerned, exhortation, Party pressure, etc.," he recalled. "I am not saying that there were not true volunteers among the Communists, but elements of pressure I would estimate affected 75% of those who went."[7]

Hundreds of Americans lost their lives. Meyer undoubtedly dragooned men into signing up for something almost like a game of Russian Roulette. And he did this after learning that his English protégé John Cornford, among the conflict's earliest foreign recruiters and fighters, had died in Spain the day after he turned twenty-one.

The U.S. Ambassador to Spain Claude Bowers and others dubbed the conflict a rehearsal for the Second World War. This grasps a truth in myriad ways, including the penchant of Communists for betrayal. The first zigzag reoriented Meyer from peace activist to military recruiter. Dizzying swerves followed. World War II started when Soviet Socialists, sworn enemies of National Socialists, entered into an agreement with their ideological cousins. They set aside their previous mutual enmity, which stemmed more from a turf war over constituents than any broad philosophical chasm, for the purpose of mutual engorgement. Each shared more in common with the other than either did with Great Britain, the United States, or France. The common denominators included a desire to subjugate beyond their borders and willingness to exterminate within them. Sometimes they did the reverse.

The day Americans heard news of an alliance between Nazi Germany and the Soviet Union, the general secretary of the Communist Party USA celebrated the Apollyon–Sathanas partnership in an evening interview on NBC. Earl Browder, who the previous month had dismissed such an alliance as about as likely as his winning the presidency of the Chamber of Commerce, explained to a stunned radio audience, "The Soviet-German agreement is . . . the best current example of the way to peace."[8]

The mutual nonaggression pact was entered into by totalitarian powers flying the blood-red flags of revolution and claiming the mantle of socialism in the very names they called themselves. This struck everyone else as a mutual aggression pact. This sentiment found validation in the September invasions of Poland. The CWS director attended the national committee meeting of the Communist Party when Germany invaded Poland.[9] Two weeks later, the Soviet Union invaded the smaller nation from the east.

Meyer defended the agreement about two weeks after the Soviet Union's invasion of Poland.[10] The ex-student denounced, at a University of Chicago event entitled "Imperialism and War," any talk of Western intervention on behalf of the invaded nations. Rather than being anti-imperialist, defending small nations from takeover by more powerful nations now constituted imperialism.[11] He sounded like the leader of his party.

By the time Browder's prophecy of the agreement bringing peace fell, the general secretary blamed the victim "for its refusal to accept the military aid of the Soviet Union." He reasoned that "the Soviet Union had no choice" as he rejected characterizing its invasion as an invasion and rationalized

the violation of the Soviet-Polish nonaggression pact as really no violation at all given that the Polish government that
had entered into that pact no longer, as of September of 1939,
governed. The interview with three New York City newspapers concluded with Browder's claim that Communist Party
membership "accelerated" after the pact and that it led to no
exodus of leading Jewish members.[12]

It definitely hurt the CPUSA in terms of external progressive elements willing to lend their names to this or that party
crusade. One could conceivably say that the pact, in a literal
sense, decimated membership by estimates most generous to
the decency of Communists. But Americans joined and left in
large numbers prior to Stalin's alliance with Hitler, so the actual percentage departing because of the pact likely amounted to some figure lower than 10 percent.[13] Meyer described
the defections outside of New York as "infinitesimal."[14]

Meyer stayed. He, like the other Jews Browder generally
mentioned, did not storm out. This does not mean that the
Jews who remained accepted the news without internal coil
and moil. Edward Shils recalled spotting Meyer on a street
corner following the pact looking so "despondent" that he
wondered whether he might break from the party.[15] Instead,
he defended the indefensible. What Browder believed, Meyer
then believed; what Browder said, Meyer then said.

The American League Against War and Fascism, an auxil-
iary of a worldwide movement that Meyer had labored for
in England, France, Holland, Canada, and the United States,
changed its name more than a year before the pact and
then immediately dissolved in its aftermath.[16] Its periodical, *Fight Against War and Fascism*, similarly altered its name
before ceasing publication in July 1939.[17] Anti-Nazism, one
of the party's primary attractions, no longer provided ra-
tionalizations to those in league with it. The Popular Front
necessarily ended.

✦ ✦ ✦

MEYER later described his primary job from 1938 to 1941 as the district's education director: "In this capacity I had complete responsibility for all of the education, agitation, and propaganda: classes of all kinds, leaflets, pamphlets, public meetings, secret party schools; in addition I was Director of the Chicago Workers School."

The director's description of his CWS role, a full-time position by any estimation, as almost an afterthought reveals the degree to which the party exploited its workers. "Other assignments, which varied from time to time, included supervision of a wide variety of organizational activities throughout the District," he noted. "I was also involved in the work of the National Educational Commission and the National Schools Commission of the Communist Party, and contributed frequently to the theoretical organ of the Communist Party, *The Communist* (later *Political Affairs*)."[18]

The party paid him a nominal amount. It expected members to donate and subscribe to its publications. He estimated that he gave twice his salary back to the party.[19] They provided him a desk, both at the school and at the local office.[20] In exchange, he turned over the hours of his life. He regarded it as a fair trade.

He traveled to campuses as the party's education director for the Illinois-Indiana District. But he loomed largest in the Chicago Workers School, wherever its periodically moving location then resided.[21] His charisma, commanding presence, and knowledge of Marxism attracted undivided attention.

Eyes on the teacher aided not just the teacher's ideology but ego and eros, too. Some of the women staring at him inevitably drifted into his daydreams. Allen Kellogg Philbrick, a Communist teaching at a local school, knew of Meyer's reputation. He warned his wife to beware of the "wolf" at the head of her classroom.[22] Like Little Red Riding Hood, she proceeded without caution.

◆ ◆ ◆

ELSIE MAY BOWN, the oldest of three sisters, lived in Somerville, Massachusetts, until the family moved to Pine Lawn, Missouri, when she was eight years old. Her father, Samuel Bown, learned the shoe trade in England, from where her mother, Maria Clarke Bown, had also emigrated before meeting her husband.[23] In St. Louis, he worked as the superintendent of patents for the International Shoe Company. He earned an income above the norm during the Great Depression.[24] The daughter's preoccupations had little to do with her father's occupation.

"She likes music, writing, good books, and study very much, all thru her high school years she would curl up with a book, or work on school papers or *Saga* [the student publication she edited] in place of playing," Samuel Bown recounted. "This caused us some concern for her health although in spite of this she has enjoyed very good health in the years she has been in west."[25]

A playground taunt of "Elsie May / She gets all A's" told a truth.[26] At Normandy High School, where she skipped gym to study and admittedly skipped social life to study, too, she left a mark in her marks.[27] Straight A's allowed her to graduate as valedictorian, first in a class of seventy-five, in 1930.[28] Preferring Boston to St. Louis and regarding Radcliffe as first among the Seven Sisters, she looked a few miles from her early home for college.[29]

"She is much inclined to stay alone rather than join in social activities," her father divulged to Radcliffe's dean of students. "[T]his we hope will be less marked now that she will be associated with many girls who have similar ideas and ambitions."[30]

She studied English literature, which at Radcliffe included *The Importance of Being Earnest, Crime and Punishment, The Blithedale Romance,* and *Jane Eyre*.[31] Areas of specialization included the Bible, Sophocles, Cicero, and Shakespeare, the last of which came to her primarily from a favorite professor, George Lyman Kittredge.[32] While she credited his class for preparing her for life, undoubtedly reading Eugene O'Neill and writing a paper judged "satisfactory" on his work prepared her for *her* life.[33]

The Show Me State student showed little and guarded much. Radcliffe professors and administrators regarded her as awkward, introverted, and meek.

"Miss Bown is as dependable as she is capable," her tutor assessed. "She modestly underestimates her ability, however, in fact, her modesty extends almost to the point of timidity. But I feel that we are overcoming this difficulty."[34]

Even the photograph taken of her for school files affirmed this judgment. Bodily gawky and facially English, she looks gray and almost glum, with her name written on a card as though for a mug shot.[35] Adults who oversaw Elsie described her as "very undeveloped socially but improving" and judged that she "needs to join in social activity."[36] She eventually found a deep connection to real people through abstract ideas.

Allen Kellogg Philbrick, the son of the noted artist and teacher Allen E. Philbrick, attended Harvard, which was blocks away from its sister school just south of the Cambridge Common. He dabbled at cross country.[37] He immersed himself in Communism. Elsie did, too. Not for the first time through a movement did a misfit fit in.

In some key ways, their experiences paralleled Frank's. The New England branch of the NSL, the Communist front that protested the expulsion of London School of Economics student Frank Meyer, started at Harvard in 1932 with Radcliffe students, possibly including Elsie, at the organizational meeting.[38] Philbrick soon served as secretary of Harvard's

NSL chapter.[39] As Frank's group at the University of Chicago dodged eggs during their strike for peace, Cambridge's Communists experienced a pelting of foodstuffs at their corresponding event in 1935.[40] At the same time that the British deported Meyer, Philbrick caused an international incident on the Boston waterfront.

A German sailor caught the Harvard junior shoving Communist flyers into the blower of a ship docked at Charlestown naval yard.

"Attention German sailors!" Philbrick's literature read. "Let not Hitler lie to you. His promises are broken daily. Salvation lies in Communism. The heroic K.P.D. [Communist Party of Germany] lives and fights. Join the fight, German sailors, for a free Soviet Germany."

Philbrick, who lied to American authorities about his address and identity, spent the night in jail.[41]

His relationship with Elsie intensified. Atop their peculiar, shared ideology, common denominators included intellectual pursuits and music. Elsie loved to listen. Allen played piano.

Samuel Bown attempted in vain to steer his daughter away from her radical beau.[42] But while her parents could, through the *in loco parentis* ethos that governed Radcliffe, restrict any trips beyond those to her aunt and uncle in Lynn and a family friend closer by, they could do nothing to prevent her from seeing a man enrolled in the college a short walk away.[43]

She graduated on June 20, 1934.[44] The end of college did not mean the end of the couple. They married during his senior year on the first Saturday of 1935.[45] Experiencing the radicalization of his daughter in Cambridge and her shock marriage to an artist-intellectual immersed in that same political milieu left the conservative father of three daughters to vow, "I'm not sending anyone else to those communist schools in the East."[46]

✦ ✦ ✦

ELSIE returned to the Midwest. She participated in the 1936–1937 Flint sit-down strike in a General Motors plant that catapulted organized labor into a position of greater power.[47] She enrolled in evening classes in education at Washington University.[48] Despite the courses and an ambition to teach, Mrs. Philbrick instead engaged in a series of clerical jobs in St. Louis before moving to Chicago around the New Year of 1938.[49] She continued secretarial work at the University of Chicago, where Mr. Philbrick, a Chicagoland native, pursued an advanced degree.[50]

"Geographic work with husband, entailing historical investigation in New England area, particularly Maine," she described her life in late 1939. "Have also engaged in interesting precinct work in connection with local elections in Chicago."[51]

That interesting work became more interesting when she met the director of the CWS in 1940.[52] Given Elsie and Allen's ties to the University of Chicago, their Hyde Park address, and their shared Communist Party activism, crossing Frank Meyer's path appeared inevitable. That such a meeting reoriented the paths of the three parties seemed, as Allen Philbrick worried, predictable.

While the face of CWS did not work in the underground, his additional duties, sometimes mysterious and often involving powerful party leaders, added to Meyer's allure. Even in a movement bewitched by fixations on equality, the school's authority figure impressively looked a rank or two above his comrades to the young women taking his courses. The Communist capitalized.

Husband

✦ ✦ ✦

THE COMMUNIST PARTY reported 1,200 students taking CWS courses in 1940.[53] One of them stood out to the teacher. The teacher stood out to that student as well.

"I thought this guy was absolutely fascinating," Elsie explained. "Unfortunately, he would never notice me at all."[54]

She did not know him as her husband did. She came to know him as commanding, charismatic, and charming. The extrovert possessed what the introvert lacked. He also reflected her passions in reading and politics. Both exhibited intelligence well above the norm. The attraction burned red hot.

In her Radcliffe alumni questionnaire for the coming 1940, Elsie listed Allen Philbrick as her husband, their address at Chicago's Mayfair Apartments, and her mother-in-law as a contact who would "ordinarily" know where to locate her.[55] But 1940 proved a far from ordinary year for Elsie Philbrick. In October, one could locate her standing before a justice of the peace with her instructor. The same week Mrs. Allen Kellogg Philbrick finalized her divorce she became Mrs. Frank Straus Meyer.

◄ 9 ►

Soldier

Within months of the bachelor's taking a bride, he received a new role from his other love. In early 1941, the party shifted its leading teacher of theory in the region from education to its other major department, organization. He regarded it as a promotion.[1] He became the assistant organizations secretary and its membership director.

He assisted Morris Childs, a twenty-year veteran of the Communist Party aided in his rise by his association with Earl Browder, in organizing the district. "The organizer is the policy man, the man with final say on all questions, so that actually the organizational department has responsibility for the carrying out of all organization decisions, for implementing of decisions, for the check-up on membership, for the functioning of organizations of the Party," Meyer noted of the role he assisted.[2]

One of Meyer's functions involved retention. He reached out to Herbert Goldhamer, a sociologist conducting research on voluntary organizations, to apply his techniques to the Communist Party. Goldhamer agreed on the condition that he publish his findings without restriction. Meyer, though sensing this to be a fool's errand, brought the matter to

Childs, who scoffed at turning over party statistics to an independent social scientist, let alone allowing him to publicize the data.[3]

Some he wished to repel. The writers Nelson Algren and Studs Terkel, whom he regarded as dilettante goofballs, he discouraged despite their enthusiasms.[4]

Just as his previous jobs as Chicago Workers School director and Illinois-Indiana District educational director overlapped, a synergistic quality colored this role. The job description did not always correspond to the job title.

The party tasked its new district membership director with recruitment, collection of dues, and oversight of membership.[5] The job proved challenging under normal circumstances. The Soviet Union had invaded Poland, Finland, Lithuania, Latvia, and Estonia and allied with the dictator long understood as the main enemy. So recruiting and keeping members demanded more. His history of catalyzing the student movement in England and transforming campus activism at the University of Chicago provided the ideal background. The times, though, felt less than ideal.

◆ ◆ ◆

WORLD events shook the Communist politically. Events closer to home jarred him personally.

Helene Meyer visited her husband's grave in B'nai Jeshurun Cemetery after attending the funeral of a friend on June 8, 1941. There Mrs. Meyer, "discovered lying semi-conscious across his grave," as the *Newark Star-Ledger* put it, suffered a stroke. The sixty-nine-year-old devoted wife and mother died in the police car on the way to the hospital. The front-page account noted, "She made it a practice to frequently visit the grave of her late husband."[6]

Two weeks later, Nazi Germany invaded the Soviet Union. This dominated discussions at the CPUSA convention Frank attended days later in New York.⁷ The forced pivot likely did little to soothe a Jew whose mother, a servant of her co-religionists, had ventured to her reward knowing her son labored for an outfit in league with Adolf Hitler.

◆ ◆ ◆

FRANK memorialized his idiocy in *The Communist*, a monthly that offered more theoretical pieces than *The Daily Worker*. Significantly, the budding party theorist attempted to meld the American Founding with Marxism. The party zeitgeist at various stages called for this maneuver. So, the significance occurred not in Meyer's deviation from his comrades but in the exaggerated degree to which the idea beguiled him. Meyer, along with his coauthor Robert Strong, juxtaposed the "treasonous" Federalists' opposition to the War of 1812 with their political heirs' push for America's involvement in World War II:

> Then, reaction fought against the prosecution of the war because it was a progressive war, a just war, a war of national independence. Today, the forces of reaction are dragging our country more and more deeply into a very different kind of war, a war of imperialist conquest, an unjust, robber war. Today, the American people, with the working class, the leading progressive class of our time, at their head, fights again as in 1812 for progress and freedom. But now that light demands a struggle against this reactionary war. And as Thomas Jefferson's party stood in the vanguard then, so the Communist Party, heir to its traditions, leads the way today, certain that now, as then, in the words of Browder, "the people are going to march forward—and to the people will belong the victory."⁸

This propaganda piece bore an unfortunate publication date of July 1941. Though editors rushed into the magazine a condemnation of Operation Barbarossa (the bloody end to the Hitler–Stalin Pact launched on June 22), Meyer's piece reflected the old line.

Contortions ensued.

◆ ◆ ◆

MEYER wrote another piece one year later that curiously relied again on Thomas Jefferson and the War of 1812. This time he emphasized the former rather the latter and made the opposite point.

"As today we, to preserve our own independence, must fight shoulder to shoulder with all who will carry the struggle against the Axis tyranny, and above all, with the Soviet Union, Great Britain and China," he wrote in *The Communist*, "so in Jefferson's day, the United States had to make its alliances, to bind itself closely with the forces which were fighting against the enemies of progress, and especially with the militant democracy of revolutionary France."[9]

Given the contradictions between the articles, rooting his beliefs in the history of his country appeared difficult. He reached. As he inspected his country's history to vindicate Communism, he encountered not substantiation but refutation. He nevertheless continued the Sisyphean effort. That boulder kept flattening him on the roll down. He eventually learned his lesson, just not then when he appeared most foolish.

Even by the standards of Communists, Meyer's about-face looked particularly absurd. In using the same historical examples to come to the opposite conclusion, he proved only the elasticity of his opinions in service to the Soviet Union. He went from vehemently denouncing Nazi Germany to opposing any war effort against it as imperialism to urging the taking up of arms against the Third Reich.

This last argument persuaded him.

✦ ✦ ✦

IN THE AFTERMATH of Pearl Harbor, Meyer sought his release from party obligations to join the military. "I didn't feel like preaching war and not doing something about it," he recalled.[10] He specifically wished to become an army officer. At regular lunches with Morris Childs at such Chicago eateries as the Harding and the Triangle, the subordinate periodically petitioned his superior for permission to take leave to join the military.

"Don't do it," Meyer recalled Childs telling him. "There is no rush. You are 3-A. You may not be drafted at all. We need forces. Hold off."[11]

The stonewalling continued. Meyer noticed the disconnect between the party's very public support for the war effort and the constraints placed upon key members seeking to volunteer. He internally juxtaposed the vast recruitment effort so recently undertaken to raise companies of Americans to fight in the Spanish Civil War with the toothless exhortations to sign up for the Second World War. Questions created cracks. As he pushed, his superiors questioned his Marxist attitude.[12] He scoffed at the criticism. In time he realized they had possessed greater sensitivity to his internal disconnect than he did. His overseers saw something in him that he could not acknowledge and Communists could not persist alongside: doubt.

"We Social Democrats have not so much faith in our own judgments," Sheila MacDonald had playfully written Frank.[13] The prime minister's daughter's taunt finally caught up to him.

♦ ♦ ♦

ANOTHER FRIEND from his halcyon days undoubtedly pricked his conscience. Meyer had lured John Cornford further and further into the party. Cornford succeeded his mentor as leader of Communist students in Great Britain. The comrade in ideology and friend in poetry submerged himself in that world because of his older American friend. One former girlfriend, noting his intense political hatreds, predicted, "I believe he'll make the Revolution, destroy and kill."[14] Following a violent course courted violent resistance. Cornford, three days after Christmas of 1936, died in the Spanish Civil War. Meyer—as sure as he breathed—wondered whether Cornford had exited this world as a result of him.

Frank wanted in. He wanted in so much he almost wanted out. But he could not go absent without leave from the party. He needed its imprimatur.

"Look," he implored Childs in late spring 1942. "I would like to try it."[15] By "it" he meant to join as a volunteer officer candidate, or VOC. Filibustering and rerouted conservations followed. Meyer persevered as the seasons changed. Childs, answering with a tone of disgust, finally relented: "All right, if you want to do it, do it."[16]

He waived his 3-A deferment to obtain a 1-A classification. Failing to obtain bars as a VOC did not mean the Army would then force enlistment. It did mean he would become subject to the draft, at his previous status, once again. Taking leave from the Communist Party toward the end of the summer of 1942 for a month to put his affairs in order, he then traded one regimented life for another.

◆ ◆ ◆

HE REPORTED to Camp Grant in early October. The Rock-ford, Illinois, facility served as an induction center—receiv-ing—for civilians becoming soldiers. The brief stay includ-ed physicals and acclimatization to Army life. Within days, an eleven-hour bus ride took the volunteer from Rockford to Little Rock, where at Camp Robinson he started basic training.

"I feel a thousand times better—we all do—I've got a rifle, a bayonet, a gas-mask, field equipment issued as soon as we got in and ate last night," he wrote of his arrival.[17] He endured the gas chamber, hiked great distances, bivouacked, dug latrines, waited chow-hall tables, and engaged in other alien tasks.[18] Along with five other men, he lived in what he likened to a wooden tent in a hutment. He led his class in academic work and scored a 159 on an intelligence quotient test.[19] His brains set him apart. Basic training nevertheless mashed him togeth-er with men from diverse backgrounds. The forced egalitari-anism and brotherhood ironically undermined his ideologi-cal commitment to all that.

Growing up in a luxury hotel, attending elite private schools, and laboring for a decade at the core of international Communism did not allow for much mixing with plumbers and bricklayers. The Army did.

"His first key experience," John Meyer said of his father's slow alienation, "was finding out that ordinary Americans in the military were not the proletariat they were cut out to be in Communist theory."[20]

If class warfare did not pervade conversations of fellow soldiers, it did saturate letters from home. Elsie emphasized news of the Red Army to her husband in the U.S. Army, com-pared *Chicago Tribune* publisher Robert McCormick to Jo-seph Goebbels, wished Franklin Roosevelt dealt with critics the way Abraham Lincoln dealt with Copperheads, and vented her frustration over the reelection of Illinois Congressman Stephen A. Day, whom she insisted held Nazi connections.[21]

Frank wrote home for Sucrets, a knife, $20, books, political news, and, repeatedly, more letters, pictures, and visits from Elsie.[22] This last request veered from the party line.

Elsie wrote on the anniversary of Pearl Harbor about "a very serious discussion today with an older man whose judgment I respect very much." It seems likely that she was referring to a party official, possibly Morris Childs. "Evidently, the question of spending time with the boys in the service—either for a considerable period, or at frequent intervals—has assumed considerable proportions and has been pretty thoroughly discussed. It seems to be generally agreed that it is a factor making for extreme disorganization all the way round—in the camps, the towns, and at home." The discussion with the older man jeopardized the marital reunion, planned for the upcoming weekend. While Elsie claimed that she left the decision to Frank, she let him know where she, or at least the man from whom she had received counsel, stood by uncharacteristically lecturing her husband that "your attitude on the whole thing is wrong, little one."[23]

Characteristically, the dutiful wife yielded to the demanding husband. They disobeyed the party. She spent this and other weekends with Frank.[24] This carried risks. Meyer later explained about party interference in family life:

> The most widespread, open, and blatant pressure of this kind on rank and filers that I know of in a legal Western party took place in the United States during World War II. Its aim was to prevent wives from visiting their husbands at Army training camps, and especially to prevent their moving to live nearby. Every political, ideological, and emotional stop was pulled, from sob-sister columns by Elizabeth Gurley Flynn in the Daily Worker to special classes for women, disciplinary actions, expulsions,

and the threat of expulsion. The Party's motive in this campaign against what it indecently labeled "camp following" was to hold on to "female forces" to replace men drafted into the Army. To my knowledge, a number of divorces were precipitated as a result of this campaign.[25]

The separation inspired thoughts of togetherness. They did not write of the possibility of death in combat. They entertained a postwar dream.

Frank wrote from Camp Robinson that "the main thing to look forward to is when this bloody business is over and the world is scavenged a little again—we won't go apart again then."[26]

Elsie, atop defying counsel to remain in Chicago, began to question the anti-monogamy stance fashionable in their circles.[27] She responded in kind to Frank's dream of permanent closeness: "I don't know what's happening to me. I have a really overwhelming desire to sort of 'settle down,' have our own house and a child or children. Just to have you here, to enjoy everything together will be unutterable joy. That's what we're fighting for, of course, and we're making such a little sacrifice compared to the peoples of Europe."[28]

◆ ◆ ◆

MEYER reported to Fort Benning for Officer Candidate School. In January 1943, the installation near Columbus, Georgia, resembled a bustling midsized city. More than one hundred thousand men came and went every few months.

He again excelled in the academic component. He scored a 97, for instance, on a test on the M1 rifle.[29]

Candidate Meyer cited a 185 out of 225 as his best score yet on the rifle range, which he estimated put him just past the threshold for sharpshooter but not nearly enough for expert.

"We've been firing on the M-1 range all day in a steady heavy downpour ¾ of the time and a nasty cold drizzle the rest of the time," the correspondence reads. "We were to fire 12 rounds slow (3 standing, 3 sitting, 3 squatting and 3 standing) I made 49 out of 60 possible; 11 rounds rapid sitting (I made 49 out of 55)—11 rounds rapid kneeling (I made 46 out of 55)—11 rounds squatting (I made 41 out of 55)—at 200 yards."[30]

Navigation, too, presented no insurmountable issue. "We had a three-hour night problem last night—getting from point to point about three miles apart over a wet wash of roads and trails with nothing but a flashlight and our aerial photograph," he wrote. "My partner and I made one wrong turn but we finally came out only 25 yards from the point we were supposed to hit."[31]

Predictably, a man who had last used his body in a vigorous manner as an Oxford undergraduate ran into an obstacle in the obstacle course. He pulled muscles and experienced continued feet trouble. The "obstacle course has me really worried," he confessed to Elsie; so much so that he decided to get a good night's sleep Saturday to practice on Sunday morning.[32]

Elsie in civilian life faced her own obstacles. Her letters told of a neighborhood scrap drive, ration cards, Chicago's State Street empty of cars but teeming with pedestrians, and the post office's insistence on thin paper for letters.[33]

The shoemaker's daughter struggled with her Communist side when the Office of Price Administration began rationing shoes and heavily regulating their manufacture and sale.

"I guess even he didn't know about shoe rationing when I spoke to him last night," Elsie wrote of her father, "or he surely would have mentioned it. They did it up brown this time, at any rate; they arrested merchants for selling shoes after 2 p.m. today ½ hour after the order came out."[34]

She regarded going with just three new pairs annually as no sacrifice but found something silly in the intrusion, itself a heterodox position for one dedicating her life to state control of the means of production. As Elsie wrote about the government's limiting the color of shoes, Frank noted it expanding the color of platoons. He marveled at the positive social change happening before his eyes in the Deep South.

"Of interest is the fact that unlike many of the other student companies I've seen around here with a platoon or half a platoon of Negroes," Frank observed, "we have 2 or 3 in each platoon—it works out very well too—despite the Southerners—one of them is platoon leader this week."[35]

The progress he saw around him eluded the officer candidate in the obstacle course. He could point to improvement in all other areas save for the course that acted as the obstacle to becoming a second lieutenant. He wondered about getting kicked out, resigning, or graduating. He confessed, "I'm, despite everything my consciousness tells me, so damned fed up with this life."[36]

The Army became fed up with him, or at least his inability to master its obstacle course, too. His lack of agility and foot problems got the better of him. He washed out of Officer Candidate School in February 1943.

◀ 10 ▶

Doubter

On February 19, 1943, authorities at Fort Benning relieved Meyer of his duties.[1] The thirty-three-year-old corporal's immobility relative to other candidates, spotlighted on the obstacle course that had so vexed him, resulted in the faculty board's determination that his qualifications, or lack thereof, did not warrant his continuation as an infantry officer candidate. They jettisoned him forty-eight days after he had reported to Fort Benning.

Significantly, the officer candidate kept the problems with his feet from the Army. Returning to New York, he saw his doctor, who back in 1939 had diagnosed anterior metatarsalgia and bilateral cavus deformity in both feet. In layman's terms, the maladies meant pain in the balls of his feet and high arches that created a multitude of issues, respectively.[2] The foot problems, dating back at least to his early days in England when he had sought medical intervention and received special alterations to the insides of his shoes, hindered him in the Army and caused increased pain due to the stress imposed upon them through training.[3] He received combination Whitman foot braces, but his doctor ultimately decided on surgery.[4]

Characteristically, he put his left foot forward. On May 25, 1943, he underwent a Hoke Arthrodesis at the Hospital for Joint Diseases in New York. Three months in a plaster cast to the knee followed. He underwent the same procedure at the same hospital on the right foot on February 11, 1944, followed by the same recovery time in a cast. In both instances, he required physical therapy.[5] The short-term implication meant confinement in a wheelchair, or relying on various walking aids, for more than a year. In the long term, his pain dissipated.

"As a result of the operations the deformities will be corrected," his New York doctor wrote the Chicago draft board. "The pains will be relieved. There will be a permanent loss of subastragalar and mediotarsal motion in both feet."[6]

He grew a beard. He obtained a cat. A sedentary Meyer nevertheless moved much. New York stints included stays in Greenwich Village, Crugers, and, significantly, the Byrdcliffe Arts Colony in Woodstock.[7] He relied on Elsie. They both relied on her father. They lived for a time in the English immigrant's home in the St. Louis area.

"Originally, when they got married, he was totally opposed for very good reason," John Meyer reflected about his maternal grandfather. "I don't think they ever got along particularly well. I think my mother was a buffer there."[8]

So, atop the physical handicap, Meyer carried the social weight of living in the house of someone who held him in low regard.

◆ ◆ ◆

THIS PERIOD of near total dependence on Elsie, heretofore emotionally dependent in a near-total way on him, brought closeness. The complete freedom from the Communist Party created distance between him and his other love.

Not since he had formed the October Club more than a decade prior did the party appear to him as an entity apart from himself. He looked at it from afar, which provided much-needed perspective.

The party's stonewalling him from joining the Army as it publicly exhorted others to do so chipped away at the exterior of the hardened Marxist. Life among the proletariat in the Army, which exposed the disconnect between Marxist theory and reality, weakened that hardness, too.

Now Meyer experienced a vacation of sorts from the party. He read. He reflected. Like a cult member separated from the group, he developed independence of mind. He questioned. Questioning and Communism did not, *could not*, peacefully coexist. Meyer became a dangerous man to keep in the Communist Party.

◆ ◆ ◆

HE did not break from the party. Instead, he wondered whether he could reform it. He vouchsafed doubts and ideas to his Chicago comrade Louis Budenz, who vouchsafed his own doubts and ideas to him.[9]

Off his feet with time on his hands, he wrote Earl Browder. He had met the American party's top man. In Chicago, he led the school Browder had founded. Their paths had crossed at various national party meetings in New York. But he did not know him beyond surface interactions.[10]

"Why can't we have a ruthless breaking with old ways of thought and action where they become wrong and harmful ways of thought and action?"[11] Meyer asked that provocative question to the leader of a revolutionary group quite rigid in conserving its beliefs, folkways, and structure. The letter-writer, disillusioned and expecting expulsion, instead saw his prestige burgeon with both Browder and party leadership.[12] After nine years in the American party, he still did not wield the influence he had exerted after less than one in the British party. This one letter elevated his standing to a point where the top people took him seriously.

The letter, dated November 29, 1943, anticipated if not influenced massive changes for American Communism and, remarkably, left clues for the provenance of massive, more lasting changes for American conservatism. He imagined a meshing of Marxism with the American tradition and imagined away the incongruity. Like a time bomb, the idea that Meyer believed would strengthen Communism in America eventually exploded in his and the party's face. But for now, during this time of Soviet–American cooperation, the idea appealed and pointing out its flaws did not.

He questioned whether class warfare remained "the best road to socialism for a world shattered and punch-drunk from these last ten years" and suggested sharing leadership after the war with those of the capitalist class. He sought a laid-back party better equipped to attract bowlers instead of the present, demanding one that mainly attracted fanatics. He suggested that democratic centralism might not work in a pluralistic society. He wondered something terribly radical for any Stalinist: "whether all the non-fascist countries have not reached the situation where the state must be regarded in the way in which Lenin described the monarchies of the 17th and 18th centuries."

Then his argument became, at least in retrospect, more interesting. He wrote,

> We have played a big part in re-evaluating American history. Practically, it has unquestionably affected our work to an enormous degree. But what I feel is still lacking is a conscious effort pervading all our work to make the Party constitution real when it speaks of our theory as the fusing of the ideas of the American leaders with the ideas of Marx, Engels and Lenin. To too great a degree our interpretation of this is still in the nature of adding on a tag here and there.

Frank Meyer in 1943, years before he became synonymous with the fusion of libertarianism with the American tradition into conservatism, lobbied the head of the CPUSA to fuse the American tradition with Communism to create a Marxism that appealed to his countrymen.

"A people's America and a socialist America must be presented all the time—not simply as an occasional article or on the 4th of July—as a natural, integral outgrowth of our whole past history, and presented in terms of our tradition," he wrote. "And this will only come about when our leaders from top to bottom are as familiar with the struggles of Jefferson and Jackson and Lincoln, and what we have inherited from those struggles, as they are with 1848, 1902, 1917, and fuse these understandings into one tool."

There was that word again: *fuse*. He wanted a fusion between Communism and the American Founding. He attempted to force Marxism upon the American tradition. A fanatic, as Meyer demonstrated with his contradictory pieces in *The Communist* using the same historical examples to protest and then push entry into the European war, could see anything, including Marxism, growing organically out of the Declaration of Independence, *Federalist Papers*, and Constitution. But this fanatic had grown wiser and more prudent since he had written those articles. He was no longer the hyperventilating, Marx-quoting nutter described in Oxford student newspapers. An honest inquiry into whether actual history meshed with this desire could not help but show that the two clashed. That realization took time. Ideas very different, it eventually dawned on him, did fit into the American tradition. This worked with other factors to push him toward new commitments.

Neither man's papers contain a direct response to the letter. The follower offered understanding if the leader could not respond given overwhelming demands but suggested doing so through his friend Louis Budenz if he felt compelled to.[13] In a sense, a response did come. Browder, whether coincidentally or consequentially, pursued almost all of the suggestions, particularly fusionism, offered by Meyer.

Eventually, comrade responded to comrade.

Meyer, not specifying whether it came through Budenz, later remembered, "I received word back from him that he had seen my letter, that he was in agreement with its general points, and that there was not much point in discussing it since I knew his public position, and that the whole position of the Party was changing."[14]

The party altered its course toward its wayward member. Then it rerouted in another direction.

The former delayed the big choice. The latter forced it.

Defector

H ope your legs are coming along as well as can be expected," Meyer's Army buddy Seymour Mullman wrote in late winter 1944. "Has the other one been operated on?"[1]

Frank had sent cookies that Mullman found "excellent" the previous fall. Mullman informed him from Fort Benning that of the ten officer candidates in their hut, just four graduated with their "cut to ribbons" class as Army officers.[2] The second lieutenant in March after venturing across the Atlantic lauded the food and conditions in his camp.[3] Then his silence suggested something else. His correspondent wrote Washington for confirmation. The Germans had killed Mullman as he helped liberate France eight days after the D-Day landing.[4]

There but for an obstacle course's obstinance goes Frank.

Death fertilizes thoughts. The slaughter of a young husband, fellow New York–area denizen, and brief brother-in-arms provided much to ponder. The mid-1940s served as a period of change and second thoughts. Meyer did not see his future clearly. His past slowly emerged from a fog to offer direction.

◆ ◆ ◆

AFTER more than a year of injury, surgery, and convalescence, he returned to his feet in a literal sense in 1944. The party's discouraging him from volunteering as it exhorted others to do so, his experiences as a soldier among Mullman and normal men, revelatory frustrations in attempting to fuse Marxism with the American tradition, and reflection in recuperation shook his faith. He moved away from the Communist Party. The Communist Party moved away from the Communist Party, too.

The Tehran Conference, the first of the three wartime summits between the leaders of the United States, United Kingdom, and Soviet Union, induced an epiphany in CPUSA General Secretary Earl Browder. If Franklin Roosevelt and Winston Churchill could meet with Joseph Stalin in late 1943, then postwar labor and capital, Communists and Democrats, and the Soviet Union and the United States could work in harmony to make a better world possible, too. This amounted to revolutionary thinking of an unexpected sort from a revolutionary imprisoned for stretches during both world wars, engaged in espionage in between them, and so all-in on Stalinism that he had participated in a Comintern meeting that sent a black American living in Moscow to the gulag, where, with teeth knocked out, he starved to death (a hand amputated, thawed, and fingerprinted provided identification).[5] Browder fared better in an American prison. Freed in 1942 by a presidential commutation order, he now effectively pardoned Roosevelt.[6]

Browder reimagined American Communism as part of a broader left-of-center coalition rather than a sectarian political cult subservient to Moscow. Roosevelt's actions betokened Browder's about-face. So did Stalin's. In 1943, the Russian dictator at least formally dissolved the Communist

International, which had fomented revolution abroad and imposed conformity to Moscow's line by native parties, to convey good faith to allies. The Communist from Kansas took this as a cue to assert independence from the Communists in the Kremlin.

In *New Masses*, where an "F. J. Meyers" semi-pseudonym began appearing midway through 1944, Browder found a committed cheerleader. Meyer's arguments in the publication curiously rested on patriotism and on progressives working within the free market. He criticized obstinate left-wing labor leaders of the John L. Lewis variety and wrote of Roosevelt as a hagiographer might. He took to heart the notion of fighting the war to attain a lasting peace rather than as a means to advance Communism in preparation for the next fight—something he did not believe his country, or the world, could tolerate after years of intense combat.[7] When internal critics questioned Browder's forecast of a rosy postwar economy, Meyer defended the leader in *New Masses*.[8] His writing became so associated with Browder's position that their essays appeared one after the other in response to criticism of Browder's economic optimism.[9]

Browder, in creatively applying old doctrine to a dynamic situation, struck his admirer as a pioneering scientist rather than a quack. "Browder, with scientific objectivity, points the most practical, indeed the only possible, road of progress in the circumstances of today; and he does not turn back in horror from that road just because the interests of decisive sections of the capitalists lead them in the same direction," wrote the younger man. Meyer parroted the Browder line— or did Browder parrot the Meyer line?—writing that Tehran "makes possible a profound transformation of the relations of the past twenty-five years between the Soviet Union and the capitalist world, between the imperialist countries and the colonial countries, between capital and labor in every country."[10]

It all recalled the Popular Front period of the mid-1930s, embodied by its slogan "Communism Is Twentieth Century

Americanism." That era Browder surely understood as the party's heyday in terms of membership and in its deepest encroachment upon the mainstream. Meyer had enjoyed better days within the party then. The Popular Front ended with the Nazi–Soviet Pact, the aftermath of which saw Browder serve his prison stint for passport fraud and the decimation of membership rolls. It saw Meyer experience his first doubts. The sequel of sorts perhaps began the moment Operation Barbarossa did. It intensified upon Roosevelt's commuting Browder's sentence and rose to new heights upon Browder's prophecy of postwar unity.

It ended upon Moscow's insistence. Before Russians intervened, two Americans did.

◆ ◆ ◆

THE RUSSIAN-BORN Communist Sam Darcy, who served as a Jimmy Higgins before his ascension as a party panjandrum, and William Z. Foster, who preceded Browder as head of the CPUSA, criticized their current leader's course. Feeling obligated to object, Foster wrote a letter.

Therein, Foster accused Browder of committing "a number of serious errors." These included forecasting postwar class collaboration instead of class conflict, accepting the two-party system as a *fait accompli*, putting the promotion of socialism on the back burner, and dangerously imagining the appetite of Western imperialists as restrained rather than "whetted" by the war. Even on questions in which they seemingly agree, such as seeing Roosevelt as an ally and the Republicans as enemies or noting the importance of the wartime no-strike pledge, Foster highlights degrees of separation. Over seventeen pages, the older but subordinate man offers respectful criticisms that nevertheless stood to jar comrades if publicized in that they focused on the one American whom American Communists only rarely and reluctantly criticized, especially on core, foundational matters, publicly.[11] Heretics, after all, cannot stay in their bishoprics.

Browder's pragmatic course struck outsiders as a sensible reorientation dictated by events. Those marinated in Marxist theory and accustomed to Comintern practice necessarily encountered it as a betrayal. Even if Foster's letter might appear to the uninitiated as cultish and divorced from current events, anyone within the party matrix would have understood its logic perfectly. For this reason, Browder suppressed it. And party people, even the theoreticians among them, outwardly embraced Browder's position for the same reason that they had outwardly embraced an alliance with Nazis. They believed it was the will of the Soviet Union. Meyer embraced it because he regarded it as wise. He had advised Browder to follow such a course, after all.

Browder ensured that most American Communists, probably including Meyer, did not read Foster's arguments.

In February, the Politburo "voted to reject the letter, with only Foster and Darcy themselves dissenting," Harvey Klehr, John Earl Haynes, and Kyrill M. Anderson wrote in *The Soviet World of American Communism*. "Browder had made it clear that Foster faced expulsion from the party leadership if he continued to cause trouble, and Foster pledged to carry the matter no further. Darcy refused to submit. As a test of Foster's loyalty, Browder ordered him to chair the commission that expelled Darcy from the CPUSA."[12]

The separation from the party that Browder engineered for one of the CPUSA's most dedicated members he soon engineered for all of its members.

✦ ✦ ✦

MEYER attended the May 1944 conference in New York in which delegates from forty-four states dissolved their party and launched a political association in its stead.[13] The

Communists began the gathering by singing not "The Internationale" but "The Star-Spangled Banner." They reverted to form in voting for Browder's resolution as a unanimous bloc. This dissolution turned party into pressure group.[14]

The "constitutional convention" established an organization that "carries forward the traditions of Washington, Jefferson, Paine, Jackson, and Lincoln, under the changed conditions of modern industrial society" and "upholds the Declaration of Independence, the United States Constitution and its Bill of Rights, and the achievements of American democracy against all the enemies of popular liberties." It essentially established a federal system of local, state, and national levels of the association, outlined rights and duties of members, and vowed to expel any Communist who acted to overthrow, or even subvert, the American system.[15] Browder, coincidentally or consciously, advanced the Communist fusionism urged upon him by Meyer.

This pulled the doubting Communist back. The failed Army officer promptly joined the Communist Political Association (CPA).[16] While not the fanatic of his England days, he experienced a partial rejuvenation as a result of Browder's reorientation.

The undisputed leader of American Communists for the past decade started to begin speeches "Ladies and gentlemen" instead of "Comrades."[17] The Young Communist League morphed into the American Youth for Democracy. The CPUSA's Politburo became the CPA's national board. Its general secretary became its president.[18] And in Greenwich Village, New York's Workers School morphed into an institution named in honor of not Marx, Engels, or Lenin but the primary author of the American Declaration of Independence.

◆ ◆ ◆

GIL GREEN, Meyer's party patron who steered him toward Chicago during the previous decade, now wanted him in

New York in an executive capacity overseeing the consolidat-
ed replacement for the city's School for Democracy and its
Workers School. Meyer made for an ideal fit to serve as the
Jefferson School of Social Science's commissar given his experience running the Chicago Workers School and his enthusiasm for the party's red-white-and-blue incarnation, advertised in the very name of the rebranded educational organ.
He harbored internal doubts about Communism and loathed
watching over Howard Selsam, whose friendship predated
their comradeship. So he demurred from an administrative
role by citing lingering feet problems.[19]

"I had known him for many years," Meyer later reasoned of
rejecting this party assignment, "and having been in the Army
for a year or so I had gotten out of the implicit Communist
type of obedience thing and I was damned if I was going in
there over an old friend in that kind of anomalous capacity."[20]

He agreed to teach.[21]

In 1944, the Meyers subleased a Greenwich Village apartment from an unsuspecting Milton Konvitz, a liberal anti-
Communist involved in the socialist-run Rand School of Social Science. Meyer's purpose, unbeknownst to his landlord,
involved teaching at the Communist-run Jefferson School of
Social Science. The rival schools, about a block apart physically
and occupying neighboring spots on the same sliver of the ideological spectrum, nevertheless operated in strictly segregated
worlds. They represented less warring factions than ignoring
factions. That Konvitz failed to recognize the neighborhood
activities of his tenants spoke to how even under a united front
against fascism the groups did not easily commingle.[22]

Resembling the education-for-the-everyman interwar
Greenwich Village People's Institute and the neighborhood's
Labor Temple as much as the Rand School, the Jefferson
School charged $4 or $10 or a similarly modest fee for continuing education–style courses on such subjects as acting,
dressmaking, and public speaking. But courses on puppetry
could not disguise the focus of indoctrinating students in

Marxism-Leninism. While "Advanced Leather Craft" and "How to Speak at Meetings" seem more Kiwanis than Communist, Meyer delivered the red-meat Marxism just as he did in Chicago.[23] Only he did not. He went through the motions. The man had changed, but his role did not reflect it.

The party attempted to place him in the new Congresswoman Helen Gahagan Douglas's office in 1945. The effort, spearheaded by Dick Sellers, an aide to Hugh De Lacy, a secret Communist ostensibly serving a Washington district in Congress, failed.[24] He stayed in Manhattan.

Meyer's Jefferson School colleagues included Josephine Truslow Adams, known to the others as a direct descendant of the second and sixth presidents who boasted a friendship with the thirty-second, the screenwriter John Howard Lawson, the labor historian Philip Foner, the novelist Howard Fast, *Amerasia*'s editor Philip Jaffe, the teachers' union activist Bella Dodd, and Robert Minor, the cartoonist who ran the CPUSA when Earl Browder went to prison.

Frank Straus Meyer appeared as "F. J. Meyers" and "Frank J. Meyer" in course catalogs.[25] He later insisted that in coming to New York he had wished to shield his work from family members.[26] The need to hide an association with the Communist Party waned to perhaps its lowest point during the Soviet–American alliance. And, in a technical sense, no party then existed. Still, Meyer, in his Communist activities, often altered his name slightly.

On Thursday nights during the first half of 1945, he taught "Principles of Scientific Socialism 1," "The Science of Society," and "History of Political Thought." This spelled a grueling schedule of teaching two classes in the winter session from 7:10 p.m. to 10:20 p.m. with a ten-minute break separating the sessions, and from 6:00 p.m. to 10:10 p.m. during the spring session with a ten-minute break buffering the two-hour courses.[27]

The catalog printed ahead of the summer session included "The Social and Political Philosophy of Franklin Delano

Roosevelt," a $4 course touted as "A study of the theoretical ideas of the greatest president since Abraham Lincoln."[28] Neither Frank Meyer nor F. J. Meyer nor anyone else taught it. By the time registration opened on July 2, Communists no longer regarded Roosevelt as the greatest anything. Frank's Communism, like Frank's course, died as a result of the party's shifting line.[29]

◆ ◆ ◆

HIS TEACHING appeared increasingly heretical. So did his writing.

The clearest signal of his reoriented thought arrived through a review shockingly published by *New Masses*. *The Road to Serfdom*, a commercial book on collectivism by the London School of Economics professor Friedrich Hayek, one-punched the former LSE student into an intellectual daze. Amid obligatory criticisms, Meyer acknowledged the book as "a real challenge" to progressives that required "careful consideration." Non-Marxist works periodically received respectful reviews in the Communist press. *The Road to Serfdom* did not read as merely outside of the Marxist tradition. It directly challenged it. And it went further by exposing all centralized planning, whether the planners called themselves New Dealers or Nazis, as inimical to individual choice. *New Masses* inevitably ignored or caricatured such books. This book, the man teaching Marxism on behalf of the party at its flagship school conceded, left "a hard residuum of theoretical argument, not new but very capably restated, which must be met upon its merits."[30]

Browderism, in its jettisoning of hardcore Marxism-Leninism in favor of anything that helped win the war that the Soviet Union rightly regarded as an existential threat, softened up a hardened Stalinist to contemplate Hayek's arguments. And Hayek's less doctrinaire brand of Austrian economics, pragmatically tolerating the existence of some aspects of the welfare state, for instance, similarly made past poison potable.

Meyer described the revelation:

> The appeal of his argument to decent, democratic people lies in the contention that government economic planning demands the accumulation of immense power in central organs and that therefore, so long as production is not unlimited, what men shall have and do will have to be decided by the arbitrary decision of other men. To the immediately obvious answer that this all depends upon whether the planning authorities are democratically chosen and controlled, he rebuts that the kind of decisions which have to be taken by such authorities are not the kind upon which a majority can ever agree. Such decisions, he says, necessitate an independent choice by governing authorities, even though they are democratic, between the claims of minorities. This necessity will in the end amount to the choice being arbitrarily made by those who exercise the power. He claims further that because agreement on such questions cannot be arrived at democratically, those who govern, no matter how democratically they are chosen, no matter how good their intentions, will then have continually to increase their use of sheer power to enforce those decisions. The net result will be a completely regimented society in which the individual would have no freedom and no real voice.[31]

Here the Communist press remarkably summarized a right-wing thinker's ideas in a way not completely alien to how a right-wing thinker might. Meyer never wrote another article for *New Masses*.

✦ ✦ ✦

THE IMPACT of another article, published in *The New York World-Telegram* and three days after that in *The Daily Worker* at about the same time *New Masses* published the Hayek review, made any such opinion in Communist organs impossible henceforth. Only during this strange spell when Communists killed their party and sacrificed its principles to save its promised land could a comrade sound like a capitalist. The nebulous group congealed again into a rigid structure that forbade such deviationism. And this other article signaled this new day of American Communism reverting to its old days.

William Z. Foster's letter, essentially stamped "return to sender" by Earl Browder, somehow made its way into the mailboxes of rank-and-file American Communists more than a year after he had composed it. Underneath the bold Paris postmark, members, if they looked hard enough, could make out a faint "Moscow," at least in their mind's eye.

The palimpsest appeared in a French Communist journal in April and traveled across the Atlantic for publication the next month. "On the Communist Political Association of the United States of America" originated not in the beautiful Paris spring but in the brutal Moscow winter. Stalin desired to neither signal the beginning of the Cold War nor advertise his control over Western parties. So Jacques Duclos put his name over an article his overlords wrote to give them cover, albeit more of a thin sheet than a thick blanket.[32] It owed to American influence. Duclos repeatedly invoked Foster by name and referred to his specific objections. The objections to Browder evoked Foster's criticisms, shared with the Kremlin, that helped engineer the CPUSA leader Jay Lovestone's ouster during the late 1920s.[33]

"Despite declarations regarding recognition of the principles of Marxism," the Duclos Letter explained, "one is witnessing a notorious revision of Marxism on the part of Browder and his supporters, a revision which is expressed in the concept of a long-term class peace in the United States, of the possibility of the suppression of the class struggle in the postwar period and of establishment of harmony between labor and capital."[34]

Shortly after its publication on May 22, several dozen members of the Jefferson School faculty convened to discuss it. Party leaders quickly lost control of the discussion. A Browderite majority, including Frank, took a negative view of the letter.[35]

Browder's chief acolyte on the faculty recalled "great enthusiasm" for Browder's position with very few exceptions and "a real hostility and objection to the Duclos article," which the teachers believed spoke for its author and not Stalin.[36]

In front of fifty or so faculty members, Meyer debated his Jefferson School colleague Francis Franklin on the Duclos letter. The audience participated in the discussion period and overwhelmingly supported with their words the speaker they had supported in other ways during the debate. He escaped for a long weekend in the country believing the Russian-controlled outfit had permanently traveled in an American direction.[37]

He so recently had pondered exiting. Now he realized his position had captured hearts and minds.

Their souls still belonged to Moscow. Over the weekend, the Communist board voted to embrace the Duclos position. In less than a week, the only world known to Frank Meyer for fourteen years had shifted underneath his feet.

He recollected, "I walked into the Jefferson School where everyone, three or four days before, had been congratulating me on my speech, and were really enthusiastic about this great theoretical point, which, after all, you have to think about for a while, and over one week every last one of them had changed their minds and were saying, 'We made so many mistakes, we shouldn't have called the meeting. All our arguments were wrong.'"[38]

Communist discussions ended in unanimity, and since the previous week's discussion sparked a debate, school director Howard Selsam, on the order of Alexander Trachtenberg, a Communist publisher and lackey for the Soviet Union, held a second meeting after the disaster of the first.[39] Selsam insisted that their first discussion had occurred too hastily and without guidance from a leading theoretician to help the faculty properly understand matters. Rather than introduce one, he carted out the Communist functionary Jack Stachel in the Jefferson School conference room.[40]

The party heavy explained that, unlike the previous week, the faculty had by now possessed the time to fully digest the letter. He petitioned the Communists to reflect on how they had sunk into revisionism. He faulted Browder's leadership, called the dissolution of the CPUSA a mistake, and lamented that the Roosevelt years resulted in a softness of American Communism. He stressed to the educators the importance of returning to Marxist roots and eradicating "the Roosevelt myth," both points indirectly explaining the cancellation of the class on the late president. He essentially told devoted ideologues of a more intellectual stripe that they had served a largely mistaken cause for much of the last decade.[41]

One of many in the audience more deeply acquainted with Marxism than Stachel gave lie to the unanimity. Perhaps thinking of Second Lieutenant Mullman, Meyer spoke "very sharply" and "more uncompromisingly" than the previous week.[42] He stated that following the path drawn by Duclos would lead to another war. He opined that if another war did break out the blame would fall on Communist shoulders. He insisted on an obligation to work for a peaceful world. Stachel described this as "provocative" even as he concluded by claiming consensus for Duclos among the faculty.[43] He responded, according to his adversary, by ignoring his argument, accusing him of "revisionism," and using other "Marxist swear words."[44]

✦ ✦ ✦

FRANK refused to let it go. Fireworks erupted between Meyer and Howard Fast at a *New Masses* editorial board meeting that spilled over into lunch.[45] He wrote a letter to *The Daily Worker* that the publication refused to print.

"I would like mine to be printed," Meyer told party bigwig Eugene Dennis, "and I know of one or two others that exist that ought to be printed to make it a discussion."

Dennis brushed him off: "Don't worry. Browder can speak for himself.'"

"I don't care personally whether Browder can speak for himself or not," Meyer recalled saying. "I have a position on this discussion which is, perhaps, not identical with Mr. Browder's, but is certainly in opposition to the line of the Duclos article.'"

Dennis reiterated: "Don't worry. He can take care of himself."[46]

Dennis took care of himself. The oafish, mustachioed man replaced Browder as leader at the late July national conference in New York, where the Communist Political Association reverted to the Communist Party, of which Dennis served, consequently, as general secretary. Despite their conflict, Meyer did not regard Dennis as a "militant" like Foster.[47] He stayed uneasily.

The former president of the Communist Political Association, unlike Jay Lovestone during the 1920s, did not eventually turn against the party he had once led. He ironically pursued the route taken by the man he had replaced as leader and who ultimately engineered his downfall. But Browder would never receive the Kremlin burial, let alone welcome within the party he led during its most consequential years, after leaving office as Foster did.

The denouement of the "O Captain! My Captain!" saga occurred in a Yonkers, New York, apartment, where two couples—Frank and Elsie and Earl and Raissa—tried to make sense of things.[48]

Another couple in their social circle went further. The broadcaster Fulton Sheen, perhaps the most famous Catholic priest in the Unted States, converted Louis Budenz, still the managing editor of *The Daily Worker*, and his wife, Margaret, to Catholicism on October 10 in a very public manner. Budenz privately described Meyer as pushing him, in all likelihood unintentionally, toward the church in the conversations leading to Meyer's fusionist letter to Browder.[49] The day after the conversion, Meyer volunteered that he respected the integrity of their decision and pledged his continuing friendship, a reaction that Margaret confessed to Elsie they had predicted—a remarkable comment given the shunning and demonization the party expected from members toward defectors.[50] "My own thinking is still caught in as yet insoluble contradictions," Meyer divulged to Budenz, "which I hope further effort and the unfolding of events will help me solve."[51]

Loyalty to the defector Budenzes and the disgraced Browders augured whither Frank Meyer. Though unclear to Frank, the party grasped his future. Elsie appeared salvageable. They opted for a dramatic gambit. Communist leaders sought to cleave Elsie, whom they did not regard as unsound, from her heretical husband. They requested she divorce him. Her mother died that summer, requiring extended time far away from the tumult of Greenwich Village in St. Louis. As when the party discouraged her from visiting Frank in Army training, she chose husband over party. In trying to save one, the party lost both.[52]

The national board, like the Yonkers club to which Browder belonged, shut down debate in the matter of Browder's expulsion.[53] The document recommending banishment referred to Browder as an "active opponent of the party."[54] Now Browder found himself in Foster's shoes. Refused the ability to address the national committee, he wrote a letter making his case.[55] But rather than submit to party discipline as Foster did, Browder again meandered outside of it. He appealed to individual members on the extensive party mailing list.[56] One member responded by judging him "an enemy of Communism" and guilty of "deliberate sabotage."[57] Another accused him of "lies and slander against Comrade Foster" and of "waging war against the entire Party."[58] The party's reversion to Soviet subservience here paid deference to American norms by erasing their former leader not through the barrel of a gun but by the big cold shun. A ghost of Earl Browder masquerading as a flesh-and-blood man roamed the earth unnoticed for more than a quarter century thereafter before belated acknowledgement of his death.

Meyer left the party less with Browder's bang than his own uncharacteristic whimper. The autumn after the Jefferson School canceled his Roosevelt course, he returned to teach "History of Modern Political Thought."[59] He then faded from view. His reemergence into the frame of his former comrades proved more memorable.

Woodstock

B rowder's life essentially ended upon the great sunder. His janissary entered into a new, second life more consequential than his first.

Whom he socialized with, what he believed, where he resided, why he existed, and how he spent his days abruptly changed in these years of transition. For one who championed the faith in the Temple newspaper and later evangelized Marxism, uncertainty abnormally agonized. He knew what he no longer accepted. In what *did* he believe? He could accept the collapse of Browderism. The question of just what the American Founding bequeathed lingered. Discovering and proselytizing the answer overwhelmed him as the forever fixation.

The letter from France that anathematized Meyer and Browder foreshadowed a different world, and one that arrived in a whirlwind. Winston Churchill's Iron Curtain Speech, Communists killing uniformed American servicemen in Korea, and the exposure of Alger Hiss, Harry Dexter White, and the Rosenbergs as Soviet agents all waited in the future. But Frank Meyer, who had not only stuck with Communism through the Hitler–Stalin Pact but performed embarrassing feats of contortionism to justify the about-face, could not predict any of that. Like Whittaker Chambers, he left the side on the march for the one backpedaling.

Meyer's own life seemed to be in retreat. With no paycheck coming from either the Army or the party, he relied on his late parents' leftovers. In 1944, the $3,093.06 listed on his income tax return came entirely from his share of rents from property left by his mother.[1] The following year, rents provided about 95 percent of his income.[2] In 1946, Frank's income derived entirely from that brick building in Newark; Elsie, filing separately that year, similarly traced her income entirely to dividends from Hoy Shoe Company stock gifted by her father, whose brother-in-law Walter Hoy had bought him out of the business.[3]

Frank might have found such an existence agreeable as a bachelor. What he once took for granted he now needed to support a wife and, as of December 31, 1944, a new son. Naming him John Cornford, a salute which pleased his fallen friend's mother even more than the gifted *Robinson Crusoe* pleased his slain friend's son whom she raised, indicated that he remained tethered to comrades if somewhat alienated from Communism.[4]

A further expense arose when the Meyers purchased a home in Woodstock, New York. It sat betwixt art and agriculture, and a persistent legend on their alp held that a nineteenth-century farmer's wife, upon her husband's death, committed a form of suttee in despair.[5] Ghosts and legends, some arriving long after the Meyers did, crowded the sparsely populated mountain. The sales contract, dated December 4, 1945, lists Crugers, a hamlet in Westchester County, as the buyers' residence.[6]

At age thirty-six, he boasted the coveted trifecta of home, wife, and child. Still, he depended almost wholly on his dead parents' wealth. Frank had spent the fifteen years since his entrepreneur father's death railing against the very capitalism that put a roof over his head. The contradiction could not have gone unnoticed.

His home hugged Ohayo Mountain Road, in contrast to so many others that distanced themselves from it. It sat on a crest not far below the 1,388-foot apex of the hillish mountain (or mountainish hill). At one end of Ohayo Mountain Road near the center of town flows the Millstream, with its short waterfalls, small pools, and rock to dry off upon. From there, one ascends the road more than a mile to reach the Meyer residence on the left side of a bend. Continuing upward, one briefly climbs to the peak before descending toward the Ashokan Reservoir.

The deed indicated 5.6 acres, but then or later the property encompassed thirteen acres. The main plot included a house, shed, carriage house, and a non-functional well. They relied on a spring before drilling a new well. A cutout across the street allowed for parking. Behind the back lawn sat a wooded area bracketed by short walls constructed with native stone. Creatures roamed about. While the mountain's incline makes a walk up it not for those in "Exercisers Anonymous," a fictitious group in recovery from the bane of exertion to which Meyer later jokingly claimed membership, the property's main rectangular plot, though jutted with rocks, uneven, and heavily wooded, boasts a relatively flat terrain.

Uneven floors denoted age. A trapdoor led from a hallway (and then from the kitchen after its expansion) to the basement, where the Meyers kept wine. A fireplace helped during winter, and an old wood stove in the kitchen helped mainly with decor. The couple slept in a bedroom off the living room. Frank worked in an office that was eventually expanded. In the upstairs sat more rooms.[7] It shouted the charm of bygone times. Its size and simplicity whispered modesty.

❖ ❖ ❖

THE SELECTION of a house so rural that it required no numbered address on postal letters came from reasons not all obvious. Living in the Byrdcliffe Arts Colony after Frank's Army stint planted the seed.[8] A neighbor was the mother of Nathaniel Weyl.

Nathaniel's father, Walter, who founded *The New Republic* along with Herbert Croly and Walter Lippmann, died before the son turned ten. He left Nathaniel a basic political outlook and his widow property. The Weyl estate bordered Meyer's land. Like Meyer, Weyl attended an Ivy League school (Columbia) before doing postgraduate work at the London School of Economics. Like Meyer, he joined the Communist Party during the early 1930s. Unlike Meyer, he served in the underground party and left immediately after the Nazi–Soviet Pact. Unlike Meyer, he cowered from coming forward. And, as John Meyer noted, "My father went to the right quicker than Nathaniel did."[9]

The migration seventy or so miles north might just as well have been seven hundred. The fledgling family essentially moved from a reasonable commute to the capital of planet Earth to a house from which one could not see the homes of most neighbors.

The social animal now wished to live apart and not among people. And he wished most of all to be able to see visitors, invited or uninvited, approaching.

Ex-Communists who did not see other Communists coming their way occasionally disappeared. In the United States, such Kremlin-ordered killings proved unusual. Juliet Poyntz, a Daughter of the American Revolution turned founding mother of the CPUSA, vanished in New York in 1937.[10] Americans meeting such a grisly fate mostly did so abroad.

"There has been no systematic compilation of the number of American radicals and Communists and their family members killed by Stalin's political police," the historians John

Earl Haynes and Harvey Klehr note, "but it is at least five hundred and probably more than a thousand."[11]

Meyer knew this instinctually. He behaved accordingly. He bought a home on a mountain. He began staying awake at night and sleeping during the day. He kept a firearm nearby.[12]

✦ ✦ ✦

HIS other existential concern involved feeding his family.

"It wasn't that we were poor," John Meyer reflected. "But we were scraping by a bit in the 1945-to-early-fifties time. He had a little income by inheritance, but it was a little. Of course, living out in Woodstock you did not have a lot of expenses, either."[13]

Meyer lost friends, social life, work, intellectual outlets, and purpose when he broke from the party. In Woodstock, an arts colony attracting proto-Beatniks and impulsively leftish migrants from the city decades before his arrival, Meyer experienced a shunning adhered to even by many local eccentric-conformists unaffiliated with the party. He turned his back on the party. So the party propelled a whisper campaign for others to turn their backs on him.

For an extrovert, albeit one living above and apart from the town, the punishment struck as especially cruel. Meyer, who largely relied on apartness to think, read, and write, more so required an argument, an audience, and alcohol to feel fully like himself. He conversed his way to ideas. This meant he needed intellectual collaborators if not friends. The furthest thing from a loner, despite his halfway hermetic accommodations, he undoubtedly felt more alone in these years than any save for his unhappy Princeton experience.

He forced himself into community affairs. He joined the American Legion, marching in 1947's Memorial Day parade and reciting Abraham Lincoln's Gettysburg Address during a ceremony that followed at a local cemetery.[14] A few weeks later, he delivered his first Woodstock lecture at the Catskill Book and Record Shop on the Village Green. The talk on "The Education of Henry Adams—The Dilemma Forecast" marked the first in a series given on Thursday afternoons that summer by Meyer and Robert Phelps, the husband of the painter Rosemarie Beck and later a popularizer of Jean Cocteau and Collette. Phelps focused on literature: W. H. Auden, Henry Miller, Henry James, E. E. Cummings. Frank took philosophy: "Genesis of the Crisis of Values: Rousseau vs. Aquinas," "The Unvaluation of Values: Marx, Freud, Spencer—Types of Moral Confusion," "The Search for New Foundations: Toynbee, Malraux, Northrop."[15] When the local paper asked the subscription-based enterprise's business manager whether the venture aimed to compete with the Woodstock Discussion Group, Elsie Meyer evaded the question.[16]

The speakers' series filled three needs. It enabled Frank to generate income. It fulfilled his inherent need for an audience to absorb his ideas and knowledge. It allowed him to fight, indirectly, the Communists for whom he once fought.

The next year Frank gave a more definitive answer as to whether the venture competed with the Woodstock Discussion Group. He participated in the takeover of the group, labeled by its critics as "pro-Red," that renamed it the Woodstock Forum and gave it a more ecumenical purpose. He sat on the board.[17]

He ensured that the clique preventing him from speaking would not prevent anyone else from speaking. By hijacking the group, he built the platform that allowed those like him to more freely lecture in his adopted hometown. But, accustomed to leading a classroom or speaking at a rally, he naturally wanted an audience larger than the one Woodstock offered.

✦ ✦ ✦

THIS DESIRE brought him back to his boyhood friend.
Just as Meyer coincidentally or consciously followed Weyl to
Woodstock, Eugene O'Neill Jr. followed Meyer in migrating
there. And like Meyer and Weyl, O'Neill, albeit as a dabbler,
joined the Communist Party during the Red Decade only to
become disillusioned.[18]

"You and Nathaniel were right about PCA, I fear, and I was
wrong," lamented O'Neill in late 1947.[19] A year earlier, the Progressive Citizens of America (PCA) had formed. During a subsequent conference, the group asked O'Neill to use his name
for promotional purposes. The involvement of the Communists Lee Pressman and John Abt in leadership, and the
likes of Dalton Trumbo and Paul Robeson in membership,
alarmed Meyer and Weyl, who were savvy about the party's
manner of exploiting famous names via front groups. They
warned their friend. Shady characters emerging from behind
the scenes eventually spooked O'Neill and other liberals. A
humbled O'Neill wrote Meyer about the public letter, "I hope
that out of this there will come publicity that will establish
me as a reasonable liberal and anti-Red."[20]

In his open letter to PCA, O'Neill lamented its zeal for the
third-party candidate Henry Wallace in part because of how
it might facilitate a Republican victory and in part because
it coincided with the aims of the Communist Party. O'Neill
expressed regret in lending his name and asked that PCA remove him as an endorser.[21]

O'Neill and Meyer supported Harry Truman in 1948.[22]
Meyer remained on his political journey away from the Communist Party. That same year he read Richard Weaver's *Ideas
Have Consequences*, a book that so profoundly influenced him
that he later called it the *fons et origo* of the conservative movement.[23] He experienced the years immediately following the

war as transitional ones. A permanent political home awaited in the future.

That future would remain there until he could address his past. O'Neill's history required a reckoning, too. Meyer's demanded one first.

◀ 13 ▶

Smith

T
hey knew each other in Chicago.

Louis Budenz edited *The Midwest Daily Record*. Frank Meyer directed the Chicago Workers School. In 1945, in New York, they both left Communism—Budenz dramatically as the managing editor of *The Daily Worker*. In the summer of 1947, Budenz lobbied Meyer to speak to the Federal Bureau of Investigation.

Meyer agreed. Shortly thereafter, an agent visited. They talked. Nobody recorded. Nobody transcribed. They conversed. Such visits occurred weekly for over a month.[1]

"When he was approached to testify, he was in considerable agony," Elsie recalled. "He finally said to me that there was no right course. On the one hand was a betrayal of friends and of trust; on the other, a betrayal of his country and his values. This was the first time he fully appreciated Grace, he said, since whatever one did one was committing a sin."[2]

Talking with FBI agents, anathema to Frank just two years earlier, budged closer to normalcy. Within a few years, Meyer wrote J. Edgar Hoover that during "painful spiritual turmoil" his agents behaved with "the most sympathetic understanding and the keenest awareness."[3] But in 1947 he moved with trepidation, and the agents wisely trod lightly. He wished to name names only in cases that involved national security.[4] His recorded statements display attempts to abide by this ideal. Ultimately, he identified dozens of Communists in testimony, interviews, and correspondence. His coming-out party as a government witness occurred on the largest stage of all less than two years after his initial contact with federal law enforcement.

◆ ◆ ◆

THE PRESS referred to him as a "mystery witness."[5] His duties in the Communist Party of the United States of America appeared less mysterious than most. Meyer worked in the aboveground organization. The Smith Act trial of the late 1940s put eleven CPUSA leaders before a jury. Meyer stuck out as one of the few prosecution witnesses who had actually served earnestly in the party. This added weight to his testimony. Others evoked the lead character of the popular radio show, movie, and all-around midcentury cottage industry, *I Was a Communist for the FBI*.

Meyer's former comrades facing Judge Harold Medina consisted of Eugene Dennis, the CPUSA leader so committed to the cause that in 1935 he abandoned his firstborn permanently in the Soviet Union; Benjamin Davis Jr., an African American who held a seat on New York's city council; John Gates, the thirty-five-year-old head of the Young Communist League who had served as a stern commissar involved in the execution of an American volunteer during the Spanish Civil War; Jack Stachel, director of agitation and propaganda; Henry Winston, an African American member of the national board; Gus Hall, a red-diaper baby of Finnish immigrants and labor agitator throughout the Midwest; John Williamson, the Scottish-born, Russian-trained organizer in the Midwest; Gil Green, who once ran the Illinois section of the party and led the Young Communist League; Robert G. Thompson, an African American veteran of the Spanish Civil War and World War II; Carl Winter, Michigan party leader; and the union leader Irving Potash.[6]

They stood accused of violating the Alien Registration Act. Known colloquially as the Smith Act, the 1940 law made it illegal "to knowingly or willfully advocate, abet, advise, or teach the duty, necessity, desirability, or propriety of overthrowing or destroying any government in the United States by force or violence, or by the assassination of any officer of any such government" and to publish, edit, or write material, or organize for any group, seeking such ends.[7]

The legislation, passed as war loomed, initially enjoyed nearly unanimous support. Who advocates the violent overthrow of a government instituted by the will of the voters? Just four representatives opposed it in the House before the Senate, controlled by a Democrat supermajority, passed it. President Franklin Roosevelt, who wielded the act in part to punish friends and reward enemies, characterized its purpose as "to preserve and build up the loyalty and confidence of those aliens within our borders who desire to be faithful to its principles. With those aliens who are disloyal and are bent on harm to this country, the Government, through its law enforcement agencies, can and will deal vigorously."[8]

Communists initially pushed hard for this vigorous application.

◆ ◆ ◆

IN 1941, less than a year after a Comintern agent assassinated Leon Trotsky in Mexico, a federal grand jury indicted his disciples under the Smith Act. The trial of leaders of the Minnesota-based Socialist Workers Party attracted Communist Party leaders because it served as a legal purge. Just as Stalin had once served alongside Trotsky, Earl Browder had once served closely with James Cannon, figurehead of the extremists on trial. In the Soviet Union, Stalin murdered real and imagined Trotskyites. In the United States, the Roosevelt administration imprisoned them.

"The Trotskyist Fifth Column in the Labor Movement," published first as an article in 1944 in *The Communist* and expanded the following year into a pamphlet, depicted the small ideological sect as akin to Nazis and the Ku Klux Klan. Its author, George Morris, placed the American Civil Liberties Union, Norman Thomas, and others defending the Trotskyists within that same KKK-Nazi axis.[9] He reasoned of this Smith Act prosecution, "It would be as incorrect as it is false to view this case as a 'civil liberties' question."[10]

Morris's article conceded that the Trotskyists did not act as saboteurs in any traditional sense. They did so by engaging in an activity the Communist Party had previously portrayed as noble: the labor strike. It also pointed to Trotskyite opposition to the United States' entrance into the war without acknowledging that during the Soviet alliance with Nazi Germany the CPUSA also held an antiwar position.[11] A few years earlier the CPUSA had regularly deployed the very descriptor—"imperialist"—that Morris specifically faulted the Trotskyites for applying to the Second World War; Browder, for instance, wrote a book called *The Second Imperialist War*.[12] Trotskyist Communists, in other words, deserved prison sentences not for holding the same opinions and partaking in the same activism as the Stalinist Communists but for doing so at the wrong time. The crimes offended the calendar as much as the law book.

The piece's obsequiousness raised the question in any discerning reader's mind whether the federal government might also use the Smith Act one day against the CPUSA. So long as the Stalin–Roosevelt alliance endured, the CPUSA enjoyed immunity. But the moment that friendship born of wartime necessity cooled, the CPUSA clearly faced legal jeopardy.

"It is a matter of the most serious hindrance to our victory drive that fifth columnists should so long have been left at large," Morris contended. "Only now has the government put twenty-nine native fascists and Bundists on trial under the same anti-sedition act."[13]

The Stalinists soon suffered the nightmare of their dream coming true.

◆ ◆ ◆

THE TRIAL opened on November 1, 1948. Meyer did not testify for nearly six months. From the stand on April 13, 1949, he witnessed the reason for the delayed summons. Judge Medina asked after one objection, "What is it you move to strike out?" "The answer of the witness," defense counsel Abraham Isserman explained. "He hasn't said anything," responded a bemused Medina, who, perhaps to humor himself, sustained the objection.[14]

It started uncharacteristically for Meyer with prosecutor John F. X. McGohey twice, and Medina once, petitioning him to speak louder. When the man in the witness box ultimately complied, perhaps too enthusiastically, Medina exclaimed, "You get 100 percent on that."[15]

The thirty-nine-year-old dropped no dramatic bombshells, *à la* Whittaker Chambers months earlier revealing film rolls in a hollowed-out pumpkin on his farm to congressional investigators looking into Alger Hiss. Whereas that case, at least in the court of public opinion, focused on Soviet espionage and infiltration of the government, this trial examined a concern with less flash: Communists taking direction from a foreign power to work on its behalf as a U.S. political party. This mattered partly because the party acted as the primary feeder system to Moscow for American spies. Conveying its importance required more complexity than articulating the significance of Julius Rosenberg's spilling atomic secrets.

Much of the postwar news-consuming public, immersed in the issue since comprehending that Stalin had transformed

Eastern Europe into a series of vassal states, navigated the case's complexity. They understood its gravity. *The New York Times* highlighted Meyer's testimony on page nineteen.[16] *Time* devoted two covers to the trial, one of which appeared around when Meyer testified.[17] The presence of four hundred policemen at the Foley Square Courthouse to open the trial, and thousands of picketers at the peak, indicated a public interest best described with a word other than benign.[18]

◆ ◆ ◆

MEYER delivered hard blows to three of his former comrades in particular: Gil Green, Jack Stachel, and Eugene Dennis. In a general sense, he bolstered the prosecution's case against all of the defendants by showing the CPUSA's fealty to Moscow, belief in violent overthrow of the government as such a central tenet that the group taught it to initiates, and authoritarian approach that allowed for no dissent once deciders had closed perfunctory debate. The two issues that dominated the witness's time on the stand pertained to the Duclos Letter and a Soviet-authored textbook.

Meyer detailed his party work in England, how Stachel referred him to Green upon arriving in 1934 at CPUSA headquarters, his discussions with Green prior to his Chicago assignment, and Green's later putting him to work at the Jefferson School.[19] He described how the party ordered the use of *The History of the Communist Party of the Soviet Union* as the primary text for students during his time at the Chicago Workers School.

"It was, so far as the school was concerned, made the central textbook for, particularly, the courses that went at that time under the name of Marxism-Leninism 1, 2 and 3—later were changed, I believe, to the name Scientific Socialism 1, 2 and 3—and what was done was to take the central theoretical sections which existed in each of the chapters, or each of the more important chapters, and use them as the center around which the principles taken up there were discussed," he testified.[20]

The fact that the book was the central text of Communist education programs mattered for the prosecution. Like the thought of American Nazis buried in the pages of *Mein Kampf*, the idea of American Communists following the guidance of Stalin and his lackeys was alarming. The book, after all, highlighted violence as the means of Bolsheviks' attainment (and maintenance) of power.

The History of the Communist Party of the Soviet Union informed, among much else, that "Marx and Engels taught that it was impossible to get rid of the power of capital and to convert capitalist property into public property by peaceful means, and that the working class could achieve this only by revolutionary violence against the bourgeoisie, by a proletarian revolution, by establishing its own political rule—the dictatorship of the proletariat—which must crush the resistance of the exploiters and create a new, classless, Communist society."[21]

Such instruction applied to the American system violated the law.

Whether the law violated the Constitution became the subject of a fierce debate, but not until after the government began using it on Stalinists. It certainly meshed with much in the American tradition (or countertradition), including the Alien and Sedition Acts, General Order Number 38, and the Sedition Act of 1918, which Roosevelt, as an integral part of the Wilson administration's war apparatus, surely understood as a precedent for the Smith Act.

Green admitted that the party used the text. He denied assigning Meyer to Chicago or urging him to take a Jefferson School position. He denied testimony by four other witnesses as well. "All these, except Mr. Meyer, served in the Communist movement as undercover agents of the Federal Bureau of Investigation. Mr. Meyer is formerly a member of the party," reported *The New York Times*.[22]

✦ ✦ ✦

THE DUCLOS LETTER, like the Hitler–Stalin Pact before it, upended and then reoriented Communists. It served as an acid test in its demand that members essentially denounce their heretofore professed beliefs and accept a new line contrary to the previous one. An exodus occurred among those less committed. The majority who stayed necessarily proved their worth as automatons.

In mid-1945, Meyer, along with dozens of faculty members of the Jefferson School, met there to discuss the Duclos Letter. Its Moscow birthplace did not occur to everyone. Some mistakenly believed that the letter really came from Paris, which, combined with the dissolution of the Comintern and the CPUSA, fostered a real debate rather than the perfunctory sort desired by most party bigwigs, Browder excepted. A second, controlled exegesis of the Duclos Letter occurred the following week.[23] As Meyer remembered it, Stachel declared that, after everyone had more fully digested the missive from France, agreement had emerged about their revisionism: it dated back a decade and would have destroyed American Communism if allowed to continue.[24]

Meyer claimed that Stachel had blamed the American way of life, American exceptionalism, and Browder. Stachel, according to Meyer's paraphrase, maintained that "the years of Roosevelt had dampened or cut off the sharpness of understanding of the class struggle character in the United States."[25]

Meyer stubbornly advocated the on-the-outs Browderite position.

"I said that the line brought forward by Duclos was a line which in the aforementioned of post-war, after the democratic people of the world had already spilt their blood in a struggle against Germany, was one that was bound to lead inevitably to a war between the United States and the Soviet Union," Meyer testified, "a war for which the Communists themselves would be responsible if that line became the line of the International Communist Movement, that peace was possible and that all democratic and progressive people should attempt in every possible way to create a peaceful world."[26]

Stachel called Meyer's remarks "provocative." The Good Communist nevertheless told the gathering that he was "happy to see the general unanimity of opinion."[27]

The Bad Communist refused to let it rest.

Meyer testified that he wrote a letter to *The Daily Worker* critical of the Duclos approach. When it neither printed nor returned his letter, he complained to the defendant Robert Thompson, who sent him up the ladder to Eugene Dennis, the party's pseudonymous general secretary. Meyer described this conversation to the court.[28]

"I told him that I would like to know when my contribution to the discussion would be printed; that in my opinion there had been nothing printed against the position of the Duclos article except a couple of small letters without theoretical substance, and Mr. Browder's own article, own letter or contribution, and over the course of some weeks all of the other contributions had been rigged the other way," Meyer testified. "I said that, before it ended, 'I would like mine to be printed, and I know of one or two others that exist that ought to be printed to make it a discussion,' which I did not believe it had been until then, as I told him."[29]

He said Dennis repeatedly brushed him off.[30]

Meyer offered more evidence of the group's abrupt reorientation. The witness testified that the Jefferson School had pulled his FDR course.[31] The man the party had essentially backed for president in 1944 by ostensibly dissolving itself and not running a candidate for the first time since 1920 struck Communists as a posthumous pariah. Meyer increasingly appeared as a living pariah.

Defense counsel, which interrupted Meyer and the prosecutor incessantly, strangely opted not to cross-examine him after characteristically petitioning the judge to postpone their questioning until the next court session on Monday. Medina, beleaguered by the stall tactics, denied the request.[32] Meyer left the witness stand around 3:00 p.m. on Wednesday.[33]

The implications of the testimony on the Duclos Letter? On orders from a foreign power, eclipsing its Moscow messenger behind the leader of the French Communist Party's moon face, American Communists obsequiously performed an abrupt pirouette on their stated beliefs of many years. Furthermore, after receiving this foreign correspondence, they rushed to condemn the man before whom they had previously performed salaams. Comrades, including Meyer, who did not do as they were told by the foreign letter-writer lost their spots.

The Daily Worker characterized, correctly though repeatedly, Meyer as a Browderite, a name that carried nefarious connotations to its readers, in its news coverage.[34] The newspaper's analysis used harsher epithets. "An unscholarly scholar, fished from the cesspools of intellectual decay, was the third of a weird and unsavory array of five prosecution witnesses to appear so far in the trial of the Communist leaders," the party's press secretary wrote. "He came to the witness stand displaying an ear-to-ear grin and what appeared to be a pathological zeal to deliver a public oral confession of a deep-seated prejudice against the Communist Party and all Communists."[35] While *The New York Journal-American* described the witness's voice as "low" and *The New York World-Telegram* called him "soft-spoken," *The Daily Worker* observed in Meyer a "large voice."[36] The analysis claimed he spoke "in spasmo[d]ic bursts of oratory" that required an unusual number of glasses of water. It accurately described Meyer as suffering from an eyebrow tic.[37] It cast the man entrusted by the party to teach its ideology to initiates as unstable, a characterization endured by Elizabeth Bentley, Louis Budenz, and so many other former Communists speaking out against their old outfit.

◆ ◆ ◆

MEYER testified on one day of a trial that lasted 347 days. It mattered, particularly in that he knew them, as Budenz did, as comrades. Other witnesses knew them as investigation subjects. But, unlike Chambers's testimony against Hiss, Meyer's account did not, and could not, deliver the knockout blow. He threw an effective punch among an accumulation of shots from other witnesses that doomed the defendants.

Nathaniel Weyl found the case weak. He wondered whether Medina might instruct an acquittal and, if not, whether the Supreme Court might render any guilty verdict moot given the civil liberties concerns the trial evoked. He told Frank he did not see evidence of an overt act of sedition.[38]

The jury, the cause for the longest delays as the defense used fifteen of its challenges to shape the body that included three African Americans, two unemployed workers, and just one member of wealth and standing (the *Miracle of the Bells* author and Broadway producer Russell Janney), deliberated for seven hours.[39] The twelve found the eleven guilty in a trial that *Life* proclaimed the "longest, most noisy, most controversial in U.S. history."[40] All received five-year sentences, with contempt convictions adding months and good behavior subtracting them. Hall, Green, Thompson, and Winston jumped bail to avoid prison, resulting in longer sentences.

Frank, by now recognizing his past enterprise as profoundly evil, felt it his civic duty to tell the justice system what he knew. The trial awarded the former Communist his loudest megaphone to renounce his former faith. It did not so much mark the coda for one tune in his life as it did strike the opening note of another. He spent the next decade naming names.

◀ 14 ▶

Speaker

Testifying in 1949's highest-profile case isolated Frank Meyer as it elevated his name. The reentrance of Eugene O'Neill Jr. into his life alleviated the former problem as it exploited the latter opportunity.

O'Neill established a home in Woodstock. In 1947, he joined Meyer and Robert Phelps to moderate "Toward a New Synthesis," which concluded their summer lecture series.[1] The Meyer–O'Neill performances mostly took place late at night in the Meyers' living room.

Garry Wills, who argued and talked all night the next decade about politics and art and religion with Meyer, noted that "Frank and Gene argued and talked all night after the war about politics and art and religion. . . . [H]e and Frank divided up all the parts of a Shakespeare play and declaimed them at each other through the night."[2]

They took their show on the road.

◆ ◆ ◆

"HIS constant opponent will be Frank Meyer, a product of New Jersey, Princeton University, Oxford, and the London

School of Economics, whom O'Neill has known since their pre-college days when, he says, both were bumptious, would-be bright boys," explained a *New York Post* article. "Their lecture platform debates, soon to be launched, grew out of living room conversations which acquired a considerable reputation in Woodstock, where O'Neill and Meyer have houses."[3]

The pair secured representation from an elite speakers' bureau. Harold R. Peat, a disabled Canadian veteran of World War I, parlayed inspiring lectures about his combat experiences and postwar recuperation into a lucrative bureau. The eponymous agency represented H. G. Wells, Alice Roosevelt Longworth, Winston Churchill, and the Americanized half-nephew of the Führer, William Patrick Hitler, at various points during its midcentury heyday.

Harold R. Peat mattered. Its two new clients? They sat low on the pecking order. But not every host could afford Thomas Mann, and not every Thomas Mann wished to travel to rural Pennsylvania. Another Nobel Prize–winner's son and his little-known cater-cousin jumped at such opportunities. They did so because lectures enabled them not just to support themselves but to do the precise thing they loved: talking.

"Close friends for almost a quarter century, Eugene O'Neill Jr. and Frank Meyer have finally been prevailed upon to transfer their exciting discussions from the living-room to the platform," began the postwar promotional material touting the Chautauqua-circuit double act.[4]

Neither the speakers' bureau nor the public prevailed upon the pair. Failure did. Both men turned to lectures as a fresh start after disaster struck.

◆ ◆ ◆

"HE refuses ever to wear dress clothes," the Harold R. Peat flyer noted of the eldest child of America's most famous playwright. "By training a Classicist and an intellectual, Mr.

O'Neill nevertheless believes that physical labor is essential to a rounded life," the thumbnail sketch further explained. It noted past work as a ranch hand, hay stacker, lumberman, turret lathe turner, metallurgist's assistant, wire strander, and professor.[5] The flyer omitted O'Neill's profound love of drunkenness.

O'Neill's Yale professorship had in part become a casualty of the Second World War. Failing in an attempt to join the Intelligence Corps, he left Yale fully expecting to enlist. But a childhood skull fracture and the shake he shared with his father meant rejection, for a man especially sensitive to it, from the Navy, like his father during the First World War, before the Army rejected him.[6] Hating Nazism and desirous of service, O'Neill labored in a wire factory to help the war effort. It lacked the excitement of the infantry or intelligence. Alcohol staved off the tedium.

On the side, he worked as an intellectual for hire in those years when broadcasting exhibited a fetish for highbrains. His card advertised his "very deep voice," ability to play senators, heavies, and pompous asses, and the British, Southern, Scandinavian, and German accents he could imitate.[7] But he mainly played orotund Orson Welles playing a narrator for ABC's production of his father's *Ah, Wilderness!*, WNYC's promotion of the Four Freedoms called *Seven Million Back the 7th*, and WNEW's *History of the Movies*.[8]

The immoderate man moderated. "I am doing Mencken's American Language for Invitation to Learning this Sunday, with Edgar Lee Masters and Malcolm Cowley," he wrote his friend. He also discussed his "grim finances" and a possible book-reading job from the Foundation for the Blind. "It ought to be a good show. I did not even know Masters was still alive; he is 77. Give a listen at noon, if awake."[9]

This new love inevitably clashed with an old love. O'Neill showed up to a television studio, much to the displeasure of the actor Adolphe Menjou, effluviating alcohol. Since the dapper Menjou habitually topped best-dressed lists, O'Neill thought it humorous to don ridiculous clothing while critiquing his book *It Took Nine Tailors*. That the worst-dressed guest did so drunk did not leave producers laughing.[10]

His dreams of becoming Clifton Fadiman giving an intellectual air to mindlessness on the air perhaps did not die there. Those dreams striking anyone but him as a possibility did. He held membership cards in the Actors' Equity Association and the American Federation of Radio Artists after his brief, broadcasting heyday.[11] He no longer obtained jobs easily.

O'Neill lectured as a last resort after a string of failures. So did his debating partner.

◆ ◆ ◆

HAROLD R. PEAT expunged Meyer's recent Stalinism just as the agency omitted O'Neill's sustained inebriation. To the extent any Americans knew Meyer, they knew him as a Communist rabble-rouser who had recently turned on his comrades.

Meyer and O'Neill, on a retail scale and in a way designed to hide rather than promote their pasts, captivated the intellectually curious public. They delivered a four-part series on "Reason, Romance, and Ritual in Twentieth Century Thought" at the Brooklyn Institute of Arts and Science.[12] The pair's presentation "Education for What?" provided the entire theme of the Central Ohio Teachers' Association convention in Columbus in October 1949.[13] They debated this topic for the Bradford, Pennsylvania, community in its high school auditorium in November.[14] On January 17, 1950, they spoke to an audience of six hundred at Marshall College, where Tom Wilkerson of High Coal, West Virginia, won the $10 prize for most imaginative question.[15]

At 10:45 the next morning, they spoke more than 250 miles away in the Hotel Cleveland ballroom, addressing the question "Can Freedom Survive Under Planning?" for the Town Hall Series.[16] O'Neill defended planning. *The Cleveland*

Plain Dealer regarded it as "the most interesting feature of the discussion" that Meyer, who had left the Communist Party about four years earlier, now regarded planning as inimical to liberty.

"The fact that the capitalist makes goods for an unknown market implies democracy—he must have the democratic vote of the consumer," Meyer told the audience. "Under planned economy the leaders must treat consumers like a father treats his children. People must be directed, must be told what to eat, where to work, what kind of schools to go to. And if they are not persuaded—and in a traditionally democratic country they cannot be persuaded—they must be coerced. That is totalitarianism."[17]

While Meyer's conservative outlook evolved, he clearly showed himself as the 1950s began as a convert to the political right. The transition that began in an Arkansas barracks continued in that Ohio ballroom.

"O'Neill-Meyer arguments are usually heated," noted the *New York Post*, "but the heat is purely intellectual, despite the fact that O'Neill confesses to a tendency to drive home points rather by voice than by logic."[18]

Though intellectuals, the pair more heavily relied on their skill set as natural performers to enthrall audiences. Both men liked the limelight. They also liked each other, normally a handicap for those in the conflict business.

"Frank and I have a notion that debates should bring out not only conflicts of opinion," O'Neill observed, "but also the basic grounds on which two intelligent intellectuals can agree."[19]

Frank lost his comrades. He regained his friend.

◀ 15 ▶

Gene

T he double act differed in their love lives. Meyer and
his wife lived in mutual devotion above Woodstock.
O'Neill and his girlfriends cohabitated in mutual
combat before parting.

"He had eighteen girls during that period," Meyer recalled
of the tall professor with a famous man's name in 1949 and
1950. "He also started drinking heavily, more than I realized
at first—although I never saw him really drunk."[1]

Others did, which calls into question Meyer's definition of
"really drunk." Meyer drank with Jimmy Tomorrow, General
Piet Wetjoen, Willie Oban, and any of the dozen or so other
down-and-outer *Iceman Cometh* characters when he drank
with Gene. He just did not know it.

"That man has the look of a man who might kill himself,"
observed a Shane O'Neill mistress.[2] Others, not venturing such
extreme physiognomic diagnoses, nevertheless sensed trouble.

"I told Gene to stop worrying about women and get back
to serious work," Meyer remembered. "Gene said he had to
have someone to work for. I told him that he had himself to
work for and asked him if he couldn't make the effort to get
back on the right track." Gene responded, "I've slipped too
far. I can't get back."[3]

✦ ✦ ✦

O'NEILL'S manic quality colored five days in September 1950. On Wednesday, September 20, at the Meyers' home, O'Neill volunteered thoughts of suicide and a wife as the cure to his depression. Candidates consisted of the artist Marion Greenwood, the future author of *Sybil* Flora Rheta Schreiber, and the art agent Ruth Lander. He picked Lander. He proposed on Thursday.

"Evidently that night and Friday were spent in a triumphal touring of the village with great celebrating," Elsie noted. "She called his mother to say they would be married the following week, and they came up here Friday night to announce the news to us. After they had left, Frank looked worried and gloomy, and I railed into him for not being happy when everyone else was. But he persisted that there was something wrong—they weren't happy, but rather almost hysterical, primarily, Ruth, of course; Gene looked dazed, worn-out, and sort of happy."

News traveled fast. On Saturday, another suitor, a married industrialist, offered Lander $25,000 to marry him instead. She said yes. Gene publicly announced his intention to kill himself.[4]

✦ ✦ ✦

MORE THAN that rejection made this moment. Gene, enjoying a solid relationship with his mother, had received little beyond a belated name and belated financial support from his father. His alcohol consumption, though prodigious, did not fill the void. His relationships, inevitably damaged by his coping mechanism, did not provide peace (or a child). Lander later blamed the bribed breakup on Gene's becoming "so weird I couldn't stand him."[5] The rejection acted as the fresh wound. His stepmother, made for that role if no other, inflicted the lingering wound.

Gene's father loved Carlotta Monterey. Others loved to avoid her.

Monterey hid drafts of her unhealthy husband's plays as a means of punishment and control.[6] In this and other ways, she manipulated the man in her thrall to change his will, essentially disinheriting his fragile and addicted son Shane and his celebutante daughter Oona, who scandalized her father and stepmother by becoming Charlie Chaplin's latest teenage bride in 1943. But senior kept junior in the will even as Carlotta left him on her lengthy enemies list.[7]

"Bless your heart—I do not want you and Sally to do any housework," she began a 1939 note to Gene, "just not expect service! You could tidy your room and hang things up."[8] Carlotta hated his Van Dyke beard, his left-wing views, and, most of all, his connection with her husband.[9] How great this hate? She burned the bedsheets after his departure from their Marblehead, Massachusetts, home.[10]

Monterey acted as a human mail cover in monitoring, censoring, and discarding letters sent from her stepchildren.[11] This served as one component of her slow isolation of an already terribly private man. One by one, Monterey extruded the children from her husband's life that he had abandoned years earlier. The eighteen-year-old Oona's marriage to the fifty-four-year-old Charlie Chaplin served as the pretext.[12] One does not need a degree in psychology to theorize why she married a man her father's age. Then, Shane's heroin addiction and the misadventures accompanying it, which included a dead child, arrests, and the selling of the contents of O'Neill's former Bermuda home, made him *persona non grata*.[13] Finally, Gene, too, experienced banishment. He grasped that his only chance of seeing his father came when he escaped the clutches of his tempestuous wife, such as during a play's rehearsal. So the contact became brief and clandestine when it happened at all.[14]

"His hatred of Carlotta was almost maniacal," the Random House editor Saxe Commins noted of his Thursday, September 21, 1950, meeting with Gene. "It was she, he insisted, who was the cause of his desperation."[15]

Others, including Gene, pointed to causes beyond Carlotta.

◆ ◆ ◆

"I DIDN'T THINK Gene would kill himself over Ruth," Meyer said of his friend's midcentury troubles at middle age, "but I knew he was capable of suicide. We'd discussed the subject many times and we were thoroughly agreed that in a case where things became intolerable for a person he should kill himself. Both of us were against the Christian viewpoint of suicide being sinful."[16]

Those conversations, in light of a forlorn Gene's erratic behavior, grew in Meyer's mind as summer became fall.

"Gene," read a handwritten note left under his door during the October part of September. "If you feel like coming up anytime you come on—don't hesitate—Frank."[17]

Gene's mood deteriorated to such a degree that the Meyers ventured out on Saturday evening, September 23, in search of his friend or his earthly vessel.

"I even searched his land," Meyer recalled, "to see if he'd tried to hang himself from a tree."[18]

Early Sunday morning, Meyer gave up the search. Gene, to the relief of the Meyers, did not give up the ghost.

He called Sunday. Meyer visited.

"He looked beat," O'Neill's best friend recalled. "I didn't want him to be alone and asked him to come to us for dinner. He didn't want to, at first, but he finally said he'd drive over in a little while."[19]

They ate. They talked. They drank.

The food and highballs distracted only so much. New concerns dissolved the Meyers' initial relief.

"At dinner we talked about our worry of the night before," Frank recalled. "Elsie told Gene he shouldn't speak of suicide, and added, 'Of course, you'll never kill yourself.' I said I realized now I had been foolish to worry, that I should have known he would never commit suicide impulsively, but would take time to plan it properly."

O'Neill corrected his friends. He admitted to wanting to hang himself with the chain blocking a private lane on his property the previous evening. A startled Frank responded, "I thought you'd plan something more thorough than that."[20]

◆ ◆ ◆

O'NEILL departed down the hill at 11:00 p.m.

"I went to bed at three but couldn't sleep," Meyer recalled of the end to his early evening. "Around 3:30, Gene returned. He said he'd slept, but was wide awake now and wanted a drink; he had no liquor in his house. I had half a bottle of bourbon, and each of us had two stiff drinks. We sat talking for about two hours, mostly reminiscing."[21]

Fears, stoked by O'Neill's earlier admission during the long night's journey into day, dissipated upon the guest's rethinking the idea of acting on his depression. Discussion between the triumvirate, interrupted upon the neighbor's departure, now resumed.

"He mentioned at one point that perhaps he had been wrong about suicide, that maybe the Christian viewpoint was the right one, after all," Meyer recalled. "Elsie was in bed in the adjoining room and she didn't get up, but she and Gene exchanged a few words through the door. He told her, 'I'm a man of iron if I come through this.'"[22]

As the sun attempted to peek over the mountains, sleep beckoned. Students relied on O'Neill to teach them. Five-year-old John required his parents to, well, parent him. O'Neill, requesting his friend leave him the remains of the bourbon, crashed on the couch.

When the Meyers awoke, the bottle was gone. So was Gene.[23]

♦ ♦ ♦

THE CONVERSATION preceding sleep reassured the Meyers. The friend of nearly a quarter century, though exiled from Yale, three marriages, airwave intellectualism, his father's life, and various guest lists, bars, and polite company, expressed an epiphany on suicide. Earlier that year Katharine White, the wife of the *Charlotte's Web* author and herself a formidable editor, followed up on an article of O'Neill's published in *The New Yorker* by writing, "I hope you'll make a habit of sending us contributions."[24] The New School for Social Research continued to employ him. Women found him attractive. Friends loved him. He could count reasons to live. And the spurning fiancée struck no one as a reason to die.

Gene's teaching duties proved fortuitous. His ex-fiancée petitioned Elsie to accompany her to retrieve her belongings from his home, presumably evacuated of its occupant. Elsie, who disliked Ruth, nevertheless agreed. With John along for the ride, she motored toward Ruth's home.[25] She came to Gene's first.

If the quiet soothed her, then the sight of Gene's jeep was alarming. His unexpected presence made bringing Ruth there a terrible idea. The absence of his vehicle from a parking lot in Poughkeepsie signaled that a New York City classroom would soon lack its teacher. In Poughkeepsie, he normally took the train. But the previous night's revelry instilled a mighty hangover that prevented the commute.

He needed to lose that job like he needed to slit his wrists. But he did just that—and slashed his ankles, too.[26]

Elsie glimpsed Gene's lifeless body at the foot of his stairs.

"Intellectually I knew he was dead," she recalled. "But emotionally I couldn't accept it."[27]

A trail of blood indicated that O'Neill had committed the murder in his second-floor bathroom. Then it indicated that O'Neill had attempted to rescue the victim by stumbling down the stairs to the front door. If O'Neill the rescuer had wished at any point to reach out for help, then O'Neill the murderer had sabotaged this by failing to pay the phone bill.[28] The Seneca-style suicide, and farewell note partially in Latin, assured that his final act owed more to the tragedies of the ancients that he studied than to his father's bleak modern dramas.

"Never let it be said of O'Neill that he failed to finish a bottle," he wrote after downing Meyer's bourbon in the bathroom. "Ave atque vale."[29] Gene, last seen in town at 10:00 A.M., did himself in at high noon.[30] And he did so by more than fulfilling Frank's wish that he act with forethought.

◄ 16 ►

Estate

T he sight left Elsie, with a five-year-old in tow, the responsibility of explaining what happened. "He's done it," she informed Frank from a neighbor's phone. She called a doctor. She broke the news to Ruth Lander, who perhaps wondered by now if Elsie's contempt for her had resulted in her standing her up.[1] John, in the back seat, remained oblivious.[2]

Eugene's mother, expecting a call from her devoted son to schedule their weekly Manhattan lunch, instead received one from a reporter, who cryptically noted an accident in Woodstock and gently referred her to the Meyers.[3] To tell the absentee patriarch, cloistered by his warden-wife and self-sequestration, the Meyers opted to recruit Saxe Commins, editor-in-chief at Random House, who in turn recruited Winfield Aronberg, O'Neill's attorney, to deliver the bad news. Aronberg delicately explained the situation. Carlotta Monterey responded, "How dare you invade our privacy!" before hanging up.[4]

Carlotta, guardian of information, merely relayed to her husband the involvement of his namesake in an accident. Gene's father corrected her. His elder son had committed suicide. He skipped the funeral, as he had his son's childhood, but provided flowers and by some accounts paid for the whole sendoff.[5] As a member of the Euthanasia Society of America's advisory council, along with Max Eastman, Robert Frost, and Robert Sherwood, the father could accept his son's chosen departure rationally without grief or dejection.[6] Except he could not. Nobody could.

Frank and Elsie, who shared the playwright's views on suicide, could not. Friends sent condolences understanding they wrote the people, with the exception of his mother, closest to Gene.

"I know that O'Neill's death must be dreadful for you," the artist Bradley Tomlin wrote. "I have thought of you and Elsie constantly. It must have been frightful for Elsie. . . . I realize that it will leave a hole in your life."[7]

An overwhelmed Kathleen Pitt-Smith, Gene's mother, who had lost him so soon after losing her second husband, effectively appointed Frank the estate's executor.[8] To that end, Frank forwarded electric bills, incoming checks, and a bank book listing $1.64 in savings to the law firm overseeing the settling of the estate.[9] He acted as the point man selling his friend's assets. The Yale professor Norman Holmes Pearson bought a recording of his college classmate Gene announcing Franklin Roosevelt's death.[10] Frank compiled a lengthy list of items and recipients. Hutchins received an axe; Julius some coins.[11] He sold his friend's record collection piecemeal.[12] One letter-writer expressed interest in owning Gene's white cat if Frank and Elsie would only hold onto it a little longer.[13] He wrote Tiffany & Co. to gauge the worth of a ship's bell clock.[14] He fielded multiple offers for Gene's Jeep that came in below the $900 asking price before accepting a full-price bid tendered before the end of the year.[15] A single woman, described as a "tear-stained face" seen "bowed over the pew at the funeral" but known as an O'Neill conquest, purchased $800 in books from Gene's extensive library and spent $50 for framed maps but backed out, after ghosting Meyer and the attorneys, from purchasing his Woodstock property for $4,000 after putting down a deposit.[16]

Frank arranged through Yale's classics department for Gene's thick collection of index cards of Greek metrical analysis to find an owner that they could benefit.[17] Along with Elsie, he organized the painstaking process of gathering Gene's letters, pictures, legal documents, and ephemera for researchers. He tried through contacts in New Haven to start a small prize for classics students in Gene's name and to pay for an annual keg at Skull and Bones, the world's most famous secret society, to which Gene belonged, or for post-dinner drinks at Jonathan Edwards College, where the alcoholic who died after drinking Frank Meyer's whiskey had lived as an undergraduate.[18] Frank and Elsie worked hard to keep their friend's memory alive.

The primary way they worked for their dead friend involved protecting his mother. This entailed favoring her over the decedent's ex-fiancée. The law firm that handled the matter insisted to Ruth that no will existed, let alone one that named her as a beneficiary. She accepted without a fight her lack of standing and merely asked that Frank hold her Leg-o-Matic table for her.[19] A will not only existed but instructed Ruth and Kathleen to "share and share alike."[20]

Whether this 1947 document became obsolete sometime prior to O'Neill's demise or the parties, including, presumably, Frank and Elsie, wished to exclude Ruth, a person they hated, remains speculation. But the existence of that written bequest belies the claims made to her by an attorney representing the estate that no such document existed.[21] Perhaps he knew of no will but Frank and Elsie knew better. John Meyer noted, "I would not be too surprised if they pushed the bounds of strict legality on that one since they felt that she was partly to blame for his suicide."[22]

✦ ✦ ✦

FRANK ran interference for Pitt-Smith on another front. This involved a man she had last seen during William Howard Taft's presidential administration.

Initially, Meyer's correspondence with her former husband exuded a warm tone. He offered to talk with the aggrieved father about his son.

"The bite was deep," he explained to the ailing father. "The woman had little to do with it—and whiskey nothing. Dispossession. Othello's occupation gone."[23]

The letter's ostensible gist involved the best way to send the son's bequest to his father.

"There is always something of Gene's he wanted you to have in case of his death—his Ph.D. diploma," he explained.[24] How did Frank know this? Gene's will, presented to Ruth as nonexistent, said it. Maybe Gene told him this independently of what he wrote in the will. Such a theoretical conversation strikes as strange.

"Your letter was a great pleasure to me; and to learn that Eugene had wanted me to have his Ph.D. diploma warmed my heart," one Princeton dropout wrote another. "Would you please send it here to our home—and thank you for your trouble."

Perhaps not remembering Meyer as the same friend of his son's whom he had met in Maine many summers ago, O'Neill responded to his correspondent's offer to meet: "I would ask you to come to see me but my health has been very poor since Eugene's death. When I am better again I will write to you, and, perhaps, we may meet some day."[25]

The signature, as though written while inside a blender, foreshadowed that "some day" would never arrive.

But another letter did six months later.

"I was very sorry to hear of your accident, and I must apologize for disturbing you, but the problem I want to ask you about has become urgent," Meyer wrote. "I should hesitate to write you about something which in a sense is not my business, were it not that Gene told me that you once asked him to let you know if his mother were ever in difficulties, so that you could help her as if it came from him."[26]

The matter concerned money owed by the playwright's son's estate.[27]

"The problem is the $4000 Guaranty Loan for Gene's land," Frank informed. "It looked for a time as though a friend of Gene's were going to buy the land for $4000, which would have solved the difficulty. But that has fallen through, and I am afraid that one might have to wait for years to find a purchaser who would pay at all what it is worth. [If it is] put up at auction to settle the estate, it will bring only a fraction of the value. With the responsibility of the loan, the estate, Mr. Palzer tells me, will be insolvent, and Mrs. Pitt-Smith will be responsible for the deficit out of Gene's insurance. That is all she has, except her job, which at her age cannot go on forever."[28]

Given O'Neill's wealth if not health, and his early nonsupport and abandonment of his firstborn, the request appeared not unreasonable. Reason factored into O'Neill family business as much as it did in Tyrone family matters in *Long Day's Journey into Night*. Meyer, perhaps grasping the delicate dynamics, worded the letter to appeal to emotion rather than reason. A cold response came not from O'Neill but from Winfield Aronberg. It read like stenography from Carlotta, who soon fired Aronberg, amid the mounting hospital bills that rationalized refusals of this sort.[29]

"There have been many attempts to get Mr. O'Neill to forget the $4,000 claim and I thought it had been made perfectly clear that he had no intention of forgetting it," the attorney wrote. He responded to the suggestion of a meeting by informing, "Mr. O'Neill is leaving the hospital within a few days and it will be impossible for you to see him."[30]

◆ ◆ ◆

LIKE GENE'S MOTHER, the Meyers experienced vexing money problems.

Their tax returns for these years reveal an income about average for American families. But beyond that bottom-line figure, the returns reveal two adults and a child living almost exclusively off passive, bequeathed income. A man in his forties could not provide for his family.

In 1950, the Meyers relied almost exclusively on the $3,296.75 derived from rent from a Schrafft's restaurant occupying the brick business building in Newark inherited through his mother. The $587.50 the family patriarch earned from lectures came not only against $903.37 in stated expenses but in the face of the lost speaking partnership.[31] The following year frozen pipes burst and inflicted damage to the Woodstock home. The lecture haul predictably dwindled with Gene gone. The $3,285.65 in rents from the Newark building amounted to more than the $3042.30 in income claimed after write-offs for 1951.[32] To add injury to the insulting income, the state of New York audited Meyer for these two years.[33] In 1952, Eugene Bown Meyer, another son named for another dead friend, arrived and along with him hundreds of dollars in medical expenses. The patriarch's listed profession paid him $135 that year (against greater expenses). Once again, the Newark building essentially accounted for all of the $3,114.15 in income claimed after expenses.[34]

They struggled. Frank drove no automobile and the family refrained through the 1950s from buying a television.[35] The sparse times required cultivating vegetables and fruit on a half-acre of the property.[36] More so did the harsh times demand that the fortysomething family breadwinner finally live up to that title.

He wondered about following Gene into the classroom.[37]

He inquired about teaching positions at Marlboro College, the University of North Carolina, and Cornell but received discouragement and outright rejection.[38] His attempt to gain employment at the State Department, facilitated by his Woodstock acquaintance Robert Bauer, went so far as to require a lengthy detailing of his history in the Communist Party.[39] He sent inquiries to publishers for a proposed collection of his former teacher Bronisław Malinowski's work presented for the educated layman but received rejections from Macmillan, Harper & Brothers, and Farrar, Straus.[40]

The unpaid work sorting out his friend's messy estate proved time-consuming, tedious, draining. It involved fits and starts dealing with flakes and friends. The presence of attorneys and demand for paperwork exacerbated his frustrations. It came at a time of transition. No longer a Communist but just a fledgling conservative, Meyer remained unsure about the path forward. The labyrinth of lawyers, the disbursement of the detritus collected over a life, and the management of personalities occupied him into 1951.

By the end of it all, he wished to escape to the Caribbean.

"I quite agree with you that it would be good for Frank to get away for a while," Kathleen Pitt-Smith wrote Elsie. "The tie between the two was very great and I know the association of lectures, study and writing, let alone missing Gene's dropping in must be very hard. I may be wrong but I should judge that Frank is a person of very deep feeling and I can well know what he is going through although maybe he, himself, does not appreciate it. I am very glad he is blessed with such a fine and understanding wife. If only Gene could have loved someone like you he probably would be with us today, in fact I am sure he would be."[41]

For Frank and Elsie, Gene's exit from his life did not mean his exit from theirs. His physical body was destroyed by exsanguination; his spirit, in ways good and bad, haunted them for the remainder. The Meyers tried to move on from Eugene O'Neill Jr. They never did.

◀ 17 ▶

Witness

A n MI5 memo from late 1934 reported that a redacted investigator "can find no trace of this man."[1] Seventeen years later, swaths of Frank Meyer suddenly enveloped British intelligence. Meyer's 1951 attempt to vacation in Jamaica pinged the empire's security apparatus because his name remained on a Home Office Security Index, from which British authorities agreed to remove him upon learning of the renunciation of his old faith (and believing him a convert to a new one, in possible confusion with Louis Budenz).[2] Around the same time, old comrades spoke in almost mythical terms to British intelligence of a 1930s American organizer. MI5 sought out Meyer—or was it Myer?—or Meyers.

A letter from MI5 to the British embassy in Washington, D.C., noted, "A source with whom we are in contact and who himself was a foundation member of the October Club at Oxford has gone so far as to describe MEYER as 'the founder of the Student C.P. movement' in this country."[3] Events made questioning him paramount.

In May 1951, the diplomats Guy Burgess and Donald Maclean, two minor players in the movement launched by Meyer, vanished as proof of their espionage surfaced. If the former comrade, albeit an Oxonian rather than a Cantabrigian, could not enlighten on Burgess and Maclean, then perhaps the early 1930s leader of young British Communists could identify others from that flock in powerful positions now.

British authorities petitioned the FBI to interview Meyer using questions it supplied. The FBI questioned him in the spring of 1952.[4]

Meyer detailed the early Communist student movement in England and the antiwar movement that the party directed. Claiming ignorance of underground work, he volunteered F. E. Warner, James Frederic Danielli, Frank Jackson, E. D. Hunt, and Peter Floud as both "sufficiently indoctrinated" and possessing "special abilities of a scientific kind" to possibly warrant Soviet recruitment.

The Brits requested a follow-up FBI interview. Meyer named many known Communists, such as the professors J. D. Bernal, Maurice Dobb, and Hyman Levy.

Among the names proffered in the initial interview, Floud (whose brother Bernard, who became a member of Parliament, raised similar suspicions), attracted credible allegations of clandestine Soviet service.[5] In the second group, Vernon Ellis Cosslett, whom he identified as the leader of the party group at Bristol University, curiously married a Soviet intelligence courier, toiled alongside the atomic spy Klaus Fuchs early in his career, and subsequent to Meyer's interview hired the atomic spy Ted Hall, which facilitated his exodus from the United States, at Cambridge.[6] Floud and Cosslett died before their treachery became public.

While British counterespionage agencies tracked down a student firebrand of the early 1930s, bringing traitors to justice—or even pushing them out of government positions—in the 1950s remained largely beyond the scope of their efforts. That British intelligence still employed spies after informants had warned of their disloyalty helps explain why it failed to follow through on Meyer's information.

Nevertheless, MI5, for whom Burgess had once performed work, judged, "The information produced by MEYER is of very great value to us and adds considerably to our records of the communist student movement in the thirties."[7]

✦ ✦ ✦

MEYER'S information disrupted the already quite disrupted Communist apparatus in America. Meyer started the fall of 1951 by appearing before the Subversive Activities Control Board (SACB) in Washington, D.C. The McCarran Act, passed over President Harry Truman's veto a year earlier, created the quasi-judicial body to identify front groups, compel operational transparency by the Communist Party and its satellites, and prevent aliens who subscribed to totalitarian tenets from staying in the country.

The witness, one of twenty-two called by the government, discussed his party work, the direction to teach the Kremlin-produced *History of the Communist Party of the Soviet Union*, and the sharp pivot taken after receipt of the Duclos Letter.[8] But he also covered ground undisturbed in earlier testimony. He described a conspiratorial outfit operating under methods generally used by gangsters.

He testified that he knew Gerhart Eisler, a Comintern agent who had fled to East Germany in 1949 after federal criminal convictions, as "Hans Berger" and "Edward."[9] The former district membership director told the board of carrying out orders not to maintain written lists of dues payers during periods of precaution, such as the Hitler–Stalin Pact.[10] He noted the party's practice to use cash except in situations, such as rent, that called for recording rather than hiding.[11]

He testified to directing secret schools held at party camps in summer and halls of foreign-language sections in winter. Here, elite members, instructed to take leave from work without offering true reasons and arrive at a safe house of sorts to receive further orders, submitted to training. "The students would meet in groups of one or two and go to the hall, timing their arrival so not more than one or two people would arrive at once and so that there would be no influx of people," he explained. "In these periods the schools were very small, eight, nine, ten or eleven students. The instructors would arrive in the same way. All papers during the day would be burned at the end of the day. The books would be removed from the room used at night in suitcases so that the hall was then in its perfectly normal appearance."[12] In other words, they did not act like Democrats or Republicans. They behaved as though they were part of a criminal conspiracy.

The former Congressman Vito Marcantonio, joining the party lawyer John Abt (himself a former Soviet agent) in providing counsel, objected to Meyer's use of the word "conspiratorial."[13] The fake names, secret meetings, and burn-after-reading material nevertheless persuaded SACB officials sitting in judgment. They ordered the Communist Party to register as a Communist-action organization.

◆ ◆ ◆

THE DEPARTMENT OF JUSTICE visited Meyer in Woodstock on September 11, 1953, with the intent of placing him under oath during an SACB case against the Jefferson School. To limit surprises, Ralph Edsall Jr., an attorney with the DOJ's Internal Security Division, interviewed Meyer months in advance.[14] So minute was the government's planning that Edsall ultimately presented Meyer with a mock transcript that he called a "guide," which included questions *and* answers based on past interviews.[15] A subpoena ordered the witness to appear at 10:00 a.m. on January 5, 1954, in the twelve-story, E-shaped Lafayette Building a short walk from the White House.[16] The detail-oriented Edsall insisted that the witness arrive in the capital on January 3 to give them the following day to again go over the testimony.[17]

Meyer told of his involvement in Communism generally and the Jefferson School specifically. He described the
discussions with Alexander Trachtenberg and V. J. Jerome
that led to the school's formation, the offer for Frank to
serve as "commissar" over it, and his role in the "curriculum
group."[18] The testimony combined with the sworn claims of
others in enabling SACB to legally, and accurately, classify
the Jefferson School as Communist-controlled. This truth-
in-advertising atop a public revulsion toward Communism
soon closed the school.

The testimony during the case that drew the most attention pertained to a Jefferson School colleague. Louis Budenz
and John Lautner depicted Josephine Truslow Adams, an
artist and teacher, as an intermediary between Franklin Roosevelt, the elected leader of the American people, and Earl
Browder, the selected leader of American Communists.

"I imagine you read in the paper the complete denial of
Josephine Truslow Adams in an AP release," Edsall wrote his
witness. "Frankly, I am not too concerned about the Adams
affair, but do think we should discuss the advisability of your
substantiating Budenz' and Lautner's story. I shall be largely
governed by your desires in this matter."[19]

Meyer's testimony displayed little desire.

"They really are a tissue of half-truths and excuses," he
nevertheless wrote Edsall of Browder's guarded response
to the allegations, "but I do think he has gone far enough
to make it difficult in the future for anyone to dispute the
story outright."[20]

He misjudged the difficulty.

◆ ◆ ◆

IN LATE 1955, he covered worn ground before SACB.[21] In-
vestigatory bodies wanted more, more, more. This zeal occasionally upended their pursuit of truth.

The Senate Internal Security Subcommittee ordered Meyer to appear before it on February 26, 1957. His appearance followed testimony delivered the previous month by Adams in executive session but selectively released and too ignored by the press for Meyer's liking.[22] Adams affirmed a story bandied about that she had acted as a Browder–Roosevelt go-between.

Meyer testified that "Franklin Roosevelt was, I believe, from the conversations I had with Miss Adams, convinced that the Soviet Union would move from its lack of civil liberties toward civil liberties while the United States moved from its constitutional and free enterprise situation to socialism, and both would end at the same point, and that, as it were, he and Browder were very close political friends, though they never met personally, working toward the same goal from somewhat different positions."[23]

He credited Adams with convincing Roosevelt to commute Browder's sentence and said Browder began writing his column for an audience of Roosevelt. The former Swarthmore art instructor and the president discussed the Chinese leader Chiang Kai-shek, the French leader Charles de Gaulle, and the upcoming Yalta conference. He further testified that her intervention reversed the government's position on several Spanish Civil War veterans blocked from World War II service. The concrete results of certain undeniable work, even if mere speculation gauged whether it was consequential or coincidental to results, amplified her influence.[24] The conversations about the shape of the postwar world intensified toward the end of Roosevelt's reign, he claimed.[25]

The relationship by proxy encouraged Browder's accommodationist line, Meyer's staying in a more mainstreamed Communist movement, and the Soviet Union's altered perception of Roosevelt. Meyer's Jefferson School colleague appears in a spy cable intercepted by the U.S. Venona Project, and other Soviet cables likely relied on information she provided.[26] Meyer, for instance, testified that Adams relayed Roosevelt's rejection of Wendell Willkie, the 1940 Republican presidential nominee who became an enthusiastic supporter of FDR's wartime leadership, as a 1944 unity-ticket running mate.[27] One of the Venona intercepts noted, via Browder's discovery of this "verbally," the president's distrust of Willkie.[28]

A game of "operator" occurred. Roosevelt spoke to Adams, who spoke to Browder, who relayed the information to spymasters, who sent it to Moscow. Alas, one link in the chain invented responses. Roosevelt almost certainly never spoke directly to Adams.

Meyer believed Adams for the same reasons as an anti-Communist as he did as a Communist. She said what he wanted to hear. The story owes to more than ideologically inspired fantasy. Adams knew Eleanor Roosevelt. She completed a commissioned painting for the First Lady, sent her another work, and met with her.[29] They served, briefly, on the board of a Communist front group together.[30] They corresponded. Mrs. Roosevelt noted she passed on her letters to the president, who demonstrated that he had read at least one by encouraging J. Edgar Hoover to launch an investigation of a supposed fascist based on a concocted claim made by Adams. This all happened.

Tales of the family dog Fala swiping documents from her or FDR's codenaming her Dr. Johnson appeared quite tall in retrospect.[31] No record exists of her meetings with the president, and records do exist of her stays in psychiatric institutions. Later, a publisher canceled an Adams project when an editor discovered that the letters she had pawned off as FDR's came from her.[32]

The truth, which surfaced a quarter century after the hearings, appeared terrible for all.[33] Meyer and Browder could not differentiate between a fellow traveler and a disturbed woman. The First Lady could not disassociate from a political extremist whose mental state also went to extremes. The president launched a federal investigation based on the word of a mental case. The subcommittee to its credit kept much within executive session before dropping the matter;

to its discredit it allowed Meyer to buttress Adams's words even though staffers knew of her mental health issues and even though the supporting witness could admittedly offer only hearsay, that is, that Meyer knew what Adams told him and what he discussed with Browder but he could not vouch for whether Adams knew the president. Meyer forever believed Adams.[34]

◆ ◆ ◆

BY THE TIME Meyer testified before the House Committee on Un-American Activities (HCUA) in 1959, the committee and un-American activities had seen better days. Three months earlier, former President Harry Truman ridiculed it as "the most un-American thing in the country today."[35] And three months before that, Martin Dies, the figure most associated with HCUA, exited public life. *The Daily Worker* had ceased publication the previous year. Neither the committee nor the Communists seemed as relevant as when Meyer first named names.

He told the committee,

> Joseph North I knew in general party activity. He is listed here as lecturer at the Faculty of Social Science. He taught classes at Jefferson School. He was editor of the Sunday Worker, editor of the New Masses, member of the Communist Party. Harry Wells—I have only a vague recollection of him. William Patterson I knew very well in Chicago as a leading member of the Chicago district of the Chicago party. He was at one time assistant editor of the Daily Record in Chicago, a Communist newspaper, and later district bureau member in Chicago. He is listed here as a member of the Faculty of Social Science. Arnold Johnson I have known as an active leader of the Communist Party. I see that he is listed as an instructor

at Jefferson School. I don't remember him there. He is
listed as a lecturer at the Faculty of Social Science. He has
been in top leadership in the party for many years. Victor
Perlo I don't know, only what I read in the newspapers.[36]

He named thirteen Communists in this testimonial itera-
tion.[37] One, returning from behind the Iron Curtain after
earlier deportation in part because of Meyer, played dumb.[38]
"To my best recollection this is the first time I see this man,"
Irving Potash, who had seen him during the Smith Act
Trial, claimed.[39]

The testimony dropped no bombshells. Many of the men
he identified already boasted Smith Act convictions thanks
in part to him. Although none admitted membership in the
secret society calling itself a "party," none really needed to for
the committee to know the truth.

◆ ◆ ◆

MEYER'S testimony helped imprison and deport people and
discredit and shutter institutions. He also helped exonerate
others and declined to name people he did not know to be
Communists who were, in fact, Communists.

At Ithiel de Sola Pool's request, his University of Chicago acquaintance provided a statement absolving the social
scientist of charges of Communist sympathies from the Industrial Review Board.[40] Pool won his case.[41] He provided a
similar affidavit for the sociologist Herb Goldhamer.[42] Asked
for information on Eugene Carson Blake, he informed his
correspondents that he knew nothing and found nothing indicating Communist affiliations for the National Council of
Churches president.[43] Ira H. Latimer, a Chicago civil rights
activist who drifted out of the Communist orbit, turned to
Frank for information on two area Communists vindictively
encouraging the Illinois bar to deny admittance to him.[44] The

names do not register for the correspondent, and the bar denied Latimer admittance.[45]

He named Communists. He did not name people personally foreign but reputationally displeasing. His former comrades depicted all witnesses in such a light. Adams, who named no names in the released sections of her testimony, fit the deranged witness caricature. But her lying mainly occurred within the party orbit and found believers within the party.

The witness stopped appearing because the congressional committees more or less caught up to his thinking. Meyer regarded the march of Communists abroad as the focus and their tiny domestic sect as more of a distraction. The external threat became his preoccupation.

◄ 18 ►

Movement

L ife became lonelier when Gene ended his. Residing in left-wing Woodstock as one who periodically resided in the headlines for testifying against Communists compounded the isolation.

"We have in the entire community two friends, and perhaps two or three other people who summon up their courage and come up and see us once a year or so," Frank confessed. "Purely from external evidence, I estimate a powerful actual Party unit, and the entire atmosphere of the artist and intellectual community—as distinguished from the 'natives,' who are staunch Republicans, generally of the Taft breed, though now somewhat eroded by Eisenhower prosperity and schmaltz—is set by it."[1]

They once counted Philip Guston, long before owners of his paintings counted millions upon sale, as a friend.

"He was one of the people we saw a good deal of until the 1952 election," Meyer told a mutual acquaintance. "He got so upset with the threat of fascism hanging over America from a Republican victory that he abruptly ceased coming to see us. As far as I can make out he held me personally responsible for the defeat of Stevenson. My own feeling toward him is of the warmest, and every time I see him in the village, I tell him to stop being a bloody fool."[2]

Danny Revzan, another local artist, refused to shun the Meyers.[3] Robert Phelps, his speaking partner in the summer of 1947, regarded Frank as his kindest friend. Meyer referred to Phelps as "pathologically kind."[4]

"A wasted weekend," Phelps journaled in 1954. "Saturday night to Frank Meyer's until 3: good talk about my 'moral values,' and Gil, which Elsie challenged. My defense—beginning with a bias for passionate people—was accepted. I even offered a censored version of G's place in my last 3 years. Both F. + Elsie listened without prejudice."[5]

They discussed Phelps's stepping out on his marriage with a male lover.[6] Frank issued harsh judgment on ideas. He dealt with people, a more fragile species, more delicately.

Phelps began contributing reviews in late 1950 to a new magazine. *The Freeman* paid homage to defunct magazines of that same name associated with Albert Jay Nock but rose out of the ashes of anti-Communist *Plain Talk*. Its outlook meshed well with that of Phelps's friend. So Frank followed Phelps.[7] The work Phelps pushed his way in Frank's lean, early-1950s paid as little as $10 for a book critique and as much as $40 for an article but rose to $100 for a lead review within a few years.[8] Though he primarily submitted reviews, Meyer's *Freeman* writings betrayed a proclivity more libertarian than literary.

He suffered because of the magazine's chronic money problems. He contributed to its ideological schisms. The junior freelancer who operated on the margins of a magazine featuring Old Right intellectuals nevertheless inserted himself into controversies.

Meyer wrote John Chamberlain seconding readers who wished the publication had endorsed Robert Taft for the Republican nomination and to discourage kid-gloves treatment of Dwight Eisenhower. He mistakenly believed the election of Adlai Stevenson a *fait accompli* but affirmed November support for Eisenhower despite misgivings.[9]

Four years earlier, Meyer had cast a ballot for the Democrat Harry Truman. Now he held his nose to vote for a Republican too liberal for his liking. He went far fast. He wanted policy change to occur as quickly and profoundly. He exhibited a revolutionary temperament conflicting with conservatism.

"The aim of conservatives between now and 1956 must be to build a consciousness of the issues sufficiently strong to nominate a candidate on the Republican ticket and elect him," he wrote Chamberlain after Taft's loss. "Milk and water attitudes toward Eisenhower at this point can only cloud that aim. After all, he thinks that the revolution of the last twenty years is established, is outside of politics, and must be accepted by every moral American."[10]

The editors, in agreement with Meyer, felt pressure from the magazine's board over their criticism of the general and support for Wisconsin's junior senator. While they succumbed to the moneymen by not endorsing Taft, they rebelled by not endorsing Eisenhower during the general election. The disputes grew so turbulent that the magazine's founding editor, Henry Hazlitt, who had inserted Forrest Davis in an editorial triumvirate believing him a sort of proxy, resigned in October when Davis joined Chamberlain and Suzanne La Follette (she had preferred Douglas MacArthur for the nomination) in taking a hard-right stance. Hazlitt wished not to associate with the "kind of magazine in which [Joe] McCarthy is a sacred character." He reemerged after the triumph of his favored presidential candidate, with the pro-Ike board's backing, in January.[11]

"You probably know by this time that the three editors of the FREEMAN—John Chamberlain, Forrest Davis and Suzanne La Follette—have resigned from the magazine. (And, confidentially, I'm not going to stay any longer than I have to)," office manager Gertrude Vogt wrote him.[12] Meyer left with his patrons. He contributed to February's issue, likely a holdover the old regime had commissioned, but published nothing else during Hazlitt's tenure.[13] Once Hazlitt left, Meyer returned to write his career's most consequential article. That meant thinking deeply about his new political credo.

♦ ♦ ♦

A PATTERN emerged. Meyer had stepped onto the speaking circuit with Eugene O'Neill Jr. He followed Robert Phelps in writing for *The Freeman*. This double-act template characterized his next intellectual venture with Nathaniel Weyl on a stage facing a much larger audience than the classic "little magazine." Whereas *The Freeman* reached twenty thousand or so readers, *The American Mercury*, founded three decades earlier by the journalism giants H. L. Mencken and George Jean Nathan, pulled quadruple the sets of eyes.[14]

They appeared in the November 1952 book section. Weyl wrote on two titles addressing the specific threat of Communist espionage.[15] His friend debuted by delivering a memorable review expounding on the general threat to a West confused about its identity. The Reform Jew turned churchless Christian asserted of Herbert Agar's book *A Declaration of Faith*, "The West is certainly in its foundations Christian." He described Agar as well intentioned but ultimately helpless to defend an ancient civilization under attack from his own principles.[16]

Meyer subsequently received a letter from Martin Greenberg not on *Mercury* letterhead as in the past but in pencil scribbled on onionskin paper. The associate editor had just resigned under "rather unpleasant circumstances." He characterized the new publisher as "an unspeakable type" who indicated "pretty sinister intentions."[17] In *Time*'s story on the dustup, *American Mercury* editor William Bradford Huie outlined his view of money as "impersonal" and expressed a willingness to accept funding from Hitler or Stalin in rationalizing the magazine's reliance on Russell Maguire.[18]

"Candidly, I am very astonished that you are doing anything for the Mercury," Weyl wrote Meyer in February. "I gleaned from the TIME story of the reorganization that it was now in the hands of scalawags and pseudo-fascists and some of the N. Y. agents have automatically ceased sending material there."[19]

Weyl, writing gently as a friend but also as a fellow ex-Communist witness, felt that they needed to exercise extra caution because of the zeal to discredit them. He understood the desire to write for pay and without a censor lurking. He nevertheless urged: steer clear.

"Personally I have not dealt with Magui[r]e, but I have done a little investigation of him, and he is no more a fascist than a lot of polite liberals were Communists when they gave money to some 'cause,'" Meyer responded. "He has been taken in once or twice to the extent of giving money to some rather unsavoury elements, but that seems to be all."[20]

Huie, unable to countenance the real Maguire the way he imagined he could hypothetical Hitlers and Stalins, soon followed Greenberg. Meyer stayed.

After it paid him $40 for the book review, the *Mercury* paid him a greater compliment in hiring him as its book review editor.[21] He assumed the role that H. L. Mencken, perhaps America's most celebrated journalist, had held a quarter century earlier. That was its past. Its present involved the perception that an anti-Semitic screwball peered over the shoulders of editors. Putting a Jew on the masthead benefited the magazine more than the Jew. Nevertheless, Meyer counted himself as "very pleased indeed."[22]

The role during his tenure entailed writing all book reviews. In his initial "Books in Review" section he explored, in brief or full, eleven titles.[23] He discussed eighteen books in the next issue.[24] The many reviews occasionally read seamlessly as one article; other times the transitions seemed forced and the reviews felt superficial.

The books editor served as an early booster of James Baldwin's *Go Tell It on the Mountain*. The magazine helped propel Baldwin's debut by excerpting the book the year prior to publication.[25] Meyer proclaimed it "a lyrical statement of true dignity about the lives of ordinary and simple people and about some of the most complex problems of human character and relationships."[26] He praised offerings by his future rival James Burnham (*Containment or Liberation?*), his future friend Richard Weaver (*The Ethics of Rhetoric*), and the future Nobelist Czesław Miłosz (*The Captive Mind*).[27]

"The book has immense power. Every page reflects the agony of Mr. Wright's effort to come to terms with the meaning of life," he wrote of *The Outsider*, by his former comrade and acquaintance Richard Wright.[28] He judged his former friend James Michener to be a mediocre talent in the May issue and then in the October number called his characters "wooden" and plot "pat and uninspired" in the "altogether too slick" *Bridges at Toko-Ri*.[29]

The experience laid the foundation for the rest of Meyer's life in establishing his *bona fides* as a book critic and in pushing him down the path of ideologist of the American right, a peculiar post for one who had recently imparted Communist dogma. Or perhaps that history made playing this part inevitable. He changed his outlook. He maintained his role. In an embryonic sense, the unlikely *fidei defensor* showed up in the review of *Shame and Glory of the Intellectuals*, a book written by the media-anointed "New Conservative" Peter Viereck, whose ideas Meyer found "neither new, nor conservative, nor very profound."[30]

Seeing Russell Kirk under this same "New Conservative" banner, Meyer offered a respectful if mixed review of *The Conservative Mind*, one of the seminal texts of the postwar conservative movement. The reviewer judged the book "valuable" but "aggravating." The annoyance came in the exclusion of the likes of Thomas Jefferson and Herbert Spencer from the tradition Kirk outlined. Meyer desired a good system of thought to combat the bad system of thought he had rejected less than a decade earlier. Kirk rejected ideological systems as inherently contrary to conservatism. "The book is rich and rewarding in the depth of its perceptions and in the warm sympathy with which Mr. Kirk explores the insights of the 18th- and 19th-century thinkers who express his concept of conservatism," Meyer conceded. "It is perhaps because of his implicit repudiation of the American fusion of individualism and conservatism that he is more disappointing when he deals directly with contemporary men and situations."[31]

There, in the summer of 1953 in the back of a thick, five-by-seven-inch, past-its-prime magazine, Meyer again wrote that word, probably without placing much significance on it, that came to define him and describe the movement that he would so shape. He now sought a "fusion" between the American tradition and liberty. This presented an alternative to Kirk's concept of conservatism, which seemed not an "ism" at all—more like a mindset than ideas directly applicable to policy. Fleshed out neither on paper nor in its proponent's mind, fusionism slowly morphed from Browderism to an alternative to the popular conception of conservatism to, ultimately, conservatism itself. This started with the Browder letter. It continued in this book review. It culminated in a book. Before that could happen, Meyer needed to break with one publication and reunite with another.

Far from pushing unseemly authors on Meyer, the *Mercury*'s editors encouraged reviews of "the type of book which lends itself to advertising and more popular appeal."[32] The reviews, in their brevity and in the popularity of the titles critiqued, veered toward a broad audience but not, evidently, far enough. The magazine killed Meyer's section after Labor Day 1953.[33] One reader objected by canceling her subscription. "Alas," Rose Wilder Lane wrote, "they won't miss my subscription as much as I'll miss your reviews!"[34]

✦ ✦ ✦

MEYER found on the right what he never quite had on the left: a mentor.

Rose Wilder Lane, more than two decades his senior, laid claim to advanced ground in the relationship in writing, reputation, and philosophy. The daughter of Laura Ingalls Wilder of *Little House on the Prairie* fame stoked his ego as she challenged his ideas. Bombarded by a one-woman intellectual battalion, Meyer defended or surrendered notions on this battlefield.

Lane forced her understudy to answer a question: What do you believe?

Lane encountered a mind to cultivate. She did that through long, dense letters. Pressing her case for unfettered immigration against her correspondent's restrictionist position, for instance, Lane wrote a postscript extending more than two pages.[35] The upstate homebodies returned the interest by, in a role reversal, visiting their pen pal's Connecticut home. Frank responded to some letters by phone.[36] He also wrote her back, but a working writer could not match Lane. An out-of-work writer couldn't, either.

The New Conservatives aroused his libertarian side. The individualist Rose Wilder Lane provoked his conservatism.

"A person who acts to defend individual persons, their innate, inalienable liberty, cannot 'conserve' the status quo; he must change it, he must abolish much of it," she insisted. "He is an abolitionist, a radical, a revolutionist. That is what he IS, and he can't change the fact by <u>saying</u> he isn't."[37]

Meyer rejected the right as revolutionary and embraced, if half-heartedly, the label attached to his outlook. "Incidentally, about the word 'conservative,' it has its difficulties, but what other label is there these days which specifically repudiates what one wants to repudiate?" he asked. "I tried for years to call myself a liberal, but it was impossible. 'Individualist' or 'libertarian' are useful, but they don't have a wide enough political connotation."[38]

She believed in revolution rather than evolution, dismissed continuity from Europe to America, and regarded the political thought that arose after the American Revolution as idiotic.[39] "Precisely what IS this 'Western tradition' for which you have 'the conservative feeling'?" she wrote.[40]

The younger man responded, "The West was the first civilization to break through that worship of Necessity and to give a charter to the individual. Freedom is not for Western man 'freedom to do right,' but freedom to choose right or wrong—the only kind of freedom that has meaning in individual terms. That, from another point of view, is original sin, a fearful burden and a gift of freedom."[41]

The philosophy so associated with Meyer developed further here. He brought together, melded, blended, joined— what's the right word?—tradition with freedom.

Whereas Lane regarded Europe as cultivating collectivism, she saw America as breeding individualism. Work and eat; sleep and die. Rather than a baton passed between the continents, individualism, she reckoned, constituted something uniquely fostered in America. Surrounding oceans, a new start, and a frontier compelled settlers to labor for themselves rather than for the group. People came to escape nationalism, monarchy, state religion, caste systems, and much else. Even if they did not want freedom, geography forced it. Lane, one of libertarianism's three founding mothers along with Ayn Rand and Isabel Paterson, exuded a red-white-and-blue libertarianism rooted in a specific time and place, the American Founding. She did not, as did others in her ideological tribe, pluck ideas from the ether.

Lane influenced Meyer profoundly. It does not detract from her sway that one of the effects involved sharpening arguments on subjects on which they disagreed.

"You see, while I still stand, and I think I will continue to stand, straddled between the conservative feeling for Western tradition and the individualist assertion of freedom and hatred of centralized power, in my letters to you I have been defending the conservative pole of my position," he wrote. "How strongly I affirm the individualist aspect I had not realized until I had to put some ideas on paper on a number of questions recently. Of course, it is also possible that your letters have had something to do with this."[42]

◆ ◆ ◆

MEYER began reviewing books for a smaller audience. In early 1954, the William Volker Fund agreed to pay him $1,000, and, more significantly, subscribe him to scores of scholarly journals, to act as a scout of sorts for the philanthropy. His guardian angel in Connecticut recommended him.[43] One of the talents Volker identified in Meyer's reviewing scholarship was Meyer.[44]

He parlayed this relationship into stronger connections and more money. He had petitioned Volker to award him a grant for a history of the United States from a libertarian perspective that he had begun as the 1940s transitioned to the 1950s coeval with the anti-Communist Democrat Meyer's transformation into a right-wing Republican.[45] Harold Luhnow, the nephew of the charity's late namesake, informed him in July 1954 of $9,500 awarded toward the project.[46]

The money validated Frank. His ego needed it less than his bank account.

Like the beneficiary, the benefactor had experienced a political epiphany upon reading Friedrich Hayek's *Road to Serfdom*. Thus, Luhnow transformed a charity primarily aimed at uplifting Kansas City to one promoting liberty everywhere. Volker almost single-handedly jumpstarted postwar libertarianism. It helped pay the salaries of Hayek at the University of Chicago and Ludwig von Mises at New York University, both of whom, significantly, taught outside of economics departments. It helped launch the Mont Pelerin Society, the Foundation for Economic Education, and the Intercollegiate Society of Individualists. It subsidized a translation of Frédéric Bastiat's *The Law*. It paid for the lectures later bound in Milton Friedman's *Capitalism and Freedom*. Henry Grady Weaver's *Mainspring of Human Progress*, Murray Rothbard's *Man, Economy, and State*, and Richard Weaver's *Visions of Order* all received support from Volker.[47] The fund soon took intense notice of another of Meyer's projects that eventually joined the auspicious list.

◆ ◆ ◆

"THE FREEMAN STORY in a nutshell is that the Eisenhower-Dupont boys forced out Chamberlain, Davis and Suzanne La Follette (the Taft sector), and brought in that old fuddy-dud, Henry Hazlitt, who wants to be polite about communism and socialism," Meyer explained to Weyl.[48]

Hazlitt's tenure as editor of *The Freeman*, during which Hayek and von Mises occasionally appeared, nevertheless alienated readers by otherwise becoming more Republican and championing an establishment anti-Communism irritating to anyone with Old Right sensibilities if imperceptible to everyone else. Meyer disappeared. Burnham, William F. Buckley Jr., and Willi Schlamm crucially appeared.

Then, a year later, Hazlitt resigned. The lack of continuity hurt. One *Freeman* successor, Frank Chodorov, a bridge between Old Right and the nascent conservative movement, recruited an enthusiastic Meyer to write a hit piece on the ideas of Kirk and the New Conservatives.

The Franks stewed, explicitly over Kirk's conception of conservatism that banished libertarians to the ideologue camp along with Marxists, bimetallists, and other cranks, and implicitly over his sudden renown. In 1955, the name Russell Kirk came to mind when learned people thought about conservative intellectuals. Chodorov, Garet Garrett, John T. Flynn, and other disparate and largely forgotten characters had labored against the state engorgement upon society embodied by both the New Deal and the drive to enter the Second World War. So thorough was progressivism's triumph that Kirk initially titled his study "The Conservative Rout."[49] *The Conservative Mind* stunned reviewers, many of whom saw an oxymoron on the cover before encountering a presentation of Anglo-American intellectual history that was not just rational but beautiful. After decades of progressive policies, the public appeared at last to be at least curious about alternatives.

But what was this outlook the left presented in caricature and the right struggled to define? *The Conservative Mind* arrived, and with it more questions. The routed conservatives did not see their champion when they came upon Kirk.

"Incidentally, Brother Kirk, although only an Anglo-Catholic, seems to have arrogated to himself the excommunicatory power of the Papal See," Meyer wrote Chodorov. "Where does he get the authority to say that a Christian cannot be an individualist? What did Buckley think of that one?"[50]

Buckley, though on the rise from his early books *God and Man at Yale* and *McCarthy and His Enemies*, did not then possess Kirk's stature. That twentysomething force of nature made pit stops at the publications where Meyer drew a dime. These two sons of privilege discussed the pending Kirk piece in person and by mail.[51]

In "Collectivism Rebaptized," the conservative catechumen who had previously complained about Kirk's excommunications brashly excommunicated conservatism's leading intellectual. Coming from Communism, the impulse to purge felt natural. Coming from Communism, Meyer understood systems but not the tone and attitude that Kirk valued. He did not grasp why Kirk preferred experience over reason and as such regarded systematizers as necessarily outside of conservatism. Meyer, looking for a system to defend against the left's system, found frustration in Kirk. He confessed his difficulty in pinning down one who left no coherent blueprint. The *Freeman* article lamented that Kirk offered no guiding principle on economics, ethics, and politics. Whereas Kirk emphasized order, duty, and authority, the word "freedom," Meyer complained, made but cameo appearances. "The New Conservatism, stripped of its pretensions, is, sad to say, but another guise for the collectivist spirit of the age," he added.[52]

The article made friends and enemies.

Robert J. Needles, a doctor from Florida, labeled the article "a sickening attack" that grossly distorted Kirk's position and introduced schisms to a besieged movement requiring unity. In seizing on Kirk's "lack of a positive program," Meyer, according to Needles, "falls into the primary and tragic error of all who would direct other men's lives."[53]

Kirk called it "the Freeman folly."[54] He spoke of reports from his "secret agents." Needles, he estimated, "has shaken [Foundation for Economic Education founder Leonard] Re[a]d."[55] General Motors bigwigs might cancel *Freeman* subscriptions. The Federation of Republican Women had deluged *Human Events* with objections to its positive notice of Meyer's article.[56] He revealed that one of his moles had informed him that Chodorov had enlisted Meyer to write a book bashing Kirk as a collectivist authoritarian on the Volker Fund's subsidy.[57]

"I don't doubt that Chodorov is opposed to you and that he doesn't like your point of view," Henry Regnery told him, "but I rather doubt that the Volker Fund would subsidize anyone to write an attack on you."[58]

Kirk's intelligence gathering, at least on this narrow point, looked not paranoid but precise. His informers fed his mania. Yet he sensed, he *knew*, that some on the right regarded him as wrong.

"Never was a skin taken more deftly, gently and precisely off," Rose Wilder Lane congratulated Meyer. "Golly, how I WISH I could watch Kirk reading that article."[59]

Meyer found a bigger fan in Harold Luhnow.

"The Directors of the Volker Fund have approved your request for a postponement of the one-year renewal of the grant for the book on American history," he explained concurrent with publication. "We have acted favorably on your request for a grant of $4,750 for the preparation of a book on the New Conservatism during the next six months."[60]

Those six months took more than six years.

◆ ◆ ◆

THE YEAR 1955 uprooted the life Meyer had planted post-Communism. Then 1955 rooted it for the remainder. As 1945 served as an alarm-bell epiphany to evacuate from the Communist Party, 1955 established him on the right.

Thwarted in its effort to nominate Taft, pilloried in the wake of Joseph McCarthy's 1954 censure, and consistently routed in policymaking, conservatives began to make headway. They saw no intellectual organ around which to coalesce. The sad experience of *The American Mercury* fostered a desire for a publication free from crackpots, and the sad experience of *The Freeman* fostered a desire for a publication free from schismatics and meddling moneymen.

"There may be a new magazine," Meyer explained to Weyl, "but nothing definite yet."[61]

Something definite appeared in Willi Schlamm's mind's eye. Whittaker Chambers, Schlamm's old colleague at the Luce magazine empire, described him as suffering from "the worst case of magazinitis."[62] He no longer wished to work at a magazine. He wanted to run one.

Buckley, an *enfant terrible* who was constitutionally unsuited to a subordinate role, came to a similar conclusion in departing *The American Mercury* after clashing with Greenberg. He explored the purchase of *Human Events* and *The Freeman* to no avail. He spoke to the publisher Henry Regnery about launching a journal. Scholarly versus opinion,

Chicago-based versus New York–based, and a monthly versus weekly, the publications imagined differed to too great a degree (Regnery launched the highbrow *Modern Age* with Russell Kirk in 1957).[63]

The Austrian émigré Willi Schlamm also discussed magazines with Regnery. He encouraged the publisher to buy *The Freeman* and discouraged him from obtaining *Human Events*. Schlamm wrote Regnery in May 1953:

> Now to that magazine. I had a fine visit with the Buckleys last week and Bill told me about his project of expanding "Human Events." I encouraged him, as did John Chamberlain. And, who knows, this is perhaps indeed all we do at the moment. But the expanded "Human Events" will solve neither our problems nor yours. You need a much more literary, much more philosophical, much more fundamental, much more radical, much more formative journal than "Human Events" can ever be. Yours must sing and dance and enthuse; it must have the scope (and the size) to create a climate of its own—the only liveable climate for the forlorn "outs."[64]

Schlamm described with great precision a journal that existed. It just did not yet exist.

◀ 19 ▶

NR

N*ational Review* "stands athwart history, yelling Stop," William F. Buckley Jr. declared in the inaugural November 19, 1955, number.[1] If the issue ended there, then readers might have regarded theirs as two dimes well spent.

It continued by audaciously defining conservatism rather than allowing its enemies to depict it as a scary straw man or a watered-down version of liberalism or a hapless, convenient, "kick me" sign–wearing foil. Conservatives believed in restrained over unlimited government, truth over relativism, victory over coexistence with the "satanic utopianism" of Communism, established excellence over fads, an adversarial two-party system over, in the parlance of the times, MeToo-Republican cooperation, free enterprise over a managed economy, and subsidiarity over remote government.[2]

"National Review is out of place, in the sense that the United Nations and the League of Women Voters and the *New York Times* and Henry Steele Commager are in place," Buckley's opening salvo explained. "It is out of place because, in its maturity, literate America rejected conservatism in favor of radical social experimentation."[3]

Liberal publications almost uniformly denied that *National Review* amounted to a conservative enterprise. They attempted to strangle it in the cradle. The second event appeared as a tacit contradiction of the first observation.

Murray Kempton described the new magazine in *The Progressive* as "for those idealists outside of the frontier of reality."[4] John Fischer in *Harper's* bizarrely characterized it as a purveyor of conspiracy theories and predicted for it "a certain interest for students of political splinter movements."[5] Harvey Breit in *The New York Times* contrasted Russell Kirk, "a thoughtful man with scruples," with William F. Buckley Jr., whose new magazine, likened therein to a right-wing version of *The Nation*, he doubted carried "the kind of intellectual leadership Mr. Kirk has in mind since Mr. Kirk calls for a discussion of 'the great questions,' such as 'What is Man?'"[6] Dwight Macdonald, who expanded a *pfft* and an eyeroll into six-and-a-half magazine pages, even attacked the new publication's letter-writers as "inarticulate, culturally underprivileged folk" (citing "Frank S. Meyer of Woodstock, N.Y." as an exception).[7]

The identikit, condescending criticism inadvertently demonstrated the need for the criticized. Even with a murderer's row of intellectuals and journalists on its roster—many of whom were widely praised just years earlier when advocating the politics of Kempton, Fischer, Breit, and Macdonald—the conservative journal of opinion won scorn. It all seemed to affirm not just the existence of the magazine but the concept articulated by Schlamm of the "outs" requiring a spot on the newsstand. The outs began their effort to become ins.

✦ ✦ ✦

MACDONALD nowhere indicated that fifteen or so years earlier the *National Review* editor James Burnham had counted him as a follower. Leon Trotsky, in lashing out at *his* follower Burnham for dumping *him*, contrasted the "intellectual snob" with Macdonald. "Dwight Macdonald is not a snob, but a bit stupid," he judged.[8] The "[e]ducated witch-doctor" Burnham, shortly after an ice ax went through Trotsky's skull, delivered not so much profundity but prophecy in 1941's *Managerial Revolution*.[9] George Orwell took Burnham and his book seriously enough to write "Second Thoughts on James Burnham" and to use his ideas as a springboard for parts of *Nineteen Eighty-Four*.[10] Yet, in embracing a full-throated anti-Communism in the intervening years, Burnham had evolved into, to borrow from Orwell's Newspeak, an unperson.

Burnham's fellow senior editor Willmoore Kendall learned to read at age two, matriculated at Northwestern at thirteen, wrote his first book at eighteen, and shortly thereafter studied as a Rhodes Scholar. In calling Kendall "a wild Yale don of extreme, eccentric, and very abstract views who can get a discussion into the shouting stage faster than anybody I have ever known," Macdonald issued at least an accurate observation in the concluding clause.[11] In temperament though not viewpoint, a reversal of some other *NR* editors, Kendall fell into the fringe category. Fixating on this reduced a complex man hailing from Oklahoma but equally at home at Oxford to a caricature of his excesses.

Macdonald's contention that Suzanne La Follette's "boiling point is even lower than Kendall's" seemed an exaggeration.[12] "When I did deal with her in person, she wasn't someone you were going to slap on the back and tell the latest joke," *NR* stringer Charlie Wiley conceded. "I mean, she was a serious lady when you did get to talk to her."[13] The daughter of a Washington congressman and cousin of the 1924 Progressive Party presidential nominee who received 17 percent of the general election vote, La Follette had marinated in politics from birth. She assisted Albert Jay Nock, a friend of Buckley's oil magnate father, in iterations of *The Freeman*. The only nineteenth-century creature in this 1955 production,

La Follette combined libertarianism with feminism to bring a perspective unrepresented by the other main players.

John Chamberlain graduated from Yale before the younger Yalies Buckley and Bozell had entered the world. His resume included stops as an editor for *The New York Times*, *Life*, and *The Wall Street Journal*. He wrote the foreword to Friedrich Hayek's American version of *The Road to Serfdom* and the introduction to Buckley's *God and Man at Yale*.

His friend Willi Schlamm, so advanced in his Marxism at age sixteen that he had met Vladimir Lenin at the Kremlin, pined to run a magazine the way five-year-olds wish for an anthropomorphic bear under the Christmas tree. "Willi was not a 'theoretician'; he was a leader of the Austrian party in the 20's," Meyer later explained. "He was expelled in the anti-Bukharanite phase, and then founded <u>Weltbuhne</u>, which was the first anti-Communist and anti-Fascist European journal, something like <u>Partisan Review</u> here."[14] He worked for Henry Luce's empire in America, where he gained citizenship in 1944, but suffered a great defeat when the magazine magnate aborted a publication helmed by Schlamm before the first issue.[15] He wanted *National Review* more than anyone wanted *National Review*.

As an undergraduate, the Nebraskan L. Brent Bozell served as the president of the campus World Federalist Movement and the Yale Political Union. But his friendship with Buckley, whose sister Patricia he married, shoved him in a conservative direction. The Catholic convert worked for Senator McCarthy, and then, along with his brother-in-law, wrote *McCarthy and His Enemies*.

William F. Buckley Jr., the sixth of ten children, spoke Spanish before he spoke French before he spoke English. Upon releasing *God and Man at Yale* in 1951, he became that rare conservative boogeyman: the personality liberals feared rather than the one they created to instill a fear of the opposition. He bounced around *The American Mercury* and *The Freeman* long enough to embrace Schlamm's counsel that he should run a magazine rather than work for one. "Bill was the conductor of an orchestra," Neal Freeman, a longtime player in the band, recalled. "One of his many great talents was he could figure out how to work with and get the best out of almost anybody. What he quickly figured out was the three amigos— the guys who put together modern conservatism: Willmoore, Frank, and Brent—were three of the most unclubbable men of the twentieth century, really difficult personalities in different ways. But somehow Bill could figure out how to work with them, how to get good product out of them."[16]

Kendall, Buckley, and Burnham had all worked for the CIA. Chamberlain and La Follette had served, impartially, on the Dewey Commission that investigated the Moscow show trials. Meyer had encountered Burnham, if from afar, as the Big Man on Campus at Princeton and Kendall had encountered Meyer, though not knowing that he did, as a frenzied radical hectoring H. G. Wells at Oxford. Kendall had taught at Yale when Bozell and Buckley attended. Schlamm and Chamberlain had worked together for Henry Luce. Everyone save Buckley had migrated right.

Mr. Buckley was fortunate in casting this *dramatis personae*. "Mr. Buckley has not been fortunate in his choice of editors," Macdonald nevertheless claimed.[17] The magazine was fortunate here in its enemies, who in attempting to caricature the endeavor instead drew themselves in cartoon.

◆ ◆ ◆

TWO NAMES sat conspicuously low on the masthead.

Meyer's name, one of ten, appeared on the blue-bordered cover ironically next to Russell Kirk's. The masthead listed neither him nor Kirk as an editor. Instead, they fell among the contributors and associates (as did Bozell and others who eventually rose). While keeping the reasons from Meyer, Buckley later divulged the story of "bilateral intellectual disagreement and a unilateral personal bitterness" creating complications in retaining both Meyer and Kirk. Specifically, Kirk, stung by Meyer's criticism of him in Frank Chodorov's *Freeman*, wished not to place his name on a masthead along-side either Frank. Kirk, according to Buckley, asked, "How could I appear cheek by jowl with them[?]"

Buckley, from day one, exhibited this greatest and most overlooked talent: managing unmanageable personalities.

"For years he was able to talk of little else whenever the general subject of Frank Meyer or Frank Chodorov or Individualism or the <u>Freeman</u> came up, and I have in my file letters from Russell in which he shows himself to be virtually possessed on the subject of that article by Frank," Buckley a few years later explained to Father Stanley Parry. "I have talked to Russell time and time and time again attempting to smooth things down, and for a long while it was touch and go whether he would write for <u>National Review</u> because the names of Frank Meyer and Frank Chodorov (who was editor of the <u>Freeman</u> when it happened) were on the masthead."[18]

Kirk did agree to write a column, "From the Academy." Apart from Buckley's desire to seduce Kirk, Meyer's status not marking him as one of the stars of the operation likely dictated his role. For instance, the prospectus touting the proposed "National Weekly" that eventually launched as *NR* omitted Meyer in the forty writers listed to appear in the publication.[19] The fact that the rival thinkers worked from home, and *National Review* required a degree of administrative work from all senior editors, likely influenced their modest titles. Kirk, undoubtedly with choice of spots short of editor, balked at a prominent position. His work with Henry Regnery to develop a competing publication, called *The Conservative Review* in the talking stages but eventually becoming *Modern Age*, probably influenced his decision.[20] His critic's involvement definitely did. Possibly compounding matters, Volker reached out to Meyer to provide an opinion on whether the foundation should fund Kirk. Rose Wilder Lane characterized Meyer as "much more tolerant of [Kirk] than I am," and Meyer acknowledged being "a little kinder to Mr. Kirk than I should have been."[21] Possibly a Kirk enthusiast would assess Meyer's treatment less charitably than Meyer did.

Meyer initially wrote "The Scholarly Journals" column. His work for Volker reviewing such publications made him the right man for the job. He took the wrong approach.

"The column you are writing, and I refer particularly to the last one, is just not for a weekly magazine, never was, never could be," Buckley bluntly informed him three months into the project. He likened it to "an essay on whatever single point or points it strikes your fancy to comment on."[22]

It read as more Meyer than the scholarly journals. Whether Buckley's vision of the reverse might have attracted more eyes seems debatable. In a mass-market magazine, writers perhaps cared about "the scholarly journals." Readers did not.

The last column by that name ran in February. Meyer soon debuted "Principles and Heresies." This proved a better fit. Embracing the commissar role from his Communist days, he knew about heresies. As a conservative assigning himself the same role in writing the *Freeman* Kirk article, he understood principles, too.

The first "Principles and Heresies" column, a two-pager, appeared in the April 4, 1956 issue. More thoughtful than conservative, the piece read, "Our ills cannot be cured on any surface level. It is at the source of evil that evil must be fought; and that means that in the fight for truth and responsibility, the decisive front is the field of ideas."[23]

The author, through "Principles and Heresies," lived those last eight words. His readers did too. They returned for that reason.

The decisive front is the field of ideas.

The words acknowledged an internal shift. In the Communist Party, Meyer, though he taught and wrote, primarily contributed as an organizer. He now devoted himself, as he had in his last years in the party, to ideas. For one so committed, no better place existed in the mid-1950s than *National Review*.

◀ 20 ▶

Discord

A month before the inaugural issue, *National Review*'s book review editor Willmoore Kendall pitched Frank Meyer about contributing. He wanted five hundred words on books suggested by the reviewers themselves. The book section paid nine cents a word.[1]

Meyer submitted to the memorable first issue a forgettable review on Robert Caponigri's *History and Liberty: The Historical Writings of Benedetto Croce*, a book noticed by *National Review* almost certainly because of its publisher, Henry Regnery. On Frank's coattails, his friend Robert Phelps more memorably reviewed the Soviet writer Ilya Ehrenburg's book *The Thaw*.[2] Here Meyer foreshadowed his value to the book section: identifying talent that he plucked from obscurity.

The laissez-faire approach that Kendall rebuffed in economics he embraced in editing. This inspired writers as it inspired something other than confidence in fellow editors. They expressed this distrust by slashing his space.

"I don't know how much you have been in on the events of the past few days. (a) My Book Review Section has been cut from 4–5 pp. to 3 minus anything that happens to turn up in the way of an ad and (b) I have been instructed to make a further cut in the stipend for reviewers," he wrote Meyer in early spring 1956.[3]

Criticisms of Kendall's section centered on the lag between the publication date of books and when their reviews ran. The professor, regarding books as an inherently slow medium, argued against the criticism but ultimately pledged to operate in fidelity to its underlying idea of timeliness.[4] The problems inherent in tasking a tenured, teaching Ivy League professor conducting scholarship with editing several pages of a weekly atop periodically submitting his own column, "The Liberal Line," overwhelmed Kendall as his resulting problems overwhelmed his colleagues.

"I interpret the expressions and silences of my fellow-editors in yesterday's discussion of the book review section as a vote of non-confidence, leaving me no alternative but to resign responsibility for it, effective immediately," he wrote on July 13, 1956. "This decision has been taken after full consultation with the two I suppose impartial observers present, namely, Brent and Frank."[5]

If Kendall had hoped that his colleagues would beg him back, then the response disappointed. He continued writing his column as he forfeited his fiefdom.

◆ ◆ ◆

WILLI SCHLAMM, a more hands-on editor than Kendall, assumed command.

Schlamm's tenure in the position was also short-lived. In the front of the book, where Schlamm provided editorial copy, he clashed with James Burnham. In a public way, this manifested in their "Should Conservatives Vote for Eisenhower-Nixon?" debate. Schlamm spoke for Meyer and others on *National Review*'s right wing. Meyer had soured on Ike before the end of year one, finding "little to distinguish the Eisenhower administration from its predecessors in the fight against creeping collectivism" and "not much more evidence of improvement in its policies for the defense of the nation against Communist world domination."[6] By 1956, he more than took Schlamm's side.

Burnham labeled conservatives who planned to withhold their vote or award it to a third party as "sectarian." His conception of parties, accurate in real time, conflicted with the vision held by several of his fellow editors. "Our parties are not ideological or class organizations," he contended, "like the parties in most other countries, but loose, shifting coalitions of diverse interest groups that join on a limited basis for the practical purposes of conducting elections and forming a government."[7] Meyer three years earlier had foretold a coming union between traditional Republicans and Southerners in "a new alignment of parties."[8]

Schlamm, who planned to leave the presidential line blank on his ballot in stalwartly Republican Vermont, likened the president to a Democrat in disguise, maintained that conservatives should prefer an Adlai Stevenson presidency because the GOP would then block what it tolerated in Ike, and said that rather than a reason to support reelection Richard Nixon on the ticket amounted to "Mr. Eisenhower's perfectly authentic running-mate."[9]

Behind the scenes, their disagreements, at Schlamm's end at least, evinced rancor. Burnham dealt with conflict not with spiritedness but strategy. It came off as passive-aggressive, which fueled the opposition's spiritedness.

Schlamm's star fell as Burnham's rose. The Austrian's ideological and personal disputes with Burnham—common among his colleagues without the last name Buckley—morphed into conflicts with the boss who increasingly looked at Burnham as his overqualified adjutant. A dispute over a "Third World War" column—Burnham's equivalent of Meyer's "Principles and Heresies"—on the Soviet invasion of Hungary catalyzed Schlamm's demise. He rightly regarded Burnham's rationalization of President Eisenhower's passive response to the invasion as a retreat from the theorist's promulgated position of rollback and liberation. Buckley rightly regarded Schlamm as encroaching upon the purview of an individual columnist. What business did one senior editor have in killing or correcting the column of another? The office situation became so uneasy that Buckley encouraged Schlamm to work, as Meyer worked, from home. Schlamm demanded a meeting of the editors, telling the magazine's cofounder: "*National Review* is as much my creation and my life's central concern as it is yours."[10]

While Schlamm had encouraged the younger man to serve as editor-in-chief, he did not quite imagine him exercising the authority that went along with the title. This misperception fixated on Buckley's age rather than his personality. He would not, but of more relevance could not, defer to Schlamm. Others insisted he should not. And Burnham, despite his status as a thinker who had influenced George Orwell and enraged Leon Trotsky, deferred to Buckley amid this cast of undeferential characters. Furthermore, others argued and philosophized; Burnham edited and put magazine issues to bed. His utility to *NR* and respect for and from Buckley made him an indispensable man.

At a Commodore Hotel throwdown-showdown in Manhattan, Schlamm insisted that Buckley, responsible for raising (and donating) funds for the enterprise and serving as the public face of the magazine, could not fire him. The dramatic scene moved senior editor John Chamberlain, Schlamm's former colleague at *Time*, to tears. It elicited a considerably cooler reaction from Schlamm's enemy. "I've seen a lot in my life that is crazy," Burnham subsequently told Buckley, "but I've never seen anybody say you can't fire me, when you are the undisputed boss of the enterprise."[11]

Schlamm did not see it that way. The magazine was his idea, after all.[12] Buckley did not fire the magazine's tempestuous cofounder. He essentially exiled Schlamm to Vermont and proscribed past provocative behavior as a condition for future employment. Schlamm submitted copy and occasionally ventured, briefly and mostly in silence, into the office.[13] The humiliation festered. It did not chasten.

Meyer wrote Schlamm that he did not object to Buckley's decision. He described their dispute as "a personal matter" quite "distinct from the ideological and tonal differences with Jim Burnham, which you and I and Brent and Suzanne share, each in his individual fashion. There have been times when I became very discouraged about the possibility of carrying on an effective struggle on these intellectual questions; but, as I told you last Wednesday after my long discussion with Brent, I am now convinced that, despite weaknesses in NR that result from the circumstances, it is a viable situation, and one with which I can live."[14]

A series of changes cascading from the Schlamm imbroglio empowered Meyer to confront that weakness. The magazine's rapid evolution catalyzed by Schlamm's diminished role in other ways empowered Burnham. Events conspired early in *National Review*'s history to pit Burnham and Meyer against one another as factional leaders within a faction's magazine.

◆ ◆ ◆

NATIONAL REVIEW desperately needed a proper publisher.

"It's always nice to hear, I'm sure, that one has a wild admirer somewhere out in the woods," L. Brent Bozell explained in the fall of 1956 to his friend in Woodstock. "You may have lots, but none more intense than Bill Rusher, who is Bob Morris' assistant on the Internal Security Committee. Bill, though he is a highly intelligent fellow, spends a good part of his time phoning his friends about Frank Meyer."[15]

Buckley hired William A. Rusher, more in tune with activist politics than anybody at the magazine, as *National Review*'s publisher the following year. It came months after Meyer testified on two separate days before the committee for which he worked. *National Review*'s existing employees showed a talent for spending money. Rusher's job concerned, in large part through subscriptions and the solicitation of advertisers, generating money. The position's crucial role in ensuring the survival of the magazine came with the added perk of a spot in editorial discussions.

So he enjoyed an equal place at the table with Meyer. The Harvard graduate never saw himself as an equal even if few equaled his multifaceted role within the magazine. A charter subscriber, Rusher drew a picture of Meyer in his mind as a chiseled Viking with penetrating steel blue eyes and "iron-gray hair." He encountered, eight months before he joined the magazine, an elfin man far from the heroic figure of his imagination even if he had correctly portrayed the hair. Rusher nevertheless openly called this physically unimpressive colleague "the Master."[16] Meyer here gained an ally as much as an admirer. Rusher's prominence, and intellectual subservience, further elevated Meyer as the master of *National Review*'s right wing.

From Rusher's first day, Meyer's power within the magazine ballooned as a result of a second happy accident. Buckley gave Rusher Schlamm's unused office. For the temperamental Austrian, this became, upon discovery, the indignity that he refused to countenance. He proposed a yearlong sabbatical effective August 12, 1957. Buckley promptly accepted.[17] Though Schlamm, who returned to Europe, occasionally contributed, he never again wielded any power within the magazine.

The blue-bordered publication needed, for the second time in thirteen months, a books editor. Enter the former position holder for *The American Mercury*.

✦ ✦ ✦

MEYER inherited a mess. Schlamm had spoiled dozens of reviews by holding them well past expiration date, which required substantial kill fees. Meyer asked Buckley, "What do you think Willi was up to?"[18]

The new editor aimed high. To do so, the Oxonian aimed east. C. S. Lewis and J. R. R. Tolkien declined his entreaties.[19]

He "succeeded" with Evelyn Waugh and W. H. Auden.

The *Brideshead Revisited* author offered a negative take on an *NR* writer's first book.[20] The Pulitzer Prize–winning poet offered a negative take on *NR*, and his tenure as an *NR* book critic ended quickly. Unfamiliar with the magazine, Auden read the issue that included his piece and noticed an item criticizing a large grant to the nuclear physicist J. Robert Oppenheimer. The ridicule, if one can call it that, seemed tame. He insisted he cared little about the politics of the journals for which he wrote. His letter implicitly said otherwise. Auden wrote from St. Mark's Place, "I can only hope that other contributors to the National Review besides myself will feel their personal honor has been tarnished by being associated with such dirt."[21]

The measure of the editor's greatness did not come in identifying writers already established and applauded. Meyer found talented but unheralded reviewers who, once cleansed of their *National Review* stain, became established and applauded.

"I have recently taken over the editorship of the book-review section of NATIONAL REVIEW, and I am hoping to give it the distinction in critical matters that the only conservative weekly of opinion in the United States should have," he wrote Hugh Kenner. "I have long admired your criticism, and I hope to persuade you to do an occasional review for us."[22]

Kenner's way of speaking passed through the unenviable accent of partial deafness by way of Ontario. The inevitable brilliance of what he said allowed him to punctuate statements with an appropriate, self-congratulatory smile. So he understandably preferred, contra his editor, correspondence to conversation.

When Meyer petitioned him, the thirty-three-year-old University of California–Santa Barbara professor had already boasted books on three unfashionable writers: G. K. Chesterton, Wyndham Lewis, and Ezra Pound. Through Kenner, Meyer landed another writer who, like Kenner, personally knew Pound.

"Meyer lives in a vortex of overwork which he copes with occasionally by running up long distance bills," Kenner told Guy Davenport, then a Haverford College professor, about Meyer's delay in contacting him. "His silences are not meaningful, just distracted."[23]

Kenner and Davenport became mainstays, with the latter for many years writing the "Random Notes" subsection and the former becoming a senior editor. "I learned from Frank how to review," Davenport later reflected. "I'd never done it before."[24] The pair appreciated Meyer for providing them a wide berth but regarded him, alongside conservatives in general, as narrow in indulging prejudices against contemporary artistic offerings.

"It does not surprise me that [Samuel] Beckett brings us smack up against Frank Meyer's limitations," Kenner wrote Davenport regarding the subject of his new biography reviewed by the latter in *NR*. "He is hagridden by *ideas*, and by a notion that everything modern somehow degenerates, unless it's programmatically patriarchal like Eliot.[25]

Their tastes ran toward William Carlos Williams, Marianne Moore, Pound, and Beckett, and away from the crowd's. This meant that *National Review*'s literary criticism was admired by the literate but criticized by mass-market magazine readers. These interests, which the duo shared to the degree that tempts one to regard them singularly, struck their editor as eccentric and his editor as nearly intolerable.

"I gather I'm about to be sacked from NR, as Bill Buckley has taken about all he can stomach of my 'academic' reviews," Davenport confessed to Kenner in 1963. "Pity. I'll try to be lighter and sassier. Frank is all for me (probably because I deliver Random Notes on time every fortnight), and I understand that you put in a kind word, too."[26]

Whenever Burnham and Buckley pushed change for a more accessible section, Kenner and Davenport undoubtedly came to mind. Since they forced those who might otherwise dismiss *National Review* to take notice, they stayed.

Schlamm's departure brought a third core reviewer to
Meyer. Minus his drama critic, Buckley filled the void with a
twenty-three-year-old former Jesuit seminarian. Very quickly,
the youngster made the obligatory pilgrimage to Woodstock.
As pilgrimages sometimes do, it created a convert. The young
Catholic did not convert to *National Review*–style conservatism. He did become Meyer's friend.

"I spent four days with Frank and Elsie Meyer—four
nights, that is—and met Robert Phelps," Garry Wills reported to Rusher of his initial nocturnal interactions, telling
Meyer that "nothing pleases me more than talking till dawn
(where the talk is as rich as at Woodstock)."[27] In addition
to food, drink, and conversation, Wills recalled declaiming
whole Shakespeare plays with Frank in the earliest a.m. hours
before an audience of Elsie and John, who remembers the
two going back and forth on the entirety of *Coriolanus*.[28] He
became a substitute Gene O'Neill. The future Pulitzer Prize–
winner returned frequently, including with his stewardess-
scholar sweetheart Natalie. They spent Thanksgiving 1958
with the Meyers.[29] Elsie gave Natalie a recipe for preparing
turkey, which she tried at a subsequent Christmas.[30]

Meyer sent Wills books for work and pleasure.[31] He put in a
recommendation with the Volker Fund, as Rose Wilder Lane
had for him, that secured Wills funding for his first book, on
G. K. Chesterton.[32] He provided letters of introduction for
his protégé to present to various personages whom he knew
during his England years.[33] On the *Empress of France* en route
to his research trip/honeymoon, the Willses received roses
and a serenade courtesy of the Meyers.[34]

Later, when the twentysomething graduate student ran
out of money, Frank secured him employment with *The
Richmond News Leader*.[35] When *NR* released a youth issue,
Wills naturally wrote the "Principles and Heresies" column.[36]
Their phone calls became so frequent that Wills advised, "You
should light candles to A. G. Bell."[37] The young writer later
estimated that he had spent more time with Meyer in the

late 1950s and early 1960s than anyone outside of his family.[38] Meyer became for Wills if not the Master then the Mentor.

✦ ✦ ✦

SCHLAMM'S departure also paved the way for Whittaker Chambers's entrance. Courted by Buckley for more than a year prior to launch, the former Communist of girth as well as stature demurred. Contrary to the public image crafted by a vengeful left, Chambers held middle-of-the-road beliefs and struck those within his orbit as jolly rather than dour. The magazine's pro-McCarthy stance, and the sectarianism perhaps best represented by Schlamm's anti-Eisenhower article, scared him off. The subtraction of Schlamm, tightness of money, health issues relatively at bay, and growing fondness for the captain of the venture resulted in the addition of Chambers in August 1957.[39]

His involvement might appear as a likely boon to Meyer. The ex-Communists had played important roles within the party and later testified in governmental hearings fraught with drama and in media-circus trials. Chambers had written a bestselling memoir, and Meyer was then working on his own book. They both dropped out of urban life in favor of rural farmhouses. They presumably knew the feeling of clutching a gun in fear. They shared rare experiences in common.

And in some ways, they did connect. Meyer visited Chambers at his farmhouse north of Frederick, Maryland, in late winter 1957 along with L. Brent Bozell.[40] A few months later, Meyer, a shareholder of the Boston Athenaeum, paid $5 for Chambers to receive mailed materials.[41] As a devourer of publications as a result of the Volker side job, he introduced his new colleague to Jean-Paul Sartre's *Les Temps Modernes*. Chambers's biographer Sam Tanenhaus described his subject as "dazzled" by a Meyer book proposal concerning his years as a Communist.[42]

But Chambers disrupted "Books, Arts, and Manners" and Meyer disturbed Chambers.

Chambers filed a late and long review of Milovan Djilas's book *The New Class*. His promised part two never arrived, and he ultimately insisted that the magazine suppress part one.[43] Meyer had rebuffed one foreign critic who had wished to review the book under the assumption that Chambers would.[44] He did not.

Chambers wrote a brilliant but flawed review of Ayn Rand's brilliant but flawed *Atlas Shrugged*. It accurately, and devastatingly, pointed out that "the author, dodging into fiction, nevertheless counts on your reading it as political reality," "deals wholly in the blackest blacks and the whitest whites," and creates a "sterile world" that "is scarcely a place for children." Then he dropped the line, as over-the-top as anything he had imagined coming from Meyer or Schlamm, for which the review and, depending upon perspective, the book or the magazine became known: "From almost any page of Atlas Shrugged, a voice can be heard, from painful necessity, commanding: 'To a gas chamber—go!'"[45] In this scouring of Rand's self-righteousness, Chambers ironically set up *National Review*'s self-righteous habit of acting as the pope of the right. As both negative branding and a sort of poetry of prose, the line succeeds in an almost preposterous way. As an accurate depiction of the work under consideration, it seems as true to the fiction as Galt's Gulch is to the fact. For better and worse, it stuck—on *Atlas Shrugged*, on Chambers, on *National Review*, on Meyer's book section.

Meyer privately criticized Rand, too, but the brutal nature of the review placed him in an awkward spot with libertarian allies.[46]

In 1958, the year massive losses turned *National Review* from a weekly into a biweekly and that spurred recriminations within the Republican Party, Chambers strangely blamed the GOP's woes not on voters' six-year itch, but, at the height of MeToo Republicanism no less, ideological purity as represented by Meyer. He wrote Buckley,

> If the Rep. Party cannot get some grip of the actual world we live in and from it generalize and actively promote a program that means something to the masses of people—why, somebody else will. There will be nothing to argue. The voters will simply vote Republicans into singularity. The Rep. Party will become like one of those dark little shops which apparently never sell anything. If, for any reason, you go in, you find, at the back, an old man, fingering for his own pleasure, some oddments of cloth (weave and design of 1850). Nobody wants to buy them, which is fine because the old man is not really interested in selling. He just likes to hold and to feel. As your eyes become accustomed to the dim kerosene light, you are only slightly surprised to see that the old man is Frank Meyer.[47]

Like what Chambers wrote about Rand, the beauty of this passage overshadowed its substance, which surely uttered a truth about Meyer's zeal for ideological purity that nevertheless seemed so far removed from why Republicans lost as to tell a truth about Chambers, too. He seemed closer to the mark in offering to Buckley a René Descartes maxim that he felt Meyer should heed, roughly translated, "To reach the truth, you must once in your life, get rid of all the opinions you have received, and rebuild the system of your knowledge from the ground up." Chambers added for Meyer that not *once* but *perpetually* better applied.[48] Both men, of course, had dispensed with Stalinism. Did Meyer retain the mental structure and ideological thinking of those days? Chambers regarded him as still a true believer, albeit of other beliefs. Meyer, in turn, spotted remora hanging about Chambers, contending that "he never got over a half-Marxist, half-Narodnik outlook on life."[49]

◆ ◆ ◆

TURNABOUT came for Chambers as Meyer, and most of the rest at *National Review*, trumpeted a virulent anti-Communism; of all issues, that sowed in him discomfort.

Meyer questioned whether the Soviet Union, deceitful about so much, had lied about Sputnik, a skepticism he continued to indulge in the wake of Vostok 2.[50] This Sputnik trutherism, prevalent in some quarters at the magazine, alienated Chambers.[51] So did an article coauthored by Meyer and Bozell but ultimately spiked by Buckley that seemed to entertain the idea of a nuclear first strike against the Soviets.[52] The bestselling author embraced a softer approach on the civil liberties of Communists, including forever *bête noire* Alger Hiss's obtaining a passport, than did the other senior editors. The dispositive event occurred when *National Review*, with Meyer and Bozell especially engaged, protested the arrival of the Soviet leader Nikita Khrushchev in the United States.[53]

Among the senior editors, Chambers occupied rare ground to James Burnham's left. His prominence and talent licensed him to write any heterodox opinion within the magazine seeking to create if not a conservative orthodoxy then a conservative mainstream. Ultimately, Chambers felt as though he did not mesh and decided to depart in late 1959.[54] Intuitively, he understood that few grains of sand remained in his hourglass.

"What happened, I think, is that his basic position which has for some time been determinist—and if not materialist, then pantheist in a peculiar scientistic form of biological mysticism—came to a political head with the Khrushchev visit," Meyer interpreted the exit to an absent Kendall in a way that that perhaps only Kendall could interpret into complete coherence. "Whit violently disapproved of NR's stand at that time and later, since he thinks that a new collectivist scientific age is dawning, in which there will be no East or West. He says he doesn't approve of it, but there is nothing to be done about it but observe it and go along with it, and he thinks that to fight the wave is childish. The Khrushchev visit and the co-existence of Camp David [where Eisenhower and his Russian counterpart met] sharpened up his split with everything NR stands for, and he felt he could no longer be associated with it."[55]

Something like this process repeated in microcosm with Max Eastman, a lesser figure within the magazine but once a major intellectual force on the left who, like Chambers, found a home in moderate-right magazines of broad reach (*Time* for Chambers and *Reader's Digest* for Eastman) before winding up at career terminus at *NR*. Both entered the magazine with names that carried weight and outlooks difficult to categorize. Their manifold similarities amplified a superficial if important difference. Chambers cut a grotesque sight with his obesity and rotten teeth. Eastman visually captivated to such a degree that his bisexual friend Claude McKay threw a fit when Eastman retrieved a naked picture of himself that McKay had long cherished, and the sight of him at a party in his eighties caused a teenaged Carly Simon to deem him the most beautiful man she had ever seen.[56] In issuing a goodbye to all that, Eastman, the son of two Congregationalist ministers, specifically cited Meyer, the descendant of a founder of Newark's oldest synagogue, arguing that conservatism was tasked with preserving the Christian nature of the West as a cause of the break.[57]

Significantly, in the cases of these two prominent men to the left of *National Review*'s middle, the magazine did not excommunicate them; rather, they disconnected. Still, the causes of their departures included Meyer and demonstrated the costs the magazine's right wing inflicted upon respectability.

✦ ✦ ✦

MEYER appeared to Chambers, Eastman, and others as a rigid ideologue. He acted as anything but within his pages at the end of each issue.

The talent he recruited to review books highlighted his split personality within the enterprise. In his column and on the council of men who guided *National Review*, he envisioned the magazine as the conservative movement's servant. As the overseer of "Books, Arts, and Manners," he brooked broad disagreement and valued talent over purity. His behavior in the former role made him seem like the worst person for the latter job. Instead, he showed himself the best man for it.

Meyer faced greater obstacles from the talent within *National Review* than from the talent he cultivated outside of it to transform the book section into the newsstand's best.

Kendall volunteered that he should write every other lead review, a suggestion Bozell regarded as an attempt to annoy Meyer. Kendall, while privately acknowledging this to Bozell as a means to put the new book review editor in his place, took offense. He accused his former student of favoring the other point in the triumvirate when interests clashed. Bozell, understanding the fragile ego with which he dealt, salved the wound of his former teacher: "I regard you as primarily responsible for whatever intellectual achievements can be attributed to me." Nevertheless, he instructed Kendall, as others so often did, to "quit quarreling about nothing."[58]

Kendall's quarrels threatened to implode the burgeoning anti-Burnham coalition. With Kendall and Bozell, Meyer enjoyed a solid bloc capable of blocking the magazine from embracing Burnhamite positions. Unlike Schlamm, Kendall remained on the masthead as a senior editor. But he hung on tenuously. For reasons including friendship and the alliance he forged to thwart Burnham, Meyer labored to keep Kendall within the magazine. Kendall, for his part, worked equally hard to give Buckley reasons to fire him.

In 1958, *National Review*'s editor, tired of missed deadlines and anemic work, outlined strict rules for Kendall's employment, which included deducting $50 from a $500 annual bonus for every deadline missed, even if by a day.[59] If the rules did not let Kendall know who was boss, then Buckley's rejection of his first column under the new arrangement reinforced the point.[60]

"Bill is an immoral monarch: he lets his ministers down; he violates his pledged word; he does not refer his decisions about the allocation of rewards and privations to the principles of justice that his religion, as also his pretensions in the realm of political discourse, commit(s) him to," Kendall fumed to Meyer. "I will have a conspicuous, central role at National Review or I will have no role at all. In my eyes, I'm the Old Man of National Review. I insist on being treated as just that. Otherwise, I simply disinherit the whole job lot of you."[61]

Meyer, two months younger than the supposed resident elder statesman, responded with tough love. He explained that Kendall did not always reciprocate the loyalty and understanding demanded of friends, particularly with regard to Buckley. He wrote,

> The first set of circumstances is the constitutional character which NR as an institution has assumed. This is irrespective of, and irrelevant to, what may have been assumed about the institution before it was established (a point to which you frequently return in conversation, but which is as unimportant as to the form of the original call to the Annapolis Convention is to the American Constitution). The fact of the matter is that, like any good journal I know anything about, NR is and should be shaped and directed by one personality. This does not mean that others do not contribute, but it does mean

that the use of those others is itself controlled, balanced and tempered by the instincts of that one personality. The only limitations upon him are the need which he may have for the talents and disparate viewpoints of others and their influence upon his decisions. It is, as I think any good magazine must be, an absolute monarchy, tempered by a willingness to hear counsel and, at the margin, by the threat of voluntary self-exile—that is, the threat of losing through resignation men whom the editor-in-chief regards as necessary to the balance he wishes to establish. This fundamental set of facts, which delimits the actual situation within NR, I feel you have never been able to accept. It is the situation, and that's that. I myself think it is a rather good situation, even though there have been times when policies developed under it have approached the edge of what I could have found acceptable.[62]

Kendall issued a lengthy response encapsulated in its first two words: "Bull shit."[63]

Meyer believed his friend transformed pettiness into principle. "Damn it, Ken," he implored, "why don't you stop fighting your friends?"[64]

As he denigrated his boss to a colleague, Kendall conscripted Buckley into solving his problems, financial, personal, and otherwise. He instructed the magazine's editor to coax his brother, nearly a stranger to Buckley, into joining him for lunch in New York, where the older man envisioned his friend extracting information from his estranged sibling. A weirded-out Buckley begged off the spying scheme.[65] Kendall succeeded in enlisting his devout boss to vouch, uncomfortably if carefully so as not to dirty his soul, for his Catholicism in his attempt to win the annulment that would allow him to marry—he had met a female admirer while teaching at Stanford—for a third time.[66] He broached the idea, likely hoping to involve him in some vague way in raising money, with

Buckley of establishing a permanent Herbert Hoover pro-fessorship at Stanford for Kendall.[67] A drunk-driving arrest in Menlo Park, and lamely fending off accusations of teaching drunk by claiming a case of flu necessitated an old family tincture of "hot-buttered rum," diminished the prospects of this plan.[68]

Meyer, a contemporary, never found himself in a hier-archical relationship with Kendall. They became sounding boards for each other, allies within *National Review*, and re-ciprocal career boosters in terms of speaking opportunities and publishing. Their conversations occurred over mail, by phone, and in periodic Woodstock bull sessions. Their close-ness allowed Kendall to comfortably confess his sins, boast of his accomplishments, and complain about colleagues. He proudly told of his two-week streak of cutting down from seventy cigarettes to less than a pack a day.[69] He divulged a three-day vomiting fit after inadvertently ingesting Ajax by eating from a pan—"all my life I have liked the crust that adheres to the side of a casserole"—somewhere in the wash-ing process.[70] One does not need a sleuthing background to deduce the time of night and the soap eater's condition. A fifty-year-old Kendall offered Meyer "the worst of possible reasons" for failing to meet a deadline: "My 19-year-old beau-ty queen pitched up at the door, after many many months of not pitching up, and I didn't send her away."[71]

Kendall gave his name to a couch at *National Review* after nearly giving Suzanne La Follette a coronary when she dis-covered him *in flagrante* with a junior staffer in her office.[72] Sometime thereafter, Kendall figured into the divorce pro-ceedings of Van Galbraith, one of Buckley's closest friends from college, who accused the Yale professor of committing adultery with his wife.[73]

Buckley could not claim ignorance. He likely knew the story of his teacher's theft of another professor's driveway. Cleanth Brooks, a noted literary critic, acted as one of the tempestuous political scientist's few boosters on the faculty.

His colleague repaid the favor in the most Kendallian way possible. "When Cleanth and his wife were away," Noel Parmentel noted, "Willmoore hired a truck and they came in and took all of Cleanth's paving to pay for Willmoore's liquor bill."[74] Given that the professorial pair had purchased land together around the time of the masonry disappearance, it possibly owed to something more convoluted.[75] Still, a letter referencing a $3,000 check confirms the gist of the legend. Kendall wrote Mrs. Brooks, "I'm sending you money for the road."[76] Buckley imagined *his* driveway, and all else, would somehow remain safe from Kendall.

Why did colleagues tolerate this one-man soap opera? "He was fun," Parmentel observed. "The right wing was fun back then."[77] Buckley and Bozell forever bore the imprint of his classroom wizardry; others knew his reputation as one of a handful of truly great political scientists. He developed an interesting interpretation of American democracy ventriloquized into Buckley's quip that he would rather the first two thousand names of the Boston phone book govern him than the Harvard faculty. And like the most beautiful women, the most brilliant men enjoy a different set of rules. Neal Freeman reflected about early *National Review*, "There were a lot of smart people around. There was one genius. That was Willmoore."[78]

◆ ◆ ◆

THE BOOK SECTION enjoyed praise and sniping from other senior editors.

"I continue to like the review section immensely—a fact which I took pleasure in airing at the last editorial lunch I attended, and rather suspected that at least one person present did not share my enthusiasm," Suzanne La Follette informed Meyer. "Whazza matter with that guy?"[79]

La Follette wrote here, presumably, of Burnham. That guy similarly complained privately to Buckley, shortly before *NR* became a biweekly, that "Principles and Heresies" did not belong in a weekly, calling the column unreadable and barely read.[80] He used the more expansive periodic editorial meetings—Agonized Reappraisals or, for short (though they were anything but), Agonies—to criticize Meyer's section. This waged the ideological war on a different battlefield. As the book section elicited contemporaneous praise, and many of its unknowns gained Pulitzer Prizes, National Book Awards, PEN Awards, and other plaudits later in their careers, the criticism concerned his personal and ideological rivalry with Meyer more than the section he edited. Reviews ran too long, too intellectual, and too heavy for a popular magazine, Burnham claimed.[81] He believed that, but Burnham primarily looked, *à la* Kendall, to put Meyer in his place. If Kendall did so out of petty motivations, Burnham's agenda involved neutering one who stood in the way of the realization of his vision. He did not wish to write for the right's version of *New Masses*.

For La Follette, either Burnham, or turning sixty-five, or the hiring of the openly liberal, twenty-year-old John Leonard over her choice of Allan Ryskind, prodded her into retirement.[82] Perhaps all three and more led to her departure. The editor's sister Priscilla Buckley gradually assumed her role as managing editor. This replaced a Burnham enemy with one who became a warm friend and close ally.

Kendall offered "my latest political theory about NR: *malgre tout*, a constitution has emerged, as I put it in a letter to Jim yesterday, Polybius plus the Divine Right of Kings: front of the book dominated by Burnham, back of the book dominated by Meyer, who can always eye each other nervously over the intervening waste of No-Man's Land, where nothing ever happens anyway; (blank) checks and (idle) balances— with one of Zeus's thunderbolts likely to strike any where any time, but not likely (fortunately, I think) to be very effective: power goes to the industrious amongst them or gets the green light. A little hard on some of the rest of us, perhaps, but I must say it gets out a good magazine."[83]

◀ 21 ▶

Quo Vadis?

Venturing into the new decade, the magazine headed in directions unanticipated, and perhaps unwanted, by some editors.

"Frank Meyer is emerging as the Voice," Whittaker Chambers acknowledged to Buckley months after his departure. "I am not being sniffy: this, I gather from stray NR readers, is just what they want to hear. And, technically, he writes it all well. It isn't my flapjack. But that is of no interest whatever. The fact is that this is what readers want."[1]

This reality annoyed one colleague.

James Burnham saw *National Review* at a crossroads in 1960. It either remained mired in that 30,000- to 35,000-subscriber range by staying doctrinaire or it boosted circulation into six digits by becoming more of a magazine and less of a conservative magazine. Purging his rival Willi Schlamm, and elbowing Suzanne La Follette, whom he placed on a list of "technical incompetents," into retirement, increased Burnham's power.[2] Road blocks, in the form of Meyer, L. Brent Bozell, and, to a lesser extent, Willmoore Kendall, remained.

So did the inconvenience that actual readers, rather than the potential subscribers Burnham envisioned, appeared to be mesmerized by a political phenomenon from the West.

229

Barry Goldwater's rising star owed in massive degree to *The Conscience of a Conservative*, a short manifesto bearing the senator's name but actually written by Bozell.

An episode in 1960 involving Burnham's scheduled review of the book encapsulated the political and personal reasons why he engendered contempt. On the day Meyer expected receipt of the review, he instead awoke to a telegram. Burnham wired, from Arizona no less, that the book struck him as a "political not literary item" that rendered it "inappropriate for lead rev[iew]." He planned instead to address it in the front of the magazine.[3] With one cable, he managed to insult Bozell, who had ghostwritten the book; inconvenience Meyer, who dropped everything to write the review himself; and alienate colleagues through his attempt to unilaterally manipulate the stance of the magazine, many of whose writers envisioned Goldwater as the political personification of their ideas. The book section editor interpreted it as "an effort to downgrade any right-wing opposition to [1960 presidential candidate Richard] Nixon."[4]

This latest skirmish in the Meyer–Burnham War, like all those before and after, occurred on multiple levels. This one involved a personal quarrel involving two distinct individuals, a battle for the soul of the magazine, and an attempt to reorient the budding conservative movement.

◆ ◆ ◆

MEYER played a long game. He saw victories as generationally sown. In 1952, he counseled colleagues at *The Freeman* not to focus on the election of Dwight Eisenhower but instead to create the conditions suitable to nominate a conservative for president in 1956. By 1960, he offered similar advice to his colleagues at *National Review*. Do not attach the publication's name to the Republican nominee, whom he envisioned as Nixon, but instead embrace Goldwater as a vessel for conservatism. Even in doing this, he argued, conservatives may need to labor until 1980 to see one of their own elected president.

The prophet, writing about the present as though from the future and about the future as though from beyond there, spelled out the position of conservatives in 1960:

> (1) The situation of conservatism in the United States presents a sharp contrast between the steady growth of conservative influence on the intellectual level and the cumulative debacle on the political level. On the one hand, NR in particular, the activities of Volker and Relm, the early stages of conservative activity by other foundations, the new active stage of work by ISI, together with the increasingly apparent bankruptcy of the Liberal position, are rapidly creating a climate in which conservatism is on the verge of emerging as the only live option for the intelligent and the independent of the new generation. On the other hand, eight years of a Liberal Republican executive have immensely weakened the political opposition in the Congress and in the states, and the opportunistic progress of Nixon farther and farther to the Left threatens to carry that process much further.
>
> (2) In such a situation there are two possibilities: either the historical circumstances will allow us the fifteen or twenty years in which a developing intellectual leadership can be translated into political reality, or before that time the bankruptcy of the Liberal leadership will produce a crisis, internal or external, in which the confidence of the American people in the leadership of the Establishment will be radically shaken and they will look for new leadership uncompromised by previous association with the Establishment (a situation similar to the breakdown of the French confidence in the systems of the Third and Fourth Republics).

(3) Whichever eventuality may occur, it seems to me that the responsibility of conservative leadership (and that means first of all NR, which is today undoubtedly the center of the movement—its <u>Iskra</u>, its <u>New</u> <u>Republic</u>) is to maintain and develop an independent position. In the first eventuality, this is the only foundation upon which a new leadership can be developed, capable of transforming present conditions. In the second eventuality (a crisis) it is absolutely vital that there exist (since we have no DeGaulle at Colombey-les-deux-Eglises) a group of persons uncompromised by association with the Establishment, to whom the country can turn in the event of a collapse of confidence in the existing leadership.

(4) Under these circumstances it seems to me absolutely vital to the future development of a conservative movement that NR under no circumstances endorse Nixon (a fortiori, not [Nelson] Rockefeller, should he yet gain the Republican nomination), either now or between the conventions and the election. The immediate practical consequences of the Democrats capturing the executive seem to me to be balanced by the opposite practical consideration: the much greater possibility of the development of a political opposition under any circumstances other than the election of a Liberal Republican president. And the basic long-term considerations I have outlined dictate that under no circumstances should the conservative movement be compromised by tailing the Nixon kite.

(5) A few months ago I would have proposed that we take a completely independent critical attitude towards all candidates. But a more positive position has recently become possible for the period between now and the conventions. The emergence of Barry Goldwater as a principled conservative gives us a public political symbol through which our position is expressed in the political arena.

(6) I would therefore propose that between now and the conventions NR (in much the way in which the New Republic committed itself to [Chester] Bowles for president) take the position that Goldwater is the only candidate whom conservatives can support; and that between the convention and the election we criticize both candidates on the basis of the standard we have established in the weeks before the conventions. I do not think that we have to sound silly in proposing Goldwater. We can make very clear (as the New Republic did in support of Bowles) that we have no illusions about the practical possibilities, but that if the Republican Party is to express conservative principles, the nomination of Goldwater is the only way to do so.

(7) I propose that we should, to a much greater degree than we have ever done before, pick a number of Senatorial and Congressional candidates and support them with the greatest of vigor, thus during the election making clear to our readers, explicitly and implicitly, that it is here that for the time we see the only hope of political improvement.[5]

Meyer largely prevailed upon his colleagues. *National Review* declined to endorse the Republican nominee for president.[6]

◆ ◆ ◆

BY 1960, *National Review* had established what Bill Rusher referred to as "our growing colony in Madrid."[7] Kendall settled there in 1959. Bozell and his wife, Tish, with their large brood in tow, followed the next year. They joined an existing diaspora of sorts in Tish's brother Reid Buckley, pursuing the family's oil business, and Frederick Wilhelmsen, a contributor to the magazine.

The sojourn in Spain profoundly affected the migrants and their magazine. *National Review*, try as it might, could not stand athwart the present yelling stop.

Rather than question how one could act as a guiding force for a magazine of American politics and culture while residing across the Atlantic, the Spanish contingent sought to recruit a third senior editor, of five on the masthead, to emigrate.

"Spain is bliss," Bozell wrote Frank and, crucially, Elsie in early 1961. "It is the only country fit to save the West. Therefore, your duties, no less than mine, are to come here and get to work. The sooner the better. The longer you stay there, the more time you will waste on a hopeless country and with an unfriendly people."[8]

As the United States inaugurated its first Catholic president, Bozell the convert touted the virtues of emigration to Francisco Franco's Spain. More startlingly, the exodus came less than a year after Bozell wrote the book that had so elevated Goldwater. In America, conservatives appeared on the cusp of finally propelling one of their own toward the presidency. Rather than parent this ephebic movement, Bozell and Kendall abandoned it—or, perhaps from their perspective, sought to guide it from afar. Bozell, seeing a country in which the leader put his face on the coin as a utopia, indulged further utopian thinking in imagining that they could shape a magazine and mold a movement by remote.

He lobbied his Cathol-ish though not Catholic colleague to uproot his family from their utopia to settle in his. The correspondents, who understood tone, hyperbole, and gasconade mostly lost on eavesdropping strangers decades later, also grasped when serious undercurrents flowed beneath jocular language. Bozell wanted the Meyers to emigrate.

"Can there be the slightest doubt in your minds that your task—the conversion of the United States—is infinitely more difficult than ours, and that the chances of you succeeding are infinitely less than ours?" Bozell queried the Meyers. "I can't believe there are two points of view about this; I am really quite serious and I need your help, for I now plan to be, not President of the U.S., but Caudillo of Spain."⁹

Meyer regarded a pilgrimage as far-fetched. He could not afford it. Neither, crucially, could *National Review*. He wanted Bozell and Kendall, two of his closest friends in the world and strongest allies within *National Review*, to return if merely for the health of the magazine. Buckley, minus the presence of his brother-in-law and the argumentative Yale faculty mentor to both, had fallen more firmly under the influence of Burnham. Meyer, scarcely venturing into the office from Woodstock, could not match the former Trotskyist's sway. But with Bozell and Kendall by his side, Meyer regarded it as more of a fair fight. To their *come here* he offered a *come home*.

"I find it hard to accept your theories on the primacy of Spain—or any other nation but the United States," he confessed. "I will, however, listen to the argument. On the concrete question of our coming to Spain, however, either for a short visit or longer—you have overlooked the interesting problem of economic survival. Have you any ideas on that— or do you propose that we bring Bill [Buckley] too, send Jim [Burnham] back to Kent, and edit NR from Madrid?"¹⁰

◆ ◆ ◆

THE DIFFICULTIES of running a magazine with a senior editor living in El Escorial, a small town located in the center of Spain whose mail crisscrossed the Atlantic slowly and whose phone lines only occasionally connected with the United States, increased tensions and created divisions within divisions. Frank's mission aimed not just to win America for conservatism but to win the factional battle within *National Review* as well. Especially in the United States, Bozell, and to a lesser extent Kendall, joined him in that crusade. Even with two in Spain, the trio also fought to remake, or restore, America.

The two interweaving aims combined in a controversy exacerbated by the distance of the editors. It ensnared not only *National Review* personnel but the personification of their movement.

In February 1961, *National Review* published a startling article critical of Arizona's junior senator. "Quo Vadis, Barry?" lamented a recent document released by Goldwater that, among other sins, allegedly established a *modus vivendi* with the New Deal.[11] Bozell wrote the critical piece. Kendall put his name on it. Bozell's association with the senator made him reluctant to acknowledge authorship over a piece critical of another ghostwritten Goldwater tract. So Bozell decided to again act as ghostwriter and recruit his fellow expat to lend him his name.

The piece exposed fissures with Goldwater and deepened them at the magazine.

Bozell, who felt dragooned into writing the piece, expressed rage, palpable in New York despite emanating from 3,500 miles away, over the editing of it. Aside the masthead, Burnham anonymously described the piece as an "unexpected personal opinion" from an infrequent contributor as of late (meaning Kendall) certain to register "vigorous objections" by friends and foes of its subject.[12] Bozell saw this as Burnham's way of neutering the piece and separating the magazine from its conclusions.[13] Bozell wished to separate himself from its conclusions to such a degree that he took his name off it. He dismissed reasons that *National Review*, also a partner in the project to propel Goldwater, might find it too provocative to attach its name to it by reminding that the magazine had asked for the article in the first place. He also objected to Burnham's lopping off his fourth and final argument against those pushing Goldwater toward the middle and the alteration of his language introducing a point, which Meyer justified as transforming the words into something less "apodictic."[14]

The edits appeared of the type normally experienced by writers even if the introductory note undermined the article in the exact manner described by Bozell. Burnham, facing a deadline, needed to make snap decisions as the piece's ostensible author and real author both remained out of reach. He rightly enlisted Meyer and Rusher, at least in one of the three offending editorial decisions, which perhaps cynically allowed him safety in numbers. He also in a genuine sense sought counsel from the two major figures at hand who were closest ideologically, and in Meyer's case personally, with the true author. Bozell regarded Burnham's note and alterations as a high-handed way of asserting his superiority over another editor of equal rank. He viewed it as a departure from the magazine's customs and a harbinger of Burnham's absorption of greater powers.[15]

Meyer, enlisted to act, adopted a calm and polite tack in a phone conversation with his *bête noire*. He got nowhere.[16] Burnham also gleefully implicated Bozell's allies as his enemies. He masterfully parlayed Meyer's and Rusher's role in the unwelcome edits into a sowing of division. This infuriated Frank and cleaved Bozell and Kendall, at least momentarily, from their allies in New York. The anger stemmed not merely from Burnham's outmaneuvering the quartet, which he clearly did. The peculiar decision to attack the man they had anointed conservative savior undoubtedly provoked Burnham to further laugh at their foolishness.

"This is the last God damned time I take any crap around NR from JB without raising bloody murder," Meyer wrote Bozell. "If I had reacted as I ought to have done to his intolerable ignoring of my memos, and snotting me when I tried to speak to him about editorials on the phone, the week before—that is, if I had acted in a natural manner and not tried your damfool idea of trying to act like Jim, this whole business would never have occurred, and you and Willmoore would not be throwing around words like 'opportunist' and 'trimmer.'"[17]

Bozell, acknowledging past counsel to his temperamental friend, refused blame for Meyer's uncharacteristically timid approach.

"While I did ask you not to make scenes at ceremonial din-
ners and to be content with fighting a cold war under terms
that seemed to give us a pretty good chance of winning,"
he conceded, "I did not ask you to act like a goddamn jerk,
to forget everything you've learned (and taught me) about
political in-fighting, to allow yourself to be mouse-trapped
in a situation obviously fraught with danger in which your
only weapon, in addition to firmness, was clarity of expression. What do you do at the supreme moment (and this is my
clinching tit [for tat]) but mumble!"[18]

Meyer felt used by Burnham. His involvement, along with
Rusher no less, in one of the three offending editorial decisions made him complicit and provided Burnham with both
a plausible excuse and an opportunity to create rifts among
the alliance in permanent conflict with him.

"I am more certain than ever of the correctness of my analysis of the long-term realities of the NR situation," Meyer
wrote Bozell. "Not only because of my continuing belief
that JB, both in metaphysical and political-philosophical
terms, stands outside of conservatism, but also because of
the apparently total impossibility of ever establishing any
frontier treaty with him or working with him as a colleague
with whom one can disagree profoundly but still come to
continuing practical conclusions. I believe this last is not dis-
sociated from his philosophical position, which, while it is
in a sense positivist and relativist, is a special brand, namely
Machiavellian-Paretan—mixed perhaps with strong elements
of the character of a sneak-bully."[19]

❖ ❖ ❖

MEYER and Burnham strongly disliked each other. Contempt took the form of cool condescension from the older
man and emotional rage from the younger one. If either
ruled, banishment of the other would follow. As counselors

and not kings, they coexisted in a prolonged cold war.

Why did they despise each other?

The men on the masthead, of course, exhibited obvious differences. Strangely, their similarities escaped notice. Both hailed from families achieving success in business: Burnham's father had served as a railroad executive; Meyer's had worked overseeing manufacturing interests. They both embraced atheism before returning to faith. Meyer matriculated at Princeton when upperclassman Burnham reigned atop his class. Meyer again followed in his footsteps at Balliol. Each separately became further radicalized in England and then enlisted in the struggle to save the fallen world through Marxism. They migrated right—Burnham first though Meyer further—and eventually found themselves present at the creation of *National Review*.

Tracing their feud to a jealous Meyer's not enjoying status at every stop as Burnham did proves a seductive if not entirely accurate thesis. Garry Wills recounted a story of a dejected Meyer, as he prepared to drop out, glimpsing Burnham, triumphantly holding court, with Princeton's popular kids. That Meyer withdrew eight months after the latter had graduated calls into question the tale.[20] While a hierarchy of sorts that prevailed within *National Review* also prevailed at Princeton, neither writes of Ivy League encounters with the other in their correspondence. In fact, when Meyer introduces himself to Burnham in a 1952 letter, he mentions his Princeton and Balliol education without any acknowledgement of the experience of Burnham at the same institutions.[21] Months later Burnham shares gossip about the lives of former schoolmates, so they clearly knew some of the same people.[22] Burnham tells Meyer of his admiration for his reviews amid much substandard material in *The American Mercury*.[23] Meyer defends Burnham from Arthur Schlesinger's attack in a letter sent to *Partisan Review*.[24]

While a decadal feud festering across continents works as a narrative device, no evidence exists of any rancor in the early 1950s derived from jealousies dating to the late 1920s. Quite possibly Burnham's success, and even look, as a Princeton man rubbed the Princeton dropout raw. But it seems unlikely that the younger man harbored jealousy for anyone who contemporaneously attended Balliol, where he strutted if not on the manicured lawns then at least as the Big Man on Campus.

More germane to their pasts invading their present, one man was a Stalinist and the other a Trotskyist. The allegiances instilled rivalry and lingering mindsets. Both men embraced Communism, but Meyer did so more intensely and as part of the Stalinist mainstream while Burnham did so on the off hours from academic work for a competing Marxist offshoot. As he taught philosophy at New York University, Burnham helped organize the American Workers Party with his fellow philosopher Sidney Hook and the do-gooder clergyman A. J. Muste—a move akin to the unemployed launching the American Millionaires Club. Burnham did not grasp the unintentional self-parody. He at least neglected to cosplay as a proletarian as others in his privileged sect did.

"Burnham gives speeches as if we were his students," the *Studs Lonigan* trilogy novelist James T. Farrell maintained.[25] "He wore hundred dollar suits," the leftist writer Harry Roskolenko observed. "He went to the theater, too."[26] Max Shachtman "felt that although he was with us and with us thoroughly, he was not, so to say, of us."[27]

His new conservative friends felt similarly. Burnham managed to change his politics. Transforming his personality demanded too much. The traits that kept comrades at arm's length distanced *National Review* colleagues as well.

The cultured and kind Arlene Croce, the famous ballet critic who eventually migrated from *National Review* to *The New Yorker*, found Burnham "a bit standoffish."[28] Spotted by Meyer in *Commonweal* in 1962, the confessedly "covert conservative" Croce responded to his entreaty to review for him by confessing a "hunger for a job—any job—on the staff of

NATIONAL REVIEW."[29] Her dream soon came true. "Of all the editors," she volunteered, "I was least close with Jim Burnham. I didn't know him personally."[30]

Here and there Burnham ingratiated himself with those lacking the last name Buckley. "The one who impressed me the most there at the office that I was closest to was Jim Burnham," recalled David Franke. "He sort of took me in as a son." When Burnham told the twentysomething editorial assistant that he reminded him of himself as a young man, Franke regarded it as one of the unforgettable compliments of his life.[31] The iceman occasionally melted.

Burnham toyed with the excitable Meyer. A continuing rib, effective because on some level its architect regarded it seriously, involved the suggestion that the book section might benefit from an overhaul, specifically briefer reviews. "I could just picture Jim just sort having this wry smile on his face as Frank is probably barking into the speaker phone," Franke offered. "Frank was volatile, passionate. Burnham was the exact opposite. He was very cool and collected."[32]

Caught up in moments of passion, a frustrated Meyer half entertained the idea that Burnham's work for the CIA had never ended and that his present assignment concerned monitoring conservatives and steering their ship toward the establishment.[33] Given the heavy presence of ex-CIA operatives within *National Review* and the agency's covert funding of *Partisan Review* and the Congress for Cultural Freedom, endeavors heavily involving Burnham, Meyer's occasional postulation looked less paranoid decades later than it did in real time.

Rusher maintained that "the difference between Frank Meyer and Jim Burnham was: Meyer wanted to know what the relationship of virtue was to freedom. Burnham wanted to know what the noted Kurd leader Salid Bhagdash was doing in Damascus last week."[34]

This assessment highlights a truth as it obscures a few. Yes, "Principles and Heresies" fixated on the philosophical underpinnings of societal trends and policy problems.

Yes, "The Third World War" sought to understand the world beyond America's shores mainly by digesting current events. But Meyer's column occasionally fixated on the headlines, and Burnham obviously showed himself, particularly in his books, as a deep philosophical thinker. The primary difference between the giants stemmed neither from politics nor principles but personality. All three nevertheless fueled the conflict.

Jim and Marcia Burnham lived a domestic existence. The drink- and drama-infused lives of Meyers, Kendalls, and Bozells did not find a counterpart in Kent, Connecticut. Burnham wanted neither long missives in green ink appearing in his mailbox nor his phone ringing at 1:00 a.m. Within the fraternity of Willi Schlamm's "outs," Burnham did not much fraternize. This at once marked him as the odd man out among the odd men at *National Review* and the indispensable man in rolling issues off the press. He participated heavily in the eleventh-hour, in-office editing of the magazine and production of the abbreviated periodical, *National Review Bulletin*. The men he clashed with, including Meyer, did not.

"His real skill was as a desk man," his junior colleague Neal Freeman noted of Burnham. "He could put together the issue of a magazine. For many years, he and I used to do a newsletter in between the fortnightly editions of the magazine. He was just a terrific deadline editor. Bill recognized that and capitalized on it."[35]

Burnham perhaps looked down on Meyer, Kendall, and Bozell because of his more useful role in producing the magazine. It appeared that when he shifted toward conservatism he, unlike Meyer, did not regard conservatives very highly. Meyer converted to conservatism; Burnham turned to it as a last available option after not just the left but liberals regarded him as *persona non grata*. And Burnham's theoretical beliefs, which attached more to power as an end in itself than how one might wield it, alienated him from his colleagues. Burnham's Svengali hold on Buckley, too, created jealousies and resentments. And then between the two rivals stood all that shared history, which, while certainly overblown, accounted for part of their feud.

David Franke, who worked at *NR* from 1960 to 1963, saw Burnham as the most influential on Buckley within the magazine. "He was just a very methodical, powerful presenter of his ideas—very logical, rational," Franke recalled. "Bill would pay most attention to him simply because of his intellect but also because he was right there. Bill would make the decisions on what we would say. There would be differences between Bill and Burnham. But most of the time I could see that Jim was the pivotal figure there. Frank was left out because he was not there."[36]

And this helped explain why the *in absentia* three amigos often found themselves defeated by the "desk man" Burnham.

◆ ◆ ◆

THIS CIVIL WAR within *National Review*, ostensibly stemming from the internecine battle for the ideological soul of Goldwater but really from the ideological soul of the magazine in the process of creating him, threatened to alienate the senator from his boosters. One of his boosters no longer looked so favorably upon the senator. The man who wrote *The Conscience of a Conservative* the year before now referred to Barry Goldwater as "our Frankenstein."[37]

Bozell judged that the crescive movement by 1960 boasted a sufficient intellectual and activist wing to recognize a natural desire for, and a lack of, a political figure around which to coalesce. The zeal for a leader, Bozell wrote Meyer, essentially created one:

> That was the setting when Goldwater and Conscience of a Conservative suddenly and prematurely walked onto the stage. I say prematurely without appealing to

> hindsight because the situation, in terms of the internal condition of the conservative movement, was not yet ripe for a leader who was not either a) under control, or b) did not need control—i.e. the paragon of our dreams. The forces within the movement were as yet too diffuse, its leadership too uncertain, its principles too vulnerable to inroads from the Nixonian left and the crackpot right; and all of those dangers were at the fore of our conversations on the subject during the early weeks and months of the Goldwater ascendency. Nonetheless, with the new impetus the movement surged forward and grew in terms of troop strength and public impact at a far greater rate than we had anticipated. Three factors were responsible for this rise: the book itself, Goldwater's semi-charismatic personality, and the latent strength of conservatism's appeal to the masses, especially youth. This altogether healthy growth reached its zenith in the hours preceding Goldwater's curtain speech at the convention. That speech marked the end of a phase.[38]

Prior to Goldwater's planned 1960 convention speech supporting the party's senatorial candidates, conservatives uncorked a tumult of cheers and horns. The uproar lasted more than eight minutes and led to much gavel-banging. The convention's sergeant-at-arms ordered revelers to clear the aisles.[39] The establishment wanted the blue blood Henry Cabot Lodge on the ticket; the energy called for Barry Goldwater.

During his curtain speech, Goldwater, a party man whose loyalty to Republicanism Bozell and Meyer regarded as treasonous to conservatism, told his well-wishers at the Chicago convention in characteristic bluntness, "Let's grow up, conservatives. If we want to take this party back—and I think we can someday—let's get to work."[40]

The "grow up" part rang louder in the ears of both Bozell and Meyer than the "take the party back" part. They saw it as the first in a series of insults toward the right wing that culminated in the treatise that Bozell, using Kendall as his beard, critiqued in *National Review*.

The delegates nominated Nixon. Lodge—not Goldwater or Walter Judd—secured a spot on the ticket. Rockefeller essentially dictated the platform. Goldwater told his followers to grow up. What about the 1960 convention appalled conservatives less than 1952?

They began to work feverishly to ensure that there would be no repeat. *National Review*'s right wing did not labor in assurance that Goldwater incarnated their ideals.

◆ ◆ ◆

GOLDWATER reciprocated. He harbored suspicions about his Eastern enthusiasts.

The senator objected to a *National Review* direct-mail letter that included his endorsement immediately after the publication of the *NR* piece "Quo Vadis, Barry?" To Rusher, the article served as the alpha and omega to explain their angered ally's response.[41] Rusher had received clearance from the senator's office. Goldwater nevertheless opposed its publication. In a conversation with the senator, Rusher confessed ignorance about whether he could have stopped the 170,000-piece mailing, which it turned out he could not have (and probably would not have), and took the blame for sending it.[42] The publisher, responsible for keeping money flowing in the right direction, felt pinched by the quibbling over their leading presidential hopeful in print. It struck him as an unforced error.

Still, Rusher, months away from propelling the Draft Goldwater Committee, gave his green light to swift-shanking Goldwater if necessary.[43] "I am not, of course, advocating an open break with BG, or that <u>NR</u> treat him with anything but loving solicitude, or that we, individually, cease our efforts to save his soul," he told Buckley. "But I am suggesting that we stop whoring after him. This advice comes, I remind you, from the Number One Pimp."[44]

A dichotomy persisted between *National Review*'s public enthusiasm for Goldwater and its private misgivings. The spotlight shined by *National Review* ensured Goldwater cast a longer shadow across America. The Arizonan repaid the attention with general crankiness and nit-picking fights.

He responded unfavorably about the prospect of Bozell's again working for him.[45] Bozell, in turn, rejected Goldwater's offer for him to ghostwrite a second bound manifesto, which Meyer regarded as an opportunity to further transform the senator into a vessel carrying their freight; he urged his friend to steer the job to M. Stanton Evans, a Yale graduate who embraced fusionism, if he indeed could not muster up the will to reprise his role.[46] Bozell indicated a silent treatment of sorts after he refused to write another book for the senator. "He's an ungracious SOB except when he wants something from you," Bozell explained to Meyer. "Oh, well."[47]

At a 1961 *Human Events* banquet, Goldwater named four publications he regarded as essential to conservatives. The list strangely omitted *National Review*.[48]

The less Barry Goldwater loved *National Review*, the more *National Review* publicly loved him. Behind the scenes, his biggest cheerleaders worried.

Meyer wrote Bozell that "no matter how he weakens (he can't really weaken beyond a certain point), he remains the rallying center politically of the movement, and unfortunately its public symbol."[49]

Meyer acknowledged the necessity of movements operating on two levels. This meant here organizing the masses around Goldwater on one level and keeping the movement philosophically sound on another. The danger involved a charismatic leader diverting the movement from its principles toward his personality cult.[50]

Meyer concluded of Goldwater that "we have got him, and if it becomes impossible to combine loyalty to principle with continuing support for him—as it may well, the way things are going—disengagement is going to be one hell of a problem."[51]

◀ 22 ▶

Moulding

I have desisted from any writing on the Communist question so far because I have felt that something in the nature of a 'retreat' was indicated, in the circumstances,"
Frank Meyer wrote various foundations in 1952. "But lately I
have been thinking of the possibility of doing a thorough job
on an aspect of the Communist Party which has never been
handled in any detail, so far as I know."[1]

The pitch came amid a great appetite for anti-Communist
literature. Meyer's friends Louis Budenz, who became a
one-man cottage industry, and Nathaniel Weyl, despite
holding back much, jumped into the genre. The field included philosophical epiphanies (1949's *God That Failed*)
and ghostwritten quickies (1951's *Out of Bondage*) lifting
the veil off a hidden world. It lacked a book detailing the
aboveground party's means and methods that produced
the Communist cadre, that contradiction in terms denot-
ing the hardened revolutionaries upon whom all else rests.
The phrase itself refuted Communism. Its centrality to
Meyer's book, though never acknowledged as a rebuttal,
served as a subconscious taunt. Everyone was equal except
the cadre. The wannabe author, entrusted by the party to
impart Marxism, looked like the right person to write the

proposed book. As importantly, 1952 seemed like the perfect time to release it.

The nonfiction bestseller list that year consistently featured Whittaker Chambers's *Witness* and Herbert A. Philbrick's *I Led 3 Lives*. The radio incarnation of *I Was a Communist for the FBI* premiered in April. At the box office, *Big Jim McLain*, *Red Snow*, and *Invasion U.S.A.* tapped into national antipathy toward Communism. As America's sons died in Korea, an expansive market existed for Frank's idea.

Duell, Sloan and Pearce expressed interest in a fictionalized version of the proposed book, which the author found great difficulty writing.[2] Meyer sent Henry Regnery an outline for the nonfiction book and the Chicago publisher expressed interest. Nothing came of it.[3]

His efforts concentrated less on publishers than foundations. A man who had toiled for the party for over a decade for meager amounts wanted proper renumeration for recounting those labors.

The RAND Corporation rejected in May 1952 a grant proposal to fund the book.[4] A year later, the private-public outfit approved a $2,000 grant only to expand it to $8,000 that summer.[5] When the beneficiary failed to produce a book the following year, the benefactor opted to continue support but at a rate of $30 per eight-hour workday.[6] With Volker Fund largesse raining down upon him, and freelance writing options that paid comparably to the revised RAND terms, the author placed the project on the back burner.

Research difficulties kept it there. Secret societies, of course, do not meticulously document their doings. And he had donated the bulk of his Marxist library to the Communist Party, so citable materials did not prove readily available. He wrote Louis Nichols, one of the FBI's top men, for access to the bureau's material from party schools.[7] As if to soften the blow to a valued witness, the rejection came from J. Edgar Hoover.[8] Meyer's collection included Jefferson School catalogs, debriefings for U.S. and U.K. authorities, some old issues of Communist publications, and testimony transcripts. Memory served as the greatest resource. In this he could rely on the remembrances of Elsie, too, as she had spent nearly as many years as he had in the party. The fact that recollection drove it determined what kind of book it would be. The journey from thought to page proved long. Working at *National Review*, parenting two boys, and fulfilling periodic requests to testify or talk all meant that he was often doing something other than writing this book.

He conceded to RAND that his book, to be titled *The Moulding of Communists*, was "dragging on for an unconscionable time after the completion of the first draft."[9] The Free Press then rejected the manuscript, which represented the last straw for the foundation.[10] While removing itself from the project, RAND imposed numerous controlling stipulations.[11] Ultimately, it let go of the project just as it had let go of its money.

Clinton Rossiter, one of the "new conservatives" Meyer sought to excoriate with his Volker grant for another book idea, rescued the moribund project. In 1957, the Fund for the Republic, for which Rossiter edited a series on Communism that featured books by Theodore Draper, David A. Shannon, Daniel Aaron, and others outside of Communism but not on the right, allotted $4,000, and $500 for expenses, for the roster's political oddball to complete *The Moulding of Communists*. The money injected adrenaline, albeit not enough to put the project over the finish line. Like RAND, the fund had initially rejected a proposal for the book.[12] Rossiter, unconcerned by occupying a spot on Meyer's ideological enemies list, told the author that he hoped for him to take more time, not less. He also explained that although he served as editor his only power owed to persuasion rather than authority.[13] The Cornell professor, who could not have known what Meyer wanted to hear, told Meyer exactly what he wanted to hear.

Did the neophyte author *need* to hear that he should hurry up and submit to an editor's direction? Probably. He took advantage of the editorial lenience.

He secured a $500 advance in early summer of 1957 from a respectable publisher in Harcourt, Brace for a due date the following summer, which passed sans book.[14] The next year, he confessed a six-week diversion because of his involvement with protesting Nikita Khrushchev's historic visit, which Rossiter called "a crusher."[15] When the tolerant editor suggested changes, the intransigent author refused to make them.[16] Rossiter, not working for the publisher but overseeing the foundation-funded series, could, as he indicated, suggest but not command. Given that Meyer heard the latter as the former and the former not at all, Rossiter's title ultimately mattered little in terms of influencing the text.

The habitual crosser of deadlines completed the manuscript in March 1960. He promptly lobbied Harcourt, Brace that "in justice and equity you should agree to publication of the book in the Fall season."[17] Neither justice nor equity called for that. Meyer, not wishing to encroach upon the release date of another project, sought with chutzpah, after repeated delays at his end, for the publisher to rush the project without reference to other scheduled commitments.[18] The publisher confirmed a compromise release date, under the short-lived Harcourt, Brace & World moniker, for the first week of the new year. The post-Christmas date that might have offended another author more or less pleased this one.[19]

◆ ◆ ◆

"COMMUNIST THEORY is powerful not because it is true; most obviously it is not," *The Moulding of Communists* explained. "It is powerful because *it is believed.*"[20]

The book, written by one who believed for fourteen years, described how the party convinced members to pour faith into falsehoods.

The former director of the Chicago Workers School essentially wrote a book about brainwashing. *The Moulding of*

Moulding

Communists explained how the party conditioned members to react rather than think. Communism indoctrinated members into seeing events through the Marxist lens of class. Initiates adopted a scrambled ethics that confused utility with morality. Assignments, accepted without question or complaint and invariably regarded as crucial no matter how trivial, brought with them the scrutiny of higher-ups that instilled accountability. Painful criticism and self-criticism sessions implanted a commissar in the soul of every Communist. The party compelled members to regard every associate as a recruit and to shut out people, including relatives, who failed to eventually join. This created a social loop that reinforced the party line and ideological dogma. Called a "party," the CPUSA more closely resembled a cult.

Communism demands a total-politics mindset, the book explained, that leaves no space, for instance, for art-for-art's-sake sensibilities. Everything—entertainment, family life, education—becomes political through the Communist lens. Views on the aesthetics of paintings or literature independent of political content bring about corrective censure.[21] One's vacations, books sitting on shelves, pictures hanging upon walls, and casual utterances all become subject to monitoring.[22]

Meyer experienced in the 1930s what others had not yet experienced by the early 1960s. The mere accusation of racism, "male chauvinism," or "petty-bourgeois" class attitudes resulted in formal watching or reeducation.[23] The Communist learned to communicate verbally and never in a format that memorialized.[24] *The Moulding of Communists* imparts that one experiences life as a "sure, well-mapped place" under Communist discipline.[25] Comfort exists in certainty.

The most jarring passage involved Frank's don't-kill-the-messenger discussion with a secret party member who had propositioned a comrade to become more than that. Neither offended nor enticed, the comrade snitched. He worried about his admirer, holding a position of great sway outside of the party, bringing discredit upon Communism. Tasked with imposing not judgment but lifestyle change, Meyer gave the man forty-eight hours to stop his active homosexuality or face expulsion. He relayed that he need not take a bride, but the party preferred it.

Meyer reported, "What private hell he went through in the next two days I do not know; but when I met with him again forty-eight hours later, he had made his decision—for the Party. I knew him and worked with him over the next seven years. From every indication, he completely transformed his life. When I last saw him he was married to a very charming woman and was the father of two children, and he rose steadily in Party responsibility."[26]

Party people were not party people. They led rigid lives subject to the direction of others.

◆ ◆ ◆

WHILE PASSAGES that detail the sexual interests or alcoholism of members demanded anonymity, the author's blanket refusal to name names as he did before committees and courtrooms hurt *The Moulding of Communists*. A vagueness beyond the omission of names in anecdotes undermined the book as well. When and where did it all happen? What role did the author play? The reader for the most part did not know.

Rose Wilder Lane noticed this flaw while reviewing chapters during the previous decade. "I needn't tell you the practical values of doing what's called 'personalizing' to the presentation of an idea or a general statement," she wrote her protégé. "It sells 'em, it puts them across, it holds the reader's popping eyes to the page."[27] Meyer failed to heed the more experienced writer's advice. In his notes for Eudocio Ravines's *Yenan Way*, one of more than fifty books from which he transcribed quotations (curiously almost none of which found their way into his book), he even critically described the work as "somewhat colored in personal detail."[28] For reasons beyond a wish to avoid naming names, the new author regarded as a minus what others saw as plus.

Beyond the absence of the whos, whens, and wheres, the way he told the story proved a curious choice. Whereas Eugene Lyons's *Red Decade* offers the reader history, Czesław Miłosz's *Captive Mind* delivers philosophy, and Aleksandr Solzhenitsyn's *One Day in the Life of Ivan Denisovich* packages its message in literature, *The Moulding of Communists* presents anthropology. The tools Bronisław Malinowski's castoff never used to describe Pueblo Indians he wielded here on a much more mysterious tribe. This made the book unique. It also necessarily tailored it to a narrower audience.

That audience, right-wingers, looked quizzically upon the involvement of the Ford Foundation–bankrolled Fund for the Republic.[29] This, however, coaxed publications that might normally overlook such a release to review it.

Meyer joked of reviews so glowing that perhaps the least enthusiastic came from the *Chicago Tribune* right-winger Willard Edwards.[30] In a mixed review, *The New York Times* judged it a "perceptive," "in some ways important book" that contained "considerable insight."[31] Raymond Moley, occupying *Newsweek*'s coveted back page, advised, "It should be read by every American engaged in the Foreign Service, from the new President down."[32]

A decade earlier, it might have been. Still, even in 1961, an appetite for literature exposing the nature of the mysterious political sect existed. Sales exceeded four thousand in the first six months, and requests arrived to publish Spanish and Burmese editions.[33] Lecture invitations inundated Meyer. Over a two-week span in April, he spoke eight times between Maine and Arizona at the University of Chicago, University of Wisconsin, Bowdoin College, and beyond.[34]

The Mike Wallace Interview showcased such A-listers as Marilyn Monroe, Bob Cousy, and Sammy Davis Jr. Other episodes acted as a sort of *This Is Your Life* for Frank Meyer. James

Michener, the prep school teacher mesmerized by him three decades prior, V. K. Krishna Menon, the fixer who elected him student president at the London School of Economics, and Ralph de Toledano, the anti-Communist journalist who connected him to the fledgling conservative movement, all appeared on the program. Meyer's past concretely confronted his present during the taping to discuss *The Moulding of Communists*. The mischievous Noel Parmentel, "to play a trick on Frank," booked Gus Hall, leader of the Communist Party whom Meyer had helped send to prison, for the same day. "They hated each other," Parmentel, who was Wallace's producer, explained. "It wouldn't have been any fun otherwise."[35] The men, according to plan, passed awkwardly. "Mike," Hall joked to Wallace while being made up, "this is really the moulding of a Communist."[36]

The interview displayed a dazzling, dynamic guest. The format, neither white-page nor lecture stage but conversation, ideally suited him. "Your book, your very interesting book, *The Moulding of Communists*, tells a little bit about the moulding of Communists but not very much about the moulding of Frank Meyer," Wallace, echoing Lane's criticism, interjected. He queried Meyer about his background and beliefs but most of all his history. Was there not a contradiction between his nebulous Christianity and his exposure of former friends?

"Of course there was," he retorted in obliquely, and perhaps subconsciously, explaining why he kept names out. "Because, despite the fact that an overriding duty required that testimony for the safety of my country and my civilization, and for truth, nevertheless, there was—and I think anyone who forgets this in my situation would be very evil—there is a breach of a trust that was once established. It was a choice of evils and a choice of goods. This is perhaps what original sin means: that too often in our lives, or most of the time in our lives, we are not faced with simple choices between absolute good and absolute evil."[37]

The conversation that showcased his brilliance could not have hurt public interest. Midway through 1963, sales surpassed seven thousand copies.[38] A subsequent Conservative Book Club edition, among other special printings, awarded further royalties.[39] The book made no bestseller list but seemed a good fit for a steady-seller list. It did well.

✦ ✦ ✦

THE MOULDING OF COMMUNISTS closed a chapter that had begun at Oxford three decades earlier. The Communist had become a *cause célèbre* who attracted the likes of Clement Attlee and Bertrand Russell, an *enfant terrible* who terrorized the likes of H. G. Wells and Robert Maynard Hutchins, a lieutenant of the East German dictator, an intimate of postcolonial India's most powerful political puppeteer, a confidante of the leader of the CPUSA, and, ultimately, a pariah to former comrades on both sides of the Atlantic upon testifying in the longest trial to that point in U.S. history. He married a Communist, named his firstborn after a martyred comrade, and ushered his best friend into and then away from the party. Not-yet-famous men wanted him close, and beautiful women both famous and anonymous wanted him closer.

He strangely said none of this in his book. He transformed a captivating story into half how-to manual, half anthropology dissertation on the folkways of reds.

Communism infused his life with exhilaration, pain, purpose, and guilt. His labors in his remaining years ensured that what once had moulded him did not define him.

◄ 23 ►

Activist

"I read his book *The Moulding of Communists*," Bob Bauman, an early chairman of Young Americans for Freedom (YAF), recalled. "I read it probably contemporaneous with the early YAF years. I remember thinking at the time, 'Well, this is where Frank got all his mojo,' from all this back-biting and destruction and so on."

Young Americans for Freedom articulated a worldview in polar opposition to the Young Communist League. Purges, machinations, extremism, sectarianism, and confrontational protest nevertheless characterized both groups.

Did Frank Meyer Bolshevize conservatism?

"I think that's definitely a key to his advice," Bauman observed of Meyer's Communist background, "because when he would call at two in the morning or one in the morning, pending, say, some YAF meeting where there was a big fight that was going to go on, he would give out meticulous information, as he saw it, from the individual characters involved, how to deal with them, what they were like. He was like a psychiatrist almost in his analysis of opponents."[1]

One Yaffer, calling self-discipline the "mainstay of the Communist organization," informed Meyer of his wish for young conservatives to imitate whom they despised.[2] Meyer responded with not correction but encouragement, albeit in a way that omitted Communism and referred not to self-discipline but "self-education."³

In playing consigliere, speaking at chapter events, hosting visitors, and providing leadership from within his brood, Meyer played a major role in YAF. Shaping its foundational ideas proved his primary legacy to the group.

◆ ◆ ◆

"I WAS really busy at *National Review*," David Franke explained of the founding meeting in September 1960. "Doug [Caddy] did most of the organizing work. Bill offered the family estate in Sharon to hold it. When we were up there at Sharon, again, Doug was the behind-the-scenes organizer."⁴

Caddy and Franke the previous year had organized the Student Committee for the Loyalty Oath. Out of the remnants of that and failed efforts to place Barry Goldwater or Congressman Walter Judd on the 1960 Republican ticket, the pair, with the encouragement of the fundraiser extraordinaire and serial committee organizer Marvin Liebman and the former New Jersey governor Charles Edison, began harnessing the energy of young conservatives to create an outlet to deliver the electricity in the air. Given Franke's employment with *National Review*, the magazine inevitably became involved.

About ninety students convened at the Buckley family's home, Great Elm, in Sharon, Connecticut, the weekend after Labor Day of 1960. "Everybody else was like me," Carol Dawson, the college chairman of Youth for Nixon, maintained. "They had their mind on changing the world."⁵

The gathering conveniently followed a quarterly *National Review* editorial conference. So it was natural that many figures associated with the magazine attended. Accounts include Meyer as present.⁶ Some of the established adults delivered formal talks but, by design, let the kids sort out the type and tenor of their organization.[7]

Finding American Youth for Freedom wanting, Jameson Campaigne Jr. suggested the more "euphonious" Young Americans for Freedom.[8] The group bandied about Young Conservatives of America and other such names. Significantly, by a vote of 44 to 40, they chose Young Americans for Freedom.[9] They were not Young Americans for Order or Young Americans for Virtue. They latched onto the word identified with Meyer, the libertarianish wing of the conservative movement, and *National Review*.

Dawson, Franke, and some others sat on a committee tasked with writing a statement. M. Stanton Evans, one of the oldest of the young Americans, arrived in Sharon with a succinct manifesto composed on the plane from Indianapolis.

"When he arrived Carol Dawson and I were in charge of drafting a statement of principles," Franke recalled. "Stan gave us what he had written. We just looked at each other and said, 'This is it.'"[10]

More so than even the credenda in the inaugural *National Review* issue, the Sharon Statement approached a Nicene Creed for conservatives. Students for a Democratic Society imitators released a Port Huron Statement twenty-one months later. Its running seventy times longer than the 368-word Sharon Statement guaranteed that it would be less read than referred to. Conservatives *read* the Sharon Statement. They believed it, too. The document, Buckley's biographer John Judis judged, "expressed *National Review*'s and Frank Meyer's attempt to fuse traditionalism, libertarianism, and anticommunism."[11]

Lee Edwards, the oldest of the young Americans in attendance, said, "I know [Meyer] is listed as being there but I cannot recall him at all, which is sort of strange, isn't it? You would think that something like that, he would very much be in the middle of it."[12] Dawson similarly wondered, "He may have been at Sharon. I don't know."[13] Campaigne reckoned, "I didn't think he was there."[14]

Conspicuous in his inconspicuousness or present in his absence, Meyer applied the correct touch—the soft touch or none at all—to the proceedings. The Sharon cipher's prized recruit, Evans, named weeks later as the youngest editor of a major city daily in the country, acted as Meyer's mouthpiece. Bread crumbs leading from Evans back to Meyer litter the trail of the former's career, with none appearing so obvious as the ones dropped at Great Elm.

The Notre Dame professor Gerhart Niemeyer cited the document as a "point of rupture" between himself and an ideologized right.[15] Thirteen days after Sharon's issuance, he submitted a rebuttal, the delay on whose publication decision Buckley blamed partly on Meyer, who had "telephoned 83 times" for the manuscript, for holding it.[16] Ultimately, Meyer urged a sympatico Buckley to reject it.[17]

The Sharon Statement's first and foremost truth enunciated the free will of the *individual*, significantly using that word embraced by Meyer. The document enumerated government's three rightful functions as preserving internal order, defending against external threats, and administering justice. It articulated victory rather than coexistence with the Soviet Union. It applied a two-pronged test to foreign policy of serving both the national interest and the end of justice.[18]

Evans left ink on paper. Meyer scattered fingerprints all over it.

He increasingly scattered fingerprints all over the rapidly expanding movement.

◆ ◆ ◆

"DAN MAHONEY just told me that we would be meeting that night at the Forrest Hills Inn for dinner," Serf Maltese recalled of a 1961 Queens gathering. "I know Kieran O'Doherty was there. I was there. Frank Meyer was there already when I arrived."[19]

They met to create a vehicle for conservatives in New York politics. The participants included disaffected Republicans, a Democrat in Maltese, and an ex-Communist fifteen years removed from the party apparatus. That night they dreamed the impossible dream.

By the early 1960s, New York Republicans laid claim to the governor's office, a U.S. Senate seat, just shy of half of the U.S. House delegation, and firm control over both legislative chambers. Conservatives saw little to cheer about. Spending in Albany dramatically increased despite Republican control. Senator Jacob Javits's reflexively liberal votes earned him the nickname of "Mr. ADA"—meaning that he voted the way Americans for Democratic Action wanted him to. Nelson Rockefeller, a veteran of the Roosevelt, Truman, and Eisenhower administrations, looked like a solid bet to take the party in an even more MeToo Republican direction than had Ike. The previous year, he had brokered the Treaty of Fifth Avenue, which forced moderate and liberal positions on presidential nominee Richard Nixon in tacit exchange for the New York governor's support.

With Republicans like these, they reasoned, who needed Democrats?

A Conservative Party, an idea explored by William F. Buckley Jr., the industrialist Gerrish Milliken, and others in early 1957, now existed because of its prime movers: Dan Mahoney, a bespectacled attorney, and his brother-in-law, fellow lawyer, and best friend Kieran O'Doherty.[20] They needed more established conservatives to back it. Enter Frank Meyer.

"His name was already accepted," Maltese noted. "He had immediate entrée to these clubs."[21] Meyer served as a reliable conduit to Buckley, whose story soon dovetailed with the party's. Unlike YAF's reliance on distilled Meyer for the Sharon Statement, the party went straight to the source for its Declaration of Principles.

The opening lines proclaimed "adherence to our original Constitutional principles by abolishing the interventions of government in affairs which are not rightly its concern, and especially by reversing the flow of power to the Federal government." It called for a restoration of "fiscal sanity" to lower taxes, unemployment, and inflation through "the creative powers of private capitalism." It singled out special privileges enjoyed by labor unions in closed-shop states, and promised "an unceasing vigilance against the undue concentration of power in any faction of our society, governmental or private." The document Meyer wrote endorsed victory over coexistence with Communism and "the restoration of this nation's autonomous control over its foreign policy in furtherance of its just national interests."[22]

The outer-borough Catholic conservatives primarily organizing the party encountered velvet ropes and obstacles, the most significant of which came from a Republican Party that grasped the challenge to its monopoly over right-of-center voters. Rockefeller likened conservatives to "cattle that aren't going anywhere." Javits called the upstarts "freakish," "out of step with the twentieth century," and "crackpot." The state GOP's executive committee resolved that no Republican could simultaneously become a member of a "splinter" party.[23]

The puppy outfit unleashed its pit bull.

"The Rockefeller-dominated State Committee of the Republican Party of New York has issued a remarkable resolution attacking a 'few'—unnamed—'individuals,'" Meyer wrote in a press release. "While obviously directed at the Conservative Party of New York, it never mentions us by name. But the resolution is permeated by an atmosphere of panic at the organizational success of the Conservative Party, and it obviously reflects the reports of our progress which are pouring into Rockefeller's headquarters. The Republican State Committee professes to be alarmed, oddly enough, by 'a few individuals who . . . are seeking to create a splinter party.'"

Meyer accused "an entrenched liberal cabal, whose members are little more than carbon copies of the [Robert] Wagners, [Herbert] Lehmans, and Eleanor Roosevelts who control the New York Democratic Party," of denying conservatives a voice on Election Day.[24]

He continued along this line in *National Review*, in whose pages he promoted the fledgling party.

Four "Principles and Heresies" columns mentioned the Conservative Party in 1962.[25] In the July 3 issue, he justified the creation of the Conservative Party by noting the corrupt convention system, absence of a primary system, and dispro-portionate power held by a few liberal GOP bigwigs that all served to mute the voices of rank-and-file Republicans. He pointed to Empire State splinter parties on the left, such as the eighteen-year-old Liberal Party, that pushed not only Democrats further left but the Republican Party, too.

"The Republican Party deserves conservative loyalty only to the degree that it is conservative," he reasoned. "The issue is simple and clear: a Republican Party conceived in the image of Taft, Knowland and Goldwater, deserves conservative loy-alty; a Republican Party conceived in the image of Rockefeller and Javits, Romney and Nixon, has no more claims upon that loyalty than the Democratic Party of Roosevelt, Stevenson and Kennedy."[26]

New York's undue influence motivated the conservatives. The Empire State boasted forty-five electoral votes, thirteen more than California or Pennsylvania—the second and third most populous states—in 1962. Every election of the twen-tieth century until that point, save for 1924 and the most recent one, had a New Yorker on one of the top two slates. Every election from 1928 through 1956 saw one of the two major parties nominate a presidential candidate who called New York home, which even the nomadic Dwight Eisen-hower sensibly did after serving as the president of Colum-bia University. Politically, economically, and even culturally, New York mattered more in 1962 than it did in 1972, 1982, and beyond.

✦ ✦ ✦

IN THE FOOTSTEPS of a YAF rally at Madison Square Garden earlier in 1962, the party followed by gathering there on October 22.

Speakers included the gubernatorial nominee David Jaquith, the senatorial candidate O'Doherty, Buckley, and Meyer. Chartered buses carried attendees from Buffalo, Syracuse, and Rochester. Unlike other political groups who hired that hall, the Conservative Party charged upwards of $2 for a ticket—and told the press about it.[27]

Five months earlier in the historic arena, Marilyn Monroe had upstaged the president on his birthday. At the Conservative Party coming-out party, the president upstaged them.

At 7:00 p.m., John F. Kennedy announced to a stunned nation the Soviet construction of missile sites in Cuba: "[T]he purpose of these bases can be none other than to provide a nuclear strike capability against the Western hemisphere."[28] Freaked-out Americans confronted the possibility of nuclear missiles pointed at them from ninety miles south of Key West by a Russian who promised to "bury" them.

Meyer offered a simple message: "Invade Cuba!"[29] Amid the brass band and bunting, he joined in the festivities by parodying the Republican leader of the state senate who did so much to impede the Conservative Party.[30] He mainly impressed on the big stage by addressing the big issue. Indeed, months before this international crisis Meyer had called for the forcible removal of Fidel Castro by Cuban patriots or American Marines.[31]

"I never saw and heard you more dynamic and stimulating than you were that night," a well-wisher wrote. "All in all it was a great rally I thought—seemed almost miraculous to me."[32]

The Cuban Missile Crisis demanded, even from a New York party, a response. Mahoney turned to the party's international affairs committee chairman. "It is time for the United States to demonstrate its adherence to the Monroe Doctrine, and its wholehearted support of the Cuban exile movement," Meyer stated in a party press release. "Senator [Gordon] Allott's proposal offers a splendid opportunity for the United States to accomplish these aims, and we call for its speedy adoption by the Kennedy Administration." The proposal advocated establishing a provisional Cuban government at Guantanamo Bay.[33] Meyer that year appeared on New York's WPIX-TV and at the Town Hall in Manhattan for the "Cuba: A Conservative Critique" forum.[34]

The party's victory in 1962 came not through any candidate's victory—its gubernatorial nominee David Jaquith outran the rest of the slate at 2.5 percent of the vote—but by its mere appearance, after surmounting GOP legal challenges and other shenanigans, on every ballot.

Meyer played a minor yet crucial role in another moral victory. Mahoney prodded Meyer to gauge Buckley's interest in running for New York City mayor. Frank, with the help of a more intuitive Elsie, reported back that a possibility existed, if played right, to coax the editor. This turned into a godsend for both candidate and party.[35] During 1965's memorable race, Buckley showcased his wit in the global media capital. When asked of his plans upon winning, he famously answered, "Demand a recount."[36]

National Review's editor-in-chief morphed from conservative gadfly to multimedia celebrity during his mayoral campaign. He held no chance of winning and a solid chance of denying the Republican victory, so the press treated him better than it ever did. "He knew he couldn't win, but he was interested in honing his own ideas on municipal problems as opposed to national and international problems," his brother Jim Buckley reflected. "So it was fun for him, and instructive for him."[37]

Events subsequently proved it instructive for Jim Buckley, too.

✦ ✦ ✦

"I HAD EXPECTED, since I knew a little about him, that he would be more ideological, making such an abrupt shift from being a Communist to being a conservative," Serf Maltese recalled. Instead, he found Meyer to be interested in the organizational aspects of their project, personable, and attentive.[38]

Meyer led the party's international affairs committee, later served as its vice chairman, presided over its platform committee, and even stood as a delegate nominee to the state's 1967 constitutional convention.[39] He spoke to local groups. He wrote press releases. "He gave us contacts," Maltese recalls. "He had a rolodex of names—he gave Dan [Mahoney] names. He would write Dan a short note saying, 'I met an old friend Charlie Brown. He might be good for a donation,' or 'He was very interested in Taft or Goldwater.'"[40]

Meyer, Maltese concluded, proved "almost indispensable in the early days of the party."[41]

◄ 24 ►

Birchers

I n the fall of 1961, Willmoore Kendall met with Edwin
Walker, who that year had become the only American
general during the twentieth century to resign his commission. Walker sought his party's nomination for governor
in Texas. Kendall sought a speechwriter position.[1] Like Kendall, he remained a conservative Democrat. He struck Kendall
as unlike himself in one trait that the academic valued most
even as he resembled him in another trait Kendall refused to
acknowledge.

"Walker, let me tell you, is a) a real egomaniac, and b) intellectually one of the stupidest men I've ever tried to discuss
anything serious with," Kendall wrote his friend in Woodstock. "He neither speaks nor understands English. And, in
any case, he's got it seems to impose his personality on every
sentence he gets from his speech-writers. But the worst of all,
of course, is that in him that Medford [Evans] feeds, i.e., the
total fascination with the idea that a conspiracy reaching in
mysterious ways into everything=he's not going to yield on
that and, of course, can't do business with us until he does."[2]

A culture clash existed between the men who composed
National Review and those of the conspiratorial right. The professor just could not see conspiracy theorists as something

other than a punch line—and he probably ranked as the most populist of the editors. The fantasies struck as too stupid to even humor. The men touting them did not wear dunce caps.

Reasoning with highly intelligent people who believed falsehoods to be the truth makes for a frustrating conversation. The Bircher Medford Evans had earned a Ph.D. from Yale and worked on the Manhattan Project. His name's presence on the masthead of *American Opinion* ensured that it appeared less within *National Review*. The previous year, the University of Illinois professor Revilo Oliver, who had translated a book from Sanskrit and knew eleven other languages, received a letter from Buckley indicating that his "position," a polite way of saying his anti-Semitic delusions, ran too far astray from *National Review*. Oliver, a founding father of the John Birch Society (JBS), appeared in an anti-Semitic publication, *Common Sense*, which Buckley characterized as setting up his unwitting colleagues for unseemly associations. *NR*'s rule of exclusion applied, he said, not just to *The American Mercury* but to any anti-Semitic publication.[3]

So characteristics other than intelligence—Prudence? Discipline? Wisdom?—were then crucially lacking in the proponents of the far-fetched ideas that nevertheless fetched a following. The conspiracy theory's logic-puzzle structure, its attempt to systematize scattered information, and the ego boost it provided the elect seeing the truth glimpsed by few others stand among the reasons that ideas so fundamentally dim attracted minds so luminous.

Breaks from Oliver, Kendall's close friend and a visitor to Woodstock, and from M. Stanton Evans's father demonstrated how pain accompanied the extrication of the right from its fringe. Friendships ended. Bitterness ensued. No congratulatory note awaited Buckley from his fashionable critics for jettisoning his uncouth allies. Only a sadist could enjoy the process. Even among men living for the fight, few wanted to anathematize. The central players knew that they must anathematize lest their burgeoning movement become

anathematized. They took the Aristotelian line that "piety requires us to honour truth above our friends."[4]

✦ ✦ ✦

A DRESS REHEARSAL occurred in 1959. Then, Buckley
decreed that no person appearing on *The American Mercury*'s masthead shall appear on *National Review*'s. This
pushed Douglas MacArthur's former chief of intelligence
Charles Willoughby, a minor contributor, outside of *NR*'s
orbit. The decision, quietly executed by Buckley but publicized by a stung Russell Maguire in *The American Mercury*,
hurt the latter publication much more than the former.[5]
The problem in 1959 involved not countenancing even a
linkage to antisemitism, which sometimes manifests itself
through wild conspiracy theories; in 1961, it involved not
countenancing wild conspiracy theories, which sometimes
include antisemitism.

Conspiracy theories flowed through a multitude of spig-
ots. A reservoir supplying many of them formed in 1958.
Robert Welch addressed twelve men of rank over two days
in Indianapolis, which, by the end of the December weekend,
resulted in an organization named after the first American
killed by Communists during the Cold War.

The explosive growth of the John Birch Society, which
spawned within a few years of its founding something approaching one hundred thousand paid members, JBS bookstores dotting the map, and highway billboards pleading
to "Impeach Earl Warren," challenged the hegemony of
National Review. Its anti-Birch crusade—initially an anti-
Welch crusade—mainly stemmed from an aversion to anti-
intellectualism, demagoguery, and conspiracy theories.
The crusaders lied to themselves when they dismissed rivalry, petty jealousy, and a controlling impulse as among
their motivations.

By early 1961, rumors flew that *National Review* prepared to condemn the John Birch Society. Calls and letters overwhelmingly opposed such a decision.[6]

The editors did not debate whether to criticize Welch. They disagreed on how and when to criticize the anti-Communist confectioner. They all found his conspiracy theories off the wall and injurious to their cause. They disagreed on how best to refute his more bizarre claims to prevent them from winning more adherents. Hawks and doves existed on the question of criticizing Welch. But nobody questioned the question. The internal debate involved the intensity, tone, and timing. Burnham, Buckley, Meyer, Kendall, Bozell, and Rusher all regarded Welch as a pariah and unanimously agreed on the need to distance the magazine from him. They disagreed on how.

The main players who were not abroad discussed the issue at an Agony held on March 28.

Rusher, the least enthusiastic about the venture, urged patience. In a memo summarizing his points from the Agony, he urged the editors to allow the society to wither on its own. He saw a death in progress. He petitioned the editors to do "the plainly necessary minimum." The publisher dealt with donors and subscribers in his vocation and activists in his avocation. He worried that in taking stands pleasing to a thankless left but repulsive to the right *National Review* would "inadvertently talk itself into a colorful, followerless eccentricity, or (almost as bad) into the only other thing left: bondage to the main line of the Republican Party." He characterized the editors as embodying a who-cares attitude toward the "simplistic Right," charging that "NR tends not to care quite enough." He advised a brief editorial praising the society but condemning the views of its leader and calling on the group to disclaim conspiracy theories.[7]

"I am not talking about subscriptions or withdrawal of financial support," he insisted of the expected fallout. "As it happens, both [Jim] McFadden and I believe that cancellations may well reach into the low thousands if Welch decrees them; and as for financial support, the controversy has already brought phone calls from (for instance) two individual members of the Milliken family, which annually furnishes, in one form or another, backing equal to about 40% of the operating deficit we anticipate for this calendar year. But I waive all such considerations: NR's survival is not at stake."[8]

Neither Rusher nor Meyer wished to pig-pile onto the JBS. They wished to call out their incorrect beliefs as they protected their civil liberties, which their enemies inside and outside the government infringed upon. Beating up the group had become *de rigueur*.

The Santa Barbara News-Press received a 1962 Pulitzer Prize for its unflattering editorials on the group.[9] Senator Stephen Young of Ohio urged the elimination of its tax-exempt status.[10] John Kennedy obliquely condemned the JBS, and a friend in the Senate later urged the president to "keep the villain alive and kicking for a year from now" to improve his reelection chances.[11] In 1961, California's Governor Pat Brown called for an investigation by his attorney general, who dismissed the JBS as harmless. The California Senate Subcommittee on Un-American Activities took up the governor's charge and investigated the group for two years.[12] FBI agents and informers, almost from the beginning, watched the JBS. J. Edgar Hoover also relied on a private organization, the Anti-Defamation League, to spy on it. The league's agents joined white supremacist organizations posing as Birchers, ran credit reports on members, and collected license plate numbers at events. They turned over embarrassing information to the press and Hoover.[13]

Neither Rusher nor Meyer knew much of this. They sensed it all.

Meyer understood the rationale of Rusher's arguments. And he agreed with Rusher on the wisdom of a course that did the least to alienate JBS members. He sought also to affirm their civil liberties. He nevertheless told Buckley in a memo copied to the other editors, "Welch's own extravagances are of such a nature that the conservative movement, and in particular NR, must in one way or another disassociate itself from them." In contrast to Rusher's case for a small editorial, Meyer conveyed that "we need considerable space."

"I should add that I do recognize extreme difficulties that any action on our part will create with Welch and his supporters," he wrote, "and some of our readers and contributors; but there seems to me to be involved here a responsibility both morally and politically to which we have to face up, in the role we have acquired (not self-sought but ours by the nature of the present situation of conservatism in America) of the conscience of American conservatism. The other side of the matter, however, must not be lost sight of—that we have to continue to exist and exert influence—and therefore, whatever we do must be carefully thought out so that we do the most good and the least harm."[14]

Buckley followed Meyer's counsel. He wrote an article just over two magazine pages long that took pains not to alienate. Its form, presented as Buckley answering questions sent to him, depicted the magazine as reluctantly dragged into the fray. Therein, he noted his nearly decade-long acquaintance with Welch, his subject's past financial support for *National Review*, and the fact that they had twice spoken from the same platform. To ensure that his point did not fall on blind eyes, Buckley defended the group's civil rights, dismissed the most fantastic of the criticisms against it, and mentioned Welch's likeability, courage, and commitment. He then announced profound differences. He specifically cited Welch's privately circulating book that depicted Dwight Eisenhower as a conscious agent of the Communist conspiracy as one such never-the-twain-shall-meet disagreement. Welch's contention that Communists controlled the U.S. government, too, received categorical rejection. If things truly were that bad, Buckley reasoned, then best to abandon persuasion and deploy force.[15]

A "Principles and Heresies" column followed. Meyer, without mentioning Welch or the society he led, stressed the importance of distinguishing between liberalism and Communism. "It must be understood that Liberalism weakens the fiber of society, but that Liberals are not, as are Communists, conscious enemies, conspiratorially organized for the conquest of world power," he wrote. "They must be fought in different ways: Communists with every resource both of the individual and of voluntary associations of individuals and of the state; Liberals by the methods of education, political organization and action."[16]

The cautious nature of "The Uproar" caused no uproar. Welch conveyed to Buckley that he regarded his article as honorable.[17] In *American Opinion*, one found not denunciations of Buckley but the writings of one of his featured columnists, the man with whom he had cofounded the magazine, and others on *NR*'s masthead. The article bylines in the November 1961 issue, for instance, all featured names—Medford Evans, E. Merrill Root, Revilo Oliver, Willi Schlamm, Russell Kirk—familiar to *NR* readers.[18] *American Opinion*'s committee of advisors, far from listing cranks and haters, continued to include some of the most accomplished Americans: the actor Adolphe Menjou, the economist Ludwig von Mises, the president of Sunoco J. Howard Pew, the former New Jersey governor Charles Edison, the retired general A. C. Wedemeyer, and the former dean of Notre Dame Law School Clarence Manion.

Buckley's and Meyer's pieces articulated clear areas of disagreement between two of the most powerful forces on the American right. No fair-minded reader could come away confusing one for the other. Still, the rather muted tone of Buckley's article and the vagueness of Meyer's failed to satisfy desires for a full-throated denunciation.

◆ ◆ ◆

WHEN *National Review* finally took on the John Birch Society in a manner pleasing to the group's critics in early 1962, it did so strategically. Volunteering caveats regarding the decency of its rank and file and the nobility of its anti-Communist aims, a lengthy piece, without a byline, that spoke for the magazine eviscerated Welch through his own words. It sought to pry good people from a deluded leader rather than denounce a diverse lot wholesale. The piece noted Welch's claims that the U.S. government colluded with Fidel Castro on the Bay of Pigs Invasion to elevate the dictator's standing, that the CIA worked for the Communists, that Eisenhower knowingly served the Communist conspiracy for all of his adult life, and that the Kremlin orchestrated 1956's Poznań June and the Hungarian Uprising for its own purposes.[19]

"We have no doubt Mr. Welch himself honestly believes that all these people are Communists—that mitigates his moral culpability," the piece explained. "But those of us who disagree are not excused if, by our silence, we egg him on."[20]

Cancel-my-subscription letters followed.

"I first heard of *National Review* through the John Birch Society," wrote Mrs. Kenneth L. Myers of Wichita. "Your below-the-belt in *NR*'s present issue is the last I want to hear, and worse, finance. Cancel my subscription effective today. The refund due me will be used for a gift subscription to *American Opinion*."[21]

The piece failed to persuade the unpersuadable.

Meyer urged Buckley to avoid creating "the impression that we are carrying on a continuing attack," and suggested that *NR* issue bland refutations of their falsehoods without highlighting their specific origins. "I think we can carry on a serious educational program on the major Welchite fallacies without naming Welch or Birch (or, for that matter, [Dan Smoot] or Walker) at all," he advised. Here he followed his own counsel.[22]

Meyer tried a softer, more oblique approach in "Principles and Heresies" two months after Buckley's excoriation. Mentioning neither Welch nor the JBS, he referred unmistakably to both and others past the fringes in writing that "at the margin, the idea of conspiracy has so passionately seized the imagination of some that they are not content with the hideous existence of the actual, documentable, powerfully functioning Communist conspiracy, but must . . . conjure up still deeper, more devilish conspiracies, hatched in the murky regions of the intellectual underworld—conspiracies encompassing Communists, international bankers, Freemasons, Jews, Catholics, and Heaven knows whom else, all directed by some mysterious 'They,' some arcane 'Invisible Government.'"[23]

By the time of the publication of that piece, letters, most of them critical, had flooded the magazine. New senior editor William Rickenbacker reported, two months after the release of the unsigned, Buckley-penned editorial, receipt of 1,065 letters that included one hundred donors and 113 correspondents who admitted JBS membership. Canceled subscriptions, actual and threatened, along with vows to not renew, amounted to 431. Just forty wrote in support. Rickenbacker counted 217 as reflecting "sober disagreement." Nearly two hundred questioned the motives of Buckley. Epistles portraying *NR* as playing into the hands of the Communists or acting unpatriotically or as something other than conservative numbered 359. "The feeling of personal allegiance to Welch, often expressed by equating our action with that of Judas Iscariot," Rickenbacker noted, "was astonishingly high, perhaps 10 percent—quite a number to confuse the Messiah with a fudge king."[24]

Homeschool

T he aim of education should be to pass on to the young the tradition of the culture—that which man has achieved—that it shall not be lost, and so that upon it we may move a little to a higher point," Frank Meyer wrote John Chamberlain shortly after the birth of his second son, Eugene. "It has taken great effort and sacrifice to achieve that small bit we know. In a minor way, and subject to the limitations of the young, it has to be transmitted at whatever cost in sweat to them."

The "totalitarian implications" of the revolution in educating children jarred him. He lamented the "gobbledygook" imparted because teachers no longer studied the subjects that they taught and presented themselves as partners facilitating learning rather than classroom authorities transmitting established methods and truths.[1] He sounded like Robert Maynard Hutchins, the great books enthusiast whom he had lambasted at the University of Chicago years earlier.

Raising two children made those beliefs personal. The state's involvement amplified the libertarian's passion. Perhaps no other issue, even Communism, ignited Meyer as education did. He decided to live his convictions by pursuing a path highly unusual then and burdensome in any age.

Despite paying taxes to support public education for strangers' children, the Meyers could not entrust the cultivation of the most precious fruits of their union to the state. While Elsie prevailed upon her husband to send John to kindergarten, after that they homeschooled through high school.[2]

◆ ◆ ◆

LEARNING started early, even if school started late.

For the early years of childhood, John and Gene encountered many classic books, including A. A. Milne's *Now We Are Six* and *When We Were Very Young*, Rudyard Kipling's *Just So Stories*, and Jean de Brunhoff's *Story of Babar*. As the boys grew, the parents exposed them to *Wild Animals I Have Known*, *Five Children and It*, *Heidi*, *Black Beauty*, *The Peterkin Papers*, *The Black Fox of Lorne*, and others.[3] Hardbacks of G. A. Henty's tales of historical fiction heavily populated the home's shelves. Young Gene became fascinated by Laura Ingalls Wilder's *Little House on the Prairie* novels.[4] The patriarch read *The Lord of The Rings* to Elsie and Gene, and boasted to its author of his elder son having read the trilogy dozens of times. "You, and certainly your son, may perhaps forgive me if I say that the heaviest of my contracts is for a further book about the world of The Lord of the Rings,"[5] J. R. R. Tolkien explained in begging off a book review for Meyer.

School hours, unlike any other school in Ulster County, started around when the opening bell rang in classrooms in Tahiti.

"I was probably waking up at one in the afternoon, something like that, twelve or one," Gene remembered. "I would sort of have assignments, three subjects a day. I would do most of it during the day, maybe until some of the later stages of high school—or the equivalent of high school. I still remember when I was preparing for the SATs—I was not as academically inclined as my brother—on Christmas night I went up to my room and took the practice exams. I was actually enjoying that part. I had very few exams; we didn't do a lot in that way. I would read things, learn things, be asked about them."[6]

The search for the right books required consultation with experts among Frank's acquaintances and trips to bookstores beyond Woodstock. He rejected the spelling books he encountered before finding a 1905 Kansas Board of Education publication in the basement of a Barnes & Noble. Modern arithmetic texts similarly repelled him, so he dug up his old textbook from his days as a student to use now as a teacher.[7] The Meyers accepted Revilo Oliver's offer to send beginner Latin books.[8] His Balliol friend Allan Hoey, then teaching languages at the Hotchkiss School, recommended *A New Organization for Geometry* and Oxford University Press's *Essential Latin* and mailed a copy of *The Latin Key to Better English*.[9] Meyer talked history books with Rose Wilder Lane.[10]

The heavier share of the faculty's division of labor fell on Mrs. Meyer. One of the school's two students judged her to be the superior teacher, at least for the early grades.[11] She had obtained a Missouri teaching certification during the 1930s, so her educational background extended beyond the subjects taught to pedagogy.[12] Both teachers excelled in certain ways.

"My mother started with geography," John recalled. "My father took it over. We had real subjects, no social studies. If we called it social studies, we were executed on the spot—history, of course." Mrs. Meyer taught arithmetic but passed the baton to her husband for algebra, which, she said, made her head spin. With her literature background at Radcliffe, Elsie naturally taught English. Her husband mainly taught Latin and science. They hired a French tutor, who died before he could teach Gene. Tutors also helped with math and science.[13]

While Mr. Meyer took a somewhat dismissive attitude toward the invariable classroom science experiments that his schoolhouse could never replicate, he did not solely rely on texts.[14] The Meyers erected an amateur weather station complete with "anemometer, rain gauge, barometer, minimum-maximum thermometer, wind vane" that allowed the boys to learn science in a practical sense, even though John remembers it as more hobby than assignment.[15]

Neither homeschool nor home devoted much time to religious instruction. Frank believed in the "Triune God," natural law, the incarnation, and the resurrection. "I accept the authority of Revelation in all matters where reason cannot function," the former rhapsodist to Satan told an inquiring frater studying for Catholic orders.[16] The children said nightly prayers in their early years, and the family read from the Bible on Christmas Eve. The Nothingarian Christians did not attend church.[17] Education was their temple and books their sacrament.

"An awful lot of the teaching was assigning reading," John reflected. "But there was systematic oversight. I would go in every day and I would have to answer questions. The Latin was painful. There was no way of hiding in the class."[18]

✦ ✦ ✦

THERE was hiding in Woodstock. Neither Roger Phelps nor Tad Crawford regarded the Meyer boys as on the radar of the town's other children. The location contributed to the social isolation. So too did the decision to keep the children out of school.

"The first thing I remember was chess boards out, and people were playing chess," Phelps explained of his first close encounter of the Meyer kind. "So I played; so I joined. We had these round-robins. The boys, the dad played, sometimes they would have a visiting friend come and they would have *invited* that person, and everybody was playing chess."

Roger, the son of his family friend Robert Phelps and the artist Rosemarie Beck, bonded with the boys over the game. They played baseball and football in a field near the Meyer house. But they mostly played games of an intellectual nature—*Tri-Tactics*, *Diplomacy*, and *L'Attaque*—with the adults included in these indoor, intellectual competitions.[19]

Chess similarly drew Tad Crawford. He visited about every other day in the summer and spent some Thanksgivings with the family. With his own parents splitting, Crawford found in the Meyers a model of an intact family and passport to "a very special grownup world" once the games ended and the conversations began. Crawford recalled Elsie's "Oh, really" exasperation when Frank tossed salt over his shoulder for luck at the dinner table. The patriarch came across as serious-minded but with a sense of humor and the matriarch as kind. "John and his mother took the kind of rational viewpoint," he observed. "Gene and his father were more mercurial and, in a way, you might say, outgoing."[20]

The family, sometimes after visitors such as Roger or Tad departed, played bridge. "We played things like *D-Day*, *Waterloo*, the original Avalon Hill *Tactics II*, *Gettysburg*," John recalled. "The advantage of the wargames was we were even. In chess, after a little while, we weren't even."[21]

Phelps and Crawford knew the patriarch as the easiest checkmate. Phelps recalled occasionally beating John, a superior player, only because he became flustered when distracted. John, Gene, and Frank belonged to King's Knight Chess Club in nearby Kingston, and later they joined the Manhattan Chess Club for more competitive play in periodic treks to Gotham.[22]

The trio played in many of the same tournaments. Chess was one of the few activities that they did together outside of the house. They traveled to tournaments in New York, Baltimore, Atlanta, and beyond. Frank became a regional director of the U.S. Chess Federation.[23] Elsie harried various editors at *The New York Times* through a nearly decade-long campaign of hectoring letters, often intemperate and occasionally wrong, about chess coverage, of which she wanted more and in the sports section.[24]

Frank peaked at a 1649 rating.[25] But at age twelve Gene already boasted a rating one hundred points higher. The boy drew with Pal Benko, winner of the 1964 U.S. Open Chess Championship, earlier that year. Before he turned nineteen, John became one of 122 chess masters in the United States.[26] Both boys entered the headlines in 1964 by John's victory in the U.S. junior chess championship and Gene's first-place finish in the under-thirteen U.S. chess championship at the same event.[27] *The New York Times*'s chess column periodically analyzed their matches move by move.[28]

Elsie enjoyed the all-male Meyer chess excursions because they allowed her to relax without the demands of her children or husband. She tended a garden and a menagerie of animals. Her habit of feeding raccoons in her kitchen prompted the moniker "Jane Goodall of Ohayo Mountain" from a friend.[29] The family cycled through two dogs. Through her husband, the wife became habituated to cats, of which they kept three or so at any one time. She grew so close to one feline, nursed back to health only for a vehicle to run over it, that she memorialized it with a grave marker on the property.[30]

◆ ◆ ◆

ROGER PHELPS visited the Meyer home once or twice a week. He enjoyed a rare glimpse into ordinary ongoings of extraordinary people. He did not see the Meyers after they had prepared to host friends. He saw them the way Larry Mondello saw the Cleavers, albeit if Barbara Billingsley and Hugh Beaumont did not come straight from hair, makeup, and wardrobe into a spotless home. Neither Crawford nor Phelps saw them as terribly out of the ordinary; ordinary struck as out of the ordinary in Woodstock.

He called her "baby," Phelps recalled, as in "Baby, will you please tell that jackass to get off the phone?" She ran interference for him to clear phone lines or shoo unwanted visitors. He mainly left the children to their own devices until noise took him away from his: "He would come to the foot of the stairs and say, 'It's pretty loud up there' or 'Just cut this out now.'"[31]

The picture of a four- or five-day unshaven, chain-smoking patriarch in a bathrobe stuck out for Phelps.

"I don't think I ever saw him walk out of that house," he explained. "I don't think I saw him outdoors ever."[32]

Frank received secretarial help a few days a week. The family employed a woman to pick up groceries and perform scattered domestic chores. Occasionally Frank employed a local cab driver to chauffeur him to airports and distant trips.[33] These tasks otherwise fell to Elsie.

"Very devoted to him, very," Phelps noted. "He was a little bit of a tyrant, kind of a friendly tyrant. He wasn't a mean person to her. He expected things his way."

She ran the house, but he directed her. This extended to their joint project to facilitate balance among the professoriate.

◆ ◆ ◆

"FRANK MEYER has gone to work like a demon to get me into a school near him (Bowdoin or Amherst or one of the OK eastern beaneries)," Guy Davenport noted in early 1963. "He has more contacts than fokes in the Academy."[34]

The examples of Davenport, a liberal who was encountering troubles at Haverford that he believed were related to his *NR* work; Jeffrey Hart, who was forced from Columbia for his right-wing outlook; and Willmoore Kendall, who had departed Yale partly due to politics all affirmed to *National Review* the wisdom of counteracting academia's crawl into a bigoted institution where no conservatives need apply.

The failed academic in the ranks did something about this situation. A tenured academic outside the magazine did something about it first.

"Don Lipsett asked me to acquaint you with my thinking concerning a possible Committee of Correspondence in Political Science," Jerzy Hauptmann wrote Meyer in late 1961. "I am glad to learn of your interest, especially since Bill Buckley showed similar interest about a year ago."[35]

Meyer wondered about the parochial aim of the professor of political science and public administration at Park College in Missouri. He did not want his efforts to be confined to one field. He viewed meetings as too expensive and instead indicated letters and calls as more efficient. Initially, Meyer wrote about joint credit for the endeavor.[36] That did not happen.

Hauptmann ceded control to William Yandell Elliott, mentor to Meyer's friend Henry Kissinger.[37] Meyer provided the Harvard professor counsel, such as that the endeavor should maintain independence from *National Review*.[38] Then the *National Review* editor seized control, which, given that Meyer subsequently spoke at Park College and Hauptmann enthusiastically reviewed his work, pleased the initial idea man.[39]

With headaches spreading from Goldwater's orbit, migraines from Yaffers, and the John Birch Society metastasizing into a brain tumor, *National Review*'s editors regarded the prospect of allowing the movement to arise organically, without input, or even control, from them as horrifying. Still, on more than a technicality, the resulting newsletter *The Exchange* owed not to *NR* but Frank and Elsie Meyer.

"Many of us have thought for some time that informal communication among dispersed scholars and writers would be useful and stimulating," the graduate school flunkout wrote in the first issue. "It would constitute a sort of Committee of Correspondence for a limited and congenial group who now are too seldom in touch with one another, either on concrete problems of their professions or on tentatives for intellectual exploration."[40]

Years before the internet, the Meyers essentially created a members-only conservative message board. The low-budget, mimeographed newsletter, which initially aspired to come out monthly during the school year, arrived in the mailboxes of 175 or so right-wing intellectuals in May 1962. It encouraged conservative academics to exchange information on reading material for courses, scholarly journals, grants, and teaching jobs offered and desired.[41]

Milton Friedman wrote on free trade in the first issue's "tentatives" section.[42] Another future Nobel Prize–winning economist, James Buchanan, petitioned successfully to submit to a later issue.[43] Quality, not quantity, also characterized recipients.

The Relm Foundation granted $2,500 on an annual basis for the project, stipulating that $1,750 go to editorial and secretarial, the publication come out four or five times annually, a board of academics from separate disciplines advise it, and it limit recipients to five hundred.[44] In 1963, Meyer successfully solicited $2,500 from the Lilly Endowment.[45] As he explained to foundations, they could pay the Intercollegiate Society of Individualists or The Educational Reviewer (a group launched long prior to *National Review* by William F. Buckley Sr. that his son revived) to keep the donations tax-exempt. Part of this money made its way to Frank and Elsie.[46]

The generous subsidies caused Meyer to return subscriber payments as small as a dollar.[47] When a Brigham Young University librarian asked for missing issues, the editor prevailed upon him to return or destroy numbers in his possession.[48] *The Exchange* represented private correspondence between likeminded academics for furtherance in a profession in which they operated as endangered species. The secrecy extended to jobs advertised and sought. One generally needed to contact the editor for further information. Exposing employers and applicants risked harm, so rules necessarily included anonymity and excluded all lacking a trusted source's recommendation.

That Russell Kirk referred candidates to Meyer suggested a cooling from previous heat.[49] Catholic University's Institute of Law and Relations hired at least three professors through *The Exchange*.[50] A deluge of job-seekers flooded the Meyers' mailbox, including the economist Paul Craig Roberts, the political scientist Ellis Sandoz, and the historian Ralph Raico.[51] Many readers regarded it primarily as a want ad to find employment. The times validated yet thwarted the mission. Conservative professors wanted jobs, but universities did not want jobs going to conservative professors. The situation created supply as it diminished demand.

The Exchange cast Meyer as the unlikely point man for conservative academics. His reputation in this milieu, despite the lack of an advanced degree, caused Governor Claude Kirk's pick on the state higher education board to petition him to apply to become president of the University of Florida.[52] An attempt was made to lure Meyer from *NR* to serve as the dean of the University of Dallas.[53]

Bill Rickenbacker launched a similar newsletter called *The Communicator's Communicator* for conservative journalists during the 1960s.[54] As the decade advanced, the need for both, but especially *The Exchange*, became obvious. Politics motivated classroom takeovers, the shouting down of speakers, premature shuttering of institutions for the semester, destruction of research, and even in a few extreme cases campus murder. This far-left environment, hostile to liberals, became especially so for conservatives.

Meyer did what he thought should get done but did not. He reverted to alpha organizer when necessity beckoned and others demurred. Here others answered. But skittishness over the movement's spontaneous formation outside of *National Review*'s orbit encouraged Meyer to commandeer a role he had mastered for different ends on campus so long ago. Again he combatted what he had helped create.

✦ ✦ ✦

THE CHILDREN he helped create went to sleep long after midnight and rose in the early afternoon, did not attend school, and checkmated adults. "In the context of Woodstock,

New York, they were peculiar but not unusual," Roger Phelps assessed. "That is to say, everybody was peculiar."[55]

Unfortunately for the inhabitants of that bubble of normalized weirdness, the outside world did not appreciate weird so much as it tolerated it.

The state did not always. When a flustered social worker pointed out to Elsie that she had not received permission to keep her children home, from the bedroom came a libertarian roar. "You need *my* permission to do anything with my children," the enemy of the state bellowed. "I don't need *yours!*"[56]

The insolence came from the state and not the individual, the protective parent essentially said.

The father nevertheless described the curriculum and the students' progress by writing an annual letter to the school district's superintendent.[57] Other authorities looked askance upon the unusual arrangement beyond grade school and into college.

"At this point I tentatively feel that he would have few academic problems; I wish I could say the same about social adjustment. In this regard, please include among the references you send the name of your family physician. Also, I would like very much to have John interviewed by a member of our medical staff at Princeton," director of admission E. Alden Dunham, wrote Frank in the fall of 1962.[58]

John Meyer's averaging above 700 on each of the college boards impressed Dunham. His homeschooling did not. He wanted the seventeen-year-old to be examined not just in math and English but by a psychiatrist.

"Your proposal that John see a psychiatrist as part of the process of admission is an unconscionable invasion of his privacy, one which I will under no circumstances tolerate," came the response.[59]

Thus commenced a six-month pissing match between Meyer and Dunham. It became testy, nasty even. Princeton relented on the psychiatrist. But the school made further requests that the father regarded as onerous and unnecessary.[60] After educating John himself, and obtaining College Board examinations as early as 1955 to prepare for this moment, Frank gleaned from Dunham that he needed to do more than other parents did after already having done more than other parents did and that he did not choose the right path from the start.[61] Yet his son, not accustomed to taking tests, aced the test colleges imposed. Why more examinations, medical and otherwise?

Guy Davenport, fresh off a wild weekend of hosting John for a college visit and Frank for an event that involved traveling from a Philadelphia dinner to a LaSalle College debate, found, like Dunham, the Meyers' child-rearing methods curious. He wrote Hugh Kenner,

> Frank had quantities of Scotch in his noggin; Garry [Wills] lives in the Empyrean; Johnny [Meyer] has never been in this world. We made it just in time; Frank debated Dwight Mac[d]onald, and afterwards we all wandered off to [historian John] Lukacs's snazzy hideout beyond Valley Forge. With great effort I got Frank detached from that party, hours later, and not until dawn did any guest (here at the stoic apartment) make a move toward bed. I had to lecture on Coleridge at ten, so I snuck over to John [Davison]'s and grabbed two hours' sleep. I have severe reservations about people who never see the sun. AND I have severe reservations about Johnny Meyer. Haverford will never let him in: he'd perish. He can talk global politix and is a whizz at chess, but he can't stand gracefully or sit with ease, or reply to a query. Disturbing and somehow wrong, such a hot-house way to bring up kiddies. We suspect that Mary Ann [Mott] was his first sight of a girl in the flesh, if he indeed recognized her as such. My softball bat and weights and bicycle were inspected by Frank and Johnny as curiosae from New Guinea; shields and pizen arrows perhaps.[62]

John ultimately chose neither Haverford nor Princeton. "Look," the Yalie Ross Mackenzie told dean Bob Ramsey about John, "I know a guy who's pretty much the pure brain that

Yale says it's looking for."[63] Unlike its Ivy League counterpart, it conveyed no unusual requests. In fact, a Yale committee's new report on the freshman year encouraged the school to seek intelligence above all else in students.[64] Mackenzie thus recommended Yale to the Meyers and a Meyer to Yale.

Acceptance into an Ivy League school marked a triumph for the efforts of the child, the teaching of the parents, and the countercultural notion of homeschooling. Awarded the moniker of "the Duke" by his Yale peers, John's routinely making the dean's list, winning the intercollegiate chess championship, and leading the school's Young Americans for Freedom chapter and its College Republicans in his senior year validated not just the school's decision but the homeschooling decision as well.[65] The Princeton debacle added some bitter to the sweet.

Why did it become so contentious?

Yes, the loving father protected his son. Yes, the homeschooling advocate felt outrage at elite condescension. Yes, he attracted bees in his bonnet more easily than others.

Something beyond all this more fully explains the back-and-forth that started at the end of summer and ended at the beginning of spring.

Did Frank Meyer see Radcliffe Heermance in E. Alden Dunham? Impossible in a literal sense given his obliviousness to Heermance's anti-Semitic interest in him, this scenario in a metaphorical sense holds true in Princeton's signifying to him painful snobbishness. Dunham, who pushed to increase African Americans at Princeton, did not share the racial tics of his long-gone predecessor.[66] But prejudices, like fashions, change. Bigotries do not disappear but generationally shape-shift. The snobbery of an earlier time targets another group later. Heermance's intolerance fixated upon those not white and Christian; Dunham's on nonconformist educations. At least Meyer saw it that way. Dunham regarded the application as unusual and probably felt the unusual precautions imposed at his end a matter of due diligence.

The notion of calling in a psychiatrist picked at another scab. Decades earlier, Meyer had parted from Princeton in the midst of a mental health crisis. The experience scarred him. Now Dunham reopened old wounds. The father protected his son from indignity. He also defended his younger self from an institution permanently at war with that younger self.

Seventeen years removed from the Communist Party, the former Marxist still understood that history occurs "the first time as tragedy, the second time as farce."[67]

Twisted Tree

B oth of us consider the evening on Ohayo Mountain one of the high spots of our year," L. Brent Bozell wrote on behalf of his wife in the fall of 1956.[1] He returned frequently to talk the night away. More frequently did he find other ways to engage his conversation partner.

"My genius is distinctly for the telephone rather than the epistolary," Meyer later confessed in a letter to Bozell.[2] He knew himself.

Initially, the devices were black, mounted, and rotary.[3] They miraculously transmitted an isolated man's voice to fellow conservatives. They also sent out a massive portion of his income. Bozell siphoned the largest part of his phone bill in these years.

"A running joke at *NR* was Willmoore Kendall's quip that an emergency phone call between Frank Meyer and Brent Bozell was a call that interrupted their usual call," Priscilla Buckley wrote. "Frank Meyer was AT&T's best customer."[4]

The calls came unexpectedly and often during sleeping hours. Their frequency led Bozell and Meyer, witnessed by Marvin Liebman, to draw up a contract of sorts ridiculing the situation:

L. Brent Bozell, the party of the first part (Natch!), and Frank S. Meyer, the party of the second part, have conferred on various matters unpleasant to relate, and have reached the following understanding:

1. That the party of the second part has thoroughly & profligately dissipated funds entrusted to him & others by incessant & interminable phone calls to no purpose;

2. That the party of the second part sincerely regrets the abuse of the authority bestowed on him by the party of the first part (i.e., the permission to use telephone);

3. That the party of the first part forgives;

4. That the party of the second part undertakes & pledges to party of first part and to one M. Liebman that any & all phone calls made by party of second part from now until 27ᵗʰ day of Sept, 1959 will be personally paid for by party of second part as justice and penance doth require.

Subscribed to this 16ᵗʰ day of September 1959

L. Brent Bozell

Frank S. Meyer.[5]

One could afford Ivy League tuition, room, and board and still go on a $1,000 spending spree with the money Meyer spent on long-distance charges.[6] The year the two friends crafted their contract, the Meyers spent $3,417 on telephone bills. This amounted to 58 percent of the salary he drew from the magazine and 30 percent of his taxable income.[7] The following year, the phone bills they wrote off calculated to 56 percent of his *National Review* income, which had ballooned by about $1,000 to $7,000.[8] Along with a lit cigarette, the telephone symbolized Frank Meyer.

The phone allowed him to influence affairs at *National Review*. The magazine directed other inner-directed men elsewhere. Meyer avoided defenestration not by any conscious act but by rarely venturing into the office and not so much as even keeping a desk there. This disadvantaged him in pushing the editorial line. It also determined that Meyer, if frequently quarreling with Burnham or occasionally annoying Buckley, never wore out his welcome. One could generally choose to deal with him or not.

Arlene Croce, one of the editors tasked with putting issues to bed, recounted, "Frank was a telephone person to me always."[9] Neal Freeman explained, "I used to joke to the Meyer boys that AT&T invented caller ID to solve the Frank Meyer problem. He would call at two in the morning knowing you would be home, but you didn't know whether it was the widow next door or if your parent might be in trouble. So you would pick it up. And, of course, it would be Frank, and you had to catch the 6:45 train in the morning. You were not eager to speak to Frank all of the time."[10]

Bozell and Meyer eagerly communicated with one another all of the time. With Bozell in Spain, mail replaced telephone and another agreement—committing recipient to respond to sender within seventy-two hours—governed correspondence.[11] Occasionally, they communicated in the magazine's pages before a paying audience.

◆ ◆ ◆

MEYER'S first *National Review* article of 1962 read as unlikely fuel for an explosive debate whose residue coated articles, conference panels, and books for decades.

"The Twisted Tree of Liberty," which ran as a standard article rather than under "Principles and Heresies," started out as taxonomy of *conservatus americanus* detailing the characteristics of the myriad genera of the growing family. Meyer noted that some strains veered so far from the family tree in emphasizing an aspect of conservatism that they wound up in opposition to it. His anti-Communism overwhelmed his libertarianism in excommunicating a subset of libertarians who advocated disarmament and pacifism in response to Soviet aggression.[12] He privately characterized them as "treasonous characters" to Bozell.[13]

Bozell regarded it as clever that a libertarian defended traditionalism from fringe libertarianism in a way that not only did not dismantle some aspect of libertarianism but elevated it to conservative orthodoxy. He playfully vowed revenge.[14]

"I am hard at work on an article reading you out of the conservative movement—and you wouldn't want to interrupt that, would you?" he offered as an excuse to a violation of their seventy-two-hour pact. "Which is to say, son, when you finally get the 'opportunity to meet [my] arguments,' you will have them in front of you in NR in a piece that will have created, unless it is laughed at, the biggest stink the movement has smelt in some time. This assumes, of course, it will be published. If it's not, I will have to resign. It's one of the things I will want to talk to you about since I am not above us arranging to have it published in Bill's absence. In general, it is an attack on freedom. Fritz [Wilhelmsen], you will be happy to know, and God, agree with me."[15]

That month, a similar sharpening of the meaning of postwar conservatism occurred in the magazine's pages when Morton Auerbach repeated his claims that the postwar right lacked coherence and overflowed with contradictions. Meyer, M. Stanton Evans, and—most effectively—Russell Kirk rebutted the liberal professor.[16] The exchange displayed the degree to which the magazine of opinion operated, contra the wishes of Burnham (a former professor of philosophy at New York University), as a journal of political philosophy.

On that side of the Atlantic, crises beyond philosophical disagreement called for the Meyers to come. L. Brent Bozell endured deep depressions, and the alcoholism of his wife required care from the psychiatrist Juan José López-Ibor, under whose spell both Bozells, Kendall, and Virginia Wilhelmsen all fell. Returning to America, a scenario Meyer strenuously argued for, Brent insisted, might mean institutionalization for Tish, a scenario Meyer strenuously argued against.[17] They all hoped for a Spanish visit from the Meyers. Problems associated with the Newark building rented out to a Schrafft's restaurant, his aunt's failing health, book deadlines, pending college tuition, Volker money drying up, and Elsie's recent struggles with pleurisy, pneumonia, and gall bladder surgery conspired to ensure that the three amigos never reunited in Spain, a place that a quarter century before had claimed the life of one Meyer confidant and here taxed friendship with others.[18]

Bozell and Meyer settled on a two-day meeting of the minds.[19] "We are looking forward, like children to Christmas, to your arrival," Meyer wrote in February.[20] Though 3,500 miles apart, the couples remained close. Bozell, around the time of their meeting, successfully pushed Buckley to give Meyer a raise.[21] Meyer lobbied Buckley to publish the article rebutting himself and talked about it with the Circle Bastiat member Ronald Hamowy, who offered to run it in *The New Individualist Review*, an option as appealing to Bozell as *New Masses* printing one of his articles.[22]

"The main point is that the farthest thing from my mind was to give any impression that our personal friendship is in any way affected," Meyer clarified following a transatlantic phone conversation. "After all, we have said much more violent things privately than we are ever going to say in print."[23]

That the odd Meyer piece reproving libertarians catalyzed Bozell to launch a six-thousand-word fusillade and do so eight months later said as much about the critic as it did the criticized. The critic heartily agreed with the article's main point anathematizing the libertarians who were countering Soviet belligerence with demilitarization. Bozell, an American Legion national oratory champion in high school and anchor of a Yale debate team whose victory over Oxford undergraduates left the stunned Brits refusing to shake hands, relished intellectual combat.[24] "The Twisted Tree of Liberty" extended an olive branch; Bozell snatched it to pummel the opponent.

Meyer, himself also of that rare breed of human beings to develop a carapace, if only operational during intellectual disagreements, appreciated in Bozell what alienated others from both. They happily went at it, grateful to the other for sharpening their arguments.

Whereas Meyer stressed common denominators of traditionalism and libertarianism, Bozell emphasized difference to the point of irreconcilability. Indeed, the articulated positions exhibited a gap between them in the power each entrusted to the state. One gifted it enormous dominion; the other jealously restrained it.

◆ ◆ ◆

IN "FREEDOM OR VIRTUE," Bozell pegged man's goal as virtue and politics as a means to aid in this pursuit. Freedom for freedom's sake, he reasoned, represented a rebellion against God and nature.

"If the link between economic and other freedoms is thus tenuous, and if freedom, in any event, is difficult to translate into a 'transcendent value,' the real reason libertarians assign absolute value to economic freedom probably lies elsewhere," he reasoned in perhaps the article's most penetrating section. "And I suspect that the explanation is as simple—and as ominous for the future of conservatism—as a group hangover from the century when the argument about the interdependency of freedoms was exactly reversed: when, that is to say, instead of demanding economic freedom for the sake of political and other freedoms, libertarians demanded the other freedoms for the sake of economic freedom."[25]

Profound insights into the libertarian mind came from a libertarian mind in recovery. He now saw a model of the good state in Francisco Franco's Spain. Bozell, if nothing else, was a seeker. His debating partner clearly, if not to himself, journeyed, too.

The article's rhetorical flashes, more so even than its gobbling up more than seven full pages in the magazine, arrested readers. Bozell ridiculed Meyer's three natural functions of government—order, justice, defense—as "the mystery of the trinitarian state" and translated the line that "virtue-not-freely-chosen is not virtue at all" as "leading inescapably to the burlesque of reason."[26]

Atop the philosophical depth and literary talents displayed, the author prophetically analyzed liberalism, despite an illusory Camelot in the White House, as a spent intellectual force awaiting political collapse.[27] What filled the void?

Bozell cited efforts of Meyer and Evans (and invoked YAF's Sharon Statement, influenced by the former and written by the latter), and goals as modest as consolidating the right to as ambitious as capturing the government.[28] Devoted readers, unaware of developments on the Iberian Peninsula, undoubtedly had regarded this Meyer–Evans project as a Bozell–Meyer–Evans project. Bozell's pivot announced that Meyer's cause, ostensibly to define conservatism and unite its disparate strands, faced opposition. Tracing that call to if not inside the house than at least to the caller so frequently on the line accentuated the effort's difficulty. If Meyer could not convince—and given Bozell's conversion from essentially a Meyerite position to one more extreme than Kirk's—the man visiting his home, invading his mailbox, and tying up his telephone line, how could he expect to persuade millions of strangers?

◆ ◆ ◆

TWO WEEKS LATER, Bozell's friend and fellow senior editor responded. He noted that YAF, ISI, and, probably as an inside joke, *The Conscience of a Conservative* all took his side. He now did not seek to invent conservatism but merely to articulate it.

"Why Freedom" described a project "very different from an ideological—and eclectic—effort to create a position abstractly 'fusing' two other positions. What I have been attempting to do is to help articulate in theoretical and practical terms the instinctive consensus of the contemporary American conservative movement—a movement which is inspired by no ideological construct, but by devotion to the fundamental understanding of the men who made Western civilization and the American republic."[29]

What appeared in *National Review* in 1962 differed greatly from what appeared in *The Freeman* in 1955. This iteration of Meyer moved away from the lingering Communist mindset that reflexively offered a system toward a conservative mindset that noted the prolonged development of tried and tested ideas. Now he depicted his political philosophy as an acknowledgement of the best that made the West rather than a system conveniently concocted for political purposes. Bozell assumed the role of the gadfly Meyer of 1955 and Meyer played, poorly, the bothered horse Kirk.

Meyer stressed that fusionism derived from the tradition of Western civilization and the American Constitution. His three-page article conveyed that freedom amounted to the tradition of the West but that the West's tradition stewarded "virtue in freedom." The former required the latter to express itself; the latter required the former to imbue meaning.

Fidelity to one to the extent that it dismissed the other necessarily ran contrary to conservatism. "Why Freedom" explained that "the rigid positions of doctrinaire traditionalists and doctrinaire libertarians were both distortions of the same fundamental tradition and could be reconciled and assimilated in the central consensus of American conservatism."[30]

Bozell's heretofore closest sounding board advocated a political philosophy profoundly different than any developed in Spain. Meyer defended a conservatism of the American Founding against a conservatism of the fruit of foreign soil.

"The denial of the claims of virtue leads not to conservatism," he explained, "but to spiritual aridity and social anarchy; and the denial of the claims of freedom leads not to conservatism, but to authoritarianism and theocracy."[31]

Not everyone agreed.

✦ ✦ ✦

Such disputations made the magazine. The debate served notice that anything could happen between its covers. Buckley wisely decided to print the drag-out debates that took place in a Woodstock living room and on the lines of its black phones. Editors did not bare-knuckle brawl elsewhere on the newsstand. They did in *National Review*.

Meyer construed Bozell's broadside as an invitation to a favorite playground. And the younger debating partner received the older man's responding with vigor rather than a yawn as a compliment. Shared belief, as evidenced by the concordance between the book the younger man had so recently written for Goldwater and the book the older man readied for publication, had characterized them as much as any pair associated with the magazine. No gully slowly formed by water but a fissure torn by a powerful earthquake carved sudden space between them.

Spain happens.

◄ 27 ►

Freedom

M y book on the New Conservatives seems to be headed for spring publication," Meyer had written the Volker Fund back in 1957, "and the probable publisher will be McDowell-Obolensky, Inc."[1]

He erred in all.

An improbable publisher rescued the project. "Either Meyer hasn't read Kirk or can't read," Henry Regnery reacted in 1955 to *The Freeman*'s hit piece on his prized author.[2] An aghast Russell Kirk, then notified by a confidential informant of the project, wrote Regnery, "Who would read such a book by Meyer, or whoever would publish it, I can't say."[3]

The swerve came when Kirk's longtime collaborator Henry Regnery decided to publish him.

In February 1960, Meyer signed a contract with the Henry Regnery Company. The Chicago publisher advanced him $250, just less than what he made for a speech and a tiny fraction of Volker's grants that had poured into the project since 1955.[4]

Why did the publisher who had once rejected Meyer finally court him?

In 1959, Regnery and Kirk had a falling-out that resulted in the latter's exit as *Modern Age*'s editor. Suddenly, Regnery's allies who ran *Modern Age* petitioned Kirk's perceived nemesis to write for it. Out of respect for Kirk, Meyer vowed not to submit a piece until after the controversy had abated. He confessed to Kendall, "I feel rather distressed about this in some ways since, whatever can be said of Kirk, it was his magazine in concept and development." Convinced that Regnery's "sharply" breaking with Kirk fueled an almost vindictive interest in publishing his book, Meyer vowed to prioritize it after finishing *The Moulding of Communists*.[5]

The pattern of missed deadlines repeated. A Regnery advertisement promoted the book for its Fall 1961 list, and, upon not receiving the manuscript, the publisher listed it for Winter 1962.[6] The author again failed to deliver. So much time had passed from 1955 seed to 1962 harvest that Meyer received notification in early 1962 of the Volker Fund's termination based upon the wishes of its long-deceased founder.[7]

The delay proved convenient. The book, as conceived, looked less like a call for arm-in-arm unity on the right than an invitation to a no-liberals-welcome rumble. Ridiculed in academia and the media, conservatives in the movement's nascence did not need internecine battles royale. Ironically, the most truculent participant in past battles royale pushed this irenic, kumbaya-conservatives unity that the times demanded. One could call this out of character. Meyer, though, contained multitudes. The sectarian yielded here to the ecumenist.

He did not initially. Responding to a draft's blind review that found the author grinding an axe against the New Conservatives, Meyer in 1960 told Henry Regnery that "the book is explicitly and openly, in its subtitle as in the construction of every chapter, a critique of the New Conservatism as well as of contemporary orthodox Liberalism. This is, in fact, one of the purposes of the book—so for it I have no apologies."[8]

But public opinion shifted away from Kirk's conception of conservatism and toward the one embraced by *National Review*. By the early 1960s, a harsh critique like the *Freeman* broadside, if devouring a whole book, might look like a *non sequitur* at best and at worst literary bullying. Meyer, too, had not only softened toward Kirk but moved, albeit by inches and not yards, in his direction. The book certainly critiqued European-style conservatives. It developed into something less parochial and more ambitious. One message pervades its 172 pages: This is what we believe.

In Defense of Freedom had reached galley stages by the time Jameson Campaigne Jr. oversaw the project. The manuscript required little editing, and Meyer tolerated less. Campaigne, who had hosted Meyer as a speaker at Williams College and visited Woodstock prior to accepting the Regnery job, praised his accomplishment as he pointed out a mixed metaphor, the missing indicator of who emphasized the italics within a quote, and the likelihood that "the emotional effect of see-ing a father-image like Lincoln criticized without argument" would likely turn some sympathetic readers into critics.[9]

"As for what you say about my book, I am immensely grat-ified," Meyer responded to the twenty-two-year-old. "I have taken account of the first two points you raise and made ap-propriate changes. I am still thinking about just how to han-dle the Lincoln question."[10] The iconoclasm stayed.

Henry Regnery used "Freedom and the New Conserva-tism" as the working title.[11] Meyer preferred "Why Free-dom."[12] By 1961, the author pushed "In Defense of Freedom: A Conservative Credo." Regnery, as it did around the same time with Willmoore Kendall's *Conservative Affirmation*, objected to a particular word.[13]

"Everyone I have talked to without exception agrees that we should not use the subtitle 'A Conservative Credo,'" Henry Regnery argued. "This will not bring in readers we wouldn't get anyway, and I am sure will scare off many we could get without it. I strongly urge you to drop this subtitle—there is no magic in the word 'conservative,' and in this case I think it would be a hindrance."[14]

An intransigent Meyer thought otherwise. He sensed a buzz about conservatism likely to boost intellectual and commercial interest. He refused to budge.[15] As with Clinton Rossiter's guidance, he knew best.

◆ ◆ ◆

IN DEFENSE OF FREEDOM begins, "My intention in writing this book is to vindicate the freedom of the person as the central and primary end of political society. I am also concerned with demonstrating the integral relationship between freedom as a political end and the beliefs of contemporary American conservatism."[16]

From page one, he lets the reader understand his dual purpose. He articulates a political philosophy ideally suited to inform the total polity. Implicitly, that requires a faction to embrace the idea. He sees American conservatism as the vehicle to deliver it to the broader polity.

Conservatism? Does not *liberalism* connote liberty? The author explains why the political labels of the nineteenth century no longer fit in the twentieth. Utilitarianism shoved liberalism off course. Preoccupations with individual rights strangely morphed into the greatest good for the greatest number. Thus, liberalism became profoundly hostile to the human person. The rights and freedoms protected by the state became rights and freedoms trampled upon by a state ostensibly seeking to do the best for the most, which led to doing best for itself. Liberalism increasingly relied on force rather than freedom. Acknowledging this reality, the book uses "collectivist liberalism" to differentiate it from "classical liberalism."[17]

Conservatives embraced the other nineteenth-century outlook he regards as insufficient for the twentieth. "They were, at the best, indifferent to freedom in the body politic; at the worst, its enemies."[18] The traditions European conservatives sought to preserve included monarchy, aristocracy, and the state's church—all concepts not only foreign but offensive to Americans. Conservatives who insisted that nations could not import alien traditions did not heed their own counsel. They imagined Edmund Burke's warnings about the French Revolution, or the Habsburgs' upholding the tradition of the Catholic Church, as directly applicable to the United States. Rather than import some other nation's conservatism, Meyer advocated conserving domestic institutions. This meant an ethos based on the Declaration of Independence, the Constitution, and the *Federalist Papers*, themselves a product of the Western heritage yet distinctly American. Here Meyer's disagreements with Rose Wilder Lane over the West's influence upon the United States shaped fusionism.

In Defense of Freedom advances individual rights, freedom, and a government dedicated to the preservation of both. And therein lies the fusionism. Americans find freedom in their tradition. Preserve the latter and one preserves the former. Fusionism brought traditionalists and libertarians together. Critics found this to be a contrived unity that allowed the right to paper over internal differences. Meyer regarded it as an organic political philosophy growing out of history. And that allowed him to more firmly root fusionism within conservatism because he could show that it came from somewhere and sometime rather than from someone. America did not tether its identity to a monarch or a sect or an ethnicity but to its founding credo: freedom.

◆ ◆ ◆

AS IN *The Moulding of Communists*, Meyer avoids citing specific examples to illustrate points. This failed in a book detailing the nuts and bolts of the creation of the Communist cadre. It succeeded in a philosophical book. The decision not to parochially mire it in 1962 gives the work a timeless quality befitting political theory. It also enables it to hone in on the disease rather than distract the reader with symptoms.

"We concentrate upon problems that seem to multiply, hydra-like, rather than upon the principles that bear upon the problems; and this creates the suffocating verbiage of so much contemporary political and social discussion," he maintains. "Like a bevy of old wives congregated about the bedside of a suffering patient, every pundit presses his own nostrum, each directed towards a conspicuous symptom; and, as the chatter arises, it drowns the voice and crazes the mind of anyone attempting to assess the underlying malady which creates the symptoms."[19]

Atop symptom fixation, he rejects scientism, that peculiar modern alchemy that transforms dogma into "science." The scientific method applies to gravity but not to the study of social man in part because of the vested interest of the man-scientist.[20] Falling for scientism practically ensures that one falls for another modern delusion that imagines that social engineers—scientists of a sort—at the control board of the state can manipulate citizens the way a watchmaker might manipulate cogs and springs to make sure that the device runs smoothly.

Meyer concedes the necessity of both order and government. He defines the government's *raison d'être* in terms obverse to that used by statists: to prevent interference upon individual freedom.[21] He parts company with other conservatives on the reliance on prescription over mere reason. He finds the use of reason necessary not only to choose between good and bad custom but to rebut the ideologies based on reason.[22]

"Society and the state were made for individual men," he argues, "not men for them."[23] Both the social engineers and New Conservatives reverse this nostrum. Whereas Kirk speaks dismissively of social atoms, Meyer regards society as the construct. For worshippers of the state, it becomes necessary to frame the state, society, community as central to every question. Meyer accentuates that the individual and human beings constitute reality and society and humanity the abstraction. He expounds,

Socially, it assumes the existence of an organism, "society," as the being to which, and to the good of which, all moral (and by the same token, political) problems finally refer. Sometimes this principle is modified, but never by intrinsic reference to the individual person, only (when the totalitarian implications of total reference to "society" loom too large) by reference to collectivist images of specialized groups of individuals: "minorities," "the underprivileged," "the elite," "scientists," "gifted children," "backward children," "labor." Concern is never for, there is no reference to, a man who is a Negro, a poor man, a rich man, a well-born man, an able man, a biologist, a child, a carpenter.[24]

A philosophy that puts mass ahead of man inevitably leads to identity politics.

The ultimate difference between his and competing philosophies concerns freedom. For others, an elastic definition prevails, such as the freedom from want that imposes burdens on third parties or the freedom in choosing the righteous path that actually limits freedom. Freedom did not mean the freedom to choose right but the freedom to choose. He writes, "A hammer when you smash your thumb with it is just as much a hammer as when you drive a nail true."[25]

Euphemism characterizes so many other presentations of freedom. Politicians, philosophers, and theologians wish to attach whatever belief they embrace to one of the few words that exudes almost uniformly positive connotations. He explains, "Freedom means freedom; not necessity, but choice between responsibility and irresponsibility; not duty but the choice between accepting and rejecting duty; not virtue, but the choice between virtue and vice."[26]

✦ ✦ ✦

"LEVIATHAN" serves as the heart of *In Defense of Freedom*. At fifty-five pages, it gobbles up nearly a third of its space. It is a short book within a short book. Drawing inspiration from *The Road to Serfdom*'s depiction of Nazism, Communism, and the New Deal as all guzzling from the same group-over-individual wellspring; Lord Acton's emphasis of liberty as a precondition of virtue; and, it seems, Albert Jay Nock's *Our Enemy, the State*'s separation of the people from the state, "Leviathan" outlines the legitimate functions of government and describes why the powerful always and everywhere engorge upon people's freedoms to increase their in-group's power. A fourth influence, J. R. R. Tolkien's *Lord of the Rings*, illustrates another of Acton's points most vividly: Power corrupts. *In Defense of Freedom* implores readers to let neither Gollum nor Gandhi wear that ring.

"The state is not co-extensive with the totality of that which it governs; it is a definite group of men, distinct and separate from other men, a group of men possessing the monopoly of legal coercive force," he writes. "And it remains thus set off, separate, whether it governs with or without the consent of the governed, with or without their participation in the choice of the governors. Even in a democratic polity, the state is not 'we,' identical with all the people, as is often claimed, it is 'they,' those who hold state power."[27]

Meyer points to the negative examples of Akhenaton and the Tower of Babel, which didn't stop others from attempting to establish heaven on earth.[28] This suggests a resilient impulse in man that is immune to the lessons of history. Collectivists, by whatever name they operate, act "to take God's place as creator, and to know better than God—to know that the enforcement of their design upon the individual man is a higher good for him than he could achieve by exercise of his own free choice."[29]

As they deposed God or usurped God's role, collectivists in turn divinized the state. Movements begun by defying the state ended by deifying it: "Jacobinism, Marxism, Fascism, collectivist liberalism, each in its own way has joined intellectually and emotionally in the deification of the state, and each in its own way has contributed to that immense growth in the power of the state which is the effective condition of totalitarianism."[30]

Vox dei imagines itself as *vox populi*, too. The deliberate confusion of group desires for "the General Will" characterizes totalitarians. "The *Volk* of the Nazis, the proletariat of the Communists, are but manifestations of this totality whose will is the General Will, lay figures draped out to gain the consent of the masses," he writes. "These figures are presented as if they were indeed the very image of the masses, but in reality they are only representations of the will of the elite: the will of the Communist Party is the true will of the proletariat; the will of the *Fuehrer* is the true will of the German *Volk*."[31]

The project sought to wage this uphill battle against not only contemporary prevailing opinion that placed the collective over the individual in spite of the recent disasters in Nazi Germany, the Soviet Union, and beyond, but also classical political philosophy that began with that assumption. He sought to desacralize the state. This began with the premise that individuals serve as an end and not means for any political philosophy worth pursuing. Most political philosophies heretofore pursued nevertheless reversed means and ends.

"The state must be limited to its proper function of preserving order," he wrote. "But this will only be possible when the person is considered as the central moral entity, and society as but a set of relations between persons, not as an organism morally superior to persons."[32]

One disturbing way the state transgresses the boundaries nature proscribes involves its desire to filter truth from falsehood. Error, propelled by charisma, mania, or some other fuel, can only persist for long periods with the aid of the state. The state cannot kill an idea. It can prop up lies, which means any disinformation fact-checker, fake-news police, or fairness doctrine necessarily becomes disinformation, fake news, and unfairness.[33] The free marketplace of ideas, not the state, effectively weeds out falsehood from fact. The state, nursing an overwhelming vested interest in shaping public opinion, perpetually seeks to try to arbitrate truth. This idea finds a relative in Meyer's contention that a person may act virtuously only when given the freedom to choose. Compulsion can neither anoint truth nor dictate virtue.

The book rebuts the contention that freedoms suppressed by majority vote correspond to something morally superior to freedoms suppressed by strongmen. "Those who possess the power of the state possess it exclusively and over against the rest of society," he points out, "whether their power is confirmed by hereditary right, landed property, wealth, or the democratic ballot."[34] The form of government that erases rights matters not at all. Freedom *über alles*.

Meyer sought to limit, not abolish, government. "The state . . . has two natural functions, functions essential to the existence of any peaceful, ordered society: to protect the rights of citizens against violent or fraudulent assault, and to judge in conflicts of right with right. It has a further third function, which is another aspect of the first, that is, to protect its citizens from assault by foreign powers."[35] He regarded police, courts, and defense as legitimate. Everything else—from programs as early in the republic as building canals to the coeval cacoethes for sending exuberant government missionaries to Africa—belonged to some sphere outside the state.

◆ ◆ ◆

THE TASK of the American right involved not so much conserving as restoring.

"For half a century or more the idea [the primacy of the person] was clearly and firmly held," Meyer writes, "and the practice of the American republic closely approximated the idea. But a process of retrogression set in, first slowly, then faster and faster—a process in which the decisive moments were the introduction of mass democratism by Andrew Jackson, the undermining of the sovereignty of the several states by Abraham Lincoln, and the naturalization in the United States of 20th-century collectivist principles and methods by Franklin D. Roosevelt."[36]

This tasked conservatives with the awkward quest of overthrowing rather than preserving. Surely none by that name sought to petrify the omnivorous state. For a former revolutionary, toppling rather than protecting did not feel so awkward.

"For the shackling of Leviathan, the limitation of the state's invasion of the free domain of individual persons," he concludes, "those instincts await only intellectual articulation, that energy needs only organization."[37]

◆ ◆ ◆

THE LENGTH of Meyer's tentacles as editor and activist guaranteed publicity. M. Stanton Evans defended the book in ISI's *Individualist* by wondering how conservatives could universally accept the linkage between statism and relativism but doubt that between freedom and moral absolutism.[38] John Chamberlain pondered in *The Wall Street Journal* whether *In Defense of Freedom* was not the most important book on the right since *The Road to Serfdom*.[39] Senator Barry Goldwater submitted Chamberlain's review into the Congressional Record.[40]

Meyer's ubiquity in the movement provoked not just admiring reviews but resentful ones. Kirk's caustic critique described the book as an "odd performance" and its author as an "eccentric," an odd word of opprobrium from a man who occasionally wore a cape. "Formerly a Communist ideologue ... Mr. Meyer now transfers his political passion to conservatism (of sorts)—which he would erect into an ideology, with slogans and dogmas," Kirk wrote. "He burns to purge this new true faith of deviationists, to create a disciplined sect of the faithful, to become the law and all the prophets to young persons marching to Zion."[41]

If it spoke more of the sensitivities of reviewer than to the reality of the reviewed, the criticism hit a truth, shrinking in relevance the longer Meyer marinated in the conservative milieu, about the ideologization of the American right. His temperament and history screamed ideologue. His philosophy, fusionism—in its elemental form a preservation of the American tradition, that is, freedom—struck its votaries as a less forced, more organic conservatism than Kirk's admonition to look to Edmund Burke, Samuel Taylor Coleridge, and others largely rooted in foreign soil for guidance.

Meyer advanced freedom not as Thomas Paine or Frédéric Bastiat or Ludwig von Mises did. He did so through his book as a patriot conscious that freedom stemmed from the American tradition, which duty compelled American conservatives to conserve.

◆ ◆ ◆

THE BOOK became a classic. It did not become a hit. It sold 1,292 copies from its November 12, 1962, release until year end and 859 the next six months. By 1970, when the Regnery edition went out of print, sales reported to the author reached an underwhelming 3,070 copies.[42] *The Moulding of Communists*, an inferior book read only as a curio if at all decades later, outsold that initial run of *In Defense of Freedom* within a few months of its release.[43] As a commercial endeavor, *In Defense of Freedom* flopped.

In terms of influence, it succeeded wildly. That triumph confuses terribly when considered in the light of its initial marketplace failure.

The afterlife of the initial run included a Regnery Gateway edition in 1973 and an expanded version released by the Liberty Fund in 1996.[44] *In Defense of Freedom* ultimately joined a conservative canon of a dozen or so books, of which right-wing intellectuals read most to grasp the ideas that animated their movement and the nuanced strains therein. Reading this canon has served as the price of admission to conversations with other serious conservatives. More so than *The Road to Serfdom*, *The Conservative Mind*, and *Ideas Have Consequences*, *In Defense of Freedom* laid out a clear credo that American right-wingers could rely upon. It told conservatives why they believed what they believed even if few conservatives amened every line. People who read, and reread it, disproportionately attained positions of great influence. If small, Meyer's audience was select.

Written on Eugene O'Neill's desk, *In Defense of Freedom* instinctively inspired, like the playwright, varied interpretations.[45] "Meyer's manifesto was designed to unite his fellow intellectuals in a polemical campaign against the Soviet Union," judged Paul Gottfried in *Chronicles*.[46] The economist Murray Rothbard quoted from *In Defense of Freedom* and then concluded of his friend's philosophy that "it is libertarian, period."[47] Michael Warren Davis judged Rothbard's assessment as likely wrong and described Meyer "at bottom" a "traditionalist" in *The Imaginative Conservative*.[48] Senator John East read the book and concluded, "Meyer is not a 'traditionalist' or a 'libertarian,' nor is he a 'fusionist': the essential Meyer is a Christian theorist."[49]

The most common misunderstanding regarded fusionism as a compromise of necessity to more easily obtain power. That conservatives more easily obtained power after essentially adopting it as the movement's default political philosophy served as this claim's gravamen. This perspective necessarily conceives fusionism as not only a cynical calculation but an ideology—not developing organically but something syncretical invented by a theorist and therefore outside of conservatism.

The smaller error misconstrues fusionism as one part traditionalism, one part libertarianism—or sees it as identical to the bromidic three-legged stool of social conservatism, smaller government, and a strong national defense. Meyer did not petition traditionalists to give here and libertarians to give there. Given his history as a philosophically uncompromising debating partner, a plea to compromise principles strikes as a rather bizarre if somewhat common interpretation.

Neither tiny "ism" nor great compromise, fusionism to Meyer simply meant conserving the American tradition. That tradition—from the Declaration of Independence through Washington's Farewell Address—derived from the broader Western tradition and developed into ordered liberty. This simplicity coaxed more complicated readings.

Though unknown to those distilling fusionism through polluted waters, that Meyer devised a similar scheme relating to Communism in 1943 likely further propelled cynicism regarding fusionism as a utilitarian construct. The temptation to cast Meyer as transposing the Popular Front of the Communist Party upon the American right—*Conservatism Is Twentieth-Century Americanism*—is seductive. Tellingly, though, his intellectual journey toward conservatism began around the time he realized the impossibility of fusing Communism with the American tradition.

The underlying idea that the American Founding's significance involved advancing freedom and that American conservatives necessarily find freedom as their nation's tradition attracted conservatives because of its simplicity and truth. Almost all of those who believe this idea remain ignorant of the term "fusionism" and the name "Frank Meyer." One grasps the most compelling proof of the book's influence by listening to conservatives who have never read it nevertheless recapitulate its themes.

◀ 28 ▶

Crackup

A book intended to unite the movement coincided with the crackup of its intellectual leadership. Meyer dedicated *In Defense of Freedom* to L. Brent Bozell, William F. Buckley Jr., and Willmoore Kendall, men he described as "companions in battle" and "whetstones of the mind."[1] The inscription on parchment made special relationships permanent. Paper disintegrates. So do friendships.

The whetstones started coming for people rather than ideas. This began before Meyer's book went on sale.

William Rickenbacker left a fourteen-page memorandum on his boss's desk at noon on September 12, 1962. A pilot like his famous father Eddie, a classically trained pianist, a successful investor, and a multilinguist, Rickenbacker's colleagues regarded him as, well, collegial. The blistering memo stunned Buckley in that aside the colon holding back "From" read not Frank S. Meyer but a *gentle* man's name. The tonal disconnect between author and text struck readers, of which existed a handful, the way a nun's punctuating a schoolhouse lesson with profanity might.

It began with the seemingly pettifogging observation that James Burnham did not answer mail. From there the pianist built a crescendo that accused Burnham of imposing

317

his views on editorial content even when they clashed with the magazine's accepted line. This occurred, Rickenbacker alleged, especially during Buckley's absences. He described a passive-aggressive personality engaged in "reckless actions, devious methods, outright lies, continuous usurpations, and irresponsible criticisms." Rickenbacker, who primarily wrote in Burnham's front-of-the-magazine fiefdom, smarted from numerous edits that he regarded as sabotage.[2] For instance, his fellow senior editor, in the wake of the Supreme Court decision earlier that summer eliminating organized school prayer, excised the more hard-hitting part of an editorial.[3] He regarded Burnham as a coward who favored smuggling his rejected, more liberal views into the magazine over openly defending them. "We have, then, the picture of a man perennially engaged in skul[l]duggery, sniping from cover, avoiding open confrontation," he wrote. "His very manner of speaking betrays an arrogant disregard for the rules of considered discourse."[4]

Rickenbacker, a soldier in Meyer's civil war against Burnham, informed his general three hours after dropping off the memo that he still awaited reaction. In the lead-up to the dramatic act, Rickenbacker reported to Meyer of the sympathies of lower-level *National Review* employees, labeling Tim Wheeler a likely ally and Don Coxe an unknown commodity.[5] "We are absolutely surrounded by friends," he assessed. "The only task is to consolidate ourselves and start bitching, all the damned time, until Burnham decides he either works <u>for</u> NR or gets off the pot."[6]

It mattered little whether allies or opponents surrounded. In the democracy of *National Review*, one man's vote counted more than the combined remainder. Buckley's mind, often open and depending on the issue occasionally deferential to the counsel of his senior editors, had long ago closed with regard to Burnham. The magazine needed him and Buckley personally liked him. Whether the boss saw Burnham through rose-colored glasses or colleagues saw him through a jaundiced lens mattered less than the reality of the difference in perspective.

The sore festered before the finale. That winter Buckley wrote "sick at heart" from Switzerland. He petitioned Meyer as a friend to rein in Rickenbacker. "What is going on here, pretty clearly, is a completely unilateral personal obsession, by Bill against Jim, which has no objective base beyond everyone's individual capacity for annoying other people," the boss judged. The consequences of failure here would mean Rickenbacker's firing, the "blackest" day in the magazine's history, Buckley conjected, should it happen. He also floated the idea, personally horrifying to Meyer and a sign of the degree to which the memo backfired, of elevating Burnham not just *de facto* above the other senior editors but *de jure* in creating an executive editor position.[7] Whether Buckley really imagined that the title would end the conflict or whether he used it as motivation for Meyer to succeed in controlling his ally remains unclear. But by 1963, it had become clear that an acrid relationship existed within the magazine between just about every major player and at least one other major player.

A chastened Rickenbacker stayed. Burnham remained senior editor in title. But Buckley sent a clear message that he regarded him as the *senior* senior editor. The Meyerite rebels suffered a Shiloh in their civil war for the soul of *National Review*. Gettysburgs followed.

◆ ◆ ◆

UNLIKE RICKENBACKER, Willmoore Kendall needed a fight the way a fish needs water. Ideology inevitably fueled Meyer's disputes. Personal slights, real and imagined, animated Kendall's uncivil war with everyone, everywhere, always. If the whetstone ground dull thoughts fine, then he also wore others thin.

Kendall wrote a review of Arthur Whitaker's *Spain and Defense of the West* in 1961 that he regarded as one of his best lessons on political theory. A spirit of patriotism beckoned to defend the honor of his temporary homeland and contributed to spending ten days writing the review. He relayed an ultimatum to Manhattan by way of Woodstock: Either *National Review* publishes his article promptly and essentially unedited or he exits.[8]

That same spring, Yale gleefully accepted a buyout proposed by Kendall.[9] Before treating *NR* like Yale, Kendall, Meyer insisted, must speak with him, provide Buckley reasons for his position minus histrionics, and remain on the board whatever happens.

"I am pretty sure, as things now stand, that he will print the piece—and soon, and I hope that his editing will be tolerable," he told Kendall. "If by any chance the piece should be mauled, would it be possible for us to talk on your return before you act decisively? I cannot disagree very seriously with your analysis of the situation between you and Bill in the NR context; but I would wish, indeed I would regard it as your moral duty and your duty from the standpoint of loyalty in friendship, that you do not take the unilateral action of resignation before telling Bill very simply, clearly, and without flourishes of the sort that can get his back up and give him an excuse to act absurdly, just what you regard as just conduct on his part."[10]

He advised someone unadvisable who acted inadvisably. The professor, reasoning that his student held him to a different standard than the other writers and behaved possessively over him, had already resigned.[11] Meyer huddled by mail with Bozell to call the next play. He praised Buckley's editing of the disputed piece and confessed that the impasse reminded him of what led to Willi Schlamm's departure. He wondered, "[I]s Willmoore determined to make all relationships with NR impossible?"[12]

✦ ✦ ✦

BOZELL informed Meyer that Kendall objected not merely to the editing on his Whitaker piece but to editors altering his work at all.[13] Among the main players, he required editing most. The professor habitually wrote complex sentences in search of a period ill-suited for commercial magazines. So editing occurred, albeit not as much as it should have. Kendall resigned, Bozell explained to Meyer, by writing "the only kind of serious letter he is capable of—a 12 page, single-spaced, psychoanalysis of Bill." Buckley, regarding Kendall as "beyond the reach of reason," regretfully accepted.[14]

"Willmoore's reaction on getting Bill's letter was a) to call me, b) go to the can and vomit, c) get drunk," Bozell explained to Meyer. "It was the first drink he had taken, I gather, in more than four months."[15]

Meyer and Bozell intervened with both parties. No Kendall in the magazine's power structure provided a greater advantage to Burnham. Beyond this, the trio enjoyed a close friendship. Bozell spoke of brokering a "peace plan" between brother-in-law and former teacher.[16] This eventually resulted in Kendall allegedly apologizing and ostensibly accepting his editor's right to edit.[17] He remained.

Another dress rehearsal for Kendall's exit took place in Seattle the following year. Meyer by now grasped that his alliance rested on shifting sand. On an annual basis, Kendall threatened divorce from the magazine. On an annual basis, he became a more peripheral character within it. If physical distance diluted his influence, then events far from *NR*'s offices periodically reminded friends and foes that Kendall's remaining influence owed entirely to that distance.

One example of this saw a drunken Kendall abuse Carl Braden at a University of Washington debate in late 1962. "Any unsteadiness on my feet anyone may have observed if someone really did observe it would have been sheer fatigue," Kendall assured Meyer. He insisted he "had honestly thought" that the debate with the left-wing activist fresh from a prison stint for refusing to cooperate with the House Committee on Un-American Activities "had been one of my more triumphant public appearances."[18] Friends thought otherwise. Young Americans for Freedom members who had attended the speech thought him drunk.[19] Conservatives canceled a subsequent event at Pomona College because of a separate accusation of drunkenness at St. Mary's College.[20] Kendall conceded that he got smashed at a dinner for graduate students at Georgetown.[21] The rest? All lies.

The accused now maintained that, rather than exhaustion, the allegations of inebriation in Seattle owed to forces beyond him. He theorized that his fiancée had mistakenly packed tranquilizers instead of vitamin C tablets.[22] "I can't think, now, how I was so stupid all those days as not to have it occur to me that I must have been drugged somehow," he claimed to Meyer. The possible culprit shifted from his unwitting bride-to-be to Communists. He hinted that perhaps his ideological enemies had drugged him, given rumors of his alleged drunkenness preceding the speech, as he acknowledged that he risked sounding "Revilo Oliverish" in advancing this idea.[23] He explained in a lame attempt to goad the former Communist to his side: "Bill [Buckley], who is always I think very naïf about these things and doesn't know how the Commies operate, seems to have fallen for it hard."[24]

Meyer knew how Kendall operated. His stories could only persuade of his inability to admit wrongdoing. The extant correspondence left no trace of its recipient telling its writer that he did not believe him. No one could have believed the alcoholic searching for an excuse, *any excuse*, to save face, the revenue stream from public speaking, and even the association he so often sought to sever with *National Review*. Buckley, who had earlier made Kendall's sobriety a condition of employment, ultimately telegrammed the accused to let him know that he chalked up the misadventure to barbiturates mistakenly ingested.[25] Buckley knew he told a lie.

Rather than use the fiasco to rid the magazine of a problem, the student sought to rehabilitate his teacher. Kendall dreaded Buckley's speaking to him as though he were a "Dutch uncle." He nevertheless vowed to tolerate the indignity because he needed the magazine on the cusp of releasing *The Conservative Affirmation*. "I don't want now to break with NR until the book is launched, for reasons you will readily understand," Kendall told Meyer. "But I am going to soon after, and confine myself more and more to purely scholarly pursuits. That, of course, is where my strengths have always been anyway, and I have been very foolish to move my bets, at any time, away from them."[26]

He knew at least his strengths.

In September 1963, Buckley demoted Kendall to contributor. The senior editor position required editorial contributions. Meyer edited the back of the magazine and Burnham the front. Kendall sporadically submitted articles and reviews on his own clock. After contributing forty-three articles in the first full calendar year of the operation, he wrote just one in the year before Buckley shifted his title.[27] His "Liberal Line" column had long ceased to appear, and his stints abroad as well as at Stanford, Georgetown, Los Angeles State, and now the University of Dallas kept him far away from the physical office. He had held, since the late 1950s, a title without responsibilities. Buckley sought to accurately describe his role.

In losing his title he lost it. Kendall demanded the editor instead remove him from the masthead.[28] Venting to Bill Rusher after the magazine had refused to run a free advertisement for the University of Dallas, Kendall likened his attitude toward *National Review* to seeing an old flame working as a call girl.[29]

Buckley responded with a "Dear John" letter that left no possibility for reconciliation. It started, "I have never had the power to prevent you from being a fool" and ended, "[A]s to the reference you make to wives and call-girls, I can only welcome the news that you have finally learned to distinguish between the two."[30]

Severed from the magazine that provided an identity outside of academia, Kendall lashed out at past defenders who did not intervene. The clear permanence of this break caused him not to question his course but others' perfidy. Buckley became the first of Kendall's many former friends at *National Review*.

The unpleasant divorce from the magazine, coupled with the welcoming home at the University of Dallas, removed even the dysfunctional internal governor that had regulated his conduct with friends. He no longer depended on them for a livelihood and rarely saw them socially.

Kendall invited Meyer to debate James Farmer, a founder of the Congress of Racial Equality, at the University of Dallas on whether the civil rights movement aimed to move too far, too fast. Kendall offered $400 plus expenses, which later became $400 inclusive of expenses *plus* the advice that "if you are not going to make ad hoc preparation, something well beyond what you did that night over at Farmington or wherever it was, I'd rather you'd take yourself out your own self: People tell me Farmer's pretty good, and I'm not running the debate series to make 'us' look bad against the opposition."[31]

Meyer balked.

"I have neither requested nor do I desire your advice on debating technique," he replied. "In any case, if you want me to debate Farmer, the terms will have to stand as originally proposed by you: $400 plus expenses."[32]

Kendall reasoned correctly that Meyer charged other groups less, and since many at the university knew this, he did not want to look as though engaged in cronyism.[33] He also noted that, although the hall sat 1,800 and admission cost $1, Meyer did not act as the draw.[34] Perhaps a desegregated Dallas event debating the topic of the hour, with Kendall involving a historically black college, did.[35]

He clarified his point about *ad hoc* preparation, largely supported by extant recordings of Meyer's lectures showing an uneven, off-the-cuff approach, by maintaining that "you sometimes do not take your speaking engagements as seriously as I happen to think you should; like Bill Buckley, you seem to have an unlimited confidence in your ability to take your stance before a public audience and count on wisdom pouring forth from your mouth; unlike Bill Buckley you do not, in my opinion, always bring it off, though I regard you as tops when you have taken the trouble to prepare."

Then, Kendall being Kendall, he added insult atop a well-reasoned argument: "You are, incidentally, acting like a child."[36]

Simultaneously, they bickered over a proposed anti-Communism book. It first involved the name to insert on the cover as author of an anthology disguised as a thematic book. It included disputes over deadlines and finally Meyer's desire to withdraw, which, given his *bona fides* both within the party and as a witness against it, undermined publication prospects.

"The letter before me doesn't improve matters as regards my sentiments about this latest failure of yours to live up to your propaganda image of yourself (I've always had some difficulties with it): all for the cause, etc.," Kendall wrote after a dispute about deadlines. "Even now, you don't offer any real excuse for your default—rather you make it sort of insultingly clear that something came up that you chose to schedule before your work on the [Congressman Donald] Bruce project—who knows what connected with your overweening ambition. You seem completely unconcerned at what you end up doing to the other persons involved in the project. But as I have indicated, I do not find this wonderful."[37]

Meyer ultimately recompensated Kendall $2,000 for bowing out of the project, which, if it bought forgiveness, did not purchase forgetting.[38] Kendall began to characterize Meyer's long ago replacing him as the book review editor—in fact Meyer had replaced Schlamm, who replaced Kendall after the professor abruptly resigned from the position—in a negative light. He confessed to Elsie, "I had swallowed Frank's having got a bread & butter job at NR by dynamiting me out of it."[39] Atop the lecture and book dispute, Frank's sins, from Kendall's vantage, included not standing up for him.[40]

Their friendship, which once included Kendall's joining the Meyers for holidays, now soured to the point of Willmoore writing Frank through the intermediary of Elsie.

"Your picture of me as quarreling all the time with all my 'friends' is quite false," he informed her. "Far as I know, the onliest quarrel I have going with anybody I've deemed a friend in recent years is a quarrel with Frank Meyer. WFB doesn't count here—nobody has heard me refer to him as a friend for many years, and it isn't a quarrel I have going with him—really the routine conduct of hostilities with an enemy."

Kendall cited Meyer's "sabotaging" his debate series at the University of Dallas, pulling out of the anti-Communism anthology, and not protesting the removal of his *NR* title as reasons for the breach. He judged: "My present picture of him is that of an unjust man who does not even pay me the courtesy of wishing to <u>appear</u> just in my eyes."[41]

◆ ◆ ◆

THE WRATH spread beyond Meyer to the triumvirate's other charter member. "My place is in the classroom," Kendall said in a spat of self-knowledge, "spotting and training the next WFB and the next LBB, with foreknowledge this time of the vices that have to be avoided. Jesus!"[42] He now regarded the pair as something other than prized students who traveled more enlightened paths than Hubert Humphrey, soon to be vice president of the United States; Russell Long, then a powerful senator from Louisiana; and other luminaries who had learned from him. He informed Bozell that he symbolized "disappointment," "disloyalty," and "treason."[43]

Whereas Kendall burned his bridges, Bozell drifted away as colleagues sought to drag him, or at least the old him, back. *Contra Mundum* captured Kendall in a book title. "Contra Me" fit Bozell, who did not so much go against everyone as engage in a continuous debate with earlier versions of himself.

Bozell's biographer Daniel Kelly contrasted the sixteen "National Trends" columns appearing in 1960 with the mere nine from 1963 through 1965. To the extent Bozell took an interest in the magazine, he did so primarily to address the faith that had so suddenly consumed him. Further, prior to 1961, none of Bozell's non-column articles and reviews in the magazine focused on religion; from August 1961 through 1965, most of them did.[44]

Bozell wished to escape his brother-in-law's shadow as he clashed with him, at least by degree, on abortion and other questions. He unsuccessfully primaried the liberal Republican Congressman Charles Mathias of Maryland in 1964, published *The Warren Revolution* (which he soon repudiated to such a degree that he involved lawyers to demand Buckley delete excerpts from it included in a later book) in 1966 to poor sales nine years after he had started writing it, and that same year launched *Triumph*, which later famously placed on its cover an image of a pregnant Statue of Liberty holding up a coat hanger in place of a torch.[45] That arresting *Triumph* cover looked like a visual representation of the dim take on freedom a decade or so earlier in "The Twisted Tree of Liberty." It did not symbolize *The Conscience of a Conservative*, which did not give expression to the earlier McCarthyite, which seemed a great distance from the collegiate World Federalist. Bozell, like so many in these years, journeyed on a long, strange trip.

◆ ◆ ◆

KENDALL spent four of his most stable years at the University of Dallas with Nellie Cooper, whom he married in 1966 after securing an annulment. He communicated to Frank when needed generally through Elsie. They corresponded, spoke on the phone, and crossed paths at conferences rarely. Upon his death from a heart attack at age fifty-eight in 1967, he remained incommunicado from Meyer, and Buckley, and his brother, and his mother. His widow, as though channeling from the grave, unsuccessfully lobbied Meyer for posthumous completion of the anti-Communism book.[46] Meyer wrote Kendall's sister Yvona that "as you say, there is a sad feeling of tragedy in his last years."[47] Schlamm, the first *NR* exile, summed up the most recent one: "What a tragedy of self-damaging alienation his whole life was!"[48]

Bozell eventually matched extreme politics with extreme behavior. In Northern Ireland, he crashed a stolen bus through a gate trying to deliver an address on time; he speechified instead in a jail cell proclaiming himself alternatively the pope and the commander of the Irish Republican Army. On the phone he successfully impersonated a U.S. cabinet member to Menachem Begin for several minutes before Israel's prime minister deduced that he conversed with a madman.[49] He got better. He got worse first.

Three amigos became one. Frank replaced those early allies with Rickenbacker and Rusher. Though formidable men—the former a genuine renaissance man, the latter one of the great writers of interoffice memos in the history of both offices and memos—their counsel could not grab Buckley by the lapels as could his teacher and his brother-in-law. The replacements for *National Review*'s first wave dripped with talent. Nevertheless, they all arrived at Buckley's doorstep as inferiors in stature. They could not claim equality or superiority as Bozell and Kendall could. Therefore, their influence could never, no matter how capable they proved themselves, match the influence of the teacher and the friend. Furthermore, whereas Kendall, Bozell, Schlamm, and other departees helped shape the magazine, the magazine to some degree shaped all of their replacements who cycled through. One who owes existence to an institution behaves differently than one who brings it into existence.

The departures of Kendall and Bozell marked the end of *National Review*. The magazine continued, *à la* Menudo, by adding new writers. But it broke up just as much as The Beatles broke up six years later. Likely, no one drawing a paycheck then, prior, or after viewed the magazine as one might a cover band paying tribute. And few readers understood this end as *the* end. But the shrinking presence and ultimate disappearance of Bozell and Kendall concluded a golden age. The high-level political philosophy that characterized its pages and fathered the various strains within conservatism—fusionist, religious, populist—largely disappeared. Rusher, for instance, held strong political commitments. He did not originate or craft a political philosophy as Bozell, Kendall, and Meyer did. Burnham experienced this as something gained more than something lost. The newsstand did not generally sell out of, or even sell, journals of political philosophy. *National Review* could now read more like any other magazine. For those revering it as unlike any other magazine, the change came as unwelcome.

After the dust settled, Willi Schlamm described himself as "horrified by the chilling atmosphere" at *National Review* upon a return after long absence at a party thrown in his honor. "When I helped starting it, I did it with a firm resolution to create a veritable conspiracy of friendship and 'sticking together' against the whole miserable world; but as the years went by, the great adventure grew into another instrument of careerism, of one self-centered s.o.b. fighting against the other, of disloyalty and animosity and juvenile ambition."[50]

Meyer continued to wage civil war. He did so as the Hiroo Onoda of *National Review*. The counterweights to Burnham—Suzanne La Follette, Schlamm, Kendall, and Bozell—no longer edited the magazine. Meyer, alone among the anti-Burnhamites who had appeared on the initial masthead, remained. His allies and ammunition largely gone, he resorted to hand-to-hand combat to make the magazine, or at least the sections that he did not oversee, the right's *Appeal to Reason*. Burnham steered it toward an American version of *Saturday Review*. With a few important exceptions, Burnham triumphed over Meyer in future interoffice disputes.

"I heard Buckley say for the first time that Burnham was the intellectual force at the magazine at one of those last Agonies," Neal Freeman remembered. "It was said to put Frank in his place. He was clearly the most important intellectual force at the magazine. Everybody laughed, except Jim Burnham, who probably took it seriously." Buckley, Freeman added, saw *National Review* not as an intellectual journal but an opinion magazine.[51] He became, therefore, more comfortable in his own pages.

The magazine increasingly resembled Burnham's vision for it. The conservative movement inspired and informed by the magazine increasingly took the shape of its books editor. The former Stalinist organizer evangelized on the phone, from the lectern, and in his living room. The former Trotskyist theorist converted his boss. Meyer's principles became what the conservative movement embraced, and his heresies became what it rejected. His most effective work increasingly took place outside of *National Review*. Meyer's katabasis within the publication paradoxically corresponded to his anabasis within conservatism.

James Burnham won the magazine. Frank Meyer went about winning the movement.

◄ 29 ►

Goldwater

In Defense of Freedom championed limited government not to win a parlor game but to spur organization to channel conservative energy and to obtrude theory upon praxis. The conservative vigor, to borrow a term popular with John Kennedy, that his successor feared as "the Great Beast" in American politics lay not slumbering but stifled. The pressure had built for more than three decades. Frank Meyer sought to unleash the fury of Lyndon Johnson's Great Beast. This warranted writing a bound manifesto. It required identifying a vessel to carry its message.

The unwritten postscript to *In Defense of Freedom* came through its author's activism. Meyer wanted fusionism to capture the conservative movement, and that conservative movement to win control of government. His life in the fray reached full circle by shifting emphasis from thinking and writing to the strategy and organizing that had consumed him in his days in London and Chicago. The success of his efforts could culminate only in the election of a president, and all that meant for freedom, from the conservative movement. He moved in his last act toward this bourne.

Subsisting in the desert of American politics, conservatives appropriately found the leader of their exodus—where else?—in the desert. It took Moses forty years to glimpse the promised land. The outs needed sixteen more years and a new Moses. But the promised land had started to appear more like a reality than a mirage.

In anticipation of an early 1963 editorial Agony, Meyer urged his fellow editors to support Barry Goldwater while attacking rivals George Romney, William Scranton, and Nelson Rockefeller.[1] He wrote the senator gauging interest in a presidential run, the response to which he interpreted as "less yielding in his opposition."[2]

James Burnham remained hostile. Buckley's support wavered. "Has it occurred to you that perhaps he isn't our man?" he asked in early 1963.[3]

"As to your remark about his perhaps 'not being our man,'" Meyer replied, "the only <u>firm</u> response I can make is: he's the only man we've got. I think it is vital to find a center around which to consolidate political conservatism."[4]

Reasons existed for *National Review* to institutionally demur beyond the Arizona senator's snub at the *Human Events* dinner or his demand for *NR* to recall an authorized fundraising appeal. It became nasty.

Goldwater's aides mousetrapped Bozell and Buckley into public embarrassment. The pair hoped to help Goldwater, a candidate sans college diploma routinely pilloried by intellectuals, by launching a "professors for Goldwater"-type organization. When they arrived for a September 1963 meeting with Goldwater advisor Dr. Charles Kelley, they found, to their surprise, William Baroody Sr. of the American Enterprise Institute (AEI) and Denison Kitchel, the candidate's longtime campaign manager, accompanying him. Their suggestions did not find a favorable audience.

The real insult occurred thereafter.

"The Goldwater-for-President ship has just repelled a boarding party from the forces who occupy the supposedly narrow territory to the right of the Arizona Senator," read a story in *The New York Times* likely planted in part to portray

Goldwater as more moderate at the expense of embarrassing two longtime allies. Buckley and Bozell, the article claimed, "cornered some Goldwater aides" to become policy advisors. "Feeling that what their candidate needs least is more support from the far right, the Goldwater advisers used an old political dodge. They played dumb."[5]

Given that Bozell ghostwrote *The Conscience of a Conservative* and once worked in the senator's Washington office, and Buckley for years promoted the Arizonan, the characterization of the pair as a "boarding party" clashed with reality. Whether primarily a cheap trick to advertise separation between candidate and conservatives or a territorial Baroody waging a turf war with rivals (as the senator later believed), Goldwater ultimately apologized.[6]

Goldwater did much, and his hired guns did more, to alienate *National Review*. To *National Review*'s credit, the repeated insults from his handlers, one imagines on some level to elicit an I'm-taking-my-ball-and-going home response, did not prompt the magazine to abandon its principles.

Goldwater certainly could not cool Meyer's enthusiasm. Neither could the terrible fate of his presumptive opponent.

✦ ✦ ✦

"SINCE I have a wager with each of you on the proposition that 'if Goldwater is nominated, he will be elected,' in view of recent events you should have the option of withdrawing," Meyer wrote Dwight Macdonald, John Gregory Dunne, Burnham, and Buckley weeks after John Kennedy's assassination. "So far as I am concerned, I would be very happy to continue the wager exactly as before."[7]

Much of the country remained stuck on November 22, 1963. Meyer fixated on November 3, 1964. His colleagues seemed little affected. Willmoore Kendall, awaiting Kennedy at a scheduled Dallas luncheon on the day of his assassination, deadpanned after hearing the Stygian announcement that at least his streak of never meeting an American president remained intact.[8]

"Whatta weekend they had in Dallas!" exclaimed Jeffrey Hart. "The news reports had a kind of 'can you top this' quality. Ghastly events. Tremendous break that JFK wasn't shot by a Bircher, though."[9]

The right wing, reflexively blamed for the assassination, exhaled upon learning that a Communist named Lee Harvey Oswald, who had earlier defected to the Soviet Union, murdered Kennedy. But by the time of the inhale, panicked Communist Party leaders, including Irving Potash and Gus Hall, whom Meyer had helped send to prison, launched the most widely believed conspiracy theory in history. They blamed their political enemies rather than admitted their group's ties, documented through letters and long-distance calls, with the assassin. Once arrested, Oswald tellingly requested that John Abt, who had repeatedly objected to Meyer's testimony before the Subversive Activities Control Board, represent him.[10]

The right-wingers-did-it Rorschach Test reaction offended decency and truth. Still, Meyer's own inkblot response, if not so brazenly crass as that of former comrades, similarly said less about the event than it did about him. He seemed more bothered by the public outcry than the assassination itself. He appreciated Hart's analyzing the political fallout without mawkishness.

"Your remarks on the events of the past two weeks, show so much more common sense than some persons who should know better and have been affected by the hullabaloo, that I congratulate you," came his reply from Woodstock. "As a matter of fact, despite all the public furor, the general judgment of those around Goldwater, is that the situation is in pretty good shape, everything considered."[11]

Goldwater disagreed. The idea of running against Kennedy to provide a clear choice between liberalism and conservatism appealed to him. He loathed the idea of a campaign against Johnson. He regarded the new president as a phony and a demagogue.[12] The bullet that had killed his friend also killed his drive to run. A Goldwater presidency became a longer shot because it asked Americans to welcome a new president into office for the third time in just over a year. Just as Kennedy's deepest mourners chose to believe what flattered politically with regard to the assassination, Goldwater's most committed enthusiasts imagined it to be no obstacle to the Arizonan's victory.

✦ ✦ ✦

GOLDWATER did not so much choose to run as his devotees chose for him. He could not let so many people down after all that hype, could he? *National Review* ultimately decided, not reflexively but with debate and consideration, to support him. The association of Goldwater with *National Review* and the synonymity of *National Review* with William F. Buckley spawn bewilderment that in the year conservatives regarded Goldwater as the "choice" rather than the "echo," several at *National Review*, including its famous editor, regarded the Arizonan as anything but the candidate *accompli*.

Burnham, the Buckley whisperer whose conservatism essentially started at the water's edge, sensed kinship with Nelson Rockefeller, a liberal Republican who accepted the premise of the Soviet Union as a menace but deviated from the right on much else. In Goldwater, he saw an off-putting rube surrounded by equally uncouth politicos. Burnham held season tickets to the Metropolitan Opera House.[13] Goldwater flew B-52s. Burnham's kind of man was the fellow Ivy Leaguer and grandson of the world's richest man, not the college dropout born in the Arizona Territory.

"The fact is, as we know, that Goldwater is a second-rate person; and he seems to be surrounded by third- and fourth-rate persons," he opined privately.[14] Burnham's view partially held sway with managing editor Priscilla Buckley but few others. "I didn't know that anyone at the *National Review* had the slightest interest in Rockefeller," Arlene Croce recalled. Excepting the "bit standoffish" Burnham, her recollection more or less accurately reflected the situation.[15] Still, rejection of Rockefeller was not tantamount to embrace of Goldwater.

"Believe it or not," Neal Freeman divulged, "*National Review* was up in the air until the California primary in June of 1964 whether we would support Rockefeller or Goldwater. I became bonded to Frank in that fight."[16]

◆ ◆ ◆

BEFORE ANY MATTER of an endorsement came the fight over tone. Striking the right balance between cheerleader and referee mattered within a journalistic enterprise. Burnham, legitimately concerned about the magazine's independence but also likely seeing an opening to kneecap Goldwater while circumscribing his in-house fan club, presented a plan. He laid out four possible outcomes, ranging from triumph to obliteration, for Goldwater in the New Hampshire primary. He asked each editor to advise what course the magazine should follow for each scenario. Should Goldwater's totals fall short of, say, Meyer's hopes, how should the magazine proceed editorially? The answers, presumably, would give Burnham greater freedom, and delimit the Goldwaterite wing, in the primary's aftermath. Whether motivated by deviousness or not, Burnham asked fair questions.

Rusher seconded a metric to predetermine the magazine's next steps as he reminded that this quantitative approach applied to Burnham, too.[17] Buckley, though expressing "my dread of sounding like Human Events," that is, a booster sheet for the candidate, thought that after acting as Goldwater's cheerleader for so long the magazine's abandonment of him would signal cowardice.[18] Meyer flatly dismissed Burnham's suggestion by labeling summer, should Goldwater lose the nomination, as the time for recalibration.[19]

The most impassioned plea came from neither Meyer nor Rusher but Bill Rickenbacker. The son of the flying ace concluded his memo with the dramatic observation that sticking by their principles meant a thank you from their grandchildren. Rickenbacker, personifying here the intensity of support unmeasured by polls that propelled Goldwater's candidacy, wrote his fellow decision-makers:

> As a magazine we have no interest in supporting the successful candidate as such. We have every motive to keep our scutcheon clean, and in Goldwater we have the rare chance to pick a practicing politician who also happens to be "our man" in a specific philosophical sense. If our political theory is in any sense translatable into politics, then we can only insult our own consciences by questioning the odds on Goldwater. As it happens, he has the best chance of getting the nomination of any candidate in the last three decades, if you measure that chance by the quantity of committed delegates in conjunction with the early stage of the political year. But even if it were not so: even if he were a dark horse: I say he is our dark horse, and we should not stint our support in view of any odds. We are willing, I take it, ultimately to sacrifice our lives in the cause of Christian civilization; we should be no less willing to dedicate our magazine to the only major public figure who proclaims our own beliefs.[20]

This did not settle matters.

♦ ♦ ♦

THE AREAS where Burnham exerted the most control, the magazine's front and the biweekly *Bulletin*, appeared more evenhanded; the individual columns, written primarily by Goldwater supporters, reflected the writers' enthusiasms.

"National Review will never be mistaken for a campaign organ, which, quite understandably, strains all news involving its candidate through a sort of euphoric dye," an unsigned item in 1964's first issue explained. In volunteering this assurance, *National Review* at once acknowledged its obvious connection to the candidate as it put readers on notice that it operated as a journalistic enterprise, requiring it to reject the temptation to play flack. The magazine colored itself as "enthusiastic endorsers of Mr. Goldwater's candidacy; as independent evaluators of his statements and his campaign; and as objective analysts of his chances."[21]

The writings of one senior editor left the impression that that passage had not left an impression. Nine of the eleven "Principles and Heresies" columns from 1964 mention Barry Goldwater.

The word "objectivity" bothered Rusher and to a greater extent Meyer, who regarded it in this instance as dishonest in that *NR* had already cast its lot with Goldwater and that fetishizing objectivity acted to undermine the magazine's clearly chosen candidate.

"As is so often the case in political matters, prediction by an active participant can itself be a factor in the outcome," Meyer wrote the editors. "Whether Goldwater defeats Johnson or not partly depends on subjective factors—the most important of which are the enthusiasms, capability and skill of the Goldwater supporters. NR can play an enormous role in maintaining and developing this. We will not do so if we overstress the kind of 'objectivity'—that is the exclusion of subjective and underlying factors—which [Rusher] is discussing."[22]

Burnham's worry that various writers could not maintain objectivity received affirmation in their moonlighting activities.

In 1963, Goldwater's circle enlisted Meyer in a counter-intelligence operation. Supporters, some overzealous, a few unsavory, sought to involuntarily place Goldwater on ballot lines other than Republican. This benefited the activist groups more than the candidate for whom they ostensibly sacrificed by solidifying impressions of him as on the fringe and the marginalized groups as occupying a place within his court. The proto-campaign found the right man in Meyer, whose cachet awarded him passport to such people. He described the New Jersey Conservative Party, for instance, to the campaign as "pretty far out" and discussed his telephonic efforts to dissuade the various groups working with the Virginia Conservative Council and to "subordinate their judgment to the national judgment."[23] Goldwater understood that he faced a difficult enough challenge merely by associations with his own opinions; with oddballs tethering his candidacy to made-for-caricature third parties the task looked grim. He needed it stopped.

A Meyer prediction amplified by United Press International in the spring of 1963 posited that Democrats awaited the worst defeat in their history at Goldwater's hands.[24] In speeches that year and the next for Ohioans for Goldwater, at Young Americans for Freedom and Conservative Party conventions, and before campus audiences, Meyer touted not just the virtues of Goldwater's ideas but the likelihood of his November victory.[25]

Meyer also helped in smaller ways. He provided advice on the announcement speech.[26] He traveled to New Hampshire ahead of the primary to volunteer.[27] It does not appear that the campaign paid him a stipend or a salary, but it did cover expenses for several months.[28]

Despite the efforts of Meyer and countless others, Henry Cabot Lodge, whose votaries launched a write-in campaign, won the New Hampshire primary. Goldwater placed, and Rockefeller, his main rival, showed. Goldwater won in such delegate-rich states as Illinois and Texas. Finally, and most consequently, came California. Buckley told underlings that should Goldwater fail in the Golden State then the magazine must call on him to withdraw.[29] Goldwater saved his candidacy, and *National Review* as well, by winning in a squeaker.

The more insecure of Goldwater's handlers mistreated Meyer as they had Buckley and Bozell. In New York, where victory awaited its favorite son Rockefeller under its convention system, Goldwater at least wished to make a statement by invading his turf. Invited to appear at a Madison Square Garden "Go with Goldwater" rally, Meyer instead watched. "I want to take this opportunity to express my appreciation for your cooperation and understanding on the platform situation at the May 12 Madison Square Garden Rally," Goldwater wrote Meyer. "At the last moment, it was decided to limit individuals on the platform to active Republican political figures in the belief that such a show of strength would have considerable impact on the press and other mass media covering the rally."[30]

◆ ◆ ◆

WITH PRIMARY SEASON OVER, Goldwater appeared to be the fair-and-square victor. Still, moderates did not reciprocate unity calls that he had provided in 1960. Pennsylvania's governor Bill Scranton launched an eleventh-hour bid to derail Goldwater. Rockefeller delivered a convention speech provoking the crowd and tarnishing the party as beholden to extremists.[31] Senator Kenneth Keating of New York staged an exodus from the Cow Palace once Goldwater had secured the nomination.[32]

His worst enemies called themselves Republicans. He was one of them. Goldwater displayed in San Francisco his love-hate relationship with his biggest boosters. On the one hand, Harry Jaffa, a friend of Meyer's and a sometime *NR* contributor, indirectly provided the Ciceronian lines for which history remembers, for better and worse, Goldwater's acceptance speech, written by Karl Hess: "I would remind you that extremism in the defense of liberty is no vice. And let me remind you also that moderation in the pursuit of justice is no virtue."[33] On the other hand, Goldwater's staff again snubbed a friend, this time at a YAF rally in which the presumptive nominee's people directed Ronald Reagan to cut the event short immediately before the scheduled start of Buckley's speech. It intensified the sting that Buckley had traveled to San Francisco to help Goldwater on the very weekend his sister Maureen—a fun and lighthearted person who in her early twenties playfully decorated Willi Schlamm's *NR* office with pictures of Dwight Eisenhower—suffered an ultimately fatal brain hemorrhage.[34] He flew across a continent for this insult atop that injury?

The campaign took on the gruff quality of Goldwater. This enabled political enemies to easily caricature him. The Daisy Girl ad, approved by the dirty trickster Bill Moyers, illustrated the no-quarter effort to smear Goldwater. It features a little girl picking the petals off a flower before a nuclear bomb explodes as a Lyndon Johnson voiceover informs viewers of the election's "stakes."[35] The convention host city's mayor, John Shelley, identified *Mein Kampf* as the political bible of the Republican Party.[36] Martin Luther King Jr. saw "dangerous signs of Hitlerism" in the candidate's program.[37] *Fact* magazine asked the 12,356 members of the American Psychiatric Association whether Goldwater was "psychologically fit" for the presidency, and received such remote assessments as "latent homosexuality," "grossly psychotic," "he has never forgiven his father for being a Jew," and "a mass-murderer at heart."[38]

Apart from the indecency and demagoguery, the attacks on Goldwater exuded overkill. As a more detached Stephen Tonsor, then a professor at the University of Michigan, had wisely informed Meyer the previous December, Goldwater's chances ended the moment Oswald ended Kennedy.[39] Meyer painted a more exuberant picture.

"Principles and Heresies" informed readers of a political realignment underway that he had first pronounced in *The American Mercury* a decade earlier. The coalition Franklin

Roosevelt had assembled no longer applied. The column claimed that "the familiar landmarks of thirty years have been obliterated; and these unfortunate souls are wondering around the highways and byways of politics with hopelessly outdated maps."[40]

Meyer attempted to obliterate them through his 1964 essay collection *What Is Conservatism?*, which ISI's Victor Milione encouraged him to compile. "We are today historically in a situation created by thirty years of slow and insidious revolution at home and a half century of violent open revolution abroad," he wrote. "To conserve the true and the good under these circumstances is to restore an understanding (and a social structure reflecting that understanding) which has been all but buried; it is not to preserve the transient customs and prescriptions of the present."[41] He introduced himself here as the revolutionary he had always been. He wished to overthrow, albeit now as a counterrevolutionary. The editor's inclusion of Russell Kirk, Wilhelm Röpke, and F. A. Hayek showcased the collection's ecumenical tone. Chapters by John Chamberlain, Father Stanley Parry, and M. Stanton Evans at least floored when they did not convert. For a reader who wanted to understand the Goldwater phenomenon, *What Is Conservatism?* did an excellent job.

Meyer's 1960 memo predicting a fifteen- to twenty-year cultivation to reap the harvest proved a measured assessment. In the emotion of this election year, he confused, as he did in 1928 with Al Smith, his fervent hope for dispassionate reality. He wasn't wrong. He was early.

He branded it "conceivable" that Goldwater could win "Eastern industrial states now seemingly firmly Johnson's." He outlined a scenario in which the Republican nominee would win much of the Midwest, the Mountain West, the Southwest, several border states, and all but a few Southern states to reach 257 electoral votes. "Texas with 25 electoral votes, or California with 40 would make Goldwater President—and without the vote of a single Eastern state," he surmised. "Should Goldwater penetrate the East also, he could well win in a landslide."[42]

The landslide happened. It just buried the wrong candidate. Johnson trounced Goldwater 486 to 52 in the Electoral College. Johnson's popular vote percentage bested every candidate dating back to James Monroe in 1820.

Republicans faced a 295–140 House disadvantage and a lopsided 68–32 Senate ratio. For the last time in U.S. history, one party held a congressional supermajority. Democrats enjoyed a 33–17 advantage among governors. Considering the liberal Republicans governing such populous states as New York, Pennsylvania, Michigan, and Massachusetts, conservatives occupied a weaker position than did Republicans. And culturally the winds shifted further faster.

It looked darkest, as it does, before dawn.

In that protracted, ink-black night after the election, Frank Meyer's Great Beast, humbled, wounded, and enervated, survived. That which did not kill it made it stronger. A goblin of the Catskills nursed it to health. An enemy leaves a Great Beast alive at great risk.

◄ 30 ►

Rebuild

T he indefatigable Frank Meyer projected enthusiasm upon the movement he had shaped. What others saw as a demoralizing failure the man who publicly predicted a great victory regarded as progress toward the ultimate goal: a movement conservative in the White House.

"The remarkable thing about post-election attitudes here," he insisted to an aged and English Sir Shane Leslie, "is that no one is discouraged and all sorts of plans were under way to carry things forward. I have, myself, been deeply involved in the project of establishing a Conservative organization of the same type as [Americans for Democratic Action] on the left, and I think it will be off the ground before Christmas."[1]

The Republican Party, led by the most ideologically pure presidential nominee in its 110 years, had just suffered one of the great routs in U.S. history, and Meyer contended (pretended?)—a belief at once certainly false and certain to pass a lie-detector test—that enthusiasm gripped conservatives. His lecture invitations, which overwhelmed a year prior, did not reflect this enthusiasm.[2] *National Review*'s subscriptions, at least in the election's initial aftermath, did not reflect this enthusiasm.[3] But Meyer felt it, and if it were not true then he would make it so.

345

He willed the conservative energy and enthusiasm that strangely followed Goldwater's defeat. The tub-thumping gospeler that had marked him as a dubious political pundit prior to November 3 made him the activist-cheerleader conservatives so desperately needed after it.

He told readers that "nothing that occurred demonstrated anything wrong or weak—morally or philosophically or logically—in the conservative position. Nor, when we consider that the campaign represented but a few months of the first opportunity on a broad national scale to confute thirty years of Liberal indoctrination, can the gaining of two-fifths of the vote be considered a 'practical disaster' of momentous consequence."

He highlighted the handicaps of a hostile media and conservatism's shift in mission from preservationist crusade to uprooter of the status quo. Conservatives, he claimed, now stood closer to victory than at any time since the election of Franklin Roosevelt.[4]

He had tightrope-walked tremulous party lines many times in the distant past. Here he crossed from one end of the big top to another because he saw this feat as no stunt at all.

In *NR*'s year-end issue, Meyer doubled down by portraying the Goldwater vote as a basis upon which to create a majority and citing the popularity of Ronald Reagan's televised campaign speech, in which the actor had amplified rather than muted conservatism.[5] He reasoned that the results should not discourage but invigorate conservatives.

Meyer acted as the coach delivering the fiery pep talk to a team down by four touchdowns. He needed to convince the players not only that victory was possible but that it was halftime in the locker room and the game was not over.

Lee Edwards remembered, "Some conservatives thought, 'That's it. We were smashed, demolished. It's all done. Let's give up. Let's retire.' Others were much more aggressive. It was Frank Meyer who said something like 'You can build a pretty good political movement with a base of twenty-seven million people.'"[6] So Meyer went about creating an organization.

The shabby treatment of Buckley and Bozell during the Goldwater campaign, allegedly by AEI's Bill Baroody, was a motivation for creating a new group. This also represented, even if on a subconscious level, the revival of the "conservative senate" that Meyer, Bill Rusher, and Marvin Liebman had floated as a means to derail media attempts to set up the John Birch Society as a movement straw man and spokesman.[7] This more directly involved establishing a conservative Americans for Democratic Action, pushed by Henry Regnery and others as early as 1953, than an alternative to AEI or JBS.[8] The idea percolated. Prior to Richard Nixon's defeat in 1960, Liebman had expended significant effort to start a group that he called Americans for Conservative Action.[9] And even as Meyer and friends organized the American Conservative Union (ACU), William Loeb, publisher of the *Manchester Union-Leader*, wrote him with more or less the same idea.[10] Others thought of it. Frank and friends did it.

"So we put together—and I was part of it, not at the top but somewhere in the doing of it—a meeting in Washington, DC, in the Capitol Hilton Hotel upstairs on the second floor in a meeting room, maybe fifty, seventy-five of us, something like that, probably on a weekend, and coming out of that was the American Conservative Union," Edwards recalled. "[Meyer], along with, I think I would say, Bob Bauman, was one of the major organizers."[11]

◆ ◆ ◆

THE KEY FIGURES retreated to hammer out the mission, constitution, and officers of the activist-oriented group.

"Frank was certainly one of four or five people instrumental in working with us and setting up the ACU," Young Americans for Freedom Chairman Bauman noted. "And that's probably why he was elected as treasurer. I don't think he particularly wanted to be. But it was a way of promoting the new organization with strong names."[12]

The minutes list board members as U.S. Representatives John Ashbrook of Ohio, Katharine St. George of New York, and Donald Bruce of Indiana; *National Review* editors Buckley, Bozell, and Meyer; and Bauman, Liebman, and *Indianapolis Star* editor Jameson Campaigne Sr. Upon Meyer's motion, the group unanimously elected Bruce, whose career in Congress ended two weeks later, chairman. Campaigne motioned for Meyer to serve as treasurer, which the group unanimously approved. Buckley advanced several motions, which passed by close margins, excluding John Birch Society members. Meyer offered an amendment preventing them from serving in leadership but not from becoming members.[13] The next day, the board rescinded the anti-Birch motion but acknowledged it as "a matter of unstated policy."[14]

Buckley, truly spooked by Welch and another crank he had once known, the American Nazi Party leader George Lincoln Rockwell (on whom he had sicced a priest to unsuccessfully extirpate the evil residing therein), marinated in Manhattan, Stamford, and Switzerland.[15] Meyer, despite leaving Woodstock for little but speeches and conservative conclaves, more thoroughly inhabited the activist world. Their perspectives on the JBS necessarily differed, albeit slightly. In late 1964, the older but junior partner regarded it as an overreaction to ban JBS members from ACU as though they subscribed to a hate group as Rockwell's followers did. So he outmaneuvered his boss.

The pair shared a contempt for what they saw as conspiratorial thinking and simpletonism within the society, which, despite *NR*'s varying efforts against it in 1961 and 1962, remained a force. Despite Meyer's alteration of Buckley's proposed policy, the duo essentially sang from the same sheet of music.

◆ ◆ ◆

A BEAM-IN-ITS-EYE left pushed mainstream conservatives to denounce the society when not conflating the two distinct cliques on the right. Steve Allen, the original host of the *Tonight Show*, for instance, sent Meyer and associates a twelve-page memorandum on "the problem of irresponsible Right-wing extremist activity" a year after a left-wing extremist had murdered the president.[16] The comedian, though relying on irony, did not grasp his own. The following year, in 1965, *NR* devoted an issue to the JBS. Whereas Welch had served as the primary target in earlier attempts to separate the right from conspiratorial thinking, this issue panned out to inspect the society itself.

In a double-length "Principles and Heresies" headlined "The Birch Malady," Meyer depicted the JBS as unsophisticated and delusional. He wrote that the group not only discredited the right but siphoned conservative energy from legitimate projects to pour down intellectual rabbit holes.

"One can find elements of belief in an Illuminati conspiracy, a Fabian conspiracy, a Bilderberger conspiracy, a Council of Foreign Relations conspiracy," he marveled. "Sometimes a number of these are held at once, without explanation of the patent contradiction, and sometimes there are dark hints of an unnamed super-conspiracy that masterminds all of them."[17]

The motivation stemmed in part from the embarrassment of profoundly intellectual men linked by political adversaries to extremists who reflexively arrived at conspiracy theories. Later Meyer's irritation at a book describing him as a Bircher resulted in an apology, Doubleday's placement of an erratum slip in existing volumes, and the deletion of the offending passages from future printings.[18] It felt easier for the right's enemies to debate JBS straw men than to engage with Meyer, Buckley, and other intellects associated with *National Review*. So they repeatedly debated the straw men and smeared non-Birchers as Birchers.

THE SOCIETY broadened its "Get US out" slogan to en-
compass Vietnam as well as the United Nations. This annoyed
Meyer. "I should say that now that Welch has joined the sit-in-
ers in proposing our getting out of Viet Nam," he explained
to Allen, "my own attitude toward them has rather changed."
Noting that he "never found them very pleasing," he told his
celebrity correspondent that he nevertheless could not countenance "reading them out of American society."[19] Midway
through 1965, he colored himself, and his conservative comrades, in support of President Lyndon Johnson's war effort.[20]

At an early 1965 meeting attended by the novelist John Dos
Passos and the recent *Time* cover boy Lammot du Pont Co-
peland in which Meyer successfully motioned to make ACU
a membership organization, the board endorsed a salary for
Meyer for his role as co-coordinator of the group's advisory
assembly and director of publications. Meyer brought up the
issue of a pamphlet on Vietnam.[21] Prior to 1965, the conflict
accounted for the deaths of fewer than five hundred American servicemen. Fatalities quintupled by year's end.

Meyer combined forces with the Yale University political
scientist David Rowe and the Hoover Institution's Stefan
Possony to publish "Vietnam." Billed as an "ACU Task Force
Study," the nineteen-page pamphlet posited that "having contributed materially to the demise of colonialism in Asia, we
were now confronted by a new order of colonialism in the
emerging states, namely Communist colonialism." The authors named as a major setback to keeping South Vietnam
from falling to the Communists the "disastrous participation
in the destruction of President Diem as the start of the political instability in South Vietnam." They bluntly charged
that "the United States lacks the will to win" and that unless it
changed strategy soon it undoubtedly would face a protracted

war likely to spread to Thailand, Malaysia, and other countries in the region.[22]

The "excellent" publication particularly enthused Dos Passos.[23] The coauthor's role as director of publications veered more toward recruiting other experts to contribute studies, which soon included the NYU law professor Sylvester Petro on the Taft–Hartley Act, the Columbia Business School professor Martin Anderson on urban renewal, and the president of Rockford College John Howard on federal student aid.[24] Not yet the ACU whose scores Republican congressmen coveted or which launched the Conservative Political Action Conference, the organization made its mark in these early years as an activist group with an intellectual bent due to Meyer.

✦ ✦ ✦

REVIEWING scholarly literature for years for the Volker Fund, editing *The Exchange* to place conservatives in the academy, and overseeing book reviews for *National Review* provided an ideal background for ACU's director of publications. It similarly suited him to help launch an organization more academic than activist.

Again, as with ACU and YAF, the younger generation groomed by Meyer took the lead. Don Lipsett acted as the prime mover.

The Hoosier served as national director of the Intercollegiate Society of Individualists, which changed its name to the Intercollegiate Studies Institute in the mid-1960s but kept its initialism, ISI. In 1964, that most consequential year for the American right, Lipsett embarked upon a project to speak to intellectuals. Whereas the group from which Lipsett drew a paycheck organized conservative students for an intellectual purpose, the group he started aimed to organize conservative thinkers for a similar purpose. A parallel structure to the institutions dominated by liberals to the exclusion of conservatives began to take shape.

The organization lists Meyer as a speaker on the very first panel at its Philadelphia meeting. Along with Willmoore Kendall and Father Stanley Parry, he addressed "The Crisis of Western Civilization" in the Washington Room at the Benjamin Franklin Hotel on April 25, 1964. Figures who spoke later that day at a Philadelphia Society meeting in San Francisco included Russell Kirk, Hoover Institution President Glenn Campbell, and the economist Karl Brandt.[25] But Stephen Tonsor wrote Meyer on April 19—six days before the supposed first meeting—wishing that the latter had been able to attend the "launching" of the Philadelphia Society in Indianapolis.[26] Others date the society's origins to later that fall.[27]

The meeting Meyer addressed fell under the auspices of ISI, which dubbed it "the Philadelphia Society." Lipsett wanted to make that new institution permanent.

"Five of us, Lipsett and myself, Bill Buckley, Milton Friedman, and Frank Meyer, held a meeting at [Manhattan's] Sheraton Atlantic Hotel," Ed Feulner, then a student at the Wharton School, recalled of a memorable day in late 1964. "It was the first time that Buckley had ever met Friedman. It was the first time I had ever met any of the three of them, the big boys. It was unbelievable. At that meeting, we decided we were going to found the U.S. equivalent of the Mont Pelerin Society."[28]

That European group, established in 1947 by such intellectual giants as Friedrich Hayek, Karl Popper, Ludwig von Mises, and Frank Knight, became less replicated than Americanized. Its more reserved and classical liberal orientation shifted. America necessarily did that. More so did an energetic man from Newark, proposed by Henry Hazlitt but tabled for membership in the European group, do that.[29]

"I think he did leave an impression on the organization," William Campbell, who served as a president and a longtime secretary, observed. "In other words, it never was a policy discussion group. In the early years, it was always just fundamental questions."[30]

Meyer became a fixture. He spoke twice at the Chicago meeting the next year and again at the fall event in Philadelphia. He delivered prepared talks at a Philadelphia Society gathering every year from its founding.[31] But the impromptu remarks always trumped the scheduled lectures.

"If somebody said something he deemed a heresy," Yaffer Ken Grubbs explained, "he would pop up to the microphone and just lace into him." He cited a spirited response to the suspected populist tone emanating from the political strategist Kevin Phillips as an example of this habit.[32]

"They would both be standing on chairs at Philadelphia Society yelling at each other across the room," Don Devine recalled of Meyer and Harry Jaffa. "Cultured isn't the right word. He was a very combative guy. Certainly with me and my friends he was like your best pal."[33]

David Keene remembered that at one meeting "Irving [Kristol] decided to describe himself, finally, as a conservative. At which point Frank, who usually wore a red flannel shirt and suspenders—he was a little skinny guy—he was sitting in the back, he jumped up on the chair, interrupted the debate, pointed at Kristol, and said, 'You, sir, are not a conservative. You are nothing but a goddamned Tory socialist.' He got up and slammed the door to a then-silenced crowd."[34]

At one meeting Meyer prefaced remarks by saying, "I don't want to appear intransigent, but," which unleashed uncontrollable laughter.[35]

More so than during prepared remarks or question-and-answer sessions, Meyer left an impression in the invariable after-hours events, in which he held court deep into the night.[36] Meyer, not Lipsett, Feulner, Friedman, or Buckley, dove headlong into the meetings as both speaker and listener. The latter role often morphed into the former role. Then the scheduled speaker might, to his discomfort, become the listener as Meyer launched into an impromptu speech born from a question. In this way, Meyer put his enduring stamp on the organization, whose liveliness occurred in debates masquerading as question-and-answer sessions and the exchanges at the bar. The Philadelphia Society ensured such vibrancy by becoming not fusionist like Meyer but ecumenical like the magazine whose back pages he edited. Here, exemplars of the various strains of conservatism talked, debated, and even yelled. Frank did all three.

"People expected a pretty high level of discourse in both the papers delivered and the questions asked," member Howard Segermark recalled. "I think they got it."[37]

◆ ◆ ◆

IF THEY COULD NOT afford the trip to the Philadelphia Society to experience the back-and-forth, they bought a subscription to *National Review*.

Harry Jaffa started it. In a thoughtful review of a book on Reconstruction, he set Meyer off.[38] Or did Meyer start it? The one who assigned the review liked a good argument, after all. In a "Books in Brief" review of Dean Sprague's *Freedom Under Lincoln*, the overseer of *National Review*'s book section wrote that the sixteenth president established "an authoritarianism that was, in terms of civil liberties, the most ruthless in American history." He applauded the author for laying out the factual record but criticized the "feeble excuses" he makes for Lincoln.[39] Nobody knows who started it. Everybody knows they brawled.

One reader wondered whether Meyer was "possibly a Confederate sympathizer."[40] Another, the magazine's editor, described the item—a 101-word brief of the type never attracting much notice—as "worse than mere tendentious ideological revisionism" and judged that it "comes close to blasphemy."[41]

"I am pleased to see Bill Buckley chopping you down on Lincoln, just as your good wife chopped him down on

Churchill!," Jaffa wrote Meyer. "Hurrah for NR! Hurrah for vigorous dissent! Hurrah for Winnie and Abe!"[42]

"On Lincoln," Meyer responded, "I have not been silenced. In fact, I compound my sin in the current issue of National Review. I shall be interested in your reactions. The difference between Churchill and Lincoln is that Churchill fought to preserve freedom, Lincoln to hobble it—or so it seems to me."[43]

The institution advertised its bias in the synopsis next to the issue's table of contents: "Frank Meyer sharply disagrees with Mr. Buckley on, of all people, Abraham Lincoln."[44] In an "Open Question," Meyer acknowledged touching a third rail. Then he performed acrobatics upon it.

"Sometimes there are judgments at which one arrives that one hesitates to state publicly, out of respect for deeply held beliefs and prejudices," he noted. "I have over a number of years come to think that the general admiration for Abraham Lincoln is ill-founded." He held that waging total war guaranteed the bitterness that followed and the disregard for civil liberties ushered in centralization and ultimately doomed federalism.[45]

National Review provided Jaffa with nearly three magazine pages to counter the words of one its senior editors. Therein, Jaffa wondered how Meyer could write "a critical essay on Abraham Lincoln and the Civil War without mentioning or even alluding to the subject of slavery." Much of the article elsewhere sidestepped Meyer's points. One line drew blood: "If states can declare their right to enslave human persons within their borders, what principle is it that they appeal to in denouncing arbitrary power in the Federal Government?"[46]

In the aptly titled "Again on Lincoln" published in January 1966, Meyer wrote that the dispute amounted to Jaffa's endorsement of loose constructionism. "Freedom and equality are opposites: the freer men are the freer they are to demonstrate their inequality, and any political or social attempt—like those so frequent in the twentieth century—to enforce equality leads inevitably to the restrictions and the eventual destruction of freedom," he maintained."[47]

That all this occurred during the centenary of Lincoln's assassination, and in the midst of the civil rights movement, raised the temperature. Undoubtedly, an ongoing fixation on hundred-year-old matters did not appeal to the editor of a current events biweekly. Buckley nevertheless welcomed conflict and smartly recognized that this tolerance for heterodoxy and heresy acted as part of the appeal (an ecumenicalism that allowed it to credibly excommunicate when the rare occasion demanded).

Excuses abound for any reader who imagined Meyer and Jaffa as bitter enemies. Their correspondence exhibited warmth.

"I would like to have that long, long bull session, without agenda, and without other company," Jaffa wrote his debating partner in the fall of 1965. "I think we are giving a dramatic example of the vitality of our differences, and why a 'conservative' society would be far more vigorous than a liberal one."[48]

✦ ✦ ✦

JAFFA attended the four-day Public Affairs Conference on Liberalism and Conservatism in the spring of 1965 when Meyer delivered a paper on conservatism.[49] Leo Strauss, an earlier pen pal who begged off reviewing books for *NR*, wrote Meyer of his plans to attend.[50] The audience included the young congressman Donald Rumsfeld and the columnist Robert Novak; the Straussian academics Edward Banfield, Joseph Cropsey, and Walter Berns; and the president of Bell & Howell and future Senator Charles Percy and his future Illinois colleague in that august body Adlai Stevenson III. The conference-goers represented a shockingly large portion of the day's idea men who shaped the next day's great conversation. Meyer jumped at the opportunity to influence the influencers.

At the conference, he listed seven principles that defined conservatism.

Conservatives, he said, believe in an objective moral order; emphasize rights and duties of real persons over the needs of the collective; reject utopian delusions of establishing heaven on earth or perfecting human beings; embrace limited government against social planners, engineers, and managers; advocate the free market; endorse the Constitution's division of power, federalism, and protection of freedoms; and defend of the West against Communism.

Meyer conceded that this specified no program or blueprint but instead provided conservatives broad principles upon which to address specific questions that periodically arise.[51] Ten years earlier, an ex-Communist defining conservatism would have seemed absurd. In 1965, he looked like the man for the job. He failed to overthrow the British monarchy and replace Franklin Roosevelt with Earl Browder. He succeeded in redefining the American right.

Frank Meyer, Communist commissar, had finally ascended to conservative pope.

◄ 31 ►

Books, Arts, and Manners

A Dr. Jekyll and Mr. Hyde quality characterized Frank Meyer. Every *National Review* issue showcased the intellectual, the overseer of the best review section in America. Every few issues, William F. Buckley allowed the ideologue free rein on a single page. Somehow, readers remembered the character who made cameos rather than the constant presence.

In "Books, Arts, and Manners," editor played director, which perhaps explains why "Principles and Heresies" rather than "Books, Arts, and Manners" more readily evoked Meyer. The director rarely appeared in a scene. Rather than write, he mainly attached the right book to the right reviewer.

The contributors generally fell into three categories: stars, conservatives, and talent. The first group, often making one-off appearances, included the likes of the author of perhaps the most ambitious poem in history, Ezra Pound; the Pulitzer Prize–winner Edgar Ansel Mowrer; and the royal Otto von Habsburg. The second group sometimes overlapped with the third but not always vice versa. The conservative group included David Brudnoy, later a popular radio host in Boston; Francis Russell, an accomplished author focusing on the same city; and the Midwestern right-winger Jameson Campaigne Jr.

Campaigne wondered whether among the young conservatives assigned a review the editor sought to develop cadres.

"My sense is that it was his teaching mechanism," he reflected. "He wanted you to read this particular book to deal with it so that you yourself in the course of reviewing it would think about it. It was like he was assigning a paper in college."[1]

The third group, reviewers hired in spite of their ideological shortcomings, exuded talent but not name recognition. Possessing the former usually resulted in the latter. Once recognition came, exits followed. But before they captivated the literary world, they wrote as Frank Meyer's best-kept secrets.

◆ ◆ ◆

REGULARS came to dominate to such a degree that they had to use pen names to avoid emitting a student newspaper vibe of a few contributors writing everything. Stephen Tonsor requested H. O. to write about John Henry Newman.[2] Reid Buckley wrote under Peter Crumpet to prevent the magazine from looking as though, like Mexican oil, it were a family enterprise.[3] Robert Phelps combined his son's first name and his wife's last in the *nom de plume* Roger Becket. M. Stanton Evans went by Christopher Logan. Garry Wills became William Roman.[4]

Even when Wills contributed a paragraph to the Books in Brief subsection, he usually wrote something worth reading. "To say there is something over nature (super-natural) is to say that nature is under; and that, you see, is an insult to the World," he explained in a review of *Teilhard and the Supernatural*. "Cosmic etiquette forbids our calling the World inferior to anything—anything, that is, except the Future, which is by definition the Better."[5]

He reviewed just about anything, including Webster's dictionary.[6] His value came not only from his ability to turn a phrase. The evisceration of Richmond Lattimore's translation of *The Odyssey* could only have come from one versed in both Greek and poetry. Frank knew such a person once, and just as Wills had stepped into Eugene O'Neill Jr.'s role as late-night debating partner, he also played classicist as well as poetry reciter, appreciator, and critic. "To achieve mathematical faithfulness," the former seminarian said of Lattimore's translation of hexameter from Greek to English, "he sacrifices the primary esthetic effect."[7]

What other magazine employed a reviewer who could point out how the author erred in translating *chamai* as "groundling"?

✦ ✦ ✦

LONG BEFORE she helped craft the screenplays of *A Star Is Born* and *True Confessions*, Joan Didion had helped establish "Books, Arts, and Manners" as a skip-the-rest-to-read-the-best section. "It was through Frank that Joan Didion," Priscilla Buckley wrote, first appeared "in *NR*'s pages."[8] She came by way of Noel Parmentel, as much a booster as a boyfriend, who introduced the "painfully shy" Didion to Meyer and other New York citizens of the Republic of Letters. This included her future husband. She wrote more than two dozen pieces for the magazine between 1959 and the end of 1965. "Frank was a great supporter of Joan," Parmentel recalled. "He was a great fan of hers."[9]

The courage the socially timid woman displayed on the printed page deepened that appreciation. Didion courageously knocked established writers and boosted unknowns. "*Franny and Zooey* is finally spurious, and what makes it spurious is [J. D.] Salinger's tendency to flatter the essential triviality within each of his readers, his predilection for giving instructions for the living," she wrote in a 1961 review of America's hottest author. "What gives the book its extremely potent appeal is precisely that it is self-help copy: it emerges finally as *Positive Thinking* for the upper middle classes, as *Double Your Energy and Live Without Fatigue* for Sarah Lawrence girls."[10] The neophyte novelist Richard Stern's *Golk*, on the other hand, appeared to Didion as "sharp, funny, intelligent, rare." She judged it "a first-rate comic novel."[11]

She pondered the mid-century curio-competitors Aroma-Rama and Smell-O-Vision, described Flannery O'Connor as "above all a *writer*, which is something different from *a person who writes a book*," and gleaned six pillars upholding women's magazines: wives come in the homemaker or housewife variety; women carry the world's work, which is never done; money cannot bring happiness, but "electrical appliances often do"; women are frigid; husbands amuse almost as much as kids; and "men can be handled."[12]

Her best *National Review* piece critiqued British novelist C. P. Snow's *The Affair*. "C. P. Snow, whose novels read as if they were the products of a collaboration, over sherry, between Anthony Trollope and a speech-writer for Adlai Stevenson, once explained that he writes the way he does because the 'wicked, absurd social attitudes' implicit in the way his contemporaries write had helped to bring 'Auschwitz that much nearer.' (This hallucination, that novels *make things happen*, is common among people who write them.) Mr. Snow's own novels are as far from Auschwitz as they are from Agincourt; they constitute instead the literature of the National Health Service, and celebrate a world of committees, compromises, decisions and revisions, a world in which Civil Service Hamlets Behave Well in Difficult Situations," she began her 1960 review of the civil servant's novel.[13]

National Review wanted Didion but not the male baggage she carried. One came off as too much a bitter snob; the other, too much a back-slapping jokester. The magazine eventually dumped both men, each talented but not worth the trouble. In doing so, it lost one of its star reviewers and wished thereafter that they all could be California girls, or at least one mousey-looking one who spoke softly but carried a big pen.

Her patron and protector Parmentel seemed destined to wear out his welcome. "I would write for *National Review*, I would write for *The Nation*, and they were diametrically opposed. In effect, I was opposed to both," he admitted.[14] Resident agelast Rusher, perhaps annoyed by Parmentel's failure to fit into an ideological box, broke up backroom poker games involving Parmentel, editors Arlene Croce and Bill Rickenbacker, and staffers including Martha Butler and Myrna Bain, one of the few African Americans aboard. "He was being a pain in the ass," Parmentel reflected. "We weren't bothering anybody. He thought it was unseemly."[15]

Meyer, in contrast to his colleagues, wished to keep using Parmentel so long as he submitted to his uncharacteristically heavy edits.[16] When the stringer lampooned the nearly two-year-old Young Americans for Freedom in *Esquire* under the title "The Acne and the Ecstasy," an article that also poked fun, for the third time in a widely read magazine, at *National Review* and Buckley family members, his time writing for the magazine ended by his own making.[17]

At an editorial meeting immediately after the article's appearance, Buckley resolved to write a "Dear John" letter to Parmentel while simultaneously breaking the news to Parmentel's protégé in a "Dear Joan" letter that essentially said, We love you but not your associate.[18] Didion stayed as the magazine conveyed *persona non grata* status to her steward.

More than a year later, Parmentel continued to mock his old friends through an LP of spoof conservative folk songs that included "I Dreamt I Saw Roy Cohn Last Night" and "Won't You Come Home, Bill Buckley." To the tune of "The Ballad of Harry Pollitt," Parmentel and the humorist Marshall Dodge wrote "Frank S. Meyer, Please": "Frank S. Meyer was a lefty, a Stalinist was said / When Frank S. broke the commie yoke, he was better dead than red. . . . Frank S. Meyer went to heaven clad in BVDs / give regard to Comrade God it's Frank S. Meyer, please."[19]

Around the same time, another of Didion's male admirers exceeded his abilities with his arrogance. His relationship with her required delicacy in separating him from the magazine.

In two letters written days apart, John Gregory Dunne describes himself as "infuriated" about an *NR* editorial criticizing Jessica Mitford, the left-wing member of an aristocratic family, and "incensed" about cuts to one of his reviews.[20] His letters show a man fluctuating between those two moods. He complains about pay.[21] When Buckley asks him to nominate a capable person to rewrite poorly crafted submissions for extra cash, Dunne rejects the job as though it had been offered to him. He segues into calling his latest piece "cruelly and barbarously mutilated in what passes for editing" at *National Review* and advises Buckley to instead edit the "deranged nonsense" recently submitted by Clare Boothe Luce, the wife of his *Time* boss Henry Luce—a recommendation the disgruntled Dunne, on his last legs at the publication, sent on *Time* letterhead.[22] He imposes a Kendallian condition upon Meyer that his reviews remain essentially unedited or they not run.[23] He in part justifies the demand by volunteering, "I'm a better writer than Garry Wills."[24] Meyer responds that for many reasons, including ones beyond his control such as available space, he could not accede.[25]

"Though I am glad that you approve of my work 'generally,' I'm afraid that I can't say the same about your so-called 'stars,'" Dunne informed Meyer. "By these, I assume you mean the 'incomparable' Francis Russell (remember him walking off into the rain, like Frederic Henry [of Ernest Hemingway's *Farewell to Arms*]) or that tendentious, sententious bore Garry Wills, about who, Evelyn Waugh got the picture, if the National Review didn't."[26] Parmentel had similarly ridiculed Wills.[27] The men who loved Joan Didion loathed Garry Wills.

The former seminarian's priggishness seemed to motivate the priggish response to him. Beyond this, Wills appeared as Meyer's golden boy. *Esquire*'s Harold Hayes allegedly held Wills in a higher regard than Dunne.[28]

Even before receipt of that bitter missive, Meyer wished to extricate the magazine from Dunne, an effort complicated by his marriage to Didion about a month earlier.

"No matter how much we want Joan (who I do not think will be affected by this, in any case), he is getting to be insufferable," he wrote Buckley. "Besides, while I did not say it in the letter, I have always had to squeeze the pomposity and verbosity out of his reviews before using them, or they would be insufferable."[29]

Mr. Joan Didion, nevertheless, returned for one last hurrah. Dunne criticized the "fictitious novel" phenomenon in 1966. "He has created what he calls a 'non-fiction novel,' and more than that, a 'new art form,'" he wrote of Truman Capote's *In Cold Blood*. "It is here that I begin to quibble."[30]

Didion did not quibble but imitated. She became a leading practitioner of Capote's New Journalism, by which time her views had already veered considerably from the conservative magazine that had so early given her a platform and toward Dunne's milquetoast Connecticut liberalism.

"Frank deserves the lion's share of the credit for the discovery, encouragement and development of Joan Didion," Parmentel wrote in *Esquire* in 1962.[31] Before decade's end, as Didion's star rose among Manhattan publishers and Hollywood producers, this view became not only unfashionable but suppressed. Didion continued to send handmade Christmas cards, invariably featuring artful, black-and-white photographs of adopted daughter Quintana Roo, to the Meyers.[32] But for her admirers, loving Joan Didion presupposed erasing Frank Meyer.

◆ ◆ ◆

DUNNE was hardly the first writer to seek to edit out the editor.

"I have seldom worked so hard on anything, most of the hard work being in cut & trim. If you must cut further, would you let me do it?" Theodore Sturgeon pleaded with Meyer about a review of the English translation of Harry Martinson's epic poem *Aniara*.[33]

Aniara's author went on to win the Nobel Prize for literature. Its *NR* reviewer soon invented *Star Trek's* prime directive, wrote Spock's "live long and prosper" line, and penned the episode that included the Vulcan hand gesture created by Leonard Nimoy. When Meyer tabbed him to replace C. R. Morse as the regular science fiction reviewer, Sturgeon enjoyed bits of mainstream success, such as NBC Radio's *X Minus One* adapting his "A Saucer of Loneliness."[34] His imprint outside of hardcore science fiction fans grew during his dozen years writing for the magazine. His *National Review* space allowed him to advance his primary legacy outside of storytelling. "Ninety percent of science fiction is unadulterated crud," Sturgeon's Law informed. "As a matter of fact, ninety percent of *everything* is."[35]

He dubbed J. G. Ballard "a name to remember, and one which will one day command the most respectful attention of the mainstream critics."[36] This soon came to pass with the publication of "Why I Want to Fuck Ronald Reagan." In *Crash* and *Empire of the Sun*, he fulfilled Sturgeon's prophecy in a manner acceptable to *NR* readers. He at once affirmed and offended sci-fi purists by judging that "Ray Bradbury is not a science fiction writer. He is a poet and a fantasist and a fabulist and a stylist extraordinary."[37] "[Arthur C.] Clarke at his worst can be an irritant," he conceded in reviewing *Tales of Ten Worlds*. "But let us add that at his worst he is considerably better than much of the competition."[38]

After reviewing *Stranger in a Strange Land*, the reviewer devoted several paragraphs about his editor, whose friendship inflicted a social cost upon him, in a letter to the reviewed. Sturgeon described Meyer to Robert Heinlein as well read but a captive to ideology. "Now it is obvious that this man has been looking all his life for a womb to crawl into equipped with a framed glazed set of All the Answers nailed to the warm wall like motel rules," he wrote. "In his current activity he exudes confidence in his discovery at long last of The Way. He is of course not capable of realizing that he must have been just as sure as this when he discovered the Christian Church and the Communist Party, and that by this man's racing form you can bet he's still a transient."[39]

Sturgeon wrote of Meyer to his fellow science fiction writer Poul Anderson that "though I find his politics appalling (and he knows it) he is my friend and one of the most thoroughly educated, thoroughly cultured, and amusingly provocative people I have ever met."[40]

He tolerated the magazine's politics. The heavy-handed editing experienced in a foray outside of "Books, Arts, and Manners" he could not.

Profoundly moved by the untimely death of Cordwainer Smith, a U.S. intelligence asset who wrote science fiction in his off hours, Sturgeon lobbied *NR* to publish his obituary, "naturally without charge," or otherwise send it to *Galaxy*.[41] When it appeared in the front of the book heavily edited, an emotional Sturgeon tendered his resignation. He described Meyer to Buckley as "unfailingly patient and courteous to me." He did not feel as though other editors exhibited these traits even as he acknowledged that for them to publish the obituary represented a favor. "You see, Bill, the issue is basically not the [Smith] obit. Not at all. It is this: conceding completely that you have absolute command of your podium, you should not—and I mean really by God <u>not</u>—make a man say that which he did not say, without his knowledge and consent."[42] Buckley wrote a propitiative though not apologetic reply that claimed *NR*'s conduct was abnormal and the punishment "cruel and unusual" to the magazine and "the quarter million people who cherish your presence in this journal."[43] Sturgeon, challenged with *Star Trek* scripts and publishing deadlines, nevertheless returned. "No matter what happens," he implored, "don't lose me, Frank."[44]

Why did Frank not lose one so beyond *National Review*'s political orbit?

Their friendship, begun in Woodstock, where Sturgeon lived for a time, predated Sturgeon's involvement with the magazine. The editor who wanted a master to critique science fiction overruled the ideologue who desired a conservative to critique science fiction. So Sturgeon's politics mattered not at all. Meyer, a quite peculiar ideologue, muted his political fixations in "Books, Arts, and Manners." A former Communist, more than most, recognized that when art mixes with politics art disappears.

Why did the editor deign it necessary to periodically review science fiction?

Reputationally, the genre then sat somewhere above professional wrestling but below cowboy fiction. The era of space travel and nuclear fears jarred magazines into highlighting sci-fi. Really, though, the editor enjoyed Frank Herbert's *Dune* novels, Isaac Asimov's *Foundation* series, and the work of Poul Anderson.[45] Frank was a fan.

◆ ◆ ◆

WILLS, DIDION, AND STURGEON graduated to greater success. The section became a springboard to fame for some and louder accolades for others. The bouquets eluded its most important contributor.

"He selected the books to review. He lined up the reviewers," Eugene Meyer revealed. "My mother did the editing."[46]

The task suited the Radcliffe English major. The times did not recognize her for it.

She stood not so much by her man as behind him. To some degree, their opposites-attract personalities ensured such an arrangement. To a greater degree, cultural conventions did. While women—Suzanne La Follette, Priscilla Buckley, Arlene Croce—played important roles at the magazine over the years, the stars remained almost exclusively male.

The roles of men and women, husbands and wives, changed for better and worse in these years. Habit immunized fifty-something couples from the cultural upheaval. Younger couples dealt with the change uneasily.

John Gregory Dunne, inferior as a writer to his spouse, wrote Frank "one caution about the sensitivity of writers and their easily bruised feelings, especially when there are two in one family. As a diplomat, you failed miserably when you told me that Joan's piece was desperately needed but that you could use mine any time. My first inclination was to tell you to stuff it."[47]

Frank and Elsie's life did not endure such jealousies. He led. She followed. She worked on his work. He received credit. This fulfilled as long as the partnership endured.

◄ 32 ►

Telephone

W hile I know that we cannot as a conservative magazine ignore the political front," Meyer wrote colleagues prior to a 1966 Agony, "I would submit that under these circumstances NR would be unfaithful to its function if it continued to give the same commitment to party politics that it did during the Goldwater years. Politics in this sense, I think, should be de-emphasized."[1]

The words perhaps struck his fellow editors as an about-face. The rah-rah after the 1964 drubbing now talked of lowering the volume. Meyer understood *National Review* to be a magazine and not a booster sheet. This retreat from party politics recognized the unusual circumstances surrounding Barry Goldwater, a candidate in part created by *National Review*. Such a figure did not materialize every election cycle. It also affirmed magazines as better positioned to perform spadework for movements than to promote candidates. So the senior editor prepared the ground and planted seeds.

All around he glimpsed strange fruit.

◆ ◆ ◆

TO SEE WHAT the culture cultivated, he needed only to venture into his ostensible farming community. One local walked about with a cat on his shoulder. A bearded, booted anarchist lived primitively in the woods.[2] The characters became paradoxically more colorful and darker as drugs drenched the town.

He wrote of LSD in 1967, "What is destroyed when under the influence of the drug—and what those who take it seek to destroy—is the intellectual ordering of experience, which is the fruit of millennia of civilization."[3]

A civilization slowly constructed he saw quickly crumbling. Woodstock provided a front-row seat. Even the conservative movement offered no donjon keeping out the onslaught.

"Some of us young libertarians were promoting the legalization of marijuana," California Yaffer Ken Grubbs recalls. "He was open to that but not very enthusiastic about it and really insisted that marijuana was some Eastern, introspective substance and the real Western drug was alcohol and we really should stick with that."[4]

One drug lubricated conversation. The other anesthetized thought.

At an anniversary dinner of Yale's Party of the Right, he drank into the night and argued against the intoxicant favored by some of the group's members. "Libertarians in the Party of the Right, like myself, had started smoking pot and the traditionalists were outraged," recalled David Zincavage. "He thought that alcohol was a Western Civilization tradition and that pot was Oriental and planted degeneracy."[5]

His position on pot closely mirrored his opposition to the draft. The same man-above-mass philosophy compelled him to object through the Council for a Volunteer Military to conscription to block against expansionary Communism in Vietnam, yet another point of disagreement with James Burnham.[6] For those content with a caricature of conservatism, Meyer's vocal opposition to the draft for the war he supported was bewildering. For readers of *In Defense of Freedom*, Meyer's opposition to codification of his prejudice struck as obvious. He could support Vietnam but oppose the draft and viscerally hate marijuana without volunteering for the war on drugs. "Unless men are free to be vicious," his magnum opus noted, "they cannot be virtuous."[7]

Policy began to catch up to culture. The changes foreshadowed a day when Meyer, Barry Goldwater, Marvin Liebman, and others who had created the conservative movement might find themselves out of step with it.

Abortion caught many by surprise as a political issue. In 1967, the Conservative Party of New York asked Meyer and Charles Rice to present their views to the rank and file.[8] Meyer considered it to be a moral evil. But as a moral question he basically regarded it as outside the sphere of politics. The relevant question pertained not to whether the mother aborted life—she did, he conceded—but to whether the mother aborted a person. Personhood amounted to a metaphysical and theological, and not a scientific, question. As such, the Conservative Party and the state could not answer it definitively and should stay out.[9]

✦ ✦ ✦

MUCH ELSE changed along with the increasingly libertine morality. Racial integration had advanced at an accelerated clip since Meyer witnessed mixed platoons at Fort Benning.

Meyer, a Northerner who had endured antisemitism and proposed a Ph.D. dissertation on African Americans, nevertheless approached the civil rights movement from a dispassionate, constitutional perspective that moved further from fashion as time passed. For instance, he called the Eisenhower administration's forced integration of Central High School the "Little Rock invasion."[10] He believed that imposing a federal vision of the good upon a community equipped to govern itself amounted to centralization and paternalism. He saw in most new civil rights laws the intrusion into private conduct to compel an integration every bit as unnatural as laws forcing segregation.[11] He regarded civil disobedience and violent rebellion as immoral in a constitutional republic that allowed for a redress of grievance. The use of nonviolence to provoke violence irked him.[12] He viewed Martin Luther King Jr. unfavorably and his rivals more unfavorably.[13]

He judged by late 1966 "that the Negro movement has passed over from a program of 'civil rights' to a program of confiscatory socialism, revolutionary in its essence." This movement, he argued, relied on a form of "blackmail by violence": essentially, give us what we want or we shall give you what you do not want.

He lambasted "the egalitarian myth that anyone who is in any way worse off than anyone else can be so only because of oppression or distortion arising from evil men or evil circumstances. If individual A fails where individual B succeeds, it is always the fault of external circumstances, never of his quality or his effort or his moral fiber. Similarly, if group x fails to achieve proportion y of the goods in life, it is forbidden to inquire (even after allowing for a harsh history) of the qualities of the group in its average; instead all the powers of the omnicompetent state must be brought to bear to take from those who have achieved and give to those who have not."[14]

Meyer's critique of the civil rights movement did not stem from racial animus; evidence of such an inclination is absent from his tens of thousands of extant letters. The movement's insistence that individuals must cede to government—and to the government most distant, no less—novel and great powers to achieve equality offended his libertarianism.

Acknowledging that "the Negro people have suffered profound wrongs," he wrote in his best piece on a subject that interested others more than it did him that "those wrongs cannot be righted by destroying the foundations of a free constitutional society, which is indeed the only basis upon which a joint and lasting solution of their problems is possible."[15]

Africans now interested him more than African Americans. Meyer edited a collection called *The African Nettle: Dilemmas of an Emerging Continent.* Here, and in subsequent projects for the American-African Affairs Association, he and Elsie worked together. They edited the *Spotlight on Africa* newsletter, produced a thirty-page pamphlet, and Elsie wrote the foreword to Kofi Abrefa Busia's *The African Consciousness: Continuity and Change in Africa.*[16] *The African Nettle*'s mere existence, and its editor's noting that the continent was becoming "the most prominent spot on earth" judging from the chatter, signaled that he took seriously what others disregarded. "They all have intimate knowledge of Africa, either as natives, or as longtime residents of African countries, or as close students and observers of African affairs," the introduction claimed of contributors. This misled. Of the twelve contributors, eleven appear about as African as Johnny Winter. The inclusion of Busia, a fellow Oxonian who later became prime minister of Ghana, at least indicated that the book's editor had chosen wisely, if frugally, among blacks. Seeing Africa, a passion of Elsie's that naturally corralled her into the project, as not a unified entity but a series of complex and diverse enclaves, the book otherwise viewed the continent through a Cold War lens. Its problems appeared numerous, but Meyer volunteered for consideration among offered solutions that "cooperation of black and white is a dire necessity."[17]

✦ ✦ ✦

HIS LACK of interest in movements springing up around him in an age filled with them owed to his focus on marionetting his own movement. He now built up not a candidate but cadres.

"Frank started calling in the wee hours of the morning," *New Guard* editor Carol Dawson recalls. "That was when the American Conservative Union was born. He just was tireless when it came to his work. He must have sat up all night making phone calls. I've never known anybody quite like that."[18]

Johannes Gutenberg overthrew the Catholic Church through his movable-type printing press. Philips, Maxwell, and Sony fertilized Iran to grow the Islamic Revolution with the Ayatollah Khomeini's cassette-tape sermons. Mark Zuckerberg and Jack Dorsey aided and abetted 2011's Arab Spring.

Ma Bell provided the weaponry of Frank Meyer's revolution. He spread fusionism by phone.

"Well, if there was a big fight going on in YAF and a board meeting pending, he would almost invariably call with his advice prior to the meeting maybe a few days prior—not only to give advice but to find out what was going on so he could give advice to others, I suppose—build on his knowledge of the current situation," Bob Bauman noted. The calls came "always around eleven, twelve, or one o'clock in the morning."[19]

The pattern followed though the groups differed. Whether YAF, ACU, Philadelphia Society, or the Conservative Party, Meyer reached out and touched someone. His calls flattered their recipients until they didn't.

"He would call Dan in his office more times than a working lawyer would want," Serf Maltese said of Meyer's interactions with the Conservative Party of New York founder Dan Mahoney. "His calls were lengthy, as I recall Dan saying."[20]

"I was calling the house of Anne and Henry Paolucci," Herb Stupp, a student at St. John's University, explained of the two professors at the school active in his political circle, "and I was looking for Henry. Anne answered the phone and said, 'Herb, you have great timing. Henry just concluded an eight-hour conversation with Frank Meyer on astronomy.'"[21]

He called to influence. He called to glean information. He called out of necessity given the handicap of living on the outskirts of a town of a few thousand. He called for friend-ship. He called to cultivate future leadership.

In 1965, when the Meyers claimed earnings just short of $20,000 on their tax returns with slightly more than half coming from *National Review,* they reported telephone and telegraph expenses of $4,830.[22] In other words, Frank spent a quarter of his income, and who knows how much of his time, on the telephone. The following year, when $10,270 of their $16,040 income derived from Frank's *National Review* salary, they wrote off $4,486 in phone expenses.[23] He could have bought two new Ford Mustangs with the money he had spent on the phone in either year. Only he didn't drive. He talked.

Ron Robinson, like Stupp a New York Yaffer, remembers a jarring experience in unwittingly tying up the household's lines. "In the midst of our call," he said of a conversation with his fellow Yaffer John, "a rather brusque Frank Meyer got on, appeared to listen for a couple of seconds, and then told us to get off the line. I gathered from the way it transpired that that was not unusual for Frank Meyer to do." This happened mul-tiple times, with the previous reach-out-and-touch-someone moment mitigating the shock of the next one. "I don't re-member anyone else's parents interrupting a conversation as abruptly as the way Frank did," Robinson reflected. "When he wanted the phone, he wanted the phone."[24]

◆ ◆ ◆

BY 1966'S END, Bill Rusher informed the editors that the magazine had endured what was likely its worst financial year. A protracted Linus Pauling lawsuit over reference to him as a fellow traveler; the Birch purge, which peeled off readers; and other options for magazine readers such as a thriving *Human Events* contributed to *NR*'s troubles.[25] A magazine flailing just like the movement built up around it proved a chime-rical sight. The tide soon came in for both the magazine and the movement. Republicans opened 1967 with an additional forty-seven House seats, three in the Senate, and eight Republican governorships as a result of that nowhere-to-go-but-up election. Among those winning executive positions strode upon the stage an actor uniquely suited for the hero role the Woodstock director so desperately sought to cast.

◄ 33 ►

Reagan

F or the first time in the past few months I find myself viscerally as well as intellectually deeply concerned about the immediate future of the country," Frank Meyer wrote in March 1968 to Willi Schlamm in Europe. "Between Vietnam, this summer's projected insurrectionary riots, and the real threat to twenty years of economic stability that the monetary situation poses, almost anything could happen."[1]

Everything did.

Lyndon Johnson soon announced his decision to neither seek nor accept the Democratic Party's presidential nomination. Days later, a career criminal on the run after escaping prison murdered Martin Luther King Jr. The tragedy, and the initial elusiveness of the murderer, fueled riots that killed dozens in Chicago, Washington, D.C., Baltimore, and points beyond. Uprisings that spring plagued campuses. Columbia, where student activists occupied university buildings and held administrators hostage, served as the focal point. In June, Sirhan Sirhan, a Palestinian immigrant incensed over U.S. aid to Israel, murdered Robert Kennedy. All the while the Vietnam War reached peak violence; more than three hundred American men died in combat each week.

The chaos jarred Meyer. Even prior to Kennedy's murder, the *National Review* columnist had described the times as the most fateful for Americans since Fort Sumter. The upheaval, he reasoned, emanated not from deprivation but abundance. This did not lead to a more contented society. Riots, campus takeovers, civil disobedience, crime, and other actions often vaguely or specifically linked to political demands counterintuitively followed. The more authorities rewarded disobedience, disorder, and disregard for law, the more disobedience, disorder, and disregard for law proliferated. The damage from nihilism and a West alienated from itself, he concluded, bore this bitter fruit of attempted civilizational suicide.[2]

His articles adopted an ominous tone. More shocking to readers, his order-liberty emphasis flipped. He still articulated libertarian positions in opposing the draft and in shunning calls for gun control in the wake of the assassinations ("An unarmed citizenry is potentially the victim, first of anarchy, then of tyranny and totalitarianism").[3] The holstered firearm spotted under his jacket at a Philadelphia Society meeting in Chicago, where American Communists knew him best, indicated he practiced what he preached.[4] The times dictated a condemnation of freedom's unsavory cousin chaos. In March, Richard Nixon identified order as the priority.[5] Meyer followed that summer by telling readers that "order is the first condition of civilizational existence, the only foundation of freedom and well-being for anyone and everyone."[6]

His son John's attendance at Columbia amid the takeover and riots laying waste to his hometown of Newark the previous summer personalized the events. So did his own history. He had once stood on the other side of the barricades. If he regarded many antiwar protestors as effectively aiding the Vietcong, then he surely recalled his own role in the 1930s peace movement that had softened Great Britain, the United States, and other countries. Meyer the Communist had shouted down speakers, disrupted meetings, and scoffed at campus authorities the way Mark Rudd now did. He saw others reliving his life and wanted to stop them from inflicting the damage that he had once caused.

"The issue facing the United States this summer is the survival of a free society," he told readers. "No society can exist in a state of endemic disorder. Specifically, a representative republic cannot function if its magistrates and its representative assemblies are subject to blackmail by mob violence."[7]

From *Death Valley Days* came a sheriff to make things right. Meyer saw in Ronald Reagan the figure to lead Americans out of the smoke, grime, and darkness of 1968 to a place more resemblant of America. Some regarded this as a pipe dream; others as unwise.

✦ ✦ ✦

HUGH KENNER wrote William F. Buckley a private letter critical of his "Ronald Reagan: A Relaxing View," an unusually long cover article.[8] Kenner explained of his letter to Guy Davenport, "It is to their honor that they want it revised for print. Imagine, per contra, the Nation running a *pro*-Reagan piece."[9]

Not everyone welcomed Buckley's tolerance. And, because of that, Kenner's view of the magazine changed.

"Communication from WFB just re[a]d from Switzerland says that my Nervous View of Ronald Reagan has been held over till April (!) at Frank Meyer's (!!) intervention, in the interests of fairness, Frank having held that Reagan (!!!) should be given a chance to reply," Kenner wrote Davenport. "If Reagan does not, the accompanying rebuttal will be by Frank (!!!!)."[10]

Behind the scenes, a January editorial meeting resulted in the board's endorsement of Meyer's personally rebutting the anti-Reagan piece.[11] In February, Bill Rusher supplied the Master with a dossier.[12] Jeffrey Hart later received the task of writing the Meyer-engineered counterpoint to an article preoccupied with Reagan's treatment of the universities. This substitution, given that it negated one English professor's charge of anti-intellectualism with another's rebuttal, struck as a master stroke to anyone paying attention but too cute by half to anyone really paying attention.

When "A Nervous View of Ronald Reagan" ran in May as an "Open Question," Kenner, though a major asset as a literary critic, appeared outside of his element. Unlike Davenport, who had threatened to resign in 1965 after being assigned to cover a Philadelphia Society meeting, Kenner *did* subscribe to the general tenets that animated *National Review*.[13] Nevertheless, the University of California–Santa Barbara professor came off as a parochial cosmopolitan in portraying California's governor as a philistine for supporting the firing of the university system's president, Clark Kerr, and for his periodic clashes with academia, which to many conservatives increasingly resembled a left-wing training ground. The philistinism, to them, occurred among the people perverting intellectual pursuits toward the service of narrow, ideological ends.

Hart, on leave from both Dartmouth and *National Review* to write speeches for Reagan, authored the "Open Question" that appeared immediately after Kenner's. He juxtaposed Reagan's widely shared critique of the campuses with Kenner's use of "zamindary," a ten-cent word even by *National Review* standards. He wondered why Kenner must psychoanalyze his subjects as though the mind holds the answer for all questions. For Kenner this undoubtedly avouched philistinism's further inroads on the intellectual right; for many readers, it likely contrasted California's man of the people with yet another of its professors above all in an ivory tower.[14] The byline did not fully obscure who lurked behind every word. As a bewildered Davenport had explained to Kenner, "Frank thinks that Reagan ought to be president of the USA."[15]

Kenner lost sleep.[16] He went from gaining respect for the magazine to losing it. Buckley, though playing a passive role, allowed this to happen. He acted as godfather to Kenner's daughter, paid for another daughter's freshman year at college, and served as best man at the widowed Kenner's second wedding.[17] The *active* involvement of his other friend of more than a decade, the editor of his book reviews, sharpened the sting. So did yet another colleague's mockery of him in print as an egghead. "I can sympathize with you," Davenport wrote, "knowing how I would feel to be hee-hawed at by a cold bastard like Hart who can scarcely hide the fact that he has been called in to wipe a well-aimed egg off a politician, and to denounce the opposition with cultivated yelps and whimpers."[18]

Meyer lost his section's most accomplished literary critic. He pleaded with Davenport to beg his friend back.[19] The last issue in May listed Kenner as an associate. Any trace of him had disappeared from the masthead by June.[20]

Meyer succeeded in shielding his favored candidate but at terrible cost. The tear revealed the frayed fabric holding together the two elements—the cynosure for conservatives and a citadel for refined literary appraisal—that made *National Review* great. Meyer could play conservative pope. He could serve as keeper of culture. Could he play both? The question did not always yield an answer in the affirmative.

◆ ◆ ◆

THE SAME WEEK that *National Review* offset Kenner's criticism with Hart's rebuttal, *The New Republic* published Meyer's "Why I Am for Reagan," one in a series from supporters of the various presidential contenders.[21] The magazine commissioned Meyer to write the piece for obvious reasons. His campaign for Reagan began the moment the campaign for Goldwater ended.

In December 1964, Meyer spotlighted Reagan as the Republican future. The veteran actor had delivered a compelling infomercial for Goldwater that aired a week before the election. He did not merely replace Goldwater's scowl with a smile. He eviscerated Great Society liberalism with humor, anecdotes, and folksy logic.[22] Reagan connected. One could almost see the studio audience, and Frank Meyer listening in his living room, wondering, "Why can't I vote for *this* man?" People who knew him as a star nevertheless experienced a revelation that night that they had watched, well, a star.

Reagan parlayed that speech into a run for governor in the state that suddenly boasted the most people. He vanquished Nixon's vanquisher. Weeks before Reagan assumed office, Meyer touted him as the next president. As with Goldwater, the enthusiasm masked a Johnny Bravo quality. Ronald Reagan nevertheless fit the suit better.

Reagan met the requirements of "a candidate who can stir conservative enthusiasm and behind whom a campaign for delegates to the Republican National Convention of 1968 can be launched," "Principles and Heresies" maintained in 1966. "By the principled positions he has taken, and by his proven ability as a campaigner, demonstrated both in 1964 and this year in California, Ronald Reagan, should he prove the governor he promises to be, qualifies for this role."[23]

Rusher shared Meyer's enthusiasms. Buckley touted Reagan, too. Again, James Burnham opposed.

"I insist that Reagan is a serious candidate," Meyer responded to Burnham's insistence to the contrary. "Furthermore, if it were journalistically advisable to support a single candidate, it would unquestionably be our duty to make Reagan our choice with Nixon as our second choice."[24]

Meyer harbored a few reservations. A mere fourteen months in office did not rank among them. First, he wanted Reagan to foreswear talk of joining a presidential ticket as the B-side to Nelson Rockefeller—whose on-again-off-again run found its greatest cheerleader, at least privately through multiple lobbying attempts, in Lyndon Johnson—as a way to make poison palatable to conservatives.[25] Six or so years earlier, he had joined the efforts to form a Conservative Party of New York in large part because of Governor Rockefeller. He was not going to allow him to become president if he could help it. Second, he would consider switching support to Nixon if Reagan's forces strategically allied with Rockefeller as a means of denying Nixon the nomination. Third, it bothered him that the governor of California had so quickly pledged to support the Republican ticket even if New York's governor led it.[26]

In March, Rockefeller feinted. He announced sitting out the race. Meyer dropped all concerns and urged his colleagues to support the actor turned politician.[27] When Rockefeller returned, Meyer did not emphasize those earlier caveats.

The nomination ostensibly remained an open question heading into the convention. Nixon, who ran a safe yet nearly perfect campaign, won it as expected on the first ballot. Reagan's losing did not bite like Taft in 1952 because of his newcomer status; Nixon's winning did not bite like 1960 because he had opted to stick by Goldwater in 1964 when so many leading Republicans skedaddled. And after Goldwater's rout, many conservatives felt comfortable prioritizing victory over purity. Nixon still aroused conservative suspicion. It softened enough to allow *National Review* to provide that fall what it had refused in 1960: an endorsement.[28]

◆ ◆ ◆

STILL OTHER luminaries of Frank Meyer's book section did not share his enthusiasms. That spring, Joan Didion planted a kick-me sign on Nancy Reagan in *The Saturday Evening Post*. Didion, a California girl normally nursing a bias for all things Golden State, atoned for past conservative sympathies that ran so deep that she had fairly recently volunteered Barry Goldwater and John Wayne as the two men she admired most.[29] Didion needed only one page to permanently caricature Mrs. Reagan. She lampooned her as a novitiate actress insincerely smiling and emphasizing every line, a woman putting on a face for the purpose of "playing out some middleclass American woman's daydream, circa 1948."[30]

No dramatic break occurred. Even though she had last contributed a piece to *National Review* three years earlier, her name remained on the masthead for another three years.[31]

Another of the talents introduced to the literary world through the back pages of the magazine no longer fit in there. Strong currents dragged Garry Wills left.

The former seminarian emerged from his chrysalis most dramatically in a series of articles. In March 1968, he wrote a plodding *Esquire* piece called "The Second Civil War" that bored considerably more than the actual Civil War. Therein, in no overt way, he presented the urban rioters and purveyors of violence as the moral equivalents of the police seeking to neutralize them.[32] In *National Review*, his articles on the Republican and, especially, Democratic convention signaled drift. The longform piece about the Democratic gathering offended the ideological precepts of readers in not words but tone. It made no easily discernable ideological point, as so many of the magazine's articles did. It described well but said little. It emitted a vibration; it never declared but implied, suggested, hinted—Mayor Richard J. Daley and the cops, Bad; Tom Hayden and the "unideological" kids, Good.[33]

Meyer felt compelled to devote the "Principles and Heresies" in the next issue to a somewhat oblique, diplomatic criticism of Wills and a full-throated defense of Daley.[34] Wills, capitalizing on opportunities outside of the magazine that established his name and inhaling the bouquet of the times, baby-stepped away from *National Review*. Just as Morris Childs had recognized cracks in Frank's Communism more than a quarter-century earlier, Frank saw Garry drifting from the ideas that, if he were being honest with himself, he could admit his protégé never fully embraced in the first place.

"He had more sons than Gene and John," the late-sixties "Books, Arts, and Manners" reviewer David Brudnoy reflected. "He was the mentor of hundreds of us over the years."[35] One of those sons reporting on the rebellion of other sons

went native. Like so many parent-child relationships during the times, estrangement marked this one.

+ + +

ELECTION DAY approached. Meyer feared. He feared Hubert Humphrey as one fears a ladybug. His unease instead centered around the candidate who could not win.

"What I really fear is a massive vote for Wallace," he explained to Schlamm, "which would set up the potentialities of an American-style proto-fascist movement—not necessarily with Wallace as the leader, but with somebody who comes out of the woodwork, tempted by the potential."[36]

Although George Wallace did not run on overt racial themes as he did in his winning Alabama gubernatorial bids (after running as the more racially tolerant candidate in his lesson-learning losing gubernatorial bid), he, "Principles and Heresies" informed, "translates the frustrations, the legitimate fears, of the solid Americans to whom he appeals, into hatred."[37] Meyer regarded Wallace as a demagogue.

Meyer voted for Nixon one more time but with feeling. Like so many, he voted to make America normal again.

Humphrey closed the gap during the last month. But he did it largely by poaching votes from his fellow Democrat running on a third party. The election played out as a reversal of 1960. Winning a squeaker in the popular vote but comfortably in the Electoral College, Nixon, hated by the left since his interrogation of Alger Hiss and yet never loved by the right at any point since, won election as the thirty-seventh president.

◄ 34 ►

Nixon

Henry Kissinger solicited Frank Meyer's counsel shortly after the election. Six years earlier, Meyer had addressed Kissinger's Harvard seminar.[1] Now he provided thoughts not to undergraduates but to the most-listened-to foreign policy voice in the incoming president's ear.

While Meyer suggested that the United States select "points of conflict and confrontation" to its advantage, he implored the Nixon administration to pursue the Vietnam War to an honorable conclusion. The bulk of the letter tendered ideas untethered to current events. He wrote,

> Fundamentally I would say that the foreign policy of the United States should be, within broad moral limits, motivated by and concerned with our national interest— which, however, in the light of the realities of power in the world today, are largely those of Western civilization also. That is to say that the social systems of other nations are no concern of our policy except insofar as they represent armed power ideologically directed toward our destruction. Nor can active benevolence, charity, be an aim of foreign policy, since charity is the privilege and responsibility of individual persons, not of the custodians

of money taken from people by taxation; and, in the specific case relevant today—backward nations—the only way seriously to advance their economies, in any case, is through investment under the controls of the market system. Nor certainly can our policy be distorted by taking seriously much unrealistic utopian concepts as world government.

Granted national interest as the criterion of our policy, however, a second major consideration enters which materially transforms the concept of national interest from what it might have been in the 18th or 19th century. That is the existence of a dynamic and messianic ideology (with much of the force of a fanatic religion), controlling and guiding the long-term policies of the second most powerful state in the world. The Communist world enterprise, seated in the state power of the Soviet Union, is by its inner nature directed to the duty and necessity of eventual world supremacy. It is this which makes 19th-century concepts of national interest be primarily directed towards the restraint and eventual dissolution of this, the only major threat to our fundamental national interest—a threat, indeed, that if unchecked imperils our national survival.[2]

Kissinger, a shrewd operator whose allegiance swiftly shifted from Nelson Rockefeller to Nixon once the latter secured the nomination, perhaps here sought to flatter a Nixon critic into becoming a well-wisher or gauge sentiment on the right. But as one who periodically exchanged ideas with Meyer— six years earlier he had convened a ninety-minute meeting between Meyer and Governor Rockefeller—he possibly just wished for informed opinion in advance of becoming national security advisor.[3]

As it turned out, Nixon's friends rarely did anything to sweeten Meyer's sour view of the thirty-seventh president. His enemies did much.

✦ ✦ ✦

"IT IS SAD about Garry—being that he has been a very close friend of mine for ten to fifteen years," he confessed. "While I saw some aspects of his ideological position which were distressing a long way back, I don't really think this development began much earlier than the time he began writing for Esquire. . . . It is getting rather serious."[4]

A decade earlier, Meyer had petitioned J. R. R. Tolkien and then Evelyn Waugh to review Wills's first book to propel his protégé's career. Now he assigned himself to review *Nixon Agonistes* to slam it.

"This is a strange book," he wrote. "Its avowed subject is Richard Nixon; yet its real subject is America today—an America about which there is nothing good to be said, an America seen from a point of view similar to, if not identical with, that of the revolutionary force intent upon our destruction (the black militants, the New Left, the counterculture)."[5]

Wills cited the review as evidence of declining "standards of veracity and honor" at *National Review*. Buckley described himself as "grievously vexed," words one could not imagine Meyer adopting as a hair shirt, because he viewed his books editor as "guilty" of misreading *Nixon Agonistes*. Meyer, Buckley told Wills, "leafed through" his book.[6] Buckley, though he dreaded the departure of talent, understood Wills's judgment had long departed. Wills's plea for academia to ban Kissinger and Daniel Patrick Moynihan, two scholars who joined the Nixon administration, from employment struck him as zealotry.[7]

That summer, Meyer wrote about his recreant former apprentice and "still . . . close personal friend." He granted that his 1968 convention coverage in *National Review* and articles in *Esquire* allowed for competing interpretations. Wills's newspaper column left no room for debate: Meyer's prized pupil had defected to the left as surely as Meyer had defected from it.

"Emotionally," Meyer wrote, "he has been, to put it bluntly, a sucker for the spirit and elan of revolutionary movements, black or white. He is intoxicated by demonstrations as some men are intoxicated by alcohol." The other fallacies undergirding his radical outlook owed to the intellect. He misunderstands the threat of the Soviet Union, scorns free enterprise, and despises Middle America, he added.[8]

Meyer here overlooked white guilt stemming from Wills starting the 1960s by writing editorials for James J. Kilpatrick, the premier intellectual defender of segregation, at *The Richmond News Leader*. Meyer landed him that job.[9] Toward the end of the 1960s, Wills petitioned Jameson Campaigne Jr. to connect him with African Americans: "He wanted to live with some blacks in Chicago and find out about them." Penance for his Richmond sins resulted in embedding with two militant African American policemen. "Duke and Hutch did a number on him," Campaigne assessed. "They did the white guilt thing; they jived him."[10] This reoriented Wills saw the world differently from his patron.

It is not as if the author of *Nixon Agonistes* and his critic diverged in speaking ill of the president's policies. What policies, though? For Meyer, expanding welfare, peopling the administration with liberals, failing to keep pace in the arms race, and seeming support for busing offended. "As far as rhetoric is concerned," he wrote, "the Nixon administration, particularly in the speeches of Spiro Agnew, has been speaking to the issues concerning the broad conservative majority of the American people. But when it comes to action, there is much less to be said."[11]

Nixon revealed a truth about Meyer: He never fully supported any Republican presidential nominee in his life other than Barry Goldwater. He did not despise Nixon. He distrusted him—or trusted him to do the wrong thing. To the extent that he defended him during the early part of his presidency, he did so as a reaction to the left's hatred.

"I have not been Mr. Nixon's warmest admirer, but this

book has raised him inestimably in my esteem," he divulged. "If he stands as symbol for the American tradition—and the insight of a hostile critic should be taken most seriously— then he is indeed a great blessing to the nation."[12]

✦ ✦ ✦

"HAVE YOU ALL recovered from the summer 'festival' out your way?" David Brudnoy inquired. "I'm with Mr. Rusher; somehow Mr. Ardery's approach didn't ring true to me. I heard enough first-hand reports to have large doubts about its 'joyous' and wonderful spirit, etc."[13]

During the Woodstock festival, which took place an hour away in Bethel, Meyer conveniently competed in a chess tournament with his sons in Atlanta.[14] Phil Ardery, the young writer who panegyrized the event as "a moment of glorious innocence," sent Meyer an album by one of the concert's final performers, The Band.[15]

Harsh reviews emanated from the Meyer household.

"I have been patiently listening to things like *Sergeant Pepper*, the Band, a Simon & Garfunkel record—what a terrible assault on the senses!" Elsie Meyer explained to William F. Buckley. "I have always loved hot jazz but apart from certain complexities in the Beatles, music wise, I find rock unrelieved, maddening noise. I don't believe you really like it."[16]

She spoke for her husband.

"He listened to classical music: Bach, Mozart," John Meyer explained. "My mother was more musical than my father. They both listened to it and appreciated it. They had records and record players and also listened to WNYC at night, which played classical music."[17]

Peter Yarrow of Peter, Paul and Mary summered in a cabin down the hill, Rick Danko and Garth Hudson of The Band lived in a place on the Ashokan Reservoir side of Ohayo Mountain, and Van Morrison and other popular musicians moved into the area later. None of this seemed to register.[18] Neither did the appearance of a quasar within that constellation of rock stars.

"The hippies would come knocking on our door and say, 'Where's Bob Dylan?' We'd just sort of feign complete ignorance. They probably thought we were totally square in every conceivable way," Eugene Meyer noted. "But he wanted to be left alone, and that's why he was in Woodstock on top of Ohayo Mountain Road."[19]

Is Dylan or Meyer the antecedent of that "he"?

In spring 1969, the human personification of the decade moved next to the Meyers. They neither cared nor noticed. In this, they offered everything the pop singer/prophet dreamed of in neighbors. Dylan, who bought the sprawling estate long occupied by Nathaniel Weyl's family, lived on property that abutted the Meyer land.[20] Whereas the Meyer house hugged the road, Dylan's sat about a quarter mile back from it and lower on the mountain closer to town. The properties touched. Still, one man could not see the other's home from his home. Both liked it that way.

Meyer essentially sang the scornful "Positively 4th Street" about Greenwich Village denizens two decades before his neighbor did. They retreated to Woodstock to escape the city, grow a family, and leave behind a scene in which they no longer saw themselves. Both writers owned guns for protection from legitimate threats.[21]

"He was somewhat reclusive," John Meyer noted. "My dad did talk to him a few times. My dad wasn't starstruck."[22]

If conversations between the men who occupied different worlds but homes on the same road strike as a surreal image of the sixties, this is due to their misleading personas. Meyer inhabited the counterculture before people called it that. He knew that world. Dylan knew it long enough to despise it. He lamented the Woodstock scene with language more extreme than his neighbor's. "Everything was wrong," Dylan observed. "[T]he world was absurd." The "moochers," "dropouts," "druggies," and "rogue radicals" violating his private property transformed him into a prisoner in his home and spurred a move to a more rural part of Woodstock: Ohayo Mountain Road. "I wanted to set fire to these people."[23]

The decade's representative came to abhor politicization; the counterculture; "turning on, tuning in, dropping out"; and so much else that was representative of the decade.

Frank "was aware of Bob Dylan," John Meyer said. "He commented something that he had a lot more sense than the people in that area and he wasn't a reflection of liberalism. I just remember the comment that he had 'reasonable sense.'"[24]

The awareness, and acknowledgment of his reasonable sense, occurred periodically in "Books, Arts, and Manners."[25] On Ohayo Mountain Road, aside from scant interactions, a general aloofness pervaded.

✦ ✦ ✦

ABOUT A HALF MILLION young people traveled to Woodstock to see Jimi Hendrix, The Who, and the rest. Some trekked to Woodstock to see Frank and Elsie. Few, save Phil Ardery, made both pilgrimages.

At the farmhouse in the actual Woodstock and the farm hosting the festival named for the town, so many stayed up so late that it became early. The Jewish conservative Max Yasgur hosted the young people because the promoters paid him $10,000. Why did Frank Meyer welcome so many young people?

"Everyone with whom the Communist is in contact is, at a greater or less remove, a potential recruit," *The Moulding of Communists* explained. "In the busy routine of activity this is always kept in mind; and all personal and social life that is not pure relaxation among Party comrades or a necessary toll of the external world should be geared to the end of immediate or eventual recruitment."[26]

Meyer did not break all habits when he broke with the party. Communism moulded him, too.

His social life served his political life. In the upstate leftish milieu, the isolated writer imported company. More often than not, guests had entered the world a quarter century or more after the Meyers did. The visit became obligatory for young conservatives. Those experiencing the rite of passage soon ran the movement that Meyer had helped create. This arrived by design.

David Franke, a young staffer at *National Review* during the early 1960s who later started the Liberty Fund's publishing arm, recalled borrowing a car from his colleague Arlene Croce, herself a fellow palmer to the house on the hill, to travel from the city to the country.

"Usually, it would be a group of three or four of us around a dinner table, Frank and Elsie and then three or four of us from the conservative community," Franke recalled. "It would be a really boisterous, fun time. One of the memories that prevailed about Frank was he was more demonstrative. He had that habit of waving his hands and everything and breaking into a rally speech."[27]

The subconscious Lenin impersonations yielded to impromptu declamations of the classics.

"I do remember when we were up there, when [Don] Lipsett and I were up there, we were talking about what was going to happen with Goldwater," noted Ed Feulner, a Wharton School of Economics student who later ran the Heritage Foundation. "All of a sudden Frank would be reciting Milton or Shakespeare, and I would think about the link as to how we got there from talking about how Barry Goldwater was going to at least carry some of the South (because it was pretty clear he wasn't going to carry Pennsylvania, where I was involved in the campaign). All of a sudden there we are listening to Frank recite poetry."[28]

Dinner sometimes occurred past most bedtimes.

"Elsie would make a big salad," Franke remembered. "Frank

would be mixing the vinaigrette into the salad in this big, wide bowl. He would be smoking a cigarette—both of them were chainsmokers. And all we could do—we were transfixed watching as the ashes grew longer and longer waiting for ashes to break off into the salad bowl."

The guests ate, albeit with a degree of trepidation.

"It was amazing how long they could get before he either flicked them away or they fell," Franke said. "I don't remember them ever falling in."[29]

Jerry Smith, mentored politically by John Meyer at Yale and often the chauffer for both brothers more enthusiastic about liberty than licenses, judged lamb curry the most famous dish prepared by Elsie, who credited Eugene O'Neill Jr. for her cooking acumen.[30] Danny Boggs of Harvard described the scotch-and-cigarettes enthusiast who held court as "voluble."[31] Both *hajis* joined the federal bench in 1987 and subsequently played important roles in major affirmative action cases.

The "house was insulated not with rock wool or Fiberglas but with the wisdom of the West," containing a "comfortable old coat of a room" that featured free-flowing conversation about baseball, Tolkien, chess, philosophy, gardening, and "always civilization and barbarians," one visitor explained. [32]

Here did the ultimate deipnosophist hold court.

"It was almost a claustrophobic house, books in piles everywhere," Ross Mackenzie, who subsequently edited the editorial page of Richmond's *News Leader* and then its *Times Dispatch*, recalled. "There was some drinking, lots of conversation. It was rarefied in the discussion. For a young guy like me who is playing on this intellectual gridiron, it was something out of this world."[33]

"I have never experienced as relaxed—and at the same time as mentally taxing—a weekend," reflected David Brudnoy.[34]

R. Emmett Tyrrell, who started *The American Spectator* at Indiana University in 1967, made the pilgrimage with a teenage Bill Kristol, later founder of *The Weekly Standard*, before hosting Meyer as a campus speaker in late 1969. Kristol recalled arriving late to accommodate the host's "crazy hours," and the older man's listening and not just lecturing.[35] "He loved students," Tyrrell understood. "He was a mentor to me and dozens of others, many of whom never went anywhere in life."[36]

Some went somewhere.

"I would occasionally have to take the bus up to Woodstock," noted David Keene, a University of Wisconsin activist who later became chair of the American Conservative Union and then president of the National Rifle Association, "and be met by Elsie and arrive just about when Frank was getting up. I was tired. Then he would rage all night long, drinking . . . and we'd argue about this, that, and the other. You'd go home. Between these visits, you would invariably get calls at two in the morning asking you what the hell you had done for freedom that day."[37]

For Jameson Campaigne Jr., the encroachment of *tsundoku*, bombardment of impromptu poetry recitations and political stemwinders, envelopment of fireplace warmth and Kent cigarette smoke, and a yin calming her excitable yang marked visits. If it were merely about a social animal satiating his need, then Meyer might have hosted the more established Jameson Campaigne Sr., who was closer to his age, instead of his namesake.

"Meyer's whole deal was what they call cadre building," Campaigne reflected. "He was trying to create people to carry on for the next two or three or four decades."[38]

The young people in that ancient and uneven living room anchored the coming conservative movement. They became the leaders, talk radio hosts, college professors, activists, congressmen, judges, and journalists who impelled America rightward in the last quarter of the twentieth century. Meyer, a one-man counterculture to the counterculture, moulded conservatives in Woodstock.

◆ ◆ ◆

WHEN THE YOUTH did not venture to him, he ventured to the youth.

"Attending a Young Americans for Freedom gathering in the mid-sixties was like entering a time capsule and being transported ten or fifteen years into the past," recalled the libertarian Jerome Tuccille.[39] By the end of the decade, a dissident group brought their own beards and beads. This sixties sight confronted a crew-cutted atavism at Manhattan's Commodore Hotel in the spring of 1969.

The student activist Arnold Steinberg organized what he called a "wild panel" for the YAF Mid-Atlantic Regional Conference featuring Meyer, the conservative Catholic Henry Paolucci, Tuccille, and the anarchist Karl Hess.[40] The YAF historian Wayne Thorburn judged, "This panel became the turning point in the division between the traditionalists and fusionists on the one side and the libertarians and anarchists on the other."[41] Hess, who applauded the vandalism and campus takeovers perpetrated by the student left, arrived late with a colorful entourage in tow. To anarcho-libertarian jeers, Meyer, who defended an ordered liberty and rejected unprincipled alliances with the left, departed early whether because of Hess's tardiness, obvious disgust with the former Goldwater speechwriter going 1960s native, or the truth of claims of a previous engagement. Steinberg, who likened the raucous event to a prizefight, observed of Meyer, "You could see the more agitated he became, the more brilliant he became."[42]

It proved the undercard to the main event in St. Louis at summer's end.

Meyer spoke at the YAF national convention there on Friday, August 29. On Saturday, anarchy broke loose when an anarchist lit a draft card—or rather a duplicate of one—and held it aloft not unlike the YAF torch insignia.[43] Prepped to regard the "F" in YAF as standing for fascism, failing to amend or replace the Sharon Statement, and describing the United States as the greatest threat to world peace, this radical caucus lost its takeover attempt.[44] Depending upon which side tells the story, they either quit as sore losers or endured a purge from a vengeful majority.

◆ ◆ ◆

THE ERA NUDGED a liberty lover to stress order. Those who already favored order over freedom entertained concepts more extreme. Order's black sheep—repression—rose.

National Review highlighted the political scientist Donald Atwell Zoll's first article for it on the December 16, 1969, cover and characterized it in the "In This Issue" section as sure "to send Frank Meyer to his typewriter."[45]

Zoll described turn-of-the-decade America in apocalyptic terms. Liberalism, which ultimately absorbed much of the Old Left, could only fail in any such endeavor with the New Left. It faced a would-be destroyer not only of the parent ideology but civilization as well. Treating this revolutionary force as though it were another competing set of ideas demonstrated liberalism's inherent death wish.

Zoll called for conservatives to learn from liberalism's mistakes and consider confronting the New Left not with reason but suppression. He advised conservatives to "prepare to fight—whatever this may entail—against the tide of contemporary Jacobinism, candidly facing the necessity of techniques generally ignored or rejected by contemporary Western conservatives."

Revolutionaries bred counterrevolutionaries and infected them with extremism.

"These remarks may cause a certain amount of shock or dismay," Zoll conceded. "But in the modern age there has been a skeleton in the conservative closet. Its name is *order*."[46]

Meyer's column in the next issue emphasized the latter concern of "Principles and Heresies."

"The choice Professor Zoll offers us between revolutionary anarchy and some iron state is as false as the choice so widely promulgated in the Thirties between fascism and Communism," he observed. "There is a third alternative, and it is the only one conservatives can embrace if they are to remain conservatives: the vindication of the American tradition, the defense of an order based upon civility and freedom."[47]

Zoll's response reaffirmed Meyer's contention that fusionism sprang from the American tradition rather than political utility and that its conservative critics (or at least this one) rooted belief in foreign soil.

Zoll pleaded no contest to Meyer's claim that he rejected the tradition bequeathed by the Founding Fathers: "But any stabbing sense of guilt on my part is assuaged by the fact that these stentorian platitudes convey very little precise meaning to me, and if I do glean their general purport one thing is clear enough: They have nothing to do with the intellectual history of conservatism, and I, like most conservatives, would be more than willing to reject a very considerable part of the 'American tradition,' dominated as it is by influences scarcely harmonious with the conservative cast of mind."

It all, including Zoll's volunteering a preference for Prince Metternich over President Washington, left readers wondering just what he wished to conserve. He admitted that he did not care much to conserve the Declaration, Constitution, or *Federalist Papers*. Zoll nevertheless ended his argument by calling his interlocutor a liberal and himself a High Tory, a peculiar label for one who not only had just praised Bismarck but who purported to speak for American conservatives.[48]

While friendship imbued Meyer's heated debates with Harry Jaffa on Abraham Lincoln and Brent Bozell about freedom and virtue, Zoll's condescending tone and intemperate language, and Meyer's likening Zoll's ideas to Hitler's and Stalin's, indicated that the exchange lacked mere respect.

Zoll, largely lacking movement credentials (that he lacked academic credentials did not become known for another two decades), resembled the upstart Meyer years earlier reading established figures out of conservatism.[49] He out-Meyered Meyer. At the same time, their upstart-versus-establishment positioning showcased how fusionism had become conservatism's dominant strain.

The senior editor, uncomfortably playing the elder statesman, responded in two additional installments. He countered that American conservatism derived from Tory *and* Whig. He affirmed that the times demanded a restoration of order and that order stood as a precondition and not in opposition to freedom, which to him meant "the right to be free from coercion, so long as one does not interfere with the freedom of others and does not give aid and comfort to the would-be destroyers, domestic or foreign, on the social order on which freedom is based."[50]

Assassinations, riots, crime, and bombings eroded the surface libertarianism to reveal a conservative. Donald Atwell Zoll reawakened his libertarianism. Frank Meyer still meant freedom.

Manhattan

P resident Richard Nixon approached New York's 1970 U.S. Senate race with a "benign neutrality," according to the Conservative Party candidate James Buckley.[1] His vice president Spiro Agnew spoke for many in the administration in describing the political shape-shifter Senator Charles Goodell as the "Christine Jorgensen of the Republican Party."[2] The senator, appointed after Robert Kennedy's assassination, joined Democrats in opposing a president too liberal for Meyer and his ilk. So the Conservative Party candidate did not face active opposition from the administration.

Dan Mahoney envisioned the party he founded as acting as "a political lever."[3] Less than a decade after the third party's birth it became apparent that it could act as not only fulcrum but heavy weight. Buckley, who characterized his 1968 run as performing "jury duty" for the party, understood 1970 as beyond perfunctory service. He believed he *could* win.[4]

With the similar positions of Congressman Richard Ottinger and Senator Goodell on Vietnam, activist government, and much else, party Vice Chairman Meyer encouraged Buckley to plant a flag on the vast but uncontested conservative segment of the political field. As he urged Buckley to make his ideological differences clear, Meyer counseled Buckley after viewing an ad to blur his associations with Republicans. "If we are going to win this election," he advised, "it is not going to be solely with Republican votes. We will have to cut deeply [into] the Democratic and labor vote, and too close an identification as a Republican will hurt badly here. 'Conservative,' let us remember, is no longer a bad word."[5]

Buckley recalled running on traditional Republican issues but nevertheless winning support from blue-collar types. He noted, "I couldn't have won without that vote."[6]

Meyer divulged personal exhilaration at the upset victory for the Conservative Party, "remembering when it was just a half-dozen people in the room with an idea."[7] The victory posted one of the early signs indicating the political reorientation underway that Meyer had anticipated in 1954. It also validated beyond the expectations of the young party's founding fathers. Meyer saw it at its inception as a vehicle to force Republicans to more faithfully represent their conservative base and explicitly not to challenge the two-party system.[8] This triumph surpassed this vision. It emboldened right-wingers. Conservatives could replace a liberal Republican senator with one of their own. Why not replace a squish president, too?

◆ ◆ ◆

MEYER aimed all of his weapons at the politician that he, Willi Schlamm, and others in their clique had opposed from the outset of the magazine. His first crusade within *National Review* became his last. And a familiar foil resumed that familiar role.

By the time Phil Ardery experienced an epiphany at a 1970 Grateful Dead concert that he should leave *National Review*, the magazine's dynamic existed as it did when he arrived in 1967.

"For me there was a Burnham side and the Frank Meyer side," Ardery explained. "Frank was the libertarian guy.

Burnham was the *if it takes empowering the state to do it then do it* [side]. There were always disagreements on that score. Buckley was kind of the referee."

Meyer hosted the twentysomething Harvard graduate on multiple occasions, encouraged him to read Ludwig von Mises's *Human Action*, and phoned him.[9] He cultivated office informants.

"Bill Rusher, still rankled by Burnham's treatment of Rhodesia, came armed with material documenting the bad behavior of the generals in Greece—Jim's pet rulers, it would seem," Ardery reported to Meyer about a summer 1969 editorial meeting. "Rusher wanted someone to write an editorial that while expressing sympathy for the problems of the Greek regime, would point out the errors of its governance. Some embarrassment all around the table. Bill (Buckley) finally handled it by conceding to Rusher that all is not good in Athens, then assigning the editorial to Burnham."[10]

Even when the Meyerites won a concession, as Rusher did here, it came wrapped in thistles and thorns. The Burnham–Meyer dynamic remained, but the balance shifted heavily in the former Trotskyist's favor.

"He was very patient and very measured in conversation," Ardery observed of Burnham. "My ears perked up whenever his mouth opened because it was always something worth hearing—really exceptional person. I have no idea what his personal life was like, absolutely zero."

Ardery intermingled more with the others. Rickenbacker took him up in his airplane and handed over the controls. Arlene Croce's biting wit dazzled him, and her writing in his opinion topped the rest. Rusher he regarded as a constant yet comic presence in the office.[11]

Even Meyer, Rusher's ideological ally, had fun at the flinty publisher's expense.

"Sensing when to stop running something into the ground has never precisely been one of your long suits," Rusher wrote Meyer a year before Ardery's arrival, "and that is why

I am resorting to a written memorandum in an effort to impress upon you the fact that I am heartily sick and tired of your bringing up at each successive editorial Agony a lascivious description of my office and its famous carpet." Meyer, apparently seeking better furnishings for others, raised this sore point on three or four occasions. "As far as I am concerned, the carpet was merely a minor item of compensation—and, I may add, cost only a tiny fraction of what I have sat on various boards and cheerfully voted to pay you, over the years, for miscellaneous services, while volunteering my own," Rusher continued. "But kindly stop using my possession of it as a sort of horror story to add spice to your quarterly charity drive."[12]

The tension now derived more from levity gone to extremes than political difference. The presence of Ardery, fresh from work on the civil rights movement, and Chris Simonds and others not invested in the internal ideological struggle, contributed to the easing of tensions. The right ideas yielded to the right talent in new hires. The final year of the 1960s saw Rickenbacker, and the unideological Croce, depart. As *NR* replaced the various figures who essentially replaced Bozell and Kendall, the magazine removed itself further from the intense early battles. As it did, Burnham dominated.

"Burnham was the main presence I felt at the editorial meetings," Ardery observed. "Buckley would make the final decisions. Burnham was the leader of the editorial group even though he represented one wing of the whole mishmash of conservatism."

The disappearance of Bozell, Kendall, La Follette, and others, and the absence of Meyer from the office, only partly explained Burnham's further ascendance.

"A lot of the other guys were philosophizing," Ardery noted. "He really looked at things in power terms. Buckley was a realist, and glad there was somebody that was talking from that point of view."[13]

Outside the magazine, Meyer and Burnham switched places. Meyer exerted a massive influence; Burnham, scant. Just as

Meyer still won battles here and there within the magazine, his rival periodically claimed movement victories.

◆ ◆ ◆

THE FIRST "Principles and Heresies" of 1971 noted "a mounting disquiet concerning the course of the Nixon Administration" among conservatives.[14] In all but one column that year, Meyer wrote about Nixon, exhibiting a monomania last seen during Barry Goldwater's presidential run. Whereas the obsession took on a uniformly positive quality in 1964, his columns on Nixon seven years later leaned in an almost entirely negative direction.

Nixon's 1971 State of the Union address, proposing a full-employment budget, additional subsidies for health care, and a scheme for Washington to further fund state and local government, confirmed Meyer's "worst apprehensions." He advised the Conservative Party leader Dan Mahoney that conservatives must block Nixon's movement leftward.[15] That summer he complimented Serf Maltese for his comments in *The New York Times*. The Conservative Party, contrary to what its lieutenant Maltese told the paper, must withhold support until the president alters course, he argued.[16]

During the February 1971 ACU meeting, in which his ally M. Stanton Evans succeeded John Ashbrook as chairman, Meyer prevailed upon his fellow board members to endorse several anti-Nixon measures. These included one looking to counteract the "collectivist impact" of the president's recent State of the Union address.[17]

Two months later, in a debate at Yale with the former Congressman Allard Lowenstein sponsored by YAF, Meyer joined his liberal opponent in slamming Nixon. Given that nearly three-fourths of the national organization's members regarded Meyer as one of their "intellectual leaders," his words carried heavy weight.[18] "I would oppose the war in Vietnam, I

would oppose all alliances, any sort of foreign aid, and participation in the United Nations . . . if it were not for the threat
of Communism," he told the audience of 150. He described
the war as a battle in a much broader conflict, saying that "if
this were not true, the whole thing would be a farce." *The
Yale Daily News* headline offered a less nuanced summation of
the entire discussion: "YAF Hears Nixon Berated."[19]

♦ ♦ ♦

THE MOST POWERFUL expression of anti-Nixon sentiment occurred in July. Meyer and a dozen or so other leading
conservatives met in William F. Buckley's Manhattan townhouse. For more than six hours, they debated and discussed
a collective response to the president who had failed to meet
their low expectations.[20]

Evans, as he did at Sharon, wrote a statement. Unlike the
youngsters at the Buckley family home, the men at Buckley's
townhouse did not uniformly embrace Evans's words. James
Burnham watered down the stronger potion served. Buckley
also wished to not anathemize but scold Nixon. Buckley's
name packed a punch more powerful than the others combined, so the others acceded to his influence as he acceded
to Burnham's. So they advanced planks rather than demands,
narrowed criticism to foreign affairs, and suspended support rather than repudiated Nixon.[21] Burnham succeeded in
moderating the statement and focusing on foreign policy, on
which he basically agreed with the others.

"The tone of the room was that he was wandering far off
the reservation in respect to domestic and foreign policy," recalled signatory Randal Teague of YAF. "But there was more
consensus, the statement would find more support, if it were
addressed toward international relations, toward China."[22]

Evans ultimately did not sign. "The reason he didn't sign on
is that he was an editor of *The Indianapolis News*," signatory

and Evans confidante Allan Ryskind explained. "The publisher was not for any kind of a contest against Nixon, and he feared that if the publisher found out about it he might fire him."[23]

A dozen conservatives affixed their names to the document suspending support for the Republican president: Meyer, Rusher, Buckley, and Burnham of *National Review*; Anthony Harrigan of the Southern States Industrial Conference; the American Conservative Union's John Jones and Jeff Bell; the Conservative Party of New York's Dan Mahoney; the publisher Neil McCaffrey; Ryskind and Tom Winter of *Human Events*; and YAF's Chairman Teague. They became known by their number and meeting place: the Manhattan Twelve.

"Domestic considerations, important as they are, pale into insignificance alongside the tendencies of the Administration in foreign policy," read the document. These included Soviet advance in the Mediterranean, the U.S. ally West Germany's leftward drift, the president's overtures to China, and the deterioration of the military.[24] It did not strike as the stuff upon which to jar a sitting president.

◆ ◆ ◆

THE CLEAREST ELUCIDATION of Meyer's assessment of the political prospects for conservatives occurred during his fall 1971 Philadelphia Society speech. He warned of a "somewhat darker" interpretation of events than the other panelists.

He defined the conservative movement that emerged during the 1950s as "a delayed reaction to the revolutionary transformation of America that began with the election of Franklin Roosevelt in 1932." He identified Roosevelt's New Deal as part of the same global phenomenon that propelled Communism and Nazism. They aggrandized state power to lord over individuals as they purported to labor on behalf of the masses. Their words said one thing; their actions the opposite.

In a crime against language, liberalism morphed into its opposite and American conservatism inherited the tradition of neither conservatives nor liberals but instead the outlook of the American Founding, which he characterized as pre-right and pre-left because it occurred before the French Revolution. This postwar movement, growing among activists and intellectuals, did not hold considerable sway in the political arena until around 1960, he judged. Within four years, it suddenly captured a political party to serve as its vehicle. In the wake of this sudden triumph, conservatives instead fixated on Goldwater's ultimate defeat. They became gun-shy.

He dramatically told the conservative intellectuals gathered in New York,

> Instead of preparing for the future, the conservative movement suffered nothing less than a colossal failure of nerve. This, I think, is the key fact of the history of the past two decades. Having within our hands a vehicle which could have been moved from presidential year to presidential year constantly gaining in strength, the conservative movement let its nerveless hands fall from the wheel. Instead of starting in 1965 to consolidate and expand the ground won, and working for the next four years to repeat the challenge of 1964 with better preparation, better tactics, better management, better leadership, conservative leaders in large and decisive numbers moved into the camp of the prize opportunist of the 20th Century, Richard Nixon, placing the hope of an easy Republican win over conservative principles.

He assessed the benefits of Nixon vis-à-vis a counterfactual Humphrey administration as a couple of possibly solid Supreme Court nominations, a somewhat slower retreat in Vietnam, and much rhetoric about law and order. He acknowledged that swinging Nixon slightly to the right amounted to the best conservatives could hope for in applying pressure. He called on them to lay the groundwork for 1976. Their effort now constituted "saving the soul of the future of the conservative movement."[25]

The concern of those in the room soon involved saving the life, and the soul, of the speaker.

◄ 36 ►

Coda

E vents exposed the weakness of the Manhattan Twelve. One of its members felt weaker than the rest.

"When he came to the meetings he always wore similar clothing: a thick, button-down, Princeton shirt, suspenders, and the khakis—his clothes were hanging on him," Ron Docksai, Randal Teague's replacement as YAF chairman, recalled. "They were very loose. His complexion was sallow."[1]

At the December 5, 1971, ACU board meeting, M. Stanton Evans provided the publications report for the program's "ill" director. The mystery sickness sounded serious. The participants talked of a possible successor. They also passed a resolution urging the group's former chairman to challenge Richard Nixon.[2]

Remnants of the Manhattan Twelve similarly moved from merely suspending support for the president to actively pushing an insurgent candidate. Ohio Congressman John Ashbrook announced a presidential run. Born in Johnstown, the candidate was made in Manhattan. Meyer and his confederates installed Ashbrook to do their bidding as chairman of ACU after forcing out the former Indiana Congressman Donald Bruce. Six years later, the same crowd backed him in his challenge of the president.

The postwar conservative movement flexed its muscles. The biceps, pumped to Jack LaLanne proportions, quickly drooped in cartoonish fashion. The outs once again ate the sand kicked in their faces.

Ashbrook hit a high water mark of 10 percent. Nixon not only trounced him but Pete McCloskey, a Bay Area Republican, generally outperformed him running from Nixon's left. The idea of an insurgency on par with Eugene McCarthy, who had captured 42 percent in the New Hampshire Democratic primary four years earlier, keeping Nixon honest or preventing his renomination appeared as a fever dream. The humbling demonstrated to conservatives their pressure-group status and the considerable distance between themselves and themselves in power.

"What was the number within twenty-four hours?" asked Teague, himself eventually poached by the Nixon Administration. "People got on the telephone. The White House staff got on the telephone. Pat Buchanan started making phone calls. We became the Manhattan Twelve, Eleven, Ten, Nine, Eight."[3]

One subtracted from the twelve did not defect due to coin or conscience.

◆ ◆ ◆

HE FELT PAIN in his shoulder in summer. By Thanksgiving, he could not eat with the family.[4] Canned cherries and fortified eggnog partly sustained him.[5]

He wrote a column for the December 3 issue. Although its title, "Isolationism?," recalled the period between the wars, it looked forward. The writer envisioned a tomorrow in which America's Soviet nemesis did not exist. Its existence warped American foreign policy; its disappearance would allow it to revert to its previous, natural shape. This American future resembled the American past.

"The United States is the only country in the world with the power to confront the Soviet Union, and the Soviet Union is devoted to a policy of domination of the world," Meyer reminded his readers. "This is the stark underlying reality of international politics since World War II."

The article very much addressed the present problem confronting the nation. The chess player thought moves ahead. Its subtext invited the experience of posterity to awaken progeny.

"After World War I the issue was posed by Woodrow Wilson's messianic and abstract dream of a utopian world settlement," the right's conscience wrote. "The American reaction against it primarily reflected not the desire for isolation at all costs, but rather a realistic understanding of the actual forces in the world at the time and the unreality of Wilsonian rhetoric. Harding's much mocked-at 'normalcy' reflected simply a turn away from the ludicrous Wilsonian crusade and a return to the world of reality."[6]

"Principles and Heresies" noted that "great emphasis has been laid upon one-world utopianism, exporting democracy, and generally acting as a social worker to the whole world" by elites that clashed with "a prevailing American desire, running back to Washington's Farewell Address, to keep aloof from the power struggles of the world."[7]

He understood he could not last forever. He saw that the Soviet Union *would not* last forever. He left ideas behind that would survive Russian Communism.

Meyer did not believe, as his early *NR* colleague Whittaker Chambers did, that he had defected from the winning side to the losers. He regarded himself as a winner. He believed in the triumph of the West. He envisioned a geopolitical stage minus the disorienting existence of the Soviet Union. He spent more than a quarter century manifesting a world without this totalitarian malefactor. He never saw this world with his eyes. He did in his mind.

Other minds wondered about Frank Meyer's place in this world.

"In December 1971," remembered *NR* staffers Linda Bridges and John R. Coyne Jr., "Priscilla [Buckley] started to worry about Frank Meyer. At first it was little more than an in house joke: many days Frank was calling her as early as 3:00 p.m.—a sure sign, in him, of insomnia. Then his voice, always husky from his interminable cigarettes, grew huskier, and he eventually confided that he was suffering pain in the chest area."[8]

That "Principles and Heresies" column fittingly came as his last. His name conspicuously went missing in bylines in late 1971.

◆ ◆ ◆

"I NEVER GUESSED I would sit here hoping I had tuberculosis," he admitted to his boss and friend that winter.

William F. Buckley called as he covered Nixon in Beijing. They spoke of Meyer's sons in college and law school, Bobby Fischer, "the awful behavior of the *New York Times*," the peculiarities of one of his reviewers, opposition to Nixon's welfarist Family Assistance Plan, a cold front from Canada, the right reviewer for Garry Wills's new book on Catholicism, and, especially, the irony of the two staunch anti-Communists conversing as one reported on an American president meeting with Mao Tse-tung. "By Frank Meyer standards," Buckley observed, "it wasn't a long conversation."

From Switzerland, Buckley noticed a "quiver" in his friend's voice.[9] Allies and admirers worried.

YAF Chairman Ron Docksai in March telegrammed, "THE WINDS ARE STRONG AND THE WHEEL IS CAPTAINLESS PLEASE GET WELL SOON."[10] He urged Yaffers to similarly send get-well messages to one of the "primary architects" of conservatism. The chairman informed the board, save, conspicuously, one John Meyer, of an "acute case of tuberculosis" plaguing him without definite prognosis.[11] "I will do my best to recover if the little bugs coursing around in me will

416

cooperate," the patient responded. "Would you also give my best to the people at the National Office of YAF who signed a card I received some weeks ago."[12]

By the end of the month, Jameson Campaigne Jr., another acolyte, received a firmer prognosis from Elsie: "I am terribly sorry to tell you that Frank has cancer and the end is not too far off."[13]

◆ ◆ ◆

UPON RECEIVING the prognosis, Frank thought months. Elsie guessed weeks.[14] God awarded days.

An inoperable case, he left the hospital in Kingston to die in Woodstock. Neither carried nor wheeled, he dramatically walked up the steps with help into the house despite his white blood cells registering a count questioning his existence.[15] He wore an oxygen mask.[16] Three days before his death, Elsie told M. E. Bradford that Frank gave the green light to review a book.[17] His children described him as medicated to the point of near incapacity.[18]

"He was going to convert to Catholicism," David Keene remembered. Delays ensued in the baptism. "I get a call in the middle of the night. It's Frank. He was really upset."

"What's the problem?" Keene recalled asking.

"Dave," he responded, "they were coming up and it didn't happen because they wrecked."

"Frank, has it occurred to you that God might be trying to tell you something?" the younger man asked.

"He didn't think that was as funny as I did."[19]

Conservative Party activist George Marlin remembered it somewhat differently. Monsignor Eugene V. Clark, Francis Cardinal Spellman's last secretary, went from "drive up" to "no, not yet" to "drive up" to "no, not yet." Marlin, who noted that Clark drove a Mercedes, deadpanned, "This went on several times."[20]

The holdup, unsurprisingly, stemmed from a philosophical disagreement between Frank and God—or at least the deity's agents inhabiting the temporal plane.

"Frank's big reservation about Catholicism was that he reserved the right to commit suicide," the Meyers' friend David Zincavage explained. "The story I heard is that at his deathbed he was seriously contemplating conversion, and he said to the priest, 'I would convert but I still believe you have the right to commit suicide. Committing suicide if you're in your right mind and have a sound basis for your decision is not a sin.' The priest said, 'Frank, you're dying. You're never going to commit suicide, so forget about it.'"[21]

This dispute, as Buckley noted, resulted in Clark's descending Ohayo Mountain on Holy Thursday without bringing Catholicism a convert. Previous concerns that gave Meyer hesitation included his Jewishness and the church's collectivism.[22] Here suicide, and not primarily in a selfish sense in that it appeared as an attractive option or in the philosophical sense that a right to it appealed to his libertarianism, motivated his recalcitrance. Emotions fueled the logical man.

The most meaningful friend Meyer made in his life outside of his wife had slashed his wrists and ankles more than two decades earlier a short walk from where cancer now devoured his body. Elsie, one corner of that friendship triangle, had discovered the bloody corpse. To share the church's position on suicide as a mortal sin required Meyer to betray his boyhood friend. Why join a church that condemned Eugene O'Neill Jr.—even if he bore a physical resemblance to a bloated, hungover Mephistopheles—to eternal damnation?

"They all had some sort of fascination with suicide," Zincavage noted. "I think it was part of their ideology of self-willfulness. I think that all three of them believed in it. They were all intellectual bohemians and they were all willful people determined to live their own lives and set their own rules."

Meyer softened to conversion. He likely did so after first obtaining cyanide.[23]

"Frank taking steps to acquire that cyanide while he had cancer seemed to me silly," Zincavage, who, along with his wife, Karen Myers, found poison after purchasing the Meyer home, observed. "He was dying anyway of cancer."[24]

L. Brent Bozell visited Tuesday urging conversion. This would join him, Meyer, and their deceased debating partner Willmoore Kendall in the same faith. Buckley visited on Good Friday.

"I said Frank, do you mean it isn't convincing, or do you mean that you do not propose to observe the Church's prohibition?" recounted Buckley regarding suicide. "His mind wandered a bit, and he told me that 'Gene' had said he would return on the next day, and I said I was no scholar on the subject but that it was my impression that the self-knowledge that one will transgress in the future and even that one will seek to justify one's transgression, is not sacramentally disqualifying, and he nodded."[25]

Monsignor Eugene Clark did indeed return on Holy Saturday. The mission of converting Meyer to Catholicism had started a few years after Clark's birth. Now God provided him a few hours to seal the deal.

At Oxford, Professor Sligger Urquhart, Father Martin D'Arcy, and Chaplain Ronald Knox presented a demanding faith, which Meyer had considered as an alternative to Communism. He had not so much rejected as tabled Catholicism.[26] Here, circumstances demanded a final answer.

"He told me that leaving Oxford when he was looking at the alternatives of becoming a Communist or a Catholic, that those are the only two that made sense," John Meyer recalled. "Unfortunately, he became a Communist." Catholicism, his son understood, he regarded as the "strongest Christian tradition" and "much more philosophical than any Protestant denomination."[27] Still, he vacillated.

He finally ended his decades-long debate with Catholicism. Bedridden, unable to eat, and dependent on Elsie for tasks as simple as the shifting of a pillow, Meyer embraced the church.[28]

"I have said to those who love him how perfectly he maintained his own style and when he came to submit himself to God, it was the full and perfectly recognizable Frank he submitted to the Lord," Monsignor Clark expressed to Elsie. "You are quite right about Frank's recitation of the creed—how unfortunate the whole world could not have heard him. But I do have a feeling that a widening circle of people, who may need the witness of Frank's integrity, will be affected by Frank's completion of his turning to God."[29]

After Meyer had submitted to God, he submitted. That evening Buckley received a call from Gene Meyer. "I told him the truth," Buckley explained, "that his father was a great man, and hung up."[30]

Garry Wills, the pupil whose deviation from the master's teachings pained his teacher so much that friends kept printed evidence of his heresies from the determiner of principles, informed *NR* readers, "Lucid in the afternoon, as he prayed aloud through cancer-ravaged lungs, he was baptized—and then the tensest of vibrant men relaxed. Six hours later he was dead; and three hours after, it was Easter."[31]

◂ ◆ ▸

Conclusion

Sympathy notes from nearby neighbors included such lines as "never having chance to say hello."[1] Faraway strangers lamented, "A very trusted friend has died and I must get used to that."[2]

The cruelest month snatched Meyer's Browderite comrade Louis Budenz, whom Meyer had nudged out of Communism and into Catholicism. Then his October Club follower Jack Dunman, so hurt by Meyer's 1949 Smith Act Trial testimony that he "wrote him the angriest possible letter," died in October still bearing a grudge.[3] Their common friend R. W. Southern publicly judged Dunman the least successful man he knew, yet the caught-in-a-time-warp Communist declared months before the end of his misspent life that "Frank was probably my best friend at Oxford, and had an enormously liberating influence on me."[4] Meyer ruined Dunman's life as he did John Cornford's.

Charisma destroys. Charisma inspires.

Joanne Lockhart, a young reader of *NR* caught like Budenz and Dunman before in this small man's great magnetism, returned home from the Apollo 16 moon launch "shocked" and "dumbfounded" at the news. "Frank Meyer was so much a part of National Review," she wrote. "He stood for what I respect in the magazine—logic and reasonableness. I always thought whatever he wrote was a product of a mind that was not defending an unchangeable position but was searching for truth, no matter how harsh. He made sense."

"I must have actually cried out when I saw the article because my mother came into the room and asked what the matter was," she continued. "When I showed her the article she asked if I knew him. I said yes. But actually I didn't, except in the pages of National Review."⁵

◆ ◆ ◆

THOSE PAGES finally recognized Elsie Meyer, who for years had performed without credit the actual work on reviews assigned by her husband, as the editor of the book section (separated from "arts and manners" late in Frank's tenure). The appointment, always intended as a stopgap, proved short-lived. The May 26, 1972, issue announced "Mrs. Frank Meyer" as the "acting book editor" and a staffer for Colorado Senator Gordon Allott as her successor beginning the first of the next year.⁶

"When I had said to Bill that he needed a Washington editor," George Will recalls, "he said, 'I do and you're it.' And he then said, 'Could you edit the back of the book?' I said, 'Of course I can.'"⁷

Will, pegged as politically suspect by Meyer's many admirers, generated great controversy even before assuming posts once occupied by L. Brent Bozell and Frank Meyer.

"Frank had been a very large, important, creative thinker—fusionism and all that," Will recalled nearly a half century later. "So he had a long pedigree. But I think the heart of the matter was that I hadn't been to those College Republican conventions and I hadn't been a Yaffer and all that stuff."⁸

A disgusted M. Stanton Evans eventually asked to be taken off the masthead. Spiro Agnew as a hero to conservatives but a piñata to Will catalyzed the resignation. So did Buckley's rejection of Evans's desire to move his column from the *Bulletin* to the magazine upon Frank's death.[9] Many regarded Evans as the heir apparent to Meyer as books editor should the magazine bypass his widow. It bypassed him, too.

"I feel increasingly out of phase with the drift of things at *National Review*," one Yalie wrote the other, "particularly the book section and the political coverage."[10]

Theodore Sturgeon authored his last *NR* review the month Will took over from Elsie.[11] Guy Davenport tendered his resignation shortly thereafter.[12] Their exit came as no coincidence. No ideological allegiance but instead Meyer's personal magnetism had drawn them to *National Review*; absent the human tractor beam they naturally drifted away. Russell Kirk reflected that, whatever his disputes with Meyer, he frequently acted as reviewer and reviewed during his stewardship, attentions which waned dramatically under his successors.[13]

Buckley encouraged Will to make a pilgrimage to the old farmhouse.[14]

Eugene Meyer said of his mother's successor, "I remember George Will came up to Woodstock to talk with her about all of this. Will said—and maybe it was politeness—'I don't know why Buckley's not just keeping you doing this. You're doing very well.'"[15]

Will encountered Elsie in a house "really dark and cluttered."[16] The observation increasingly applied to the state of its occupant.

❖ ❖ ❖

AFTER WILL assumed her role, Elsie, continuing her late husband's work on the African bulletin, took a bittersweet trip to South Africa and Rhodesia planned for the previous year for her and Frank until cancer canceled it.[17] She attempted to escape her Ulster County outpost by moving part time to the 32 Gramercy Park South building where her friend Flora Rheta Schreiber lived, in the midst of striking gold through her blockbuster book *Sybil*. The *pied-à-terre* allowed for a fifteen-block walk to work. Though John visited and Gene lived there one summer, an empty apartment after so many years of a full house with her as the focal point upended her life.[18] Alone in the most populous city in the United States, she suddenly fell into a tenebrous existence as a widow *and* an empty-nester. Circumstances began to challenge her definition of herself. Newly single and almost sixty, she ventured out on one date with no call back. She suffered an injury in a fall and pneumonia.[19] She tried antidepressants; they didn't work.[20] She began to drink beyond what was normal for her.[21]

Normalcy meant dutiful dedication to advancing her husband's work. She could not resurrect her husband, so she sought to resurrect the out-of-print *In Defense of Freedom*; her frustrations in dealing with Regnery caused her to mail back in pieces a measly royalty check to the company.[22] She kept *The Exchange* alive.[23] A posthumous book dedicated to American soldiers "who fell in Indochina" written "to fill a gap created by the aesthetic prejudices of these times—to bring together in a single volume outstanding examples of heroic and patriotic poetry in the English language" rolled off the press in 1973. *Breathes There a Man: Heroic Ballads & Poems of the English-Speaking Peoples* came about through late-night Woodstock recitations between Jared Lobdell and Meyer of such poems as Alfred Tennyson's "The Revenge," Thomas Babington Macaulay's "Horatius," and G. K. Chesterton's "Lepanto." In the spirit of how he amassed the collection, Meyer encouraged reading the poems not silently but aloud.[24]

Hardly anyone read *Breathes There a Man*, either silently or aloud. Nobody read several of the other projects he had worked on prior to his death. An encyclopedia of Communism, contracted by Arlington House in 1965, died by neglect.[25] He started the "Dynamics of History," which became the "Shape of History," in 1949.[26] Upon his death, it existed as notes and eight rough chapters in a file cabinet, an article in *Modern Age*, and thoughts released into the ether but not, alas, anything resembling a book.[27] "The archeological developments came so fast and furiously during the last decade that Frank was constantly revising in his own mind," Elsie explained. "Or perhaps, like Acton, he talked out his ideas and relatively little got on paper."[28] It seems as likely that any compulsion to organize history to fit a theory waned as he immersed himself in conservatism.

Buckley altered the nature of *National Review* by allowing its regular column of political philosophy to die with its author. He tasked Gerhart Niemeyer, a traditionalist who had nearly untethered his connection to *National Review* the previous decade as a result of fusionism's rise, with periodically filling the void of political theory, which had once defined the publication.[29] Perceptive longtime readers gathered that the disappearance of "Principles and Heresies" put the exclamation point on an era's end. Meyer was the last difficult man standing within *NR* of the Meyer–Kendall–Schlamm–Bozell clique seeking to define, or even invent, conservatism.

The changing magazine's acting book editor changed into the special projects editor, a general title disguising that she primarily proofread. That title morphed into assistant editor. Her patron paid her more generously than he had her husband and allowed her an abbreviated in-office schedule.[30] Still, she moved from editor of a prestigious section of the magazine to an extra set of eyes spotting mistakes, from carrying on her husband's legacy to the important if unheralded job of spotting misuses of "wave" for "waive." "This was devastating to her," David Zincavage noted. "Buckley obviously had no idea how much this hurt her."[31]

One Buckley did.

A disconsolate Elsie confessed her hurt over the lofty title masking what she regarded as a *mise au placard* job to the Meyers' family friend Tad Crawford. The contributor of a few minor pieces to the magazine relayed to Priscilla Buckley

Elsie's anguished feeling that she was "just a copy editor." Crawford saw hurt on the managing editor's face upon saying what he then almost wished he had not.[32]

In 1975, Elsie welcomed family friends Bob Breedlove and David Zincavage to Woodstock, where they played hearts, talked politics, and, at Elsie's request given her isolation in the country, provided instruction on how to operate her .22 handgun, which Zincavage recalled as an H&R revolver. After receiving the instruction, she spoke of missing Frank, various ailments, loneliness, and, especially, the humiliation of her *National Review* duties. The downside of contentedness in playing for so long an uncredited, behind-the-scenes role in her husband's career had become jarringly apparent to her. And the true reason for the firearms tutorial became jarringly apparent to the young men as she began to ruminate aloud on ceasing to exist. They attempted between fly-fishing expeditions in the Catskills to "jolly" her up and assure her of her desired presence in the world. They urged her to reach out should she need a friend.[33] The friend she needed no longer inhabited the temporal plane. Soon neither did she.

Three years, three weeks, and five days after she lost the love of her life, Elsie Meyer walked outside and sat above the remains of precious ones residing in the backyard's pet cemetery. She was alone—as she had been even in the company of others for much of the past three years—on that Sunday save for the firearm she had brought with her. After much forethought and deliberation, she exercised the right to exit this world on her own schedule as Eugene O'Neill Jr. had done a few hundred yards down the hill a quarter century earlier.

That farmer's wife, the one so despondent over her husband's death that she partook in a sort of American-style suttee a century or so earlier, never existed. The Ohayo Mountain folktale, in a game of generational telephone, surely began as a reference to Elsie Meyer but by the whisper chain's terminus referred to a nineteenth-century farmer's wife. She ended her life on April 27, 1975.

✦ ✦ ✦

FRANK MEYER, Nosferatuan in his aversion to natural light, conjured up nobody's idea of a farmer even (or perhaps especially) during his fifties-era foray into planting green beans. Yet, from his Woodstock acreage, he grew the American conservative movement. In the spring of 1972, the crop the farmer had planted appeared deader than him. The Communists marched ahead in Vietnam, and at home Richard Nixon, a Republican declaring himself a Keynesian and imposing price controls, effortlessly crushed a kamikaze primary opponent, cheered by Meyer and company, en route to a forty-nine-state reelection landslide.

Dead does not describe all things underground. The farmer's crop, tended for decades, experienced a delayed harvest. Meyer, as he did after Goldwater's defeat, proved himself indefatigable.

In Defense of Freedom, a book that sold just over three thousand copies during its author's life, roared back into print through Regnery and later the Liberty Fund. As the conservative movement grew, so did the book's readership. That its message of fusionism better translated to the political arena than, say, *The Conservative Mind* or *Ideas Have Consequences*, contributed to a vibrant afterlife not unlike those of Malcolm X, John Kennedy, Jimi Hendrix, and other 1960s icons. What did conservatives believe and why did they believe it? *In Defense of Freedom*, along with a handful of other books destined for classic status on the right, answered these increasingly asked questions. The author became through his book synonymous with fusionism, an idea increasingly synonymous with American conservatism.

The issue—education or, more precisely, homeschooling—that arguably stoked his passion more than any other found vindication in his sons.

John became his father's fifth columnist of sorts. In an almost cosmic joke, he made a career after law school not only inside the federal leviathan but for the government entity perhaps most loathsome to the right: the Legal Services Corporation.

John shared the U.S. Open Chess Championship in 1981. Gene went 15–3–1 in a Yale exhibition of simultaneous matches against all campus comers.[34] He provided commentary on the public television coverage of the Bobby Fischer–Boris Spassky Match of the Century, attained the title of International Master, and at his peak outranked all but eighteen other players in the United States.[35] His most devastating checkmate occurred on another chessboard.

Gene Meyer helped start and became president of the Federalist Society. In his first term, President Donald Trump relied on a list provided by the group to fill three vacancies on the Supreme Court, which subsequently overthrew *Roe v. Wade*; banned affirmative action in college admissions; and restrained bureaucrats from acting like lawmakers. "Gene in being one of the founders of the Federalist Society has carried on his father's work that went beyond what Frank could have done," Crawford observed, "sort of like Alexander and Philip. Philip wanted to conquer Persia, but Alexander conquered that and much more."[36]

His figurative children took over the conservative movement. Pilgrims to the remote farmhouse came to hold leadership positions in the Heritage Foundation, National Rifle Association, Philadelphia Society, Fund for American Studies, *American Spectator*, Liberty Fund, American Conservative Union, and National Journalism Center; they occupied seats on the federal bench, in Congress, and within the president's cabinet; and they edited mass-circulation newspapers and magazines, became popular talk radio hosts, and started their own publishing houses.

They left their own impression in the ground independently of Meyer. Still, one saw their footprints all over Ohayo Mountain—and Meyer's fingerprints all over their careers.

✦ ✦ ✦

MEYER posthumously looked less like a pundit than a prophet.

He foresaw the United States' political realignment before Kevin Phillips, Richard Nixon, and Ronald Reagan did. As early as 1954, he wrote of "the coalition of traditional Republicans and Southern Democrats in the Congress. Out of the struggle which already seems to be shaping up between this coalition on the one hand, and the administration supported by 'liberal Republicans' and New Deal Democrats on the other, there may well come a new alignment of parties, giving the voters in 1956 at last a real choice of the kind they have not had for many years."[37]

A quarter century before Ronald Reagan told Mikhail Gorbachev to "tear down this wall," Meyer told Nikita Khrushchev to do the same. "We should give Khrushchev ample warning, perhaps a week or two," he said to a University of Illinois audience. "We should tell him to tear down the Berlin wall or we will throw an air and sea blockade around the Soviet Union."[38]

He believed the United States could win the Cold War without firing a shot.

Calling "peace as our first objective" a form of "appeasement," he urged America, more than thirty-five years before the fall of the Iron Curtain, to "place as our objective the overthrow of the Kremlin," which he saw as "a possibility that that may be achieved without all-out warfare. And there is a thousand times-better chance that, if it comes to it, we will win."[39]

In his 1960 memo to the *National Review* editorial board, Meyer foretold that something Reagan this way comes. He detailed the accelerated influence of the young conservative movement. Yes, a Boston liberal would soon sit in the Oval

Office. He nevertheless insisted that liberalism ran on fumes. It might take as long as until 1980. But conservatives would elect one of their own to the presidency within two decades.[40]

It all seemed preposterous. And then, preposterously, it all happened. It happened not because the man who foretold it possessed powers of prophecy but instead because he wielded great powers of persuasion, charisma, and organization. He did not so much predict the future as he constructed it along with a small collection of other very able and exceptionally committed men and women. What he did in miniature at Oxford as a Communist he brought to scale in the United States as a conservative. The conservative movement, America, and the world changed because of him.

✦ ✦ ✦

ALMOST NINE YEARS after the American Conservative Union first considered a "national conference along the lines outlined by Mr. Meyer," the group with YAF launched the Conservative Political Action Conference (CPAC).[41] At the 1981 CPAC, Ronald Reagan, elected president in 1980 after a delayed recount of the 1964 contest, name-dropped Russell Kirk, Henry Hazlitt, James Burnham, and others who had planted the intellectual seeds for the conservative movement's 1980 ballot-box triumph. Then he expounded on "Frank Meyer," who, among other teachings cited by the president, "reminded us that the robust individualism of the American experience was part of the deeper current of Western learning and culture."

A sitting U.S. president at a convivium of conservatives speaking as one of their own surely struck the celebrants as surreal. The inability of the one who foresaw the moment—the conference, a conservative president, the political realignment that made that presidency possible, the very politician speaking, Willi Schlamm's outs finally becoming the ins—to actually experience the moment struck many as bittersweet.

Reagan demonstrated an understanding that he addressed the conservative cadre forged by the leader present in his absence. Outside the room, the name meant nothing. Inside, it stirred up emotion.

"It's especially hard to believe that it was only a decade ago, on a cold April day on a small hill in upstate New York, that another of these great thinkers, Frank Meyer, was buried," Reagan reminded. "He'd made the awful journey that so many others had: He pulled himself from the clutches of 'The God That Failed,' and then in his writing fashioned a vigorous new synthesis of traditional and libertarian thought—a synthesis that is today recognized by many as modern conservatism."[42]

In the 1940s, Frank Meyer changed his mind. By the end of the 1980s, he had changed the world.

◀ ◆ ▶

Acknowledgments

D eep gratitude extends to David Zincavage and Karen Myers for warehousing Frank Meyer's papers: no David and Karen, no book—at least not one resembling this one. I thank Neal Freeman, a font of ideas, sounding board, and repository of the conservative past, for supporting this project. Jameson Campaigne Jr. dug into the file cabinets in his home and his mind to provide old letters and stories. John and Gene Meyer tolerated too many questions; thank you.

Daniel McCarthy, Hannah Rowan, and Jennifer Conner of the Intercollegiate Studies Institute helped immensely with editorial guidance; all errors belong to me and not them. I am grateful for the work expended on this project by Elizabeth Bachmann, Sam Schneider, Lauren Miklos, and Analisa Gomez of Encounter Books.

Dozens of librarians and archivists helped make this book possible. It is to my discredit that I can recognize but a few here, to include Dr. Eric Wakin, the deputy director of the Hoover Institution and the Everett and Jane Hauck Director of the institution's library and archives; Dr. Bethany Hamblen, formerly an archivist at Balliol College, University of Oxford; Jill A. Hershorin, archivist at New Jersey's Jewish

Historical Society of Greater MetroWest; and Sarah Hutcheon, research librarian of the Schlesinger Library on the campus of the former Radcliffe College.

R. Emmett Tyrrell, a terrific friend, granted me the first interview for this book. Wlady Pleszczynski, who subscribes to more publications than I do, always helps liberate articles from behind paywalls for me. I appreciate them and my other colleagues at *The American Spectator*, to include Paul Kengor, Melissa Mackenzie, Leonora Cravotta, Ellie Gardey Holmes, Scott McKay, Lori Mashburn, Seth Forman, Grace Reilly, Steve Kapustka, Aubrey Harris, Lyrah Margo, and Elyse Apel.

While the dozens of men and women who granted me interviews earn my forever gratitude, a special acknowledgment goes out to those who died between speaking to me and the publication of this book. These include Arlene Croce, Charlie Wiley, James Buckley, Noel Parmentel, David Franke, William Dennis, and Lee Edwards. Rest in peace.

A most heartfelt thank you to Joseph and Juliet Flynn. They shared their home, involuntarily, for three years with something approaching a quarter-million documents that made their way into all but the bathrooms and two bedrooms. Sorry, not sorry.

◄ ◆ ►

Notes

INTRODUCTION

1   "Meyer," S Form 81, May 16, 1949, British National Archives (TNA), KV 2/3501, PDF-1, 56–57.

2   Trial Transcript: U.S. v. Dennis, U.S. District Court for the Southern District of New York, April 13, 1949, 3198–3296.

3   "Meyer," S Form 81, May 16, 1949, TNA, KV 2/3501, PDF-1, 56–57.

4   George Orwell, *Nineteen Eighty-Four* (New York: Signet Classics, 1949, 1983), 32.

5   Kristine McKenna, "Eno: Voyages in Time & Perception," *Musician*, October 1982, accessed June 26, 2023, http://music. hyperreal.org/artists/brian_eno/interviews/musn82.htm.

6   "Freedom or Virtue: Meyer vs. Bozell," Intercollegiate Studies Institute, February 18, 2013, accessed June 26, 2023, https://isi.org/intercollegiate-review/freedom-or-virtue-meyer-v-bozell; Alexandra Ossola, "Exorcising the Ghosts of Fusionism and Frank S. Meyer," Hamilton College, August 16, 2010, accessed June 26, 2023, https://www.hamilton.edu/ news/story/exorcising-the-ghosts-of-fusionism-and-frank-s-meyer; Matthew Sitman and Sam Adler-Bell, "Know Your

Enemy: Frank Meyer, the Founder of Fusionism," *Dissent Magazine*, November 10, 2021, accessed June 26, 2023, https://www.dissentmagazine.org/blog/know-your-enemy-frank-meyer-the-father-of-fusionism.

7   Jason Mincey to Daniel J. Flynn, email, May 2, 2022, 2:11 p.m.; Jason Mincey to Daniel J. Flynn, email, May 2, 2022, 2:56 p.m.

CHAPTER 1

1   Certified Copy of Record of Birth: Frank Meyer, City of Newark, August 29, 1928, Frank Straus Meyer papers in author's possession (hereafter referred to as FSM Papers); Newark City Directory, 1910, 882, accessed March 8, 2023, https://archive.org/details/NewarkCityDirectory1910.

2   Helene [Meyer] to Jack [Meyer], February 10, 1910, FSM Papers.

3   Helene [Meyer] to "My Dearest" [Jack Meyer], February 11, 1910, FSM Papers.

4   Abner R. Gold, "Pilgrims in a New Land," *The Jewish News*, June 24, 1949, 12; "Mrs. Straus Dies, Was Well Known," *Newark Jewish Chronicle*, circa summer 1921, FSM Papers.

5   Milton R. Konvitz to Frank S. Meyer, January 2, 1951, FSM Papers; Franklin Conklin Jr. to Whom It May Concern, April 6, 1943, FSM Papers.

6   *The Jewish Community Blue Book of Newark* (Newark, NJ: The Jewish Community Blue Book Publishing Co., 1926), 767, 839.

7   Cyrus Adler, ed., *The American Jewish Year Book, 5661* (Philadelphia: The Jewish Publication Society of America, 1900), 319.

8   "Proceedings of the Council of Jewish Women," St. Louis, Missouri, November 11–16, 1923, 354, 348, 350–351, 317.

9   William Helmreich, *The Enduring Community: The Jews of Newark and Metrowest* (New Brunswick, NJ: Transaction Publishers, 1998), 74, 126; *The Jewish Community Blue Book*, 105–107.

10   *The Jewish Community Blue Book*, 489, 549.

11   Frank S. Meyer, "Again on Lincoln," *National Review*, January 25, 1966, 71.

12   Frank S. Meyer to Bill [Buckley], August 23, 1957, FSM Papers.

13   *The Jewish Community Blue Book*, 450.

14   Certified Copy of Record of Birth: Frank Meyer, City of Newark, August 29, 1928, FSM Papers.

15   "New Incorporations," *The India Rubber World*, October 1, 1913, 27.

16   "Direct from the Factory for You for $13.50," *Popular Science Monthly*, December 1920, 112.

17   Newark City Directory, 1922, 1016.

18   Newark City Directory, 1924, 1247.

19   Princeton University Application: Frank S. Meyer, May 26, 1925, Frank Straus Meyer, Undergraduate Academic Files, Series 2, AC198-2, Princeton University Archives, Special Collections, Princeton University Library.

20   Edward F. Unger to Frank Meyer, November 8, 1918, FSM Papers.

21   Helmreich, *The Enduring Community*, 237–238.

22   Minutes of Founding Meeting of B'nai Jeshurun, August 20, 1848, Box 8, Folder 2, B'nai Jeshurun Papers, Jewish Historical Society of Greater Metro West, New Jersey; Gold, "Pilgrims in a New Land," *The Jewish News*, 12; Rabbi Faith Joy Dantowitz, *Generations and Reflections: A History of Congregation B'nai Jeshurun* (Short Hills, NJ: B'nai Jeshurun, 1997), ix, 10; Nathan Kussy, "Early History of the Jews of Newark," in *The Jewish Community Blue Book*, 27–28.

23   *The Jewish Community Blue Book*, 100; Excerpt of David Sarnoff, "Radio of Today and Tomorrow," *New York Sunday Herald*, May 14, 1922, Box 4, Folder 4, Series 3, Papers of Rabbi Solomon Foster, Jewish Historical Society of Greater Metro West, New Jersey.

24   Frank S. Meyer, "Significance of Succoth," *The P.C.*, October 1923, 9, Box 6, Folder 2, Series 4, Papers of Rabbi Solomon

Foster, Jewish Historical Society of Greater Metro West, New Jersey.

25   "New Patrol Lieutenant," *The Scroll*, March 1924, 5, Box 6, Folder 2, Series 4, Papers of Rabbi Solomon Foster, Jewish Historical Society of Greater Metro West, New Jersey.

26   *The Jewish Community Blue Book*, 174.

27   Kevin J. Smant, *Principles and Heresies: Frank S. Meyer and the Shaping of the American Conservative Movement* (Wilmington, DE: ISI Books, 2002), 1.

28   Helmreich, *The Enduring Community*, 110.

29   Princeton University Committee on Admissions, "General Estimate," Frank Straus Meyer, Undergraduate Academic Files, Series 2, AC198-2, Princeton University Archives, Special Collections, Princeton University Library.

30   "Fifth Form Elections—1926," *The Polymnian*, Graduation 1926, 26.

31   Frank Meyer, "Principal's Report on Applicant," questionnaire completed by Newark Academy and provided to Princeton University, March 11, 1925, Frank Straus Meyer, Undergraduate Academic Files, Series 2, AC198-2, Princeton University Archives, Special Collections, Princeton University Library.

32   Frank Straus Meyer, "Cum Laude," June 3, 1925, FSM Papers; Diploma: Frank Straus Meyer, Newark Academy, June 10, 1925, FSM Papers.

33   Radcliffe Heermance to Jacob Frank Meyer, August 7, 1925, Frank Straus Meyer, Undergraduate Academic Files, Series 2, AC198-2, Princeton University Archives, Special Collections, Princeton University Library.

34   "School Directory," *The Polymnian*, January 1926, 19; "Frank Straus Meyer," *The Polymnian*, Graduation 1926, 59; "Sports," *The Polymnian*, January 1925, 15, 16; *The Polymnian*, January 1926, 17.

35   "Frank Straus Meyer," *The Polymnian*, 25.

36   *The Polymnian*, Graduation 1926, 5.

37   "Frank Straus Meyer," *The Polymnian*, 25.

38   "YS Kracs," *The Polymnian*, October 1925, 14; "Personals," *The Polymnian*, January 1926, 11; "School News," *The Polymnian*, February 1926, 13.

39   Helmreich, *The Enduring Community*, 96.

40   Helmreich, *The Enduring Community*, 52.

41   "Class Will," *The Polymnian*, Graduation 1925, 17; "Class Prophecy," *The Polymnian*, Graduation 1925, 15.

42   "Frank Strauss Meyer," *The Polymnian*, 10.

43   "Frank Straus Meyer," *The Polymnian*, 25.

44   Author interview of John Meyer, October 4, 2021.

45   Frank S. Meyer, "Our Debt to the Puritans," *The Polymnian*, May 1926, 13, 28.

46   Arthur Gelb and Barbara Gelb, *O'Neill* (New York: Harper and Brothers, 1962), 610.

47   Stephen A. Black, *Eugene O'Neill: Beyond Mourning and Tragedy* (New Haven, CT: Yale University Press, 1999), 104, 271–272.

48   Louis Sheaffer, *O'Neill: Son and Artist* (Boston: Little Brown, 1973), 211–212; Robert M. Dowling, *Eugene O'Neill: A Life in Four Acts* (New Haven, CT: Yale University Press, 2014), 325–326.

49   Sheaffer, *O'Neill: Son and Artist*, 211–212.

50   Gelb and Gelb, *O'Neill*, 610.

51   Quoted in Sheaffer, *O'Neill: Son and Artist*, 211–212.

52   Sheaffer, *O'Neill: Son and Artist*, 216–218, 230; Black, *Eugene O'Neill*, 351–352; Dowling, *Eugene O'Neill*, 323–235.

53   College Entrance Examination Board Certification for June 1924 and June 1925 for Frank Straus Meyer, Princeton University, Radcliffe Heermance, Director of Admissions, Frank Straus Meyer, Undergraduate Academic Files, Series 2, AC198-2, Princeton University Archives, Special Collections, Princeton University Library.

54   Wilson Farrand to Frank Meyer, July 24, 1924, Frank Straus Meyer, Undergraduate Academic Files, Series 2, AC198-2, Princeton University Archives, Special Collections, Princeton University Library.

55   Author interview of John Meyer, October 4, 2021.

CHAPTER 2

1. Radcliffe Heermance to Jacob Frank Meyer, August 7, 1925, Frank Straus Meyer, Undergraduate Academic Files, Series 2, AC198-2, Princeton University Archives, Special Collections, Princeton University Library.

2. Radcliffe Heermance to Wilson Farrand, May 26, 1925, Frank Straus Meyer, Undergraduate Academic Files, Series 2, AC198-2, Princeton University Archives, Special Collections, Princeton University Library.

3. "General Estimate," assessment of Frank Meyer from Newark Academy to Princeton University Committee on Admission, Frank Straus Meyer, Undergraduate Academic Files, Series 2, AC198-2, Princeton University Archives, Special Collections, Princeton University Library.

4. Princeton University Application, Frank S. Meyer, May 26, 1925, Meyer, Frank Straus, Undergraduate Academic Files, Series 2, AC198-2, Princeton University Archives, Special Collections, Princeton University Library.

5. Frank Meyer to Mr. & Mrs. J. F. Meyer, undated (circa early October 1928), FSM Papers. Sent from the Blue Boar Hotel, Cambridge, England.

6. Transcript: James Burnham, Princeton University, Class of 1927, Class of 1927, Office of the Registrar Records, AC116, Princeton University Archives, Department of Special Collections, Princeton University Library.

7. Frank S. Meyer, paper, "Paradise Lost as an Epic," English 102a Professor Elsasser, 1927, FSM Papers.

8. Frank S. Meyer, poem, "Evocation," Princeton, December 9, 1927, FSM Papers.

9. Frank Meyer, untitled, unpublished poem, undated, FSM Papers. Handwritten on paper.

10. Frank Meyer, untitled, unpublished poem, undated, FSM Papers. Two handwritten drafts on two scraps of paper.

11. Frank Meyer, poem, "Homage to the Daughter of the Moon (For D.M.)," May 1928, FSM Papers.

12   Frank Meyer, poem, "Three Poems of Remembrance (For D.M.)," Christ Church Meadows, Oxford, September 30, 1928, FSM Papers.

13   Frank Meyer, "For R. H. (Dead for Love of One I Love)," unpublished poem, undated, FSM Papers. Handwritten on Hotel Riviera stationery.

14   Dorse to Frank Meyer, November 23, 1928 (postmarked as such), FSM Papers. Newark to England.

15   Dorse to Frank Meyer, April 6, 1929, FSM Papers. New York to Paris.

16   Frank Meyer, "Cross-Section," *Nassau Literary Magazine*, November 1, 1927, 128; Frank Meyer, untitled, unpublished poem, undated, FSM Papers. Handwritten on stationery from Park Lane Hotel in London.

17   Frank Meyer to Jacob Meyer, postcard, October 14, 1926, FSM Papers.

18   Frank Meyer to Helene Meyer, July 4, 1931, FSM Papers.

19   Transcript: Frank Straus Meyer, Princeton University, Class of 1930, Office of the Registrar Records, AC116, Princeton University Archives, Department of Special Collections, Princeton University Library.

20   Transcript: James Burnham, Princeton University.

21   Transcript: Frank Straus Meyer, Princeton University.

22   Christian Gauss to the Committee on Admissions, St. John's College, Cambridge University, September 6, 1928, FSM Papers.

CHAPTER 3

1   Eugene O'Neill Jr. to Frank Meyer, undated (circa 1928), FSM Papers.

2   Eugene O'Neill Jr. to Frank Meyer, December 7, 1927, FSM Papers.

3   Eugene O'Neill Jr. to Frank Meyer, April 3, 1928, FSM Papers.

4   Frank Meyer to Mr. & Mrs. J. F. Meyer, undated (circa late October 1928), FSM Papers.

5 Carrington Cabell Tutwiler Jr. to Frank Meyer, March 31, 1928, FSM Papers. Postmarked April 2, 1928.

6 [Frank Meyer], "Total Abstinence," circa late 1920s, Box 8, Folder 1, Frank S. Meyer Collection, Hoover Institution Library & Archives.

7 [Frank Meyer], "Public Opinion," undated (circa late 1920s), Box 8, Folder 1, Frank S. Meyer Collection, Hoover Institution Library & Archives; [Frank Meyer], untitled essay fragment on religious toleration in the Soviet Union, undated (circa late 1920s), Box 8, Folder 1, Frank S. Meyer Collection, Hoover Institution Library & Archives.

8 Peter Nehemkis to Frank Meyer, September 6, 1929, FSM Papers.

9 Frank Meyer to Mr. & Mrs. J. F. Meyer, August 9, 1928, FSM Papers.

10 Frank Meyer to Mr. & Mrs. J. F. Meyer, undated (circa shortly after August 25, 1928), FSM Papers.

11 Frank Meyer to Mr. & Mrs. J. F. Meyer, undated (circa August–September 1928), FSM Papers.

12 Frank Meyer to J. F. Meyer, September 24, 1928, FSM Papers.

13 Frank Meyer to Mr. & Mrs. J. F. Meyer, October 12, 1928, FSM Papers.

14 Frank Meyer to Mr. & Mrs. J. F. Meyer, October 12, 1928, FSM Papers.

15 Frank Meyer to Mr. & Mrs. J. F. Meyer, undated (circa October 1928), FSM Papers.

16 Frank Meyer to Mr. & Mrs. J. F. Meyer, undated (circa late 1928), FSM Papers.

17 Frank Meyer to Mr. & Mrs. J. F. Meyer, undated (circa late 1928), FSM Papers.

18 Frank Meyer to Mr. & Mrs. J. F. Meyer, undated (circa late 1928), FSM Papers; Frank Meyer to Mr. & Mrs. J. F. Meyer, January 25, 1929, FSM Papers.

19 Frank Meyer to Mr. & Mrs. J. F. Meyer, undated (circa post–December 11, 1928), FSM Papers.

20 Frank Meyer to Charles Morris, October 25, 1928, Frank

Meyer [1928] Dossier, Membership 16, Balliol College Archives, Oxford University.

21 Frank Meyer to Charles Morris, January 25, 1929, Frank Meyer [1928] Dossier, Membership 16, Balliol College Archives, Oxford University; Frank Meyer to Charles Morris, February 26, 1929, Frank Meyer [1928] Dossier, Membership 16, Balliol College Archives, Oxford University.

22 Frank Meyer to Jacob and Helene Meyer, August 15, 1928, FSM Papers.

23 Frank Meyer to Mr. & Mrs. J. F. Meyer, November 29, 1928 (undated but indicated in text), FSM Papers; Frank Meyer to Mr. & Mrs. J. F. Meyer, November 21, 1928, FSM Papers; Frank Meyer to Mr. & Mrs. J. F. Meyer, undated (circa late September–early October 1928), FSM Papers.

24 Frank Meyer to Mr. & Mrs. J. F. Meyer, undated (circa late 1928), FSM Papers; Frank Meyer to Mr. & Mrs. J. F. Meyer, January 20, 1929, FSM Papers.

25 Frank Meyer to Mr. & Mrs. J. F. Meyer, January 20, 1929, FSM Papers.

26 Frank Meyer to Mr. & Mrs. J. F. Meyer, November 23, 1928, FSM Papers.

27 Jacob Meyer to Frank Meyer, October 30, 1928, FSM Papers.

28 Frank Meyer to Mr. and Mrs. J. F. Meyer, undated ("Sunday," circa August, 1928), FSM Papers.

29 Frank Meyer to Mr. & Mrs. J. F. Meyer, undated (circa post–December 11, 1928), FSM Papers.

30 Frank Meyer to Mr. & Mrs. J. F. Meyer, undated, FSM Papers. Written on Savoy Hotel London stationery.

31 Frank Meyer to Mr. & Mrs. J. F. Meyer, January 20, 1929, FSM Papers.

32 Postal Telegraph-Commercial Cables, telegram, April 27, 1929, FSM Papers.

CHAPTER 4

1.   "England," June 1952, FSM Papers; "Oxford Union Society Life Membership," F. S. Meyer, June 1, 1932, FSM Papers; Frank Meyer to Mr. & Mrs. J. F. Meyer, November 27, 1929, FSM Papers.

2.   Frank Meyer to Mrs. Jack F. Meyer, October 28, 1930, FSM Papers; Frank Meyer to Helene Meyer, undated (circa May 1931, typed "mother my dear"), FSM Papers.

3.   Frank Meyer to Mrs. Jack F. Meyer, October 28, 1930, FSM Papers.

4.   "Balliol College Boat Club: The Eights," program, May 28, 1930, FSM Papers.

5.   "Balliol College Boat Club: Morrison Fours," program, November 20, 1929, FSM Papers. Inscription by Toddie Webb.

6.   Dick Southern to [Frank] Meyer, November 13, 1972, FSM Papers.

7.   H. B. Squire, program inscription, "Balliol College A.F.C.: Winners of the Intercollegiate Association Cup," March 4, 1931, FSM Papers.

8.   Frank Meyer to Mr. & Mrs. J. F. Meyer, undated (circa May 1930), FSM Papers. "Working rather hard for . . ." Balliol College, Oxford stationery.

9.   Fred Bartlett to Frank Meyer, August 12, 1930, FSM Papers.

10.   Frank Meyer to Mrs. J. F. Meyer, July 24, 1930, FSM Papers.

11.   Western Union, telegram, unsigned, undated, FSM Papers. Paris to Newark.

12.   "Deaths," *Newark Star-Eagle*, August 13, 1930, 12; Helene Straus Meyer, will, FSM Papers.

13.   Peter [Nehemkis] to Frank Meyer, August 17, 1930, FSM Papers.

14.   James A. Michener to Frank Meyer, October 30, 1930, FSM Papers.

15.   Carrington Cabell Tutwiler Jr. to Frank Meyer, September 26, 1929, FSM Papers.

16.   Diana [Hubback] to Frank Meyer, January 8, 1930 (postmarked), FSM Papers.

17 Sheila MacDonald to Frank Meyer, undated ("Saturday," circa 1931), FSM Papers.

18 Frank Meyer to Winifred Gillett, undated ("Sunday," circa 1930), FSM Papers.

19 Frank Meyer to Winifred Gillett, undated ("Sunday," circa spring 1930), FSM Papers.

20 Sally to Frank Meyer, undated, FSM Papers. From Somerville College to Balliol College.

21 Frank Meyer to Winifred Gillett, undated (circa 1930), FSM Papers. "Balliol still my address—they forward . . ."

22 Frank Meyer to Helene Meyer, July 18, 1931, FSM Papers.

23 Frank Meyer to Helene Meyer, undated (circa July–August 1931), FSM Papers.

24 Frank Meyer to Helene Meyer, July 31, 1931, FSM Papers.

25 Frank Meyer to Helene Meyer, undated (circa August 1931), FSM Papers.

26 Frank Meyer to Helene Meyer, August 30, 1931, FSM Papers.

27 Handshaking Notes: Meyer, F. S., 1929–1932, Studies and Discipline 8, Balliol College Archives, Oxford University.

28 Frank S. Meyer, "The Government of the University," undated (circa late 1920s/early 1930s), Box 8, Folder 1, Frank S. Meyer Collection, Hoover Institution Library & Archives.

29 Author interview of John Meyer, February 4, 2020.

30 [Elsie Meyer] to Mr. [Jack] Dunman, July 14, 1972, FSM Papers.

31 Handshaking Notes: Meyer, F. S., 1929–1932, Studies and Discipline 8, Balliol College Archives, Oxford University.

32 "England," June 1952, FSM Papers.

33 S. I. Form 0.6, "Relating to: F. S. Meyer," January 16, 1932. Originated with C.C. Oxford.

34 "Cross-Reference: Subject—Meyer," January 27, 1932.

35 "Cross-Reference—F. S. Meyer," memo, February 21, 1932, TNA, KV 2/3501, PDF-2, 73; D. C. Driver, "Meyer," May 11, 1932, June 15, 1932, TNA, KV 2/3501, PDF-2, 74; D. C. Driver, "Meyer," November 2, 1932, TNA, KV 2/3501, PDF-2, 76; D. C. Driver, "Meyer," January 27, 1932, TNA, KV 2/3501,

PDF-2, 81; D. C. Driver, "Meyer," January 28, 1931, May 13, 1931, October 31, 1931, December 2, 1931, TNA, KV 2/3501, PDF-2, 82.

36   "The Passing Hour," *Isis*, November 2, 1932, 2; D. C. Driver "F.2/U.R.G," TNA, KV 2/3501, PDF-2, 74.

37   D. C. Driver, memo, "January 27, 1932 issue of *Isis*," undated, TNA, KV 2/3501, PDF-2, 47.

38   "The Passing Hour," *Isis*, June 15, 1932, in D. C. Driver "F.2/U.R.G," TNA, KV 2/3501, PDF-2, 74.

39   "The Passing Hour," *Isis* December 2, 1931, in D. C. Driver, "Meyer," TNA, KV 2/3501, PDF-2, 82.

40   "The October Club," brochure, 1932, FSM Papers; "England," June 1952, FSM Papers.

41   Frank Meyer, testimony, Senate Internal Security Subcommittee, "Scope of Soviet Activity in the United States," February 27, 1957, 3579; "England," June 1952, FSM Papers.

42   Eleanor [Woolley] to Frank [Meyer], note, undated (circa January 1932), "Monday night," FSM Papers.

43   Eleanor Woolley to Frank Meyer, January 22, 1932, FSM Papers.

44   Eleanor to Frank [Meyer], January 9, 1932, FSM Papers.

45   Eleanor to Frank [Meyer], January 9, 1932, FSM Papers.

46   Eleanor Woolley to Frank Meyer, February 2, 1932, FSM Papers.

47   Eleanor Woolley to Frank Meyer, January 27, 1932, FSM Papers.

48   Eleanor Woolley to Frank Meyer, January 24, 1932, FSM Papers.

49   Fred Bartlett to Frank Meyer, January 28, 1932, FSM Papers; Eleanor Woolley to Frank Meyer, January 29, 1932, FSM Papers. Woolley wrote "Thursday night" but January 29 was a Friday.

50   Eleanor [Woolley] to Frank [Meyer], January 9, 1932, FSM Papers.

51   Eleanor [Woolley] to Frank Meyer, January 12, 1932, FSM Papers.

52 Eleanor [Woolley] to Frank [Meyer], January 9, 1932, FSM Papers.

53 Eleanor Woolley to Frank Meyer, January 24, 1932, FSM Papers.

54 Fred Bartlett to Frank Meyer, January 28, 1932, FSM Papers; Eleanor Woolley to Frank Meyer, January 22, 1932, FSM Papers.

55 Eleanor Woolley to Frank Meyer, January 22, 1932, FSM Papers.

56 Fred Bartlett to Frank Meyer, January 28, 1932, FSM Papers.

57 Fred Bartlett to Frank Meyer, January 28, 1932, FSM Papers.

58 Frank Meyer to Dorothy [Canning Miller] & Peter [Nehemkis], April 20, 1930, FSM Papers. Although dated 1930, the letter clearly received subsequent revision.

59 Frank Meyer to Helene Meyer, June 1932, FSM Papers.

60 Author interview of Tad Crawford, October 2, 2023.

61 "The Passing Hour," *Isis*, June 15, 1932, in D. C. Driver "F.2/U.R.G," TNA, KV 2/3501, PDF-2, 74.

62 Handshaking Notes: Meyer, F. S., 1929–1932, Studies and Discipline 8, Balliol College Archives, Oxford University.

63 Special Branch Sergeant Evans and Inspector W. Hay to MI5, memo, "F. S. Meyer," December 10, 1932, TNA, KV 2/3501, PDF-1, 70–71; S. I. Form 0.6, "Relating to: F. S. Meyer," October 31, 1932 (January 9, 1934, date of extract), TNA KV 2/3501, PDF-1, 75.

64 J. Howard McGrath v. Communist Party USA, Subversive Activities Control Board, Washington, D.C., September 24–26, 1951, 5810–5812.

CHAPTER 5

1   Harold Laski to Frank Meyer, July 29, 1932, FSM Papers; Harold Laski to Frank Meyer, August 7, 1932, FSM Papers. July letter was sent from West Kensington to Oxford. August letter was postmarked August 8 and sent from London to London.

2   Helene S. Meyer to Frank Meyer, November 1, 1931, FSM Papers. Addendum dates January 25, 1932, and August 3, 1932.

3   A. D. Lindsey to Frank Meyer, December 17, 1932, FSM Papers; Reinstatement Committee to the Chairman of the Court of Governors of the London School of Economics, petition, circa May 1934, FSM Papers.

4   London School of Economics and Political Science Rockefeller Research Fund Committee, minutes, "Rockefeller Research Fund: Estimated Expenditure 1933–1934 and 1934–1935," July 5, 1934, 179, LSE Minutes 12/3, Rockefeller Research Fund Committee Minute Book, London School of Economics Library; "England," June 1952, FSM Papers. This particular document appears both in Meyer's papers and in the British National Archives and constitutes the record of the FBI debriefing of Meyer at the request of British intelligence.

5   J. Mair to the Academic Registrar, June 22, 1934, Student File for Frank Meyer, LSE Library, London; "Name: F. S. Meyer," undated (circa 1932), Student File for Frank Meyer, LSE Library, London.

6   Bronisław Kasper Malinowski to Frank Meyer, January 19, 1934, FSM Papers.

7   Bronisław Kasper Malinowski to Frank Meyer, January 19, 1934, FSM Papers.

8   Meyer, F. S., "London School of Economics and Political Science Attendance Record Sheet, 1932–1933," Student File for Frank Meyer, LSE Library; Meyer, F. S., "London School of Economics and Political Science Attendance Record Sheet, 1933–1934," Student File for Frank Meyer, LSE Library.

9   Bronisław Kasper Malinowski to Frank Meyer, January 19, 1934, FSM Papers.

10   Bronisław Kasper Malinowski to Frank Meyer, January 19, 1934, FSM Papers.

11   Special Branch Sergeant Evans and Inspector W. Hay to MI5, memo, "F. S. Meyer," December 10, 1932, TNA, KV 2/3501, PDF-2, 70–71.

12   Untitled partial document signed by Sergeant Gordon A. Brown, TNA, KV 2/3501, PDF-2, 1–2.

13   Colonel Sir Vernon Kell to [Ernest] Holderness, March 13, 1934, TNA, KV 2/3501, PDF-2, 33–34.

14   Special Branch Sergeant Evans and Inspector W. Hay to MI5, memo, "F. S. Meyer," December 10, 1932, TNA, KV 2/3501, PDF-2, 69–70.

15   Educational Worker, advertisement "Tours to the U.S.S.R.," *Student Vanguard*, May 1933, 30; Charles Madge, "All Out on May Day," *Student Vanguard*, May 1933, 8, Folder CORN I /2/6, Papers of F. M. Cornford, Wren Library, Cambridge University; "The Universities Under the Soviets," *Student Vanguard*, February 3, 1934, 20, LSE Minutes, 6/3/3/, LSE Emergency Committee, 1933–1934, LSE Library Archives; "Social Murder," *Student Vanguard*, February 3, 1934, 23, LSE Minutes, 6/3/3/, LSE Emergency Committee, 1933–1934, LSE Library Archives.

16   John Cornford, "Art and the Class Struggle: A Reply to Rayner Heppenstall," *Student Vanguard*, May 1933, 12–13, Folder CORN I /2/6, Wren Library Papers of F. M. Cornford, Trinity College, Cambridge University. For examples of Cornford's early fiction, see John Cornford, "His Discovery," March 1923, or John Cornford, "The Baby," March 1923, Folder CORN I 4/1, Papers of F. M. Cornford, Wren Library, Trinity College, Cambridge University.

17   F. J., "Revolutionary Preludes," *Student Vanguard*, May 1933, 32, Folder CORN I /2/6, Wren Library Papers of F. M. Cornford, Trinity College, Cambridge University.

18   Peter Stansky and William Abrahams, *Journey to the Frontier:*

Two Roads to the Spanish Civil War (Boston: Little, Brown and Co., 1966), 190–193.

19   Stansky and Abrahams, *Journey to the Frontier*, 199–200; Author interview of Peter Stansky, January 22, 2023. In discussions with Stansky, he did not know the identity of the unnamed American. According to Cambridge archivists, who corresponded with the author and later discussed in-person their collection, the letters in their possession neither cover the ground discussed by Abrahams and Stansky, who believes he possibly gleaned the information from a letter made available to him from the Cornford family six decades prior to the publication of this book, nor mention Meyer. Within the FSM Papers, a letter from Cornford's brother confirmed Meyer as the American referred to by Stansky and Abrahams.

20   Frank S. Meyer to Christopher Cornford, March 25, 1961, FSM Papers; C. F. Cornford to Frank S. Meyer, May 15, 1961, FSM Papers.

21   "England," June 1952, FSM Papers.

22   Director-General to G. T. D. Patterson, memo, "Confidential: Frank Strauss Meyer," November 28, 1951, TNA, KV 2/3501, PDF-1, 44.

23   "Student Activities: London School of Economics," *Student Vanguard*, May, 1933, 23–24, Folder CORN I 2/6, Papers of F. M. Cornford, Wren Library, Trinity College, Cambridge University.

24   "Federation of Student Societies," *Student Vanguard*, May 1933, 20, Folder CORN I 2/6, Papers of F. M. Cornford, Wren Library, Trinity College, Cambridge University.

25   Senate Internal Security Subcommittee, transcript, "Scope of Soviet Activity in the United States," February 26, 1957, 3580.

26   Michael Straight, *After Long Silence* (New York: W. W. Norton and Co., 1983), 48.

27   London School of Economics and Political Science Rockefeller Research Fund Committee, minutes, "Rockefeller

Research Fund: Estimated Expenditure 1933–1934 and 1934–1935," June 14, 1933, 115, LSE Minutes 12/3, Rockefeller Research Fund Committee Minute Book, London School of Economics Library; London School of Economics and Political Science Rockefeller Research Fund Committee, minutes, "Rockefeller Research Fund: Estimated Expenditure 1933–1934 and 1934–1935," July 6, 1933, 133, LSE Minutes 12/3, Rockefeller Research Fund Committee Minute Book, London School of Economics Library.

28 "Marxism and 'Marxism at L.S.E.,'" *Student Vanguard*, February 3, 1934, 13, LSE Minutes 6/3/3, LSE Emergency Committee, 1933–1934, LSE Library Archives.

29 "Marxism and 'Marxism at L.S.E.,'" *Student Vanguard*, February 3, 1934, 13, LSE Minutes 6/3/3, LSE Emergency Committee, 1933–1934, LSE Library Archives; London School of Economics Emergency Committee, minutes, "Life Membership of the Students' Union," February 22, 1934; LSE Emergency Committee, agenda, April 26, 1934; William Beveridge, "Changes of Students' Union," April 19, 1934, LSE Minutes 6/3/3, LSE Emergency Committee, 1933–1934, LSE Library Archives; Straight, *After Long Silence*, 50.

30 The London School of Economics and Political Science (University of London) Annual Commemoration Dinner, program, December 13, 1933, FSM Papers.

31 Willmoore Kendall Jr. to Willmoore Kendall, October 27, 1932, in *Oxford Years: The Letters of Willmoore Kendall to His Father*, ed. Yvona Kendall Mason (Bryn Mawr, Pennsylvania: Intercollegiate Studies Institute: 1993), 79.

32 [Yvona Kendall Mason] to George [Carey], February 4, 1974, Box 2, George Carey Folder, Willmoore Kendall Collection, Cowan-Blakley Memorial Library, University of Dallas.

33 "The Passing Hour," *Isis*, November 2, 1932, 2.

34 S. I. Form 0.6, "Relating to: F. S. Meyer," December 13, 1932, TNA, KV 2/3501, PDF-2, 69.

35 C. F. C. [Christopher Cornford] to Mum [Frances Cornford], 1932, BL, MS 58412, Darwin and Cornford Papers.

36   S. I. Form 0.6., "Relating to: Frank Myer," January 9, 1933, TNA, KV 2/3501, PDF-2, 67.

37   V. S. S. I. Form 0.6., Extract Relating to F. S. Meyer, April 12, 1933 (original document dated April 10, 1933, covering events from April 8, 1933), TNA, KV 2/3501, PDF-2, 62.

38   Special Branch to MI5, "Frank Strauss MEYER," April 18, 1933 (sent April 19, 1933), TNA, KV 2/3501, PDF-2, 61. Signatures indecipherable.

39   K. M. M. S. to G. P. O. Captain Booth, April 28, 1933, TNA, KV 2/3501, PDF-2, 61; "Result of List of Letters to Frank Strauss MEYER, 12, Morningside Crescent, N.W.," April 28, 1933 to May 17, 1933, TNA, KV2/3501, PDF-2, 56. The message from K. M. M. S. is marked "Secret."

40   Superintendent (initials indecipherable), "Frank Straus Meyer," August 23, 1933, TNA, KV 2/3501, PDF-2, 51. Stamped "Special Branch. . . . To MI5."

41   ". . . War," *Student Vanguard*, May 1933, 4, Folder CORN I 2/6, Papers of F. M. Cornford, Wren Library, Trinity College, Cambridge University.

42   "Extract from a report on the Anti-War Congress (held in Bermondsey Town Hall on 4th and 5th March, 1933) published in the issue of WAR dated 15.3.33," undated (circa March–April 1933), TNA, KV 2/3501, PDF-2, 63.

43   "England," June 1952, FSM Papers; Frank Meyer, testimony, Senate Internal Security Subcommittee, "Scope of Soviet Activity in the United States," February 26, 1957, 3581.

44   "England," June 1952, FSM Papers.

45   "Without Comment," *Student Vanguard*, May 1933, 2, Folder CORN I /2/6, Papers of F. M. Cornford, Wren Library, Trinity College, Cambridge University.

46   "England," June 1952, FSM Papers.

47   Martin Ceadel, "The 'King and Country' Debate, 1933: Student Politics, Pacifism, and the Dictators," *The Historical Journal*, June 1979, 405–406.

48   "Oxford's Union Motion," *Information*, February 24, 1933, 394–395, CHAR 9/104, Churchill Archive, Churchill

College, Cambridge University; "Mr. Wal Hannington," *Information*, February 23, 1933, 395–396, CHAR 9/104, Churchill Archive, Churchill College, Cambridge University; "Appeal to Students," *Information*, February 24, 1933, 396, CHAR 9/104, Churchill Archive, Churchill College, Cambridge University.

49 "Student Activities: London School of Economics," *Student Vanguard*, May 1933, 23–24.

50 Elisabeth to unknown, undated, BL, Darwin and Cornford Papers, MS 58412.

51 "England," June 1952, FSM Papers.

52 "F. S. Meyer: (Students' Group)," Personal M/12, March 1, 1934, TNA, KV 2/3501, PDF-2, 44.

53 "S. B. Report 301/AFAS/4 re Ennst Jablinski," September 6, 1933, TNA, KV 2/3501, PDF-2, 53.

54 Untitled partial document signed by Sergeant Gordon A. Brown, TNA, KV 2/3501, PDF-2, 1–2.

55 "Very Secret: Communist Literature," November 16, 1934, TNA, KV 2/3501, PDF-2, 6.

CHAPTER 6

1 "Frank Straus MEYER," March 10, 1934, TNA, KV 2/3501, PDF-2, 42; Vernon Kell to Ernest Holderness, March 13, 1934, TNA, KV 2/3501, PDF-2, 33–34.

2 "'Unwanted' Advice," *The Student Vanguard*, February 3, 1934, 22, LSE Minutes 6/3/3, LSE Emergency Committee 1933–1934, London School of Economics Library.

3 The London School of Economics and Political Science (University of London) Emergency Committee, "Case of Student Discipline," March 5, 1934, LSE Minutes, 6/3/3, LSE Emergency Committee, 1933–1934, LSE Library Archives.

4 The London School of Economics and Political Science (University of London) Emergency Committee, "Case of Student Discipline," March 5, 1934, LSE Minutes, 6/3/3, LSE Emergency Committee, 1933–1934, LSE Library Archives.

5   "Reinstate Meyer and Simons," *The Student Vanguard*, circa
    March 1934, 3–4, FSM Papers; Frank Meyer, Jack Simons,
    Phyllis Freeman et al., to William Beveridge, March 2, 1934,
    FSM Papers.

6   F. S. Meyer to Director [William Beveridge], February 28,
    1934; The London School of Economics and Political Science
    (University of London) Emergency Committee, "Case of
    Student Discipline," March 5, 1934, LSE Minutes 6/3/3, LSE
    Emergency Committee 1933–1934, London School of Eco-
    nomics Library.

7   The London School of Economics and Political Science
    (University of London) Emergency Committee, "Case of
    Student Discipline," March 5, 1934, LSE Minutes, 6/3/3, LSE
    Emergency Committee, 1933–1934, LSE Library Archives;
    Agenda for March 22, 1934 meeting of the London School
    of Economics and Political Science (University of London)
    Emergency Committee, "Disciplinary action with respect
    to certain students," March 15, 1934, LSE Minutes 6/3/3, LSE
    Emergency Committee 1933–1934, London School of Eco-
    nomics Library.

8   Frank Meyer, Jack Simons, Phyllis Freeman et al., to William
    Beveridge, March 2, 1934, FSM Papers.

9   Frank Meyer to William Beveridge, March 4, 1934, FSM
    Papers.

10 W. H. B. to Frank S. Meyer, March 1, 1934, Frank Straus
    Meyer Student Dossier, LSE Library; Frank S. Meyer to the
    Director, March 4, 1934, Frank Straus Meyer Student Dos-
    sier, LSE Library.

11 "Reinstate Meyer and Simons," *The Student Vanguard*, circa
    March 1934, 4, FSM Papers.

12 "Reinstate Meyer and Simons," *The Student Vanguard*, 3–4,
    FSM Papers.

13 Agenda for March 22, 1934, meeting of the London School
    of Economics and Political Science (University of London)
    Emergency Committee, "Disciplinary action with respect
    to certain students," March 15, 1934, LSE Minutes 6/3/3, LSE

Emergency Committee 1933–1934, London School of Eco-nomics Library.

14   Meeting minutes of the London School of Economics and Political Science (University of London) Emergency Com-mittee, "Case of Discipline—Supplementary Information," March 22, 1934, LSE Minutes 6/3/3, LSE Emergency Com-mittee 1933–1934, London School of Economics Library; "Resolution of Emergency Committee," March 22, 1934, LSE Minutes 6/3/3, LSE Emergency Committee 1933–1934, London School of Economics Library.

15   Agenda for March 22, 1934 meeting of the London School of Economics and Political Science (University of London) Emergency Committee, "Disciplinary action with respect to certain students," March 15, 1934, LSE Minutes 6/3/3, LSE Emergency Committee 1933–1934, London School of Economics Library; Meeting minutes of the London School of Economics and Political Science (University of London) Emergency Committee, "Case of Discipline—Supplemen-tary Information," March 22, 1934, LSE Minutes 6/3/3, LSE Emergency Committee 1933–1934, London School of Eco-nomics Library.

16   Colonel Sir Vernon Kell to [Ernest] Holderness, March 13, 1934, TNA, KV 2/3501, PDF-2, 33–34.

17   Bronisław Kasper Malinowski to Frank Meyer, April 4, 1934, Frank Straus Meyer Student Dossier, LSE Library.

18   Sheila MacDonald to Frank Meyer, undated (circa 1934), FSM Papers.

19   Special Branch to MI5, document, "Myer," December 2, 1932, TNA, KV 2/3501, PDF-2, 71; S. I. Form 0.6, "F. S. Meyer," document extracted from Oxford C.C., February 10, 1932 by MRPH on December 16, 1932, TNA, KV 2/3501, PDF-2, 77; Personal M/12, document, "F.S. Meyer: (Students' Group)," March 1, 1934, TNA, KV 2/3501, PDF-2, 44.

20   "Report No. 227," August 9, 1933, TNA, KV 2/3501, PDF-2, 58. Indecipherable initials.

21   Sheila MacDonald to Frank Meyer, May 24, 1934, FSM Papers.

22 "Cross-Reference: Subject—Frank MAYER," May 14, 1934; S. Form 81, TNA, KV 2/3501, PDF-2, 29; "Cross-Reference," March 15, 1934; S Form 81, TNA, KV 2/3501, PDF-2, 30; Special Branch to MI5, "Frank Meyer," May 4, 1934, TNA, KV 2/3501, PDF-2, 15; Meeting minutes of the London School of Economics and Political Science (University of London) Emergency Committee, "Case of Discipline—Supplementary Information," March 22, 1934.

23 *Fred Fiske Show*, WAMU-FM, January 26, 1983, accessed on August 14, 2023, https://www.cia.gov/readingroom/docs/CIA-RDP88-01070R000100570002-1.pdf.

24 "Case of Mr. Meyer an American Student in London," *The Times*, May 11, 1934, TNA, KV 2/3501, PDF-2, 8; S Form 81, "Cross Reference—Subject: Meyer, Mr. Frank," April 24, 1934; "University Socialists," *Manchester Guardian*, April 23, 1934, TNA, KV 2/3501, PDF-2, 32; "Copy of Press Cutting from the 'Daily Telegraph,'" April 26, 1934, TNA, KV 2/3501, PDF-2, 35.

25 "Reinstatement at L.S.E.," *Student Vanguard*, undated (circa April 1934), 24, FSM Papers.

26 "Reinstatement at L.S.E.," *Student Vanguard*, 24, FSM Papers.

27 Telegraph to Press TASS Moscow, Great Northern Telegraph Company, Limited, May 22, 1934, TNA, KV 2/3501, PDF-2, 22.

28 "Student Control of Student Affairs: 5 Students Suspended from London School of Economics," press release, London School of Economics Bureau of Federation of Student Societies, undated (circa March 1934), FSM Papers.

29 Reinstatement Committee to the Chairman of the Court of Governors of the London School of Economics, petition, undated (circa spring 1934), FSM Papers; "England," June 1952, FSM Papers.

30 *The Student Vanguard*, February 3, 1934, LSE Minutes 6/3/3, LSE Emergency Committee 1933–1934, London School of Economics Library.

31 "Case of Mr. Meyer an American Student in London," *The*

Times of London, 26.

32   Quoted in Reinstatement Committee to the Chairman of the Court of Governors of the London School of Economics, petition, undated (circa spring 1934), FSM Papers; "Milestones," *Time*, May 23, 1927, 27.

33   Reinstatement Committee to the Chairman of the Court of Governors of the London School of Economics, petition, undated (circa spring 1934), FSM Papers.

34   Reinstatement Committee to the Chairman of the Court of Governors of the London School of Economics, petition, undated (circa spring 1934), FSM Papers.

35   "England," June 1952, FSM Papers; Bronisław Kasper Malinowski to Frank Meyer, April 27, 1934, Frank Straus Meyer Student Dossier, LSE Library.

36   Reinstatement Committee to the Chairman of the Court of Governors of the London School of Economics, petition, undated (circa spring 1934), FSM Papers.

37   Lord Beveridge, *The London School of Economics and Its Problems* (London: George Allen & Unwin, 1960), 43–44.

38   Bronisław Kasper Malinowski to Frank Meyer, April 27, 1934, Frank Straus Meyer Student Dossier, LSE Library.

39   "Further Developments in the Case of Frank Meyer," *The Student Vanguard*, circa spring 1934, TNA, KV 2/3501, PDF-2, 4; "Frank Strauss Meyer," O. A. H., Extract from H. O. File 632672, May 30, 1934, TNA, KV 2/3501, PDF-2, 16. A copy of the unsigned *Student Vanguard* editorial also appears in the FSM Papers.

40   Sheila MacDonald to Meyer, undated, FSM Papers. Addressed to 10 Downing Street, S.W.1.

41   "England," June 1952, FSM Papers.

42   "Meyer Leaves: Under Protest: Rally to Victoria at 8.00 p.m. TODAY," undated (circa early June 1934), FSM Papers.

CHAPTER 7

1   Herbert Brownell v. Jefferson School of Social Science, Subversive Activities Control Board, Washington, D.C., January 5, 1954, 1116–1117.

2   Quoted in Max Eastman, *Love and Revolution: My Journey Through an Epoch* (New York: Random House, 1964), 107.

3   "Cross-Reference: Subject—Frank Meyer," S Form 81, July 6, 1934, TNA, KV 2/3501, PDF-2, 11. The intercepted letter signed by Meyer, which included the "Ulrich" enclosure, bears the date June 19, 1934.

4   K. M. M. S. to Major V[alentine] Vivian, June 21, 1934, TNA, KV 2/3501, PDF-2, 9.

5   Martin Ceadel, "The 'King and Country' Debate," 397–422. Even Ceadel, whose main interest appeared to be downplaying the influence of the pledge on the continent, concedes that "the debate was undoubtedly widely reported in Germany" and that several sources recalled Mussolini discussing it.

6   Colonel Sir Vernon Kell to Sir Ernest Holderness, June 12, 1934, TNA, KV 2/3501, PDF-2, 10. Holderness in Home Office.

7   Number 375 Passport: Frank S. Meyer, Consulate General of the USA, London, England, May 13, 1933, FSM Papers.

8   Herbert Brownell v. Jefferson School of Social Science, 1118–1119; Herbert Brownell v. California Labor School, Washington, D.C., December 5, 1955, 19.

9   U.S. v. Dennis, 3201–3214.

10   U.S. v. Dennis, 3213.

11   U.S. v. Dennis, 3214.

12   Herbert Brownell v. Jefferson School of Social Science, 1119–1120.

13   J. Howard McGrath v. Communist Party USA, 1951, 5526.

14   Frank Meyer to Mark Graubard, December 1, 1955, FSM Papers.

15   [Bronisław Malinowski] to Fay-Cooper Cole, March 24, 1934, Frank Straus Meyer's Student Dossier, LSE Library;

Bronisław Malinowski to William Beveridge, April 27, 1934, Frank Straus Meyer's Student Dossier, LSE Library.

16 Bronisław Kasper Malinowski to Frank Meyer, April 27, 1934, Frank Straus Meyer Student Dossier, London School of Economics Library. Typed addendum to that letter.

17 Transcript: Frank Straus Meyer, University of Chicago, Office of the Registrar, Social Sciences, Graduate, Frank S. Meyer Student File, Hanna Holborn Gray Special Collections Research Center, University of Chicago.

18 "Frank S. Meyer Talks to First Meeting of NSL," *Daily Maroon*, October 9, 1934, 1.

19 "Today on the Quadrangles," *Daily Maroon*, October 11, 1934, 2.

20 "Opponents Point to Methods of the NSL as Harmful to Campus," *Daily Maroon*, November 8, 1934, 1.

21 Edward Shils, "Totalitarians and Antinomians," in *Political Passages: Journeys of Change Through Two Decades, 1968–1988,* ed. John H. Bunzel (New York: Free Press, 1988), 11.

22 Transcript: Frank Straus Meyer, University of Chicago; Martin Gardner to Frank Meyer, September 11, 1961, FSM Papers.

23 Shils, "Totalitarians and Antinomians," 11.

24 Transcript: Frank Straus Meyer, University of Chicago.

25 Martin Gardner to Frank Meyer, September 11, 1961, FSM Papers.

26 Martin Gardner, *Undiluted Hocus-Pocus: The Autobiography of Martin Gardner* (Princeton, NJ: Princeton University Press, 2013), 95–96; Martin Gardner to Frank Meyer, September 11, 1961, FSM Papers.

27 "Daily Maroon Initiates Political Union for Discussion by All Campus Partisans," *Daily Maroon*, October 12, 1937, 1.

28 "Set Up Ten Polling Places for Campus-Wide Election of Members of Political Union," *Daily Maroon*, November 23, 1937, 1.

29 "Campus Casts 835 Votes for Political Union Candidates," *Daily Maroon*, November 24, 1937, 1.

30 "Political Union Selects Fritz, Meyer as Heads," *Daily Maroon*, December 8, 1937, 1.

31 Author interview of Jameson Campaigne Jr., May 7, 2020.

32 "Six International House Residents Lead Symposium," *Daily Maroon*, May 20, 1936, 1. Two decades after his University of Chicago experience, Frank Meyer received, in confidence, a series of letters to and from Communists using alternate names from Senate Internal Security Subcommittee aide Robert Morris. See Bob Morris to [Frank Meyer], memo, March 25, 1957, FSM Papers. The International House figures in some. See, for example, Tsuru to Bill [W.T. Parry], August 31, 1936, FSM Papers. The letter instructs to "answer care of The International House."

33 Charles Chatfield, *For Peace and Justice: Pacifism in America, 1914–1941* (Knoxville, TN: University of Tennessee Press, 1971), 259–260.

34 Chatfield, *For Peace and Justice*, 260–261.

35 James Lerner, "Youth Congress," *Fight Against War and Fascism*, November 1934, 13–14; "Forward Against the Forces of Death," *Fight Against War and Fascism*, November 1934, 8–10.

36 Chatfield, *For Peace and Justice*, 258–261.

37 Quoted in "Forward Against the Forces of Death," *Fight Against War and Fascism*, November 1934, 10.

38 "Committee Issues Call for Annual Anti-War Strike," *Daily Maroon*, April 17, 1936, 1; "Campus Joins in Anti-War Demonstration," *Daily Maroon*, April 23, 1936, 1–2.

39 "Campus Joins in Anti-War Demonstration," *Daily Maroon*, April 23, 1936, 1–2.

40 "Communists Meet Minus Trotskyists," *Daily Maroon*, October 20, 1937, 1.

41 "Communists Meet Minus Trotskyists," *Daily Maroon*, October 20, 1937, 1.

42 "Committee on Resolutions to Convene Today," *Daily Maroon*, March 5, 1937, 1.

43 Frank Meyer, "Corrects Statement," *Daily Maroon*, April 19, 1935, 2.

44   "ASU Protest Results in Ban of Hearst News," *Daily Maroon*, February 21, 1936, 1.

45   Milton Friedman and Rose D. Friedman, *Two Lucky People* (Chicago: University of Chicago Press, 1998), 184.

46   Daniel J. Flynn, *Blue Collar Intellectuals: When the Enlightened and the Everyman Elevated America* (Wilmington, DE: ISI Books, 2011), 43–45.

47   Robert Maynard Hutchins, *The Higher Learning in America* (New Brunswick, NJ: Transaction, 1936, 1995), 110–112, 33–58, 59–87, 31–32, 36.

48   "Educational Trends Interpreted by Students at ASU Parliament," *Daily Maroon*, January 19, 1937, 2.

49   Frank Meyer, "The Fire Burning," *Daily Maroon*, May 18, 1937, 1, 3.

50   Sam Hair, "The Travelling Bazaar," *Daily Maroon*, May 20, 1937, 2.

51   Mark Rosenthal, "A Defense of Unreality," *Daily Maroon*, May 28, 1937, 3.

52   Sam Hair, "The Travelling Bazaar," *Daily Maroon*, May 1, 1935, 2.

53   "People," *Echo*, June 1938, 26.

54   Frank Meyer to Mrs. J. F. Meyer, April 29, 1937, FSM Papers.

55   Transcript: Frank Straus Meyer, University of Chicago.

56   Untitled document, 1937, Box 10, Folder 4, Frank S. Meyer Collection, Hoover Institution Library & Archives.

57   Herbert Brownell v. Jefferson School of Social Science, 1130–1132.

58   Transcript: Frank Straus Meyer, University of Chicago.

CHAPTER 8

1   Cam Stewart to Frank S. Meyer, September 29, 1966, FSM Papers.

2   James Farr, "Educating Communists: Eugene Bechtold and the Chicago Workers School," *American Communist History* 19, nos. 1–2 (2020): 67–106.

3   Morris Childs, *Unite the People of Illinois: Jobs, Security, Peace and Democracy—Report to the Illinois State Convention of the Communist Party* (Chicago: Illinois State Committee of the Communist Party, 1938), 87–88, Box 24, Folder 22, Louis Budenz Papers, Providence College Archives and Special Collections.

4   U.S. v. Dennis, 3245.

5   "Organize Group for Scientific Culture Study," *Daily Maroon*, October 26, 1939, 1; "Today on the Quadrangles," *Daily Maroon*, November 17, 1939, 2.

6   Frank Meyer to Dean Russell D. Niles, statement, "At the request of Professor Arad Riggs, I am submitting the following statement," March 3, 1955, FSM Papers.

7   Frank S. Meyer to Cameron Stewart, January 5, 1965, Box 2, Folder 3, Cameron Stewart Collection, California State University Fullerton Special Collections. A duplicate of this original letter appears the FSM Papers.

8   Transcript: National Broadcasting Corporation Interview with Earl Browder, August 26, 1939, Box 63, Folder "1939 Jul–Dec," Earl Browder Papers, Bird Library, Syracuse University, New York; James G. Ryan, *Earl Browder: The Failure of American Communism* (Tuscaloosa, AL: University of Alabama Press, 1997), 159.

9   Herbert Brownell v. Jefferson School of Social Science, 1142–1143.

10   "Communists Tell How They Feel," *Daily Maroon*, October 3, 1939, 4.

11   "Today on the Quadrangles," *Daily Maroon*, October 27, 1939, 2; "Today on the Quadrangles," *Daily Maroon*, November 3, 1939, 2.

12   Transcript: "Interview of Earl Browder with Representatives from New York Post, World-Telegram, and Journal American," September 18, 1939, Box 63, Folder "1939 Jul–Dec," Earl Browder Papers, Bird Library, Syracuse University.

13   Harvey Klehr, John Earl Haynes, and Kyrill M. Anderson, *The Soviet World of American Communism* (New Haven: Yale

University Press, 1998), 72–73.

14   William Bilderback to Frank S. Meyer, April 27 1967, FSM
     Papers; enclosed therein: Transcript: Interview of Frank S.
     Meyer by William Bilderback, undated, FSM Papers; Frank
     S. Meyer to Cameron Stewart, January 5, 1965, Cameron
     Stewart Papers, University Archives and Special Collections,
     California State University-Fullerton.

15   Shils, "Totalitarians and Antinomians," 12.

16   Harvey Klehr, John Earl Haynes, and Fridrikh Igorevich
     Firsov, *The Secret World of American Communism* (New
     Haven, CT: Yale University Press, 1995), 10–11; James Water-
     man Wise, "Forward from Pittsburgh," *The Fight for Peace
     and Democracy*, January 1938, 5–7, 30, https://mc.dlib.nyu.
     edu/files/books/tamwag_fawf000053/tamwag_fawf000053_
     lo.pdf.

17   New York University's Tamiment Library posts a complete
     collection of *Fight against War and Fascism*, including its last
     issue: *The World for Peace and Democracy*, July 1939, https://
     hdl.handle.net/2333.1/vhhmgshq.

18   Form 57: Frank Straus Meyer, State Department, December
     24, 1950, FSM Papers.

19   J. Howard McGrath v. Communist Party USA, 5780.

20   J. Howard McGrath v. Communist Party USA, 5778.

21   James Farr, "Educating Communists," 67–106.

22   Author interview of Eugene Meyer, February 3, 2020.

23   Samuel Bown, "The Story of an English Emigrant," undated,
     FSM Papers.

24   Elsie Bown, Radcliffe College: Application for a Schol-
     arship, June 1, 1931 (family income: $5,000); Elsie Bown,
     Radcliffe College: Application for a Scholarship, April
     18, 1932 (family income: $8,700); Elsie Bown, Radcliffe
     College: Application for a Scholarship, May 3, 1933 (fam-
     ily income: $8,100), Box 89, Elsie May Bown File, Rad-
     cliffe College Student Files RG XXI Series 2, Schlesinger
     Library, Radcliffe Institute for Advanced Study, Har-
     vard University.

25 Samuel Bown to Radcliffe College Office of the Dean, September 16, 1930, Elsie May Bown File, Box 89, Radcliffe College Student Files RG XXI Series 2, Schlesinger Library, Radcliffe Institute for Advanced Study, Harvard University.

26 Author interview of Eugene Meyer and John Meyer, January 19, 2024.

27 Samuel Bown to Radcliffe College Office of the Dean, September 16, 1930, Elsie May Bown File, Box 89, Radcliffe College Student Files RG XXI Series 2, Schlesinger Library, Radcliffe Institute for Advanced Study, Harvard University.

28 Elsie Bown, Radcliffe College Application for Admission, April 7, 1930, Elsie May Bown File, Box 89, Radcliffe College Student Files RG XXI Series 2, Schlesinger Library, Radcliffe Institute for Advanced Study, Harvard University.

29 Elsie Bown, Radcliffe College Application for Admission, April 7, 1930, Elsie May Bown File, Box 89, Radcliffe College Student Files RG XXI Series 2, Schlesinger Library, Radcliffe Institute for Advanced Study, Harvard University.

30 Samuel Bown to Radcliffe College Office of the Dean, September 16, 1930, Elsie May Bown File, Box 89, Radcliffe College Student Files RG XXI Series 2, Schlesinger Library, Radcliffe Institute for Advanced Study, Harvard University.

31 "Elsie May Bown," Divisions of Ancient and Modern Languages—Tutorial Board "Consultation" notes, Elsie May Bown File, Box 89, Radcliffe College Student Files RG XXI Series 2, Schlesinger Library, Radcliffe Institute for Advanced Study, Harvard University.

32 Consultations: "Bown," October 8, 1931–May 3, 1934, Elsie May Bown File, Box 89, Radcliffe College Student Files RG XXI Series 2, Schlesinger Library, Radcliffe Institute for Advanced Study, Harvard University.

33 "Elsie May Bown," Divisions of Ancient and Modern Languages—Tutorial Board "Consultation" notes, Elsie May Bown File, Box 89, Radcliffe College Student Files RG XXI Series 2, Schlesinger Library, Radcliffe Institute for Advanced Study, Harvard University.

34 R. L. Scott, "Bown, Elsie May," Tutor's Report, January 13, 1932; Report Card: Bown, Elsie May, 1931–1932, "Personal Information," Box 89, Elsie May Bown File Radcliffe College Student Files RG XXI Series 2, Schlesinger Library, Radcliffe Institute for Advanced Study, Harvard University.

35 "Bown, Elsie," 1934, Wilson Photo, Box 89, Elsie May Bown File Radcliffe College Student Files RG XXI Series 2, Schlesinger Library, Radcliffe Institute for Advanced Study, Harvard University.

36 Card: Laura F. Gilbert, "E. Bown"; Report Card: "Bown, Elsie May," 1930–1931, "Personal Information," Box 89, Elsie May Bown File Radcliffe College Student Files RG XXI Series 2, Schlesinger Library, Radcliffe Institute for Advanced Study, Harvard University.

37 "Harvard Enters Three Harriers in I.C.C. Race," *The Harvard Crimson*, October 26, 1933, accessed January 11, 2023, https://www.thecrimson.com/article/1933/10/26/crimson-enters-three-harriers-in-icc.

38 Eesha D. Dave and Jose A. Delreal, "FM Investigates: The Kremlin on the Charles," *The Harvard Crimson*, February 16, 2012, accessed January 10, 2023, https://www.thecrimson.com/article/2012/2/16/kremlin-on-the-charles.

39 "Philbrick Jailed for Attempt to Load 'Karlsrue' with Posters," *Harvard Crimson*, May 16, 1934, accessed January 6, 2023, https://www.thecrimson.com/article/1934/5/16/philbrick-jailed-for-attempt-to-load.

40 Dave and Delreal, "FM Investigates: The Kremlin on the Charles," *The Harvard Crimson*.

41 "Philbrick Jailed for Attempt to Load 'Karlsrue' with Posters," *Harvard Crimson*.

42 Author interview of Eugene Meyer, February 3, 2020.

43 "Elsie Bown," Radcliffe College Office of the Dean, October 18, 1930, Elsie May Bown File, Box 89, Radcliffe College Student Files RG XXI Series 2, Schlesinger Library, Radcliffe Institute for Advanced Study, Harvard University.

44 Transcript: Radcliffe College, Bown, Elsie May, Box 2, Radcliffe College Office of the Registrar Records RG XII Series

3, Schlesinger Library, Radcliffe Institute for Advanced Study, Harvard University.

45 Radcliffe College Alumnae Information: Elsie Bown Philbrick, October 31, 1931, Mrs. Frank S. Meyer (E. Bown) File, Box 218, Records of the Radcliffe College Alumnae Association, Schlesinger Library, Harvard University.

46 Author interview of Eugene Meyer, February 3, 2020; Samuel Bown, "The Story of an English Emigrant," undated, FSM Papers.

47 Author interview of John Meyer, March 10, 2021.

48 Transcript: Elsie May Bown Philbrick, Washington University–University College, May 12, 1937, Box 89, Elsie May Bown File, Radcliffe College Student Files RG XXI Series 2, Schlesinger Library, Radcliffe Institute for Advanced Study, Harvard University.

49 Elsie Bown Philbrick, "Radcliffe College Alumnae Information," October 31, 1939, Box 218, Elsie May Bown File, Schlesinger Library, Radcliffe Institute for Advanced Study, Harvard University; Elsie Bown, Radcliffe College: Application for a Scholarship, June 1931, Box 89, Elsie May Bown File, Radcliffe College Student Files RG XXI Series 2, Schlesinger Library, Radcliffe Institute for Advanced Study, Harvard University.

50 Elsie Bown Philbrick, "Radcliffe College Alumnae Information," October 31, 1939, Box 218, Elsie May Bown File, Schlesinger Library, Radcliffe Institute for Advanced Study, Harvard University.

51 Elsie Bown Philbrick, Radcliffe College Alumnae Information—1940, October 31, 1931, Box 218, Mrs. Frank S. Meyer (E. Bown) File, Records of the Radcliffe College Alumnae Association, Schlesinger Library, Harvard University.

52 Frank Meyer to Mark Graubard, December 1, 1955, FSM Papers.

53 Farr, "Educating Communists," 67–106.

54 Author interview of Eugene Meyer, February 3, 2020.

55 Elsie Bown Philbrick, "Radcliffe College Alumnae Information," October 31, 1939, Box 218, Elsie May Bown File,

Schlesinger Library, Radcliffe Institute for Advanced Study, Harvard University.

CHAPTER 9

1   Herbert Brownell v. Jefferson School of Social Science, 1138–1139.

2   Herbert Brownell v. California Labor School, 35.

3   Frank Meyer, affidavit, June 9, 1953, FSM Papers.

4   Author interview of Jameson Campaigne Jr., May 7, 2020; Author interview of Jameson Campaigne Jr., November 5, 2023.

5   Herbert Brownell v. Jefferson School of Social Science, 1138.

6   "Stricken at Grave: Meyer's Widow Dies," *Newark Star-Ledger*, June 9, 1941, 1.

7   Herbert Brownell v. Jefferson School of Social Science, 1142–1143

8   Frank Meyer and Robert Strong, "The Treason of Reaction in America's Second War of Independence," *The Communist*, July 1941, 651.

9   Frank Meyer, "Thomas Jefferson—Leader of the Nation," *The Communist*, July 1942, 522.

10   J. Howard McGrath v. Communist Party USA, 5536.

11   J. Howard McGrath v. Communist Party USA, 5538.

12   J. Howard McGrath v. Communist Party USA, 5534–5539; J. Howard McGrath v. Communist Party USA, 5791–5795.

13   Sheila MacDonald to Frank Meyer, May 24, 1934, FSM Papers.

14   Elisabeth to unknown, undated, BL, Darwin and Cornford Papers, MS 58412.

15   J. Howard McGrath v. Communist Party USA, 5536.

16   J. Howard McGrath v. Communist Party USA, 5539.

17   Frank Meyer to Elsie Meyer, October 22, 1942, FSM Papers. Addressed to Camp Robinson.

18   Frank Meyer to Elsie Meyer, undated (circa late October 1942), FSM Papers. Labelled "8:30 Sunday."

19   Frank Meyer to Elsie Meyer, undated (circa fall 1942), FSM Papers.

20   Author interview of John Meyer, February 4, 2020.

21   Elsie Meyer to Frank Meyer, November 24, 1942, FSM Papers; Elsie Meyer to Frank Meyer, November 27, 1942, FSM Papers; Elsie Meyer to Frank Meyer, December 2, 1942, FSM Papers; Elsie Meyer to Frank Meyer, November 3, 1942, FSM Papers.

22   Frank Meyer to Elsie Meyer, October 22, 1942, FSM Papers; Frank Meyer to Elsie Meyer, undated, Tuesday evening 10:30, FSM Papers; Frank Meyer to Elsie Meyer, undated (circa November 26, 1942), Thursday evening 10:00 p.m., FSM Papers; Frank Meyer to Elsie Meyer, undated, Wednesday, 11:00 p.m., FSM Papers. Wednesday letter sent from Fort Benning.

23   Elsie Meyer to Frank Meyer, December 7, 1942, FSM Papers.

24   Elsie Meyer to Frank Meyer, December 15, 1942, FSM Papers.

25   Frank Meyer, *The Moulding of Communists* (New York: Harcourt, Brace & World, 1961), 128–129.

26   Frank Meyer to Elsie Meyer, undated (circa November 21, 1942), Saturday evening, FSM Papers.

27   Elsie Meyer to Frank Meyer, February 7, 1943, FSM Papers.

28   Elsie Meyer to Frank Meyer, November 28, 1942, FSM Papers.

29   Frank Meyer to Elsie Meyer, undated, Saturday night, FSM Papers. Sent from Fort Benning.

30   Frank Meyer to Elsie Meyer, undated, Wednesday, 11 p.m., FSM Papers. Sent from Fort Benning.

31   Frank Meyer to Elsie Meyer, undated, FSM Papers. Sent from Fort Benning.

32   Frank Meyer to Elsie Meyer, undated (circa early 1943), FSM Papers. Sent from Fort Benning.

33   Elsie Meyer to Frank Meyer, November 10, 1942, FSM Papers; Elsie Meyer to Frank Meyer, November 19, 1942, FSM Papers; Elsie Meyer to Frank Meyer, December 8, 1942, FSM Papers.

34 Elsie Meyer to Frank Meyer, February 7, 1943, FSM Papers.

35 Frank Meyer to Elsie Meyer, undated, Saturday night, FSM Papers. Sent from Fort Benning.

36 Frank Meyer to Elsie Meyer, undated Tuesday, 11:00 p.m., FSM Papers. Sent from Fort Benning.

CHAPTER 10

1 Fred C. Ash to Corporal Frank S. Meyer, order, "Relief as an Officer Candidate," Headquarters Infantry School, Fort Benning, Georgia, February 19, 1943, FSM Papers.

2 Joseph Buchman, M.D., to Selective Service Board 88, June 11, 1943, FSM Papers.

3 Frank Meyer to Mr. & Mrs. J. F. Meyer, November 23, 1928, FSM Papers; Frank Meyer to Mr. & Mrs. J. F. Meyer, undated (circa November 1928), FSM Papers.

4 Joseph Buchman, M.D., to Selective Service Board 88, June 11, 1943, FSM Papers.

5 Joseph Buchman, M.D., to Selective Service Board 88, June 11, 1943, FSM Papers.

6 Joseph Buchman, M.D., to Selective Service Board 88, June 11, 1943, FSM Papers.

7 Maurice Leigh Robinson to Elsie [Meyer], April 7, 1972, FSM Papers.

8 Author interview of John Meyer, March 10, 2021.

9 Louis [Budenz] to Frank [Meyer], October 16, 1945, FSM Papers.

10 Herbert Brownell v. Jefferson School of Social Science, 1145–1146.

11 Frank Meyer to Earl Browder, November 29, 1943, Box 24, Folder M 1940–1963, Earl Browder Papers, Special Collection Research Center, Syracuse University Libraries.

12 William Bilderback to Frank S. Meyer, April 27 1967, FSM Papers; enclosed therein Transcript: Interview of Frank S. Meyer by William Bilderback, undated, FSM Papers. Though described as a transcript, the ten-page document seems more likely notes on the interview.

13   Frank Meyer to Earl Browder, November 29, 1943, Box 24, Folder M 1940-1963, Earl Browder Papers, Special Collection Research Center, Syracuse University Libraries.

14   Frank Meyer, Herbert Brownell v. Jefferson School of Social Science, 1145.

CHAPTER 11

1   Seymour Mullman to Frank Meyer, March 15, 1944, FSM Papers.

2   Seymour Mullman to Frank Meyer, August 11, 1943 FSM Papers.

3   Seymour Mullman to Frank Meyer, March 15, 1944, FSM Papers.

4   Edward F. Witsell to Frank Meyer, October 7, 1944, FSM Papers.

5   Ryan, *Earl Browder*, 136-141, 154-157; Klehr, Haynes, and Anderson, *The Soviet World of American Communism*, 218-227.

6   Franklin D. Roosevelt commutation order of Earl Browder, May 15, 1942, Box 39, Folder "Clemency, 1942," Earl Browder Papers, Bird Library, Syracuse University.

7   F. J. Meyers, "FDR's Sense of Our History," *New Masses*, January 30, 1945, 8-9; F. J. Meyers, "The New Bases for Peace," *New Masses*, January 16, 1945, 13-15.

8   Meyers, "The New Bases for Peace," *New Masses*, 13-15; F. J. Meyers, "How Large a Market," *New Masses*, March 20, 1945, 13-14.

9   Meyers, "How Large a Market," *New Masses*, 13-14; Earl Browder, "How Large a Market," *New Masses*, March 20, 1945, 14.

10   Meyers, "The New Bases for Peace," *New Masses*, 13-15.

11   William Z. Foster, "To the Members of the National Committee, CPUSA," January 20, 1944, Box 19, Folder "Foster, William Zebulon," Earl Browder Papers, Bird Library, Syracuse University.

12   Klehr, Haynes, and Anderson, *The Soviet World of American Communism*, 94.

13   "Minutes of the Communist Party Convention," May 20, 1944, accessed November 7, 2022, https://www.marxists.org/history/usa/parties/cpusa/1944/05/0520-cpusa-convminutes.pdf; U.S. v. Dennis, 3216–3217.

14   "Minutes of the Communist Party Convention," May 20, 1944, accessed November 7, 2022, https://www.marxists.org/history/usa/parties/cpusa/1944/05/0520-cpusa-convminutes.pdf.

15   "Constitution of the Communist Political Association," May 20–22, 1944, accessed November 7, 2022, https://www.marxists.org/history/usa/parties/cpusa/1944/05/0522-cpa-constitution.pdf.

16   U.S. v. Dennis, 3216–3217.

17   Ryan, *Earl Browder*, 235.

18   Klehr, Haynes, and Anderson, *The Soviet World of American Communism*, 93–94.

19   U.S. v. Dennis, 3218–3220; Herbert Brownell v. Jefferson School of Social Science, 1161–1165.

20   Frank Meyer, Herbert Brownell v. Jefferson School of Social Science, 1162.

21   U.S. v. Dennis, 3218–3220.

22   Milton R. Konvitz to Frank S. Meyer, January 2, 1951.

23   The Jefferson School of Social Science, course catalog, Winter Term, February–April, 1945, 45, 28, FSM Papers.

24   Transcript: Senate Internal Security Subcommittee, "Scope of Soviet Activity in the United States," February 26, 1957, 3585–3586.

25   The Jefferson School of Social Science, course catalog, Winter Term, February–April, 1945, 24, 73, FSM Papers; The Jefferson School of Social Science, course catalog, Spring, April–June, 1945, 19, 20, 56, FSM Papers; The Jefferson School of Social Science, course catalog, Summer Session, July–August, 1945, 10, 27, FSM Papers.

26   Herbert Brownell v. Jefferson School of Social Science, 1266.

27   The Jefferson School of Social Science, course catalog, Winter Term, February–April, 1945, 24, 73, 84, FSM Papers; The

Jefferson School of Social Science, course catalog, Spring Term, April–June, 1945, 19, 20, 56, 64, FSM Papers.

28 The Jefferson School of Social Science, course catalog, Summer Session, July–August, 1945, 10, 27, 31, FSM Papers.

29 U.S. v. Dennis, 3239–3240.

30 F. J. Meyers, "The Road to Confusion," *New Masses*, June 5, 1945, 16.

31 Meyers, "The Road to Confusion," *New Masses*, 17.

32 Ryan, *Earl Browder*, 246–261; Klehr, Haynes, and Anderson, *The Soviet World of American Communism*, 91–106.

33 Ryan, *Earl Browder*, 35–37; Harvey Klehr, "Leninism and Lovestoneism," *Studies in Comparative Communism*, Spring/Summer 1974, 12–14.

34 Jacques Duclos, "On the Dissolution of the Communist Party of the United States," in *Marxism-Leninism vs. Revisionism*, ed. William Z. Foster et. al. (New York: New Century Publishers, 1946), accessed December 25, 2022, https://www.marxists.org/history/usa/parties/cpusa/1945/04/0400-duclos-ondissolution.pdf.

35 U.S. v. Dennis, 3221–3229.

36 Herbert Brownell v. Jefferson School of Social Science, 1242.

37 Herbert Brownell v. Jefferson School of Social Science, 1242–1246.

38 Herbert Brownell v. Jefferson School of Social Science, 1245.

39 Herbert Brownell v. Jefferson School of Social Science, 1245.

40 Herbert Brownell v. Jefferson School of Social Science, 1245–1246.

41 Herbert Brownell v. Jefferson School of Social Science, 1245–1251; U.S. v. Dennis, 3228–3231.

42 Herbert Brownell v. Jefferson School of Social Science, 1248–1249.

43 U.S. v. Dennis, 3221–3232.

44 Herbert Brownell v. Jefferson School of Social Science, 1249.

45 Frank S. Meyer to Howard Fast, November 21, 1957, FSM Papers; Howard Fast to Frank Meyer, November 24, 1957, FSM Papers.

46   U.S. v. Dennis, 3236–3237.

47   William Bilderback to Frank S. Meyer, April 27 1967; enclosed therein, transcript: Interview of Frank S. Meyer by William Bilderback, undated, FSM Papers. The transcript seems more likely a summation of his interview with Meyer.

48   J. Howard McGrath v. Communist Party USA, 5742–5755.

49   Louis [Budenz] to Frank [Meyer], October 16, 1945, FSM Papers.

50   Frank [Meyer] to Louis [Budenz], October 11, [1945], FSM Papers; Margaret [Budenz] to Elsie [Meyer], undated (circa mid-October 1945), FSM Papers.

51   Frank [Meyer] to Louis [Budenz], October 11, [1945], FSM Papers.

52   Author interview of John Meyer, July 11, 2023; Frank [Meyer] to Louis [Budenz], October 11, [1945], FSM Papers.

53   "Minutes of the Meeting of the Yonkers Club of the Communist Party, February 12, 1946," report, February 13, 1946, Box 45, Folder "Yonkers Club 1946," Earl Browder Papers, Bird Library, Syracuse University.

54   National Committee, Communist Party of the United States of America, "Statement of the National Board on Earl Browder," undated [February 5, 1946], Box 13, Folder "National Committee 1938–1946," Earl Browder Papers, Bird Library, Syracuse University.

55   Earl Browder to National Committee, Communist Party, February 7, 1946, Box 12, Folder "Communist Party USA Central Committee Memoranda, Earl Browder Papers, Bird Library, Syracuse University.

56   Earl Browder to Comrades ("An Open Letter from Earl Browder to the Members of the Communist Party U.S.A."), undated (circa winter 1946), Box 2, Series 1, Earl Browder Papers, Bird Library, Syracuse University. The source information here refers to the pre-2008 classification of the Browder Papers. Attempts to locate this document for the purpose of updating the source citation failed. All other citations involving the Browder Papers reference the current boxes and folders containing the document relied upon in the text.

57 Frank Collier to Earl Browder, March 8, 1946, Box 8, Folder "Correspondence—C 1939–1961," Earl Browder Papers, Bird Library, Syracuse University.

58 R. E. Goforth to Earl Browder, March 4, 1946, Box 19, Folder "Correspondence—G 1939–1660," Earl Browder Papers, Bird Library, Syracuse University.

59 U.S. v. Dennis, 3239.

CHAPTER 12

1 U.S. Individual Income Tax Return: Frank S. and Elsie Meyer, 1944, FSM Papers.

2 U.S. Individual Income Tax Return: Frank S. and Elsie Meyer, 1945, FSM Papers; Addendum to 1945 return: Memorandum A to Schedule E, FSM Papers.

3 U.S. Individual Income Tax Return: Frank S. Meyer, 1946, FSM Papers; U.S. Individual Income Tax Return: Elsie Meyer, 1946, FSM Papers; Walter [Hoy] to Frank and Elsie [Meyer], December 18, 1962, FSM Papers.

4 Frances Cornford to Frank S. Meyer, August 7, 1945, FSM Papers; James Cornford to Mr. and Mrs. Meyer, January 31, 1947, FSM Papers.

5 Author interview with current homeowner of the Meyer residence, June 16, 2022.

6 Joseph S. Friedberg (seller) and Frank S. Meyer (buyer), indenture, December 4, 1945, private papers of David Zincavage and Karen Myers.

7 Author interview of John Meyer, February 4, 2020; Author interview of John and Eugene Meyer, January 19, 2024; Joseph S. Friedberg (seller) and Frank S. Meyer (buyer), indenture, December 4, 1945, private papers of David Zincavage and Karen Myers. The description of the home and surrounding land also stems from a June 2022 visit.

8 Maurice Leigh Robinson to Elsie [Meyer], April 7, 1972, FSM Papers.

9 Author interview of John Meyer, April 25, 2022.

10   Herbert Romerstein and Eric Breindel, *The Venona Secrets: Exposing Soviet Espionage and America's Traitors* (Washington, DC: Regnery, 2000), 149; Alen Weinstein and Alexander Vassiliev, *The Haunted Wood: Soviet Espionage in America—The Stalin Era* (New York: Random House, 1999), 88–89.

11   John Earl Haynes and Harvey Klehr, *In Denial: Historians, Communism & Espionage* (San Francisco, CA: Encounter Books, 2003), 119.

12   Author interview of Eugene Meyer, February 3, 2020.

13   Author interview of John Meyer, February 4, 2020.

14   Peg Hard, "Special Ceremony to Mark Township Memorial Day," *Kingston Daily Freeman*, May 26, 1947, 9.

15   "Book Shop Plans Weekly Lectures," *Kingston Daily Freeman*, May 21, 1947, 3.

16   "Book Shop Plans Weekly Lectures," *Kingston Daily Freeman*, 3; Peg Hard, "Meyer Will Open Lecture Series," *Kingston Daily Freeman*, June 11, 1947, 3.

17   Peg Hard, "19 Board Members Named to Conduct Woodstock Forum," *Kingston Daily Freeman*, May 10, 1948, 14.

18   Black, *Eugene O'Neill*, 430.

19   Eugene O'Neill Jr. to Frank Meyer, December 1947, Box 1, Folder 22, Eugene O'Neill Jr. Collection, Beinecke Library, Yale University.

20   Eugene O'Neill Jr. to Frank Meyer, December 1947, Box 1, Folder 22, Eugene O'Neill Jr. Collection, Beinecke Library, Yale University.

21   Eugene O'Neill Jr. to Progressive Citizens of America, December 18, 1947, Box 1, Folder 22, Eugene O'Neill Jr. Collection, Beinecke Library, Yale University.

22   Author interview of John Meyer, October 4, 2021.

23   Frank S. Meyer, "Richard M. Weaver: An Appreciation," *Modern Age*, Summer 1970, 243.

CHAPTER 13

1   J. Howard McGrath v. Communist Party USA, 5881–5885.

2   [Elsie Meyer] to [Jack] Dunman, July 14, 1972, FSM Papers.

3   Frank Meyer to J. Edgar Hoover, July 26, 1954, FSM Papers.

4   J. Howard McGrath v. Communist Party USA, 5785.

5   "Red Trial 'Mystery Witnesses,'" *The Titusville Herald*, April 18, 1949, 9.

6   For a discussion of the son Gene Dennis left behind in the Soviet Union, see James Gregory interview of Gene Dennis Vrana, November 13, 2010, accessed July 18, 2022, https://depts.washington.edu/dock/vrana_interview.shtml; see also Klehr, Haynes, and Anderson, *The Soviet World of American Communism*, 352–353. For description of the activities of John Gates in Spain, see Herbert Romerstein, *Heroic Victims: Stalin's Foreign Legion in the Spanish Civil War* (Washington, DC: Council for the Defense of Freedom, 1994), 13–14, 35–40.

7   The Alien Registration Act of 1940, Title 1, Section 2, accessed August 18, 2023, https://loveman.sdsu.edu/docs/1940AlienRegistrationAct.pdf.

8   Franklin Roosevelt, Alien Registration Act Signing Statement, June 29, 1940, accessed July 2022, https://www.presidency.ucsb.edu//documents/statement-signing-the-alien-registration-act.

9   George Morris, "The Trotskyite Fifth Column in the Labor Movement," *The Communist*, August 1944, 714, 716–723.

10   Morris, "The Trotskyite Fifth Column in the Labor Movement," *The Communist*, 717.

11   Morris, "The Trotskyite Fifth Column in the Labor Movement," *The Communist*, 718.

12   Morris, "The Trotskyite Fifth Column in the Labor Movement," *The Communist*, 722; Earl Browder, *The Second Imperialist War* (New York: International Publishers, 1940).

13   Morris, "The Trotskyite Fifth Column in the Labor Movement," *The Communist*, 723.

14   U.S. v. Dennis, 3211.

15   U.S. v. Dennis, 3199.

16   Russell Porter, "Jury Hears Stalin Ordered Violence," *New York Times*, April 14, 1949, 19.

17   "Eugene Dennis, U.S. Communist Boss," *Time*, April 25, 1949, 1; "Judge Medina," *Time*, October 24, 1949, 1.

18   "The Trial Was the Longest, Most Noisy, Most Controversial in U.S. History," *Life*, October 24, 1949, 34.

19   U.S. v. Dennis, 3205–3215.

20   U.S. v. Dennis, 3245.

21   *The History of the Communist Party of the Soviet Union* (Moscow: Foreign Language Publishing House, 1939), 9.

22   Russell Porter, "Communist Trial in its 24th Week," *New York Times*, June 28, 1949, 13.

23   U.S. v. Dennis, 3226–3232.

24   U.S. v. Dennis, 3228–3229.

25   U.S. v. Dennis, 3230.

26   U.S. v. Dennis, 3231.

27   U.S. v. Dennis, 3231.

28   U.S. v. Dennis, 3233–3234.

29   U.S. v. Dennis, 3236–3237.

30   U.S. v. Dennis, 3237.

31   U.S. v. Dennis, 3239–3240.

32   U.S. v. Dennis, 3293–3296.

33   "FBI Men Testify at Red Trial," *New York Sun*, April 13, 1949, 1, 8; Phillip Santora, "Ex-Red Describes 'Call to Arms,'" *New York Daily Mirror*, April 14, 1949, 3, 23.

34   Max Gordon, "2 FBI Stoolies 'Disclose' C. P. Aids Strikers," *The Daily Worker*, April 14, 1949, 1, 11.

35   Harry Raymond, "McGohey Fishes in Specimen from Cesspool," *The Daily Worker*, April 14, 1948, 3.

36   "2nd Secret Witness Tells Red Teaching," *New York Journal-American*, April 13, 1949, 1, 4; "Warning of War Cost Him Card, Ex-Red Says," *New York World-Telegram*, April 13, 1949; Harry Raymond, "McGohey Fishes Another Specimen from Cesspool," *The Daily Worker*, April 14, 1948, 3.

37   Raymond, "McGohey Fishes Another Specimen from Cess-pool," *The Daily Worker*, 3.

38   Nathaniel Weyl to Frank Meyer, April 15, 1949, FSM Papers.

39   "Communist Trial Ends with 11 Guilty," *Life*, October 24, 1949, 32–33.

40   "The Trial Was the Longest, Most Noisy, Most Controversial in U.S. History," *Life*, 34.

CHAPTER 14

1   "Book Shop Plans Weekly Lectures," *Kingston Daily Freeman*, May 21, 1947, 3.

2   Garry Wills, *Confessions of a Conservative* (Garden City, NY: Doubleday, 1979), 41.

3   Mary Braggiotti, "Giant, Mighty Arguer," *New York Post*, November 3, 1948, 57.

4   "Harold R. Peat Presents Eugene O'Neill, Jr. and Frank Meyer," flyer, undated (circa late 1940s), Box 245, Redpath Chautauqua Collection, University of Iowa Special Collections and University Archives.

5   "Harold R. Peat Presents Eugene O'Neill, Jr. and Frank Meyer," flyer, undated (circa late 1940s), Box 245, Redpath Chautauqua Collection, University of Iowa Special Collections and University Archives.

6   Black, *Eugene O'Neill*, 456; Croswell Bowen, *The Curse of the Misbegotten: A Tale of the House of O'Neill* (New York: McGraw-Hill, 1959), 86, 293.

7   "O'Neill, Eugene, Jr.," Box 6, Folder 204, Eugene O'Neill Jr. Collection, Beinecke Library, Yale University.

8   "Ah, Wilderness!," program, *The Theatre Guild on the Air*, ABC, October 7, 1945; "Program Parade," *Radio Daily*, July 6, 1945; "History of the Movies," *Variety*, September 16, 1945, Box 13, Folder 302, Eugene O'Neill Jr. Collection, Beinecke Library, Yale University.

9   Eugene O'Neill Jr. to Frank Meyer, August 1946, Box 1, Folder 22, Eugene O'Neill Jr. Collection, Beinecke Library, Yale University.

10 Dowling, *Eugene O'Neill*, 464; Bowen, *The Curse of the Misbe-gotten*, 345.

11 Eugene O'Neill Jr., Actors' Equity Association Card #A41339, December 19, 1945; E. G. O'Neill, American Federation of Radio Artists, Card #148518, punched May 1, 1948, Box 6, Folder 204, Eugene O'Neill Jr. Collection, Beinecke Library, Yale University.

12 "Harold R. Peat Presents Eugene O'Neill, Jr. and Frank Meyer," flyer, undated (circa late 1940s), Box 245, Redpath Chautauqua Collection, University of Iowa Special Collections and University Archives.

13 The Central Ohio Teachers' Association, program, 1949, 1, 4, 6, FSM Papers.

14 "Noted Educators to Be Presented in Debate by Civic Forum Here," *Bradford Era*, November 10, 1949, 5.

15 Mary Jenkins, "Campus Life at Marshall," *Charleston Daily Mail*, January 22, 1950, 9; Curtis Baxter to Bernice Blond, January 18, 1950, FSM Papers.

16 "Town Hall Series Year Book, 1949–1950," 18, FSM Papers.

17 Marjorie Johnson, "Debate Government Planning at Town Hall Program," *Cleveland Plain Dealer*, January 19, 1950, 17, FSM Papers. Quote therein.

18 Braggiotti, "Giant, Mighty Arguer," *New York Post*, 57.

19 Braggiotti, "Giant, Mighty Arguer," *New York Post*, 57.

CHAPTER 15

1 Arthur Gelb and Barbara Gelb, *By Women Possessed: A Life of Eugene O'Neill* (New York: G.P. Putnam's Sons, 2016), 680.

2 Quoted in Bowen, *The Curse of the Misbegotten*, 280

3 Quoted in Gelb and Gelb, *By Women Possessed*, 680.

4 Elsie Meyer to Lois Bry, September 3, 1951, Box 2, Folder 30, Lois Williams Bry Collection of Eugene O'Neill Jr., Beinecke Library, Yale University.

5 Quoted in Flora Rheta Schreiber to Frank [Meyer], undated (circa fall 1957), FSM Papers. Labeled "Sunday."

6   Dowling, *Eugene O'Neill*, 447–448.

7   Dowling, *Eugene O'Neill*, 462.

8   Carlotta Monterey to Eugene O'Neill Jr., May 29, 1939, Box 1, Folder 25, Eugene O'Neill Jr. Collection, Beinecke Library, Yale University.

9   Black, *Eugene O'Neill*, 484.

10   Black, *Eugene O'Neill*, 465.

11   Bowen, *The Curse of the Misbegotten*, 245, 282, 286, 304–305; Black, *Eugene O'Neill*, 361, 433.

12   Black, *Eugene O'Neill*, 459; Sheaffer, *O'Neill: Son and Artist*, 541–542.

13   Sheaffer, *O'Neill: Son and Artist*, 563, 567, 615–616; Black, *Eugene O'Neill*, 484, 497.

14   Black, *Eugene O'Neill*, 487.

15   Quoted in Dowling, *Eugene O'Neill*, 465.

16   Quoted in Gelb and Gelb, *By Women Possessed*, 680–681.

17   Frank Meyer to Eugene O'Neill Jr., undated (circa late September 1950), Box 1, Folder 23, Eugene O'Neill Jr. Collection, Beinecke Library, Yale University.

18   Quoted in Gelb and Gelb, *By Women Possessed*, 681.

19   Gelb and Gelb, *By Women Possessed*, 681.

20   Quoted in Gelb and Gelb, *By Women Possessed*, 681.

21   Gelb and Gelb, *By Women Possessed*, 681.

22   Gelb and Gelb, *By Women Possessed*, 681–682. Quote therein.

23   Sheaffer, *O'Neill*, 629–631.

24   K. S. White to Eugene O'Neill Jr., February 23, 1950, Box 1, Folder 23, Eugene O'Neill Jr. Collection, Beinecke Library, Yale University.

25   Sheaffer, *O'Neill*, 631; Gelb and Gelb, *By Women Possessed*, 682.

26   In Bowen, *The Curse of the Misbegotten*, 348, the author writes of O'Neill cutting both wrists and ankles. In Black, *Eugene O'Neill*, 499–500, the author writes of O'Neill slitting the left wrist and ankle. In Dowling, *Eugene O'Neill*, 465, the author writes that he slashed his wrist and both ankles. New York's laws pertaining to death certificates severely restrict who may obtain them.

27   Quoted in Gelb and Gelb, *By Women Possessed*, 682.
28   Dowling, *Eugene O'Neill*, 465; Sheaffer, *O'Neill*, 631.
29   Quoted in Sheaffer, *O'Neill*, 631.
30   Sheaffer, *O'Neill*, 631.

CHAPTER 16

1   Gelb and Gelb, *By Women Possessed*, 682–684. Quote therein.
2   Author interview of John Meyer, October 4, 2021.
3   Gelb and Gelb, *By Women Possessed*, 683–684.
4   Sheaffer, *O'Neill: Son and Artist*, 631–632; Gelb and Gelb, *By Women Possessed*, 683–684. Quotes therein.
5   Kathleen Pitt-Smith to Carlotta Monterey, October 13, 1950, Box 2, Folder 62, Series 1, Eugene O'Neill Jr. Collection Beinecke Library, Yale University; Louis Sheaffer, *O'Neill*, 631–632; Black, *Eugene O'Neill*, 499–500.
6   Gelb and Gelb, *By Women Possessed*, 677; Bowen, *The Curse of the Misbegotten*, 342–343.
7   Bradley Tomlin to Frank Meyer, September 29, 1950, Box 2, Folder 83, Series 1, Eugene O'Neill Jr., Beinecke Library, Yale University.
8   Nathaniel Palzer to Frank Meyer, September 29, 1950, Box 2, Folder 75, Series 1, Eugene O'Neill Jr. Collection, Beinecke Library, Yale University; Kathleen Pitt-Smith to Frank Meyer, October 20, 1950, Box 2, Folder 76, Series 1, Eugene O'Neill Jr., Beinecke Library, Yale University.
9   Frank Meyer to Nathaniel Palzer, November 12, 1950, Box 2, Folder 76, Series 1, Eugene O'Neill Jr. Collection, Beinecke Library, Yale University.
10   Norman Holmes Pearson to Frank Meyer, November 2, 1950, Box 2, Folder 78, Series 1, Eugene O'Neill Jr. Collection, Beinecke Library, Yale University.
11   Estate List Compiled by Frank Meyer, undated, Box 6, Folder 200, Series 1, Eugene O'Neill Jr. Collection, Beinecke Library, Yale University.
12   Elise McStea Whitney to Frank and Elsie Meyer, undated,

Box 2, Folder 85, Series 1, Eugene O'Neill Jr. Collection, Beinecke Library, Yale University.

13   Barbara Burton to Frank Meyer, November 22, 1950, Box 2, Folder 67, Series 1, Eugene O'Neill Jr. Collection, Beinecke Library, Yale University.

14   Frank Meyer to Tiffany and Co., December 5, 1950, Box 2, Folder 82, Eugene O'Neill Jr. Collection, Beinecke Library, Yale University; Tiffany and Co. to Frank Meyer, December 7, 1950 Box 2, Folder 82, Eugene O'Neill Jr. Collection, Beinecke Library, Yale University.

15   Frank Meyer to Nathaniel J. Palzer, November 1, 1950, Box 2, Folder 76, Series 1, Eugene O'Neill Jr. Collection, Beinecke Library, Yale University; Frank Meyer to Nathaniel J. Palzer, December 5, 1950, Box 2, Folder 77, Series 1, Eugene O'Neill Jr. Collection, Beinecke Library, Yale University; Nathaniel J. Palzer to Frank Meyer, December 29, 1950, Box 2, Folder 77, Series 1, Eugene O'Neill Jr. Collection, Beinecke Library, Yale University.

16   Norman Holmes Pearson to Frank Meyer, November 19, 1950, Box 2, Folder 78, Series 1, Eugene O'Neill Jr. Collection, Beinecke Library, Yale University; Nathaniel Palzer to Elise McStea Whitney, March 1, 1951, Box 2, Folder 77, Series 1, Eugene O'Neill Jr. Collection, Beinecke Library, Yale University; Bowen, *The Curse of the Misbegotten*, 346.

17   Frank Meyer to Alfred Bellinger, December 5, 1950, Box 2, Folder 64, Series 1, Eugene O'Neill Jr. Collection, Beinecke Library, Yale University; Alfred Bellinger to Frank Meyer, February 8, 1951, Box 2, Folder 64, Series 1, Eugene O'Neill Jr. Collection, Beinecke Library, Yale University; Frank Meyer to Alfred Bellinger, March 14, 1951, Box 2, Folder 64, Series 1, Eugene O'Neill Jr. Collection, Beinecke Library, Yale University.

18   Frank Meyer to Norman Holmes Pearson, December 5, 1950, Box 2, Folder 78, Series 1, Eugene O'Neill Jr. Collection, Beinecke Library, Yale University; Norman Holmes Pearson to Frank Meyer, January 24, 1951, Box 2, Folder 78, Series 1, Eugene O'Neill Jr. Collection, Beinecke Library, Yale University.

19   Nathaniel Palzer to Ruth Lander, December 26, 1950, Box 2, Folder 55, Series 1, Eugene O'Neill Jr. Collection, Beinecke Library, Yale University; Ruth Lander to Nathaniel Palzer, October 21, 1950, Box 2, Folder 55, Series 1, Eugene O'Neill Jr. Collection, Beinecke Library, Yale University.

20   Eugene O'Neill, will, March 7, 1947, Box 6, Folder 181, Series 1, Eugene O'Neill Jr., Beinecke Library, Yale University.

21   Nathaniel Palzer to Ruth Lander, October 24, 1950, Box 2, Folder 55, Series 1, Eugene O'Neill Jr. Collection, Beinecke Library, Yale University; Ruth Reade Lander to Nathaniel Palzer October 21, 1950, Box 2, Folder 55, Series 1, Eugene O'Neill Jr. Collection, Beinecke Library, Yale University.

22   Author interview of John Meyer, April 25, 2022.

23   Frank Meyer to Eugene O'Neill, November 12, 1950, Box 2, Folder 74, Series 1, Eugene O'Neill Jr. Collection, Beinecke Library, Yale University.

24   Frank Meyer to Eugene O'Neill, November 12, 1950, Box 2, Folder 74, Series 1, Eugene O'Neill Jr. Collection, Beinecke Library, Yale University.

25   Eugene O'Neill to Frank Meyer, November 20, 1950, Box 2, Folder 74, Series 1, Eugene O'Neill Jr. Collection, Beinecke Library, Yale University.

26   Frank Meyer to Eugene O'Neill, May 14, 1951, Box 2, Folder 74, Series 1, Eugene O'Neill Jr. Collection, Beinecke Library, Yale University.

27   Guaranty Trust Company of New York to Eugene O'Neill, promissory note, March 4, 1949, Box 6, Folder 180, Series 1, Eugene O'Neill Jr., Beinecke Library, Yale University; Bowen, *The Curse of the Misbegotten*, 320-321.

28   Frank Meyer to Eugene O'Neill, May 14, 1951, Box 2, Folder 74, Series 1, Eugene O'Neill Jr. Collection, Beinecke Library, Yale University.

29   Louis Sheaffer, *O'Neill: Son and Artist*, 657; Winfield Aronberg to Frank Meyer, May 16, 1951, Box 2, Folder 57, Series 1, Eugene O'Neill Jr. Collection, Beinecke Library, Yale University.

30 Winfield Aronberg to Frank Meyer, May 16, 1951, Box 2, Folder 57, Series 1, Eugene O'Neill Jr. Collection, Beinecke Library, Yale University.

31 U.S. Individual Income Tax Return for Calendar Year 1950, Form 1040: Frank S and Elsie Meyer, undated; see also the accompanying Schedule C, Schedule of Profit (or Loss) from Business or Profession; FSM to Sam [Bown], September 25, 1964, FSM Papers.

32 U.S. Individual Income Tax Return for Calendar Year 1951, Form 1040: Frank and Elsie Meyer; see also the accompanying, "Memorandum A to Losses from Casualty," FSM Papers; New York State Income Tax Resident Return for the Calendar Year 1951, Form 201: Frank S. Meyer, FSM Papers.

33 Morton T. Valley to Frank S. Meyer December 8, 1953, FSM Papers.

34 U.S. Individual Income Tax Return for Calendar Year 1952, Form 1040: Frank S. and Elsie Meyer, May 14, 1953; see also, accompanying Schedule C, Profit (or Loss) for Business or Profession 1952, FSM Papers.

35 Author interview of John Meyer, February 4, 2020; Author interview of John Meyer, July 11, 2023.

36 Frank Meyer to Herbert Goldhamer, May 12, 1952, FSM Papers.

37 Frank Meyer to Norman Holmes Pearson, December 5, 1950, Box 2, Folder 78, Series 1, Eugene O'Neill Jr. Collection, Beinecke Library, Yale University.

38 Frank Meyer to Walter Hendricks, April 24, 1950, FSM Papers; Walter Hendricks to Frank Meyer, April 27, 1950, FSM Papers; Frank Meyer to [Gordon Gray], August 21, 1952, FSM Papers; Milton R. Konvitz to Frank S. Meyer, January 2, 1951, FSM Papers. Letter to Gordon Gray was addressed to "The Chancellor"; Gray, who responded to the correspondence, served as president.

39 Form 57, State Department, Frank Straus Meyer, December 24, 1950, FSM Papers.

40 James Putnam to Frank Meyer, May 26, 1950, FSM Papers;

Joan Daves to H.W. Jansen, March 17, 1950, FSM Papers; John Farrar to Frank Meyer, March 29, 1950, FSM Papers.

41   Kathleen Pitt-Smith to Elsie Meyer, undated, Box 2, Folder 80, Series 1, Eugene O'Neill Jr. Collection, Beinecke Library, Yale University.

CHAPTER 17

1   LDT for VV to Miss Sissmore, memo, "Frank Strauss Meyer," December 14, 1934; MI5 memorandum labeled "Secret," TNA, KV 2/3501, PDF-2, 3.

2   Director-General to S.L.O. Jamaica, memo, July 6, 1951, TNA, KV 2/3501, PDF-1, 48; Home Office Aliens Department to Miss Prince, memo, June 29, 1951, TNA, KV 2/3501, PDF-1, 49.

3   Director-General to G. T. D. Patterson, memo, "Frank Strauss MEYER," November 28, 1951, TNA, KV 2/3501, PDF-1, 44.

4   G. T. D. Patterson to the Director-General, memo, "Frank Strauss MEYER," June 26, 1952, TNA, KV 2/3501, PDF-1, 23; Director-General to G. T. D. Patterson, memo, October 11, 1952, TNA, KV 2/3501, PDF-1, 21; Director-General to G. T. D. Patterson, memo, June 9, 1952, TNA, KV 2/3501, PDF-1, 23–24); G. T. D. Patterson to the Director-General, memo, "Frank Strauss MEYER," May 7, 1952, TNA, KV 2/3501, PDF-1, 25; Director-General to G. T. D. Patterson, memo, "Frank Strauss MEYER," November 28, 1951, TNA, KV 2/3501, PDF-1, 44.

5   "England," June 1952, FSM Papers. The same material appears in the archives of British intelligence as "FOR STOTT: RE: FRANK STRAUSS MEYER," May 6, 1952, TNA, KV 2/3501, PDF-1, 26–34. The date conflict indicates that Meyer possibly mixed up dates or that there is a discrepancy between the interview date and British receipt of the transcript.

6   T. Mulvey, "Vernon Ellis Cosslett," *Biographical Memoirs of Fellows of the Royal Society*, November 1994, 63–80;

A Compassionate Spy, directed by Steve James, (Los Angeles: Magnolia Pictures, 2022), DVD.

7   Director-General NR to G.T.D. Paterson, memo, June 9, 1952, TNA, KV 2/3501, PDF-1, 23.

8   J. Howard McGrath v. Communist Party USA, 5554–5557.

9   J. Howard McGrath v. Communist Party USA, 5606.

10   J. Howard McGrath v. Communist Party USA, 5615–5616.

11   J. Howard McGrath v. Communist Party USA, 5617.

12   J. Howard McGrath v. Communist Party USA, 5550–5551.

13   J. Howard McGrath v. Communist Party USA, 5552.

14   [Edsall to Meyer], "Memorandum," undated; "Comments on Your Memorandum of Interview September 11, at Woodstock," undated; Ralph J. Edsall to Frank [Meyer], memo, "Jefferson School of Social Science," November 20, 1953, FSM Papers.

15   "Direct Examination of Frank Straus Meyer Before the Subversive Activities Control Board by Justice Department Attorney Ralph J. Edsall," undated, FSM Papers; Ralph J. Edsall to Frank [Meyer], memo, "Jefferson School of Social Science," November 20, 1953, FSM Papers.

16   Thomas J. Herbert to Frank Straus Meyer, subpoena, United States of America Subversive Activities Control Board, January 5, 1954, FSM Papers.

17   Ralph J. Edsall to Frank Meyer, December 23, 1953, FSM Papers.

18   "'Link' to Browder Retold at Inquiry," *New York Times*, January 6, 1954, 12; "Offered Post of Commissar, Ex-Red Says," *Washington Post*, January 6, 1954, 5. A Library of Congress microfilm edition of the *Post* excludes the article but the edition digitized in ProQuest, as well as the original held by author, includes this Associated Press article.

19   Ralph J. Edsall Jr. to Frank S. Meyer, December 23, 1953, FSM Papers.

20   Frank S. Meyer to Ralph J. Edsall Jr. January 26, 1954, FSM Papers.

21   Herbert Brownell v. California Labor School, 16–101.

22   [Frank Meyer] to Louis [Budenz], April 3, 1957, FSM Papers.

23   Frank Meyer, testimony, Senate Internal Security Subcommittee, "Scope of Soviet Activity in the United States," February 26, 1957, 3588.

24   Frank Meyer, testimony, Senate Internal Security Subcommittee, "Scope of Soviet Activity in the United States," February 27, 1957, unpaginated transcript, FSM Papers.

25   Frank Meyer, testimony, Senate Internal Security Subcommittee, "Scope of Soviet Activity in the United States," February 27, 1957, unpaginated transcript, FSM Papers.

26   Klehr, Haynes, and Firsov, *The Secret World of American Communism*, 249–258; Romerstein and Breindel, *The Venona Secrets*, 171–181.

27   Frank Meyer, testimony, Senate Internal Security Subcommittee, "Scope of Soviet Activity in the United States," February 27, 1957, unpaginated transcript, FSM Papers.

28   Klehr, Haynes, and Firsov, *The Secret World of American Communism*, 249–250.

29   Eleanor Roosevelt, "My Day, April 12, 1941," *The Eleanor Roosevelt Papers Digital Edition*, 2017, accessed February 25, 2023, https://www2.gwu.edu/~erpapers/myday/displaydocedits.cfm?_y=1941&_f=md055860.

30   Romerstein and Breindel, *The Venona Secrets*, 174.

31   Josephine Truslow Adams, testimony, Senate Internal Security Subcommittee, "Scope of Soviet Activity in the United States," January 16, 1957, unpaginated but excerpted section spans pages 1651, 1653–1667, 1678, 1679, 1688, FSM Papers.

32   Harvey Klehr, "The Strange Case of Roosevelt's 'Secret Agent,'" *Encounter*, December 1982, 84–91.

33   Klehr, "The Strange Case of Roosevelt's 'Secret Agent,'" *Encounter*, 84–91.

34   William Bilderback interview of Frank Meyer, undated, 7–8; included as attachment to a letter, William Bilderback to Frank Meyer, April 21, 1967, FSM Papers.

35   Quoted in Archives Experience Newsletter, September 27, 2022, accessed September 27, 2023, https://www.archives-foundation.org/newsletter/the-loyalty-test/.

36   Frank S. Meyer, testimony, "Communist Training Opera-
     tions—Part 1," House Committee on Un-American Activi-
     ties, July 21, 1959 (Washington, DC: Government Printing
     Office, 1959), 1018.

37   Frank S. Meyer, testimony, "Communist Training Opera-
     tions—Part 1," House Committee on Un-American Activi-
     ties, 1007–1024, 1037, 1040–1041.

38   Frank S. Meyer, testimony, "Communist Training Opera-
     tions—Part 1," House Committee on Un-American Activi-
     ties, 1040.

39   Frank S. Meyer, testimony, "Communist Training Opera-
     tions—Part 1," House Committee on Un-American Activi-
     ties, 1037.

40   Ithiel de Sola Pool to Frank Meyer, November 13, 1950, FSM
     Papers; Francis M. Wray to Ithiel de Sola Pool, November 3,
     1950, FSM Papers; Frank S. Meyer to "whom it may con-
     cern," November 20, 1950, FSM Papers.

41   Ithiel de Sola Pool to Frank Meyer, postcard, December 29,
     1950, FSM Papers.

42   Frank Meyer, affidavit, "On the Subject of Herbert Gold-
     hamer," June 9, 1953, FSM Papers.

43   Frank S. Meyer to Lt. Col. and Mrs. H.C. Goodell, June 11,
     1961, FSM Papers.

44   Ira H. Latimer to Frank S. Meyer, June 25, 1956, FSM Papers.

45   Frank Meyer to Ira Latimer, July 28, 1956, FSM Papers.

CHAPTER 18

1   Frank Meyer to Mark Graubard, September 25, 1955, FSM
    Papers.

2   Frank Meyer to Mark Graubard, December 1, 1955, FSM
    Papers.

3   Author interview of John Meyer, February 4, 2020; Author
    interview of John Meyer, October 4, 2021.

4   Robert Phelps, journal entry, October 14, 1954, Rosemarie
    Beck Foundation.

5   Robert Phelps, journal entry, October 11, 1954, Rosemarie Beck Foundation.

6   Author interview of Roger Phelps, May 29, 2022. For a fictionalized, desexualized depiction of the affair, see Robert Phelps, *Heroes and Orators* (New York: McDowell, Obolensky, 1958).

7   Gertrude E. Vogt to Frank Meyer, May 27, 1952, FSM Papers.

8   Eve E. Boyden to Frank Meyer, February 13, 1953, FSM Papers; Barbara Sellers to Frank Meyer, November 17, 1952, FSM Papers; Barbara Sellers to Frank Meyer, August 27, 1952, FSM Papers; Helen M. Beatty to Frank Meyer, May 7, 1952, FSM Papers; Frank Meyer to Frank Chodorov, July 18, 1954, FSM Papers; Frank Chodorov to Frank S. Meyer, July 22, 1954, FSM Papers.

9   Frank Meyer to John Chamberlain, August 31, 1952, FSM Papers.

10 Frank Meyer to John Chamberlain, August 31, 1952, FSM Papers.

11 "The Press: Battle for the Freeman," *Time*, January 26, 1953, 74–75.

12 Gertrude E. Vogt to Frank Meyer, January 23, 1953, FSM Papers. NYC.

13 Frank S. Meyer, "Word-Juggling," *The Freeman*, February 23, 1953, 392–393.

14 John B. Judis, *William F. Buckley: Patron Saint of the Conservatives* (New York: Simon and Schuster, 1988), 103; "The Press: Battle for the Freeman," *Time*, 74–75.

15 Nathaniel Weyl, "Ways of Treason," *American Mercury*, November 1952, 111–113.

16 Frank Meyer, "Cliches and Shibboleths," *American Mercury*, November 1952, 108–110.

17 M[artin] Greenberg to [Frank] Meyer, December 1, 1952, FSM Papers.

18 "Trouble for the Mercury," *Time*, December 8, 1952, 42.

19 Nathaniel Weyl to Frank Meyer, February 11, [1953], FSM Papers.

20   Frank Meyer to Nathaniel Weyl, February 18, 1953, FSM Papers.

21   Patricia Hunsinger to Frank Meyer, October 27, 1952, FSM Papers.

22   John A. Clements to Frank S. Meyer, March 3, 1953, FSM Papers; Frank Meyer to John A. Clements, March 5, 1953, FSM Papers.

23   Frank Meyer, "Books in Review," *American Mercury*, March–April, 1953, 118–128.

24   Frank S. Meyer, "Books in Review," *American Mercury*, May 1953, 68–78.

25   James Baldwin, "Exodus," *American Mercury*, August 1952, 97–103.

26   Frank S. Meyer, "Books in Review," *American Mercury*, September 1953, 141.

27   Frank S. Meyer, "Books in Review," *American Mercury*, September 1953, 73–74, 135–136; Frank S. Meyer, "Books in Review," *American Mercury*, October 1953, 141–142.

28   Frank S. Meyer, "Books in Review," *American Mercury*, June 1953, 143; Frank Meyer to Granville Hicks, April 27, 1953, FSM Papers. Therein, Meyer explains, "I knew Wright slightly—I think it was when I was educational director of the South Side section of the Party in Chicago; but I am afraid my attitude toward him was much more Party functionary than human."

29   Frank S. Meyer, "Books in Review," *American Mercury*, May 1953, 78; Frank S. Meyer, "Books in Review," *American Mercury*, October 1953, 143.

30   Frank S. Meyer, "Books in Review," *American Mercury*, May 1953, 71–72.

31   Frank S. Meyer, "Books in Review," *American Mercury*, July 1953, 142.

32   Jack A. Clements to Frank Meyer, May 12, 1953, FSM Papers.

33   John A. Clements to Frank S. Meyer, September 9, 1953, FSM Papers.

34   Rose Lane to [Frank] Meyer, September 24, 1953, FSM Papers.

35 R[ose] W[ilder] L[ane] to Frank Meyer, May 12, [1955], FSM
Papers.

36 R[ose] W[ilder] L[ane] to Frank Meyerses, October 10, 1954,
FSM Papers; [Frank S. Meyer] to Mrs. Lane, July 18, 1954,
FSM Papers; [Frank S. Meyer] to Mrs. Lane, March 23, 1958,
FSM Papers.

37 R[ose] W[ilder] L[ane] to Meyers, September 18, 1956, FSM
Papers.

38 [Frank S. Meyer] to [Rose Wilder] Lane, October 2, 1953,
FSM Papers.

39 Rose Lane to [Frank] Meyer, September 24, 1953, FSM Pa-
pers; RWL to [Frank] Meyer, October 23, 1953, FSM Papers;
RWL to [Frank Meyer], undated (circa March 1955), FSM
Papers; R[ose] W[ilder] L[ane] to Frank [Meyer], June 6, 1955,
FSM Papers; R[ose] W[ilder] L[ane] to Meyers, September 18,
1956, FSM Papers.

40 R[ose] W[ilder] L[ane] to [Frank] Meyer, January 28, 1954,
FSM Papers.

41 [Frank Meyer] to Rose Wilder [Lane], March 12, 1954, FSM
Papers.

42 [Frank S. Meyer] to [Rose Wilder] Lane, January 26, 1954,
FSM Papers.

43 R[ose] W[ilder] L[ane] to [Frank] Meyer, October 23, 1953,
FSM Papers.

44 Morris A. Cox to Frank S. Meyer, March 8, 1954, FSM Papers.

45 Flora Rheta Schreiber to Elsie, November 23, 1951, FSM Papers.

46 H. W. Luhnow to Frank S. Meyer, July 8, 1954, FSM Papers.

47 Nicole Hoplin and Ron Robinson, *Funding Fathers: The Un-
sung Heroes of the Conservative Movement* (Washington, DC:
Regnery, 2008), 26–33; George H. Nash, *The Conservative
Intellectual Movement in America Since 1945* (Wilmington,
DE: Intercollegiate Studies Institute, 1996), 169, 348n, 349n.

48 Frank Meyer to Nathaniel Weyl, February 18, 1953, FSM Papers.

49 Henry Regnery, "The Making of *The Conservative Mind*," in
Russell Kirk, *The Conservative Mind: From Burke to Eliot—
Seventh Revised Edition* (Washington, DC: Regnery 1953,

1995), iv; Russell Kirk, *The Sword of the Imagination: Memoirs of a Half-Century of Literary Conflict* (Grand Rapids, MI: Eerdmans, 1995), 146.

50   Frank Meyer to Frank Chodorov, March 21, 1955, FSM Papers.

51   Frank Meyer to William F. Buckley, Jr., May 27, 1955, Box 3, Folder 120, Series 1, William F. Buckley Jr. Papers, Sterling Memorial Library, Yale University; William F. Buckley, Jr. to Frank Meyer, June 24, 1955, Box 3, Folder 120, Series 1, William F. Buckley Jr. Papers, Sterling Memorial Library, Yale University.

52   Frank S. Meyer, "Collectivism Rebaptized," *Freeman*, July 1955, 559–562.

53   Robert J. Needles to the Editor, *Freeman*, July 8, 1955, Folder 120, Box 3, Series 1, William F. Buckley Jr. Papers, Sterling Memorial Library, Yale University.

54   Russell Kirk to Henry Regnery, August 13, 1955, Box 39, Folder 10, Henry Regnery Papers, Hoover Institution Library & Archives.

55   Russell Kirk to Henry Regnery, July 21, 1955, Box 39, Folder 10, Henry Regnery Papers, Hoover Institution Library & Archives.

56   Russell Kirk to Henry Regnery, August 13, 1955, Box 39, Folder 10, Henry Regnery Papers, Hoover Institution Library & Archives.

57   Russell [Kirk] to Henry [Regnery], June 25 [1955], Box 39, Folder 10, Henry Regnery Papers, Hoover Institution Library & Archives.

58   Henry Regnery to Russell Kirk, June 29, 1955, Box 39, Folder 10, Henry Regnery Papers, Hoover Institution Library & Archives.

59   R[ose] W[ilder] L[ane] to Frank Meyer, July 6, 1955, FSM Papers.

60   H. W. Luhnow to Frank S. Meyer, June 24, 1955, FSM Papers.

61   Frank Meyer to Nathaniel Weyl, February 18, 1953, FSM Papers.

62   Quoted in Judis, *William F. Buckley*, 115.

63   Judis, *William F. Buckley*, 103–104, 114, 114n.

64   William S. Schlamm to Henry Regnery, May 5, 1953, FSM Papers.

CHAPTER 19

1   William F. Buckley, Jr., "Publisher's Statement," *National Review*, November 19, 1955, 5.

2   "The Week: The Magazine's Credenda," *National Review*, November 19, 1955, 6.

3   Buckley, "Publisher's Statement," *National Review*, 5.

4   Murray Kempton, "Lost-One Scape Goat," *The Progressive*, December 1955, 15.

5   John Fischer, "The Editor's Easy Chair: Why Is the Conservative Voice So Hoarse?," *Harper's*, March 1956, 16–19.

6   Harvey Breit, "In and Out of Books," *New York Times*, November 27, 1955, 324.

7   Dwight Macdonald, "Scrambled Eggheads on the Right," *Commentary*, April 1956, 367–373.

8   Leon Trotsky, *In Defense of Marxism* (New York: Pioneer Publishers, 1942), 180.

9   Trotsky, *In Defense of Marxism*, 176.

10   George Orwell, "Second Thoughts on James Burnham," last modified December 29, 2019, accessed September 11, 2023, https://www.orwell.ru/library/reviews/burnham/english/e_burnh. For discussions of Burnham's influence on *Nineteen Eighty-Four*, see R. B. Reaves, "Orwell's 'Second Thoughts on James Burnham' and *1984*," *College Literature* 11, no. 1 (1984): 13–20; George Kateb, "The Road to 1984," *Political Science Quarterly* 81, no. 4 (December 1966): 572–580.

11   Macdonald, "Scrambled Eggheads on the Right," *Commentary*, 368.

12   Macdonald, "Scrambled Eggheads on the Right," *Commentary*, 368; Author interview of Allan Ryskind, September 12, 2023. Allan Ryskind, who knew La Follette well, insists he

never saw this supposed volatility.

13   Author interview of Charles Wiley, November 19, 2021.

14   [Frank Meyer] to Jeffrey Hart, March 26, 1966, FSM Papers.

15   Judis, *William F. Buckley*, 115–116; Nash, *The Conservative Intellectual Movement*, 133.

16   Author interview of Neal Freeman, May 19, 2020.

17   Macdonald, "Scrambled Eggheads on the Right," *Commentary*, 368.

18   Wm. F. Buckley, Jr. to Father Stanley Parry, December 2, 1957, FSM Papers.

19   William F. Buckley, Jr., "Memorandum: Re: A New Magazine," 6–8, Box 10, Folder 3, James Burnham Papers, Hoover Institution Library & Archives.

20   Russell Kirk, *The Sword of Imagination: Memoirs of a Half-Century of Literary Conflict* (Grand Rapids, MI: Eerdmans, 1995), 182; Nash, *The Conservative Intellectual Movement*, 132–133.

21   [Frank Meyer] to [Rose Wilder] Lane, October 10, 1953, FSM Papers; R[ose] W[ilder] L[ane] to [Frank] Meyer, January 28, 1954, FSM Papers.

22   Wm. F. Buckley, Jr. to Frank S. Meyer, February 23, 1956, FSM Papers.

23   Frank S. Meyer, "Politics and Responsibility," *National Review*, April 4, 1956, 21.

CHAPTER 20

1   Willmoore Kendall to Frank Meyer, October 10, 1955, FSM Papers.

2   Frank Meyer, "Croce on Liberty," *National Review*, November 19, 1956, 29–30; Robert Phelps, "Motion from the Floor," *National Review*, November 19, 1956, 29.

3   Willmoore Kendall to Frank Meyer, March 29, 1956, FSM Papers.

4   Willmoore Kendall to Frank Meyer, undated (circa spring 1956), FSM Papers. Letter begins, "As I've just written Robert . . ."

5   Willmoore Kendall to William F. Buckley, Jr., memo, July
     13, 1956, FSM Papers; CC: Willi Schlamm, James Burnham,
     Suzanne La Follette, Frank Meyer, Brent Bozell.

6   Frank S. Meyer, "Where Is Eisenhower Going?," *The Ameri-
     can Mercury*, March 1954, 125.

7   James Burnham, "Should Conservatives Vote for
     Eisenhower-Nixon? Yes," *National Review*, October 20, 1956,
     12, 14.

8   Meyer, "Where Is Eisenhower Going?," *The American Mercu-
     ry*, 126.

9   William S. Schlamm, "Should Conservatives Vote for
     Eisenhower-Nixon? No," *National Review*, October 20, 1956,
     13–15.

10   Quoted in Judis, *William F. Buckley*, 155.

11   Judis, *William F. Buckley*, 155–156. Quote therein.

12   Bill [Buckley] to Jim [Burnham], undated (circa 1957), Box
     5, Folder 26, James Burnham Papers, Hoover Institution
     Library & Archives.

13   Judis, *William F. Buckley*, 156.

14   Frank Meyer to Willi Schlamm, April 28, 1957, FSM Papers.

15   L. Brent Bozell to Elsie and Frank [Meyer], October 20, 1956,
     FSM Papers.

16   William A. Rusher, "N. R. Newsletter," June 1972, FSM Pa-
     pers; William A. Rusher to John M. Ashbrook, June 26, 1963,
     FSM Papers.

17   Willi [Schlamm] to Bill [Buckley], July 24, 1957, FSM Papers;
     Wm. F. Buckley, Jr. to Willi [Schlamm], July 25, 1957, FSM
     Papers.

18   Frank S. Meyer to Bill [Buckley], September 23, 1957, FSM
     Papers.

19   C. S. Lewis to Frank Meyer, May 23, 1958, FSM Papers;
     J. R. R. Tolkien to Frank Meyer, January 20, 1961, FSM
     Papers.

20   Evelyn Waugh, "Chesterton," *National Review*, April 22,
     1961, 251.

21   W. H. Auden to the Editors, January 26, 1959, FSM Papers.

22   Frank S. Meyer to Hugh Kenner, September 9, 1957, FSM Papers.

23   Hugh Kenner to Guy Davenport, May 6, 1961 in *Questioning Minds: The Letters of Guy Davenport and Hugh Kenner*, ed. Edward M. Burns (Berkeley, CA: Counterpoint, 2018), 34.

24   Quoted in Smant, *Principles and Heresies*, 131.

25   Hugh Kenner to Guy Davenport, January 18, 1962, in Burns, ed., *Questioning Minds*, 70.

26   Guy Davenport to Hugh Kenner, October 26, 1963, in Burns, ed., *Questioning Minds*, 436.

27   Garry Wills to William Rusher, undated (circa 1958), Box 98, William A. Rusher Papers, Library of Congress; Garry Wills to Frank and Elsie Meyer, undated (circa 1958), FSM Papers.

28   Wills, *Confessions of a Conservative*, 41–42; Author interview of John Meyer, July 11, 2023.

29   Garry Wills to Frank Meyer, undated (circa fall 1958), FSM Papers; Wills, *Confessions of a Conservative*, 41.

30   Garry Wills to Frank Meyer, undated (circa January 1960), FSM Papers. "Tel. 1/9/60."

31   Garry Wills to William Rusher, undated (circa 1957–1958), Box 98, William A. Rusher Papers, Library of Congress; Wills, *Confessions of a Conservative*, 38.

32   Garry Wills to Frank Meyer, undated (circa spring 1959), FSM Papers.

33   Frank Meyer to Garry Wills, July 1, 1959, FSM Papers. Letters of introduction enclosed.

34   Garry Wills to Frank Meyer, June 12, 1959, FSM Papers.

35   Wills, *Confessions of a Conservative*, 44.

36   Garry Wills, "Nero in Our Camp," *National Review*, September 12, 1959, 332–333.

37   Garry Wills to William Rusher, undated (circa 1957–1958), Box 98, William A. Rusher Papers, Library of Congress.

38   Wills, *Confessions of a Conservative*, 43.

39   Sam Tanenhaus, *Whittaker Chambers: A Biography* (New York: Modern Library, 1998), 491–500.

40   Whittaker Chambers to William F. Buckley, March 10, 1957,

in *Odyssey of a Friend: Whittaker Chambers' Letters to William F. Buckley, Jr., 1954–1961*, ed. William F. Buckley Jr. (New York: G. P. Putnam's Sons, 1969), 160–161.

41   Frank S. Meyer to Frederick B. Adams, January 28, 1955, FSM Papers; Frank S. Meyer to Frederick B. Adams, February 21, 1955, FSM Papers; Tanenhaus, *Whittaker Chambers*, 499; Anne Palmer to Frank S. Meyer, May 21, 1957, FSM Papers; Frank S. Meyer to Anne Palmer, May 26, 1957, FSM Papers.

42   Tanenhaus, *Whittaker Chambers*, 499.

43   Tanenhaus, *Whittaker Chambers*, 501; Frank S. Meyer to Slobodan M. Draskovich, September 13, 1957, FSM Papers.

44   Frank S. Meyer to Slobodan M. Draskovich, September 13, 1957, FSM Papers.

45   Whittaker Chambers, "Big Sister Is Watching You," *National Review*, December 28, 1957, 594–596.

46   Frank S. Meyer to Donald Haverstrom, February 10, 1968, FSM Papers.

47   Whittaker Chambers to William F. Buckley, November 23, 1958, in Buckley, ed., *Odyssey of a Friend*, 216.

48   Whittaker Chambers to William F. Buckley, November 31, 1958, in Buckley, ed., *Odyssey of a Friend*, 217–218. Date listed as the 31st in book despite November ending after thirty days.

49   FSM to Hiram Caton, March 3, 1970, FSM Papers.

50   Stefan Possony (dictated to Regina Possony) to Frank S. Meyer, August 25, 1961, FSM Papers; Willmoore Kendall to Elsie Meyer, undated (circa early spring 1959), FSM Papers; Tanenhaus, *Whittaker Chambers*, 506. Kendall vaguely references the controversy; his letter begins, "You know better than that . . ."

51   Tanenhaus, *Whittaker Chambers*, 506; Judis, *William F. Buckley*, 174n.

52   Judis, *William F. Buckley*, 174.

53   Tanenhaus, *Whittaker Chambers*, 512.

54   Wm. F. Buckley to The Editors, memo, November 6, 1959,

FSM Papers.

55 Frank Meyer to Willmoore Kendall, December 12, 1959, FSM Papers.

56 Christoph Irmscher, *Max Eastman: A Life* (New Haven, CT: Yale University Press, 2017), 244–245, 1.

57 Irmscher, *Max Eastman*, 347.

58 Brent Bozell to Willmoore Kendall, September 10, [1958], FSM Papers.

59 William F. Buckley to Willmoore Kendall, September 10, 1958, FSM Papers. Burnham and Meyer carbon-copied.

60 Willmoore Kendall to Frank Meyer, postcard, September 12, 1958, FSM Papers.

61 Willmoore Kendall to Frank Meyer, undated (circa late winter 1959), FSM Papers. Letter begins, "As you see I have fallen."

62 Frank Meyer to Willmoore Kendall, January 10, 1959, FSM Papers.

63 Willmoore Kendall to Frank Meyer, undated (circa January 1959), "Saturday," FSM Papers.

64 Frank Meyer to Willmoore Kendall, January 26, 1959, FSM Papers.

65 [William F. Buckley Jr.] to Willmoore Kendall, March 25, 1959, MS576, Part 1, Box 8, William F. Buckley Jr. Papers, Yale University.

66 Wm. F. Buckley, Jr. to Father Eugene A. Moriarty, May 19, 1959, MS 576, Part 1, Box 8, William F. Buckley Jr. Papers, Yale University; Christopher H. Owen, *Heaven Can Indeed Fall: The Life of Willmoore Kendall* (Lanham, MD: Lexington Books, 2021), xvi–xvii.

67 [Willmoore Kendall] to Bill [Buckley], undated (circa 1959), MS 576, Part 1, Box 8, William F. Buckley Jr. Papers, Yale University.

68 Owen, *Heaven Can Indeed Fall*, 140.

69 Willmoore Kendall to Frank Meyer, undated, (circa summer 1960), "Saturday," FSM Papers. Letter begins, "I must not let another day go . . ."

70 Willmoore Kendall to Frank Meyer, undated (circa late October, 1958), FSM Papers; Frank Meyer to Willmoore Kendall, November 1, 1958, FSM Papers; Willmoore Kendall to Frank Meyer, postcard, November 6, 1958, FSM Papers.

71 Unsigned letter, undated (circa, May 1959), FSM Papers. The letter, appearing on *National Review* stationery, contains Willmoore Kendall's penmanship in Frank Meyer's folders.

72 Priscilla L. Buckley, *Living It Up at* National Review*: A Memoir* (Dallas, TX: Spence Publishing, 2005), 18.

73 Owen, *Heaven Can Indeed Fall*, 154.

74 Author interview of Noel Parmentel, February 12, 2023.

75 Willmoore [Kendall] to Charles [Hyneman], July 6, 1950, Box 16, untitled Charles Hyneman folder, Willmoore Kendall Papers, Hoover Institution Library & Archives.

76 [Willmoore] Ken[dall] to Tinkum [Brooks], undated (circa late 1950 to early 1951), Box 6, Folder 148, Cleanth Brooks Papers, Beinecke Library, Yale University.

77 Author interview of Noel Parmentel, February 12, 2023.

78 Author interview of Neal Freeman, November 7, 2022.

79 Suzanne La Follette to Frank [Meyer], August 10, 1959, FSM Papers.

80 Smant, *Principles and Heresies*, 56.

81 Frank Meyer to Willmoore Kendall, May 28, 1960, FSM Papers.

82 James Burnham to Wm. F. Buckley Jr., memo, "Strategic Development of NATIONAL REVIEW," undated (circa late spring 1960), FSM Papers. Here Burnham lists La Follette as one of the magazine's "technical incompetents," i.e., the mistaken hires from whom *National Review* moved past. Judis, *William F. Buckley*, 172; Jeffrey Hart, *The Making of the American Conservative Mind:* National Review *and Its Times* (Wilmington, DE: ISI Books, 2005), 61. Ryskind, for his part, does not even recall *National Review* considering him for a job though he acknowledges La Follette knew him well and perhaps internally pushed him within the magazine. Author interview of Allan Ryskind, September 12, 2023.

83 Willmoore Kendall to Frank Meyer, undated (circa June 1960), FSM Papers. Letter begins, "As usual, a quick answer . . ."

CHAPTER 21

1   Whittaker Chambers to William F. Buckley, January 12, 1960, in Buckley, ed., *Odyssey of a Friend*, 280.

2   James Burnham to Wm. F. Buckley Jr., memo, "Strategic Development of NATIONAL REVIEW," undated (circa late spring 1960), FSM Papers.

3   James Brunham [*sic*] to Frank Meyer, telegram, April 1 [1960], FSM Papers; Frank Meyer to Willmoore Kendall, March 14, 1960, FSM Papers. The telegram was sent from Tuscon, Arizona, to Woodstook, New York.

4   Frank Meyer to Willmoore Kendall, March 14, 1960, FSM Papers.

5   FSM to WFB Jr., LBB, JB, JC, WAR, FLB, memo, "NR position on Presidential candidates," May 10, 1960, FSM Papers.

6   "National Review and the 1960 Elections," *National Review*, October 22, 1960, 233–234.

7   William A. Rusher to L. Brent Bozell, March 6, 1961, FSM Papers.

8   Brent [Bozell] to Elsie and Frank [Meyer], February 7, [1961], FSM Papers.

9   Brent [Bozell] to Elsie and Frank [Meyer], February 7, [1961], FSM Papers.

10 [Frank Meyer] to Brent [Bozell], February 23, 1961, FSM Papers.

11 Willmoore Kendall, "Quo Vadis, Barry?," *National Review*, February 25, 1961, 107–108, 127.

12 "In This Issue," *National Review*, February 25, 1961, 99; Kendall, "Quo Vadis, Barry?," *National Review*, 107–108, 127.

13 B[rent Bozell] to Francisco [Meyer], February 26, [1961], FSM Papers.

14 [Frank Meyer] to Brent [Bozell], February 23, 1961, FSM

Papers.

15 [Brent Bozell] to William A. Rusher, February 28, [1961], FSM Papers; [Brent Bozell] to James Burnham, Frank Meyer, and William Rusher, March 19, 1961, FSM Papers.

16 [Frank Meyer] to Brent Bozell, March 7, 1961, FSM Papers.

17 [Frank Meyer] to Brent Bozell, March 7, 1961, FSM Papers. "Trimmer," like "squish" and "RINO" later, essentially meant a milquetoast moderate or someone even further left.

18 Brent [Bozell] to Frank [Meyer], March 16 [1961], FSM Papers.

19 [Frank Meyer] to Brent Bozell, March 7, 1961, FSM Papers.

20 Wills, *Confessions of a Conservative*, 46; Transcript: James Burnham, Princeton University.

21 Frank S. Meyer to James Burnham, May 21, 1952, FSM Papers.

22 Jim [Burnham] to Frank [Meyer], July 11, 1952, FSM Papers.

23 Jim [Burnham] to Frank [Meyer], April 23, 1953, FSM Papers.

24 Frank S. Meyer to the Editors, *Partisan Review*, March 25, 1953, FSM Papers.

25 Quoted in Daniel Kelly, *James Burnham and the Struggle for the World: A Life* (Wilmington, DE: ISI Books, 2002), 57.

26 Quoted in Kelly, *James Burnham and the Struggle for the World*, 70.

27 Quoted in Kelly, *James Burnham and the Struggle for the World*, 70.

28 Author interview of Arlene Croce, July 28, 2021.

29 Frank S. Meyer to Arlene Croce, April 18, 1962, FSM Papers; Arlene Croce to Frank S. Meyer, May 7, 1962, FSM Papers.

30 Author interview of Arlene Croce, July 28, 2021.

31 Author interview of David Franke, April 8, 2020.

32 Author interview of David Franke, April 8, 2020.

33 Kelly, *James Burnham and the Struggle for the World*, 273.

34 Quoted in David B. Frisk, *If Not Us, Who? William Rusher, National Review, and the Conservative Movement* (Wilmington, DE: ISI Books, 2012), 79.

35 Author interview of Neal Freeman, May 19, 2020.

36   Author interview of David Franke, April 8, 2020.

37   Brent [Bozell] to Frank [Meyer], March 16, [1961], FSM Papers.

38   Brent [Bozell] to Frank [Meyer], March 16, [1961], FSM Papers.

39   Barry Goldwater, "1960 Republican Convention Speech," July 25, 1960, accessed October 9, 2023, https://www.c-span. org/video/?4009-1/1960-republican-convention-address.

40   Barry Goldwater with Jack Casserly, *Goldwater* (New York: Doubleday, 1988), 119; Rick Perlstein, *Before the Storm: Barry Goldwater and the Unmaking of the American Consensus* (New York: Hill and Wang, 2001), 92–95; "The 1960 Republican Convention," video, accessed August 27, 2023, https://www. youtube.com/watch?v=BXxUIsaThMc.

41   William A. Rusher to Bill [Buckley], February 27, [1961], FSM Papers.

42   William A. Rusher to L. Brent Bozell, March 6, 1961, FSM Papers.

43   William A. Rusher to L. Brent Bozell, March 6, 1961, FSM Papers.

44   William A. Rusher to Bill [Buckley], February 27, [1961], FSM Papers.

45   Brent [Bozell] to Frank [Meyer], March 16, [1961] FSM Papers.

46   [Frank Meyer] to Brent [Bozell], June 9, 1961, FSM Papers.

47   Brent [Bozell] to Frank and Elsie [Meyer], undated (circa spring 1961), "Monday night," FSM Papers.

48   Judis, *William F. Buckley*, 222.

49   [Frank Meyer] to Brent [Bozell], February 23, 1961, FSM Papers.

50   [Frank Meyer] to Brent Bozell, March 7, 1961, FSM Papers.

51   [Frank Meyer] to Brent Bozell, March 7, 1961, FSM Papers.

CHAPTER 22

1   Frank Meyer to Herb [Goldhamer], April 14, 1952, FSM

Papers.

2   Frank Meyer to Charles A. Pearce, July 18, 1952, FSM Papers; Frank Meyer to Charles A. Pearce, April 29, 1952, FSM Papers. The July letter was addressed to "NYC."

3   Frank S. Meyer to Henry Regnery, December 8, 1952, FSM Papers; Henry Regnery to Frank S. Meyer, February 24, 1954, FSM Papers; Frank S. Meyer to Henry Regnery, March 10, 1954, FSM Papers.

4   Herbert Goldhamer to Frank Meyer, May 8, 1952, FSM Papers.

5   Purchase Order: The RAND Corporation, "Frank S. Meyer," Account 619, May 20, 1953; Purchase Change Order, The RAND Corporation, "Frank S. Meyer, Account 619, September 11, 1953, FSM Papers.

6   Purchase Order: The RAND Corporation, "Frank S. Meyer," Account 681, November 1, 1954, FSM Papers.

7   Frank Meyer to Louis Nichols, July 18, 1954, FSM Papers.

8   J. Edgar Hoover to Frank Meyer, July 23, 1954, FSM Papers.

9   Frank Meyer to Hans Speier, February 25, 1956, FSM Papers.

10   G. H. Putt to Frank S. Meyer, December 5, 1956, FSM Papers.

11   Hans Speier to Frank S. Meyer, April 26, 1956, FSM Papers; Hans Speier to Frank S. Meyer, June 23, 1960, FSM Papers.

12   David F. Freeman to Frank S. Meyer, June 8, 1954, FSM Papers.

13   Clinton Rossiter to Frank Meyer, April 26, 1957, FSM Papers.

14   Frank S. Meyer and Harcourt, Brace and Company, contract for *The Moulding of Communists*, June 25, 1957, FSM Papers; J. H. McCallum to Frank S. Meyer, June 20, 1957, FSM Papers; Jeannette E. Hopkins to Frank S. Meyer, December 10, 1957, FSM Papers; Jeannette Hopkins to Frank S. Meyer, April 16, 1958, FSM Papers.

15   Frank Meyer to Clinton [Rossiter], September 20, 1959, FSM Papers; Clinton Rossiter to Frank [Meyer], September 28, 1959, FSM Papers.

16   Clinton Rossiter to Frank S. Meyer, April 14, 1960, FSM Papers; Frank Meyer to Clinton Rossiter, April 18, 1960, FSM Papers.

17   Frank S. Meyer to J. H. McCallum, April 15, 1960, FSM
        Papers.

18   Frank S. Meyer to J. H. McCallum, April 1, 1960, FSM Papers;
        Frank S. Meyer to J. H. McCallum, April 15, 1960, FSM
        Papers.

19   J. H. McCallum to Frank S. Meyer, September 6, 1960, FSM
        Papers.

20   Meyer, *The Moulding of Communists*, 66.

21   Meyer, *The Moulding of Communists*, 38–40.

22   Meyer, *The Moulding of Communists*, 127.

23   Meyer, *The Moulding of Communists*, 29–30.

24   Meyer, *The Moulding of Communists*, 122, 127.

25   Meyer, *The Moulding of Communists*, 52.

26   Meyer, *The Moulding of Communists*, 83–84.

27   "RWL" to Meyer, July 21, 1954, FSM Papers.

28   "Raines, Eudocio, 'The Yenan Way,'" notes, undated, Box 4,
        Folder 3, Frank S. Meyer Collection, Hoover Institution
        Library & Archives.

29   Robert H. Strahan Jr. to Frank S. Meyer, undated (circa
        November 1961), FSM Papers; Rosalie M. Gordon to Frank S.
        Meyer, January 14, 1961, FSM Papers.

30   [Frank Meyer] to Brent Bozell, February 8, 1961, FSM Papers.

31   Alexander Dallin, "What It Takes to Be a Card-holder in
        Good Standing," *The New York Times*, January 8, 1961, B3.

32   Raymond Moley, "The Communist Fanatic," *Newsweek*, Feb-
        ruary 6, 1961, 88.

33   Jeannette E. Hopkins to Frank S. Meyer, July 20, 1960, FSM
        Papers; Edward A. Hodge to Frank S. Meyer, September 27,
        1961, FSM Papers.

34   JEH to JHM, memo, "Re: Frank Meyer," September 13, 1962,
        FSM Papers.

35   Author interview of Noel Parmentel, July 25, 2023.

36   Author interview of Noel Parmentel, September 9, 2023.

37   *The Mike Wallace Interview*, TV interview audio recording,
        January 5, 1961, Oversize 6, Mike Wallace Papers, Bird Li-
        brary, Special Collections, Syracuse University, New York.

38   Jeannette E. Hopkins to Frank S. Meyer, July 30, 1963, FSM Papers.

39   Carl A. Kohlman to Frank Meyer, May 3, 1965, FSM Papers.

CHAPTER 23

1   Author interview of Bob Bauman, April 23, 2020.

2   Conrad Chapman to Frank S. Meyer, March 7, 1966, FSM Papers.

3   Frank S. Meyer to Conrad Chapman, March 13, 1966, FSM Papers.

4   Author interview of David Franke, April 8, 2020.

5   Author interview of Carol Dawson, April 20, 2020.

6   Smant, *Principles and Heresies*, 91.

7   Frisk, *If Not Us, Who?*, 123.

8   Author interview of Jameson Campaigne Jr., November 5, 2023.

9   Wayne Thorburn, *A Generation Awakes: Young Americans for Freedom and the Creation of the Conservative Movement* (Ottawa, IL: Jameson Books, 2010), 27.

10   Author interview of David Franke, April 8, 2020.

11   Judis, *William F. Buckley*, 189.

12   Author interview of Lee Edwards, September 15, 2020.

13   Author interview of Carol Dawson, April 20, 2020.

14   Author interview of Jameson Campaigne Jr., November 5, 2023.

15   Gerhart Niemeyer to James Burnham, October 4, 1960, Box 10, Folder 7, James Burnham Papers, Hoover Institution Library & Archives.

16   Wm. F. Buckley, Jr., to Gerhart Niemeyer, October 12, 1960, Box 11, Folder Gerhart Niemeyer 1960, William F. Buckley Jr. Papers, Sterling Memorial Library, Yale University; Gerhart Niemeyer, submitted manuscript, "Letter to Young Conservatives," September 24, [1960], Box 11, Folder Gerhart Niemeyer 1960, William F. Buckley Jr. Papers, Sterling Memorial Library, Yale University.

17   Frank S. Meyer to Bill [Buckley], undated ("10/19" written on

document), Box 11, Folder Gerhart Niemeyer 1960, William
F. Buckley Jr. Papers, Sterling Memorial Library, Yale Univer-
sity; Gerhart [Niemeyer] to [Bill] Buckley, October 21, 1960,
Box 11, Folder Gerhart Niemeyer 1960, William F. Buckley
Jr. Papers, Sterling Memorial Library, Yale University.

18   Young Americans for Freedom, "The Sharon Statement,"
September 11, 1960, accessed June 12, 2023, https://www.yaf.
org/news/the-sharon-statement.

19   Author interview of Serphin Maltese, May 14, 2021.

20   Wm. F. Buckley, Jr., to "All Concerned," memo, January 22,
1957, Box 7, Folder 37, Raymond Moley Papers, Hoover
Institution Library & Archives.

21   Author interview of Serphin Maltese, May 14, 2021.

22   New York Conservative Political Association, "Declaration
of Principles" in *A Political Prospectus: Confidential*, June 6,
1961, FSM Papers; J. Daniel Mahoney, *Actions Speak Louder*
(New Rochelle, NY: Arlington House, 1968), 26.

23   George J. Marlin, *Fighting the Good Fight: A History of the
New York Conservative Party* (South Bend, IN: St. Augustine's
Press, 2002), 45; Mahoney, *Actions Speak Louder*, 37.

24   Conservative Party, press release, "New York Conservative
Party Answers Republican State Committee Attack," June 21,
[1962], Box 1, Series 4, Conservative Party of New York State
Records, M. E. Grenander Department of Special Collec-
tions & Archives, State University of New York–Albany;
Mahoney, *Actions Speak Louder*, 54.

25   Frank Meyer, "New York Conservatives and the Two-Party
System," *National Review*, July 3, 1962, 486; Frank Meyer,
"Kennedy, Cuba, and the Voters," November 6, 1962, 352;
Frank Meyer, "Us Simple Americans," *National Review*, July
31, 1962, 64; Frank Meyer, "The 1962 Elections: The Turning
of the Tide," *National Review*, December 4, 1962, 434–435.

26   Meyer, "New York Conservatives and the Two-Party System," *National Review*, 486.

27   Conservative Party, press release, "For Immediate Release,"
October 17, 1962, Box 1, Series 4, Conservative Party of New

York State Records, M. E. Grenander Department of Special Collections & Archives, State University of New York–Albany; Conservative Party, press release, "For Immediate Release All A.M. and P.M. Papers," October 18, [1962], Box 1, Series 4, Conservative Party of New York State Records, M. E. Grenander Department of Special Collections & Archives, State University of New York–Albany.

28 John Kennedy, speech, October 22, 1962, accessed October 17, 2023, https://www.jfklibrary.org/learn/about-jfk/historic-speeches/address-during-the-cuban-missile-crisis.

29 Mike Newberry, "Ultras Rally Shrieks for Invasion of Cuba," *The Daily Worker*, October 28, 1962, Box 18, Folder 1, Frank S. Meyer Collection, Hoover Institution Library & Archives.

30 Mahoney, *Actions Speak Louder*, 102, 108.

31 Don Baker, "Seminar Called Major Defense for Home Front," *Indianapolis Times*, February 23, 1962, Box 18, Folder 1, Frank S. Meyer Collection, Hoover Institution Library & Archives.

32 M. N. Bonbrake to [Frank] Meyer, undated (circa early 1963), FSM Papers.

33 Conservative Party, press release, "Conservative Party Endorses Allott Proposal to Install Provisional Cuban Government at Guantanamo," July 3, [1962], Box 1, Series 4, Conservative Party of New York State Records, M. E. Grenander Department of Special Collections & Archives, State University of New York–Albany.

34 Mahoney, *Actions Speak Louder*, 160; Marlin, *Fighting the Good Fight*, 74.

35 Marlin, *Fighting the Good Fight*, 97.

36 Quoted in Neal Freeman, foreword to *The Unmaking of a Mayor*, by William F. Buckley, Jr. (New York: Encounter Books, 1966, 2015), xi.

37 Author interview of James Buckley, May 1, 2021.

38 Author interview of Serphin Maltese, May 14, 2021.

39 John P. Lomenzo to Frank S. Meyer, September 12, 1967, FSM Papers; James D. Griffin to County and Club Chairmen,

memo, July 8, 1968, FSM Papers; State Headquarters to All Committee Members, memo, "State Convention," August 24, 1966, FSM Papers; Mahoney, *Actions Speak Louder*, 327–328.

40 Author interview of Serphin Maltese, May 14, 2021.

41 Author interview of Serphin Maltese, May 14, 2021.

CHAPTER 24

1 Owen, *Heaven Can Indeed Fall*, 159.

2 Willmoore Kendall to Frank Meyer, postcards, December 15, 1961, FSM Papers. This refers to two postcards stapled together.

3 Wm. F. Buckley, Jr. to Revilo P. Oliver, May 16, 1960, FSM Papers.

4 Aristotle, *Nicomachean Ethics*, in *Great Books of the Western World*, vol. IX, ed. Robert Maynard Hutchins (Chicago: Encyclopedia Britannica, 1952), 341.

5 Judis, *William F. Buckley*, 173–174.

6 [Frank Meyer] to Brent [Bozell], March 27, 1961, FSM Papers.

7 Bill Rusher to Bill Buckley, Brent Bozell, Jim Burnham, Willmoore Kendall, Frank Meyer, and Priscilla Buckley, memo, April 3, 1961, FSM Papers.

8 Bill Rusher to Bill Buckley, Brent Bozell, Jim Burnham, Willmoore Kendall, Frank Meyer, and Priscilla Buckley, memo, April 3, 1961, FSM Papers.

9 Matthew Dallek, *Birchers: How the John Birch Society Radicalized the American Right* (New York: Basic Books, 2023), 71.

10 Dallek, *Birchers*, 77.

11 Dallek, *Birchers* 78, 101. Quote therein.

12 Edward H. Miller, *A Conspiratorial Life: Robert Welch, the John Birch Society, and the Revolution of American Conservatism* (Chicago: University of Chicago Press, 2021), 242–243; "The Harmless Ones," *Time*, August 11, 1961, 15.

13 Dallek, *Birchers*, 37–40, 140–143, 145, 147–148.

14 FSM to WFB, CC: LBB, JB, WK, WAR, memo, "For editorial

conference, Tuesday, March 28," March 26, 1961, FSM Papers.

15   Wm. F. Buckley, Jr., "The Uproar," *National Review*, April 22, 1961, 241–243.

16   Frank S. Meyer, "The Conservative Movement: Growing Pains," *National Review*, May 6, 1961, 281.

17   Robert Welch to William F. Buckley, Jr., April 25, 1961, Box 14, John Birch Society Folder, William F. Buckley Jr. Papers, Sterling Memorial Library, Yale University.

18   "Contents—November, 1961," *American Opinion*, November 1961, ii.

19   "The Question of Robert Welch," *National Review*, February 13, 1962, 83–88.

20   "The Question of Robert Welch," *National Review*, 88.

21   "To the Editor: The Question of Robert Welch," February 27, 1962, *National Review*, 140.

22   [Frank S. Meyer] to Bill [Buckley], March 17, 1962, FSM Papers.

23   Frank S. Meyer, "What Is Under the Bed?," *National Review*, April 10, 1962, 244.

24   Bill Rickenbacker to Brent Bozell, Bill Buckley, Priscilla Buckley, Jim Burnham, Willmoore Kendall, Frank Meyer, Bill Rusher, and Bill Rickenbacker, memo, "Survey of the Correspondence Arising from Our Editorial on Robert Welch in the 13 February 1962 Issue of NR," April 14, 1962, FSM Papers.

CHAPTER 25

1   Frank Meyer to John Chamberlain, October 23, 1952, FSM Papers.

2   Author interview of John Meyer, February 4, 2020.

3   [Elsie Meyer] to Garry [Wills], August 26, 1963, FSM Papers.

4   [Elsie Meyer] to [Rose Wilder] Lane, November 26, 1962, FSM Papers.

5   J. R. R. Tolkien to Frank Meyer, January 20, 1961, FSM Papers.

6   Author interview of Eugene Meyer, February 3, 2020.

7   Frank Meyer to Allan Hoey, October 7, 1954, FSM Papers.

8   Frank Meyer to Revilo Oliver, January 23, 1958, FSM Papers.

9   Allan Hoey to Frank Meyer, September 15, 1954, FSM Papers; Allan Hoey to Frank Meyer, June 6, 1958, FSM Papers; Allan Hoey to Frank Meyer, March 4, 1958, FSM Papers; Allan Hoey to Frank Meyer, February 21, 1955, FSM Papers; Allan Hoey to Frank Meyer, July 28, 1956, FSM Papers.

10 Frank S. Meyer to [Rose Wilder] Lane, August 27, 1953, FSM Papers; Rose Lane to [Frank] Meyer, September 5, 1953, FSM Papers.

11 Author interview of Eugene Meyer, February 3, 2020.

12 Transcript: Washington University, University College, Elsie May Bown Philbrick, October 1, 1934 to May 22, 1935, May 12, 1937, Elsie May Bown File, Box 89, Radcliffe College Student Files RG XXI Series 2, Schlesinger Library, Radcliffe Institute for Advanced Study, Harvard University.

13 Author interview of John Meyer, February 4, 2020.

14 Author interview of John Meyer, February 4, 2020.

15 Elsie Meyer to *The New York Herald Tribune* Review editor, April 19, 1956, FSM Papers.

16 Frank Meyer to Frater Leo R. Gaffney, June 12, 1960, FSM Papers; Frank Meyer to George Sokolsky, August 12, 1959, FSM Papers.

17 Author interview of Eugene Meyer, July 10, 2023.

18 Author interview of John Meyer, February 4, 2020.

19 Author interview of Roger Phelps, May 29, 2022.

20 Author interview of Tad Crawford, October 2, 2023.

21 Author interview of John Meyer, February 4, 2020.

22 "Woodstock Chess Wizards: Meyer Brothers Annex National Chess Titles," *Kingston Freeman*, August 17, 1964, 18; Hans Kmoch to Frank S. Meyer, May 31, 1965, FSM Papers.

23 Peter Berlow to Frank Meyer, June 8, 1965, FSM Papers.

24 Mrs. Frank S. Meyer to Turner Catledge, August 18, 1964, FSM Papers; Mrs. Frank S. Meyer to George Palmer, August 27, 1964, FSM Papers; George Palmer to Mrs. Frank S. Meyer,

September 2, 1964, FSM Papers; Mrs. Frank S. Meyer to
George Palmer, September 19, 1964, FSM Papers; Mrs. Frank
S. Meyer to Clifton Daniel, December 30, 1965, FSM Papers;
Mrs. Frank S. Meyer to A. M. Rosenthal, December 21, 1966,
FSM Papers; A. M. Rosenthal to Frank S. Meyer, December
22, 1966, FSM Papers; Mrs. Frank S. Meyer to Arthur Gelb,
April 4, 1970, FSM Papers; Mrs. Frank S. Meyer to Arthur
Gelb, June 8, 1971, FSM Papers; Mrs. Frank Meyer to A. M.
Rosenthal, August 18, 1972, FSM Papers.

25   Author interview of John Meyer, February 4, 2020.

26   Author interview of Eugene Meyer, July 10, 2023.

27   "Woodstock Chess Wizards: Meyer Brothers Annex National Chess Titles," *Kingston Freeman*, 18; "Prize Winners," announcement, U.S. Junior Chess Championship, Towson State College, Towson, Maryland, August 10–14, 1964.

28   Al Horowitz, "Chess: New Junior Open Champion Shows Sophisticated Style," *New York Times*, September 13, 1964, 26; Al Horowitz, "Chess: Intercollegiate Battle," *New York Times*, January 30, 1966, X27; Al Horowitz, "Chess: Exchanges Often Expose the Flaws in a Formation," *New York Times*, July 3, 1967, 14; Al Horowitz, "Chess: 15 Year Old Expert Defeats a Strong Field in Pittsfield," *New York Times*, May 2, 1968, 44. Editions of the same *New York Times* contain profound variation, but the paper's online search lists the aforementioned as the correct page numbers. Microfilm cross-referencing did not always yield identical page numbers.

29   Eva [Donaldson] to Elsie [Meyer], December 2 (circa early 1970s), FSM Papers; Author interview of David Zincavage, October 6, 2021; Author interview of Eugene Meyer, July 10, 2023; Author interview of Tad Crawford, October 2, 2023.

30   The grave marker that remains reads, "Kim: Died 1973." Author interview of Eugene Meyer, January 28, 2024. Various veterinary forms give a sense of the family animal collection: Frank Meyer, "Blackie," Dog Anti-Rabies Protection Certificate, July 1, 1957, FSM Papers; Frank Meyer, "Elizabeth," Dog Anti-Rabies Protection Certificate, July 1, 1957, FSM Papers; Frank S. Meyer, Dog License State of New York, December 28, 1964,

830491; Veterinarian Form, John R. Jeffrey, shots listed from September 29, 1961 to December 27, 1967, FSM Papers; Frank S. Meyer, Pet Papers: An Immunization Record and Valuable Documents Folder Pertaining to Kim, FSM Papers. The state listed "dog" on the anti-rabies forms that it used for cats as well.

31 Author interview of Roger Phelps, May 29, 2022.

32 Author interview of Roger Phelps, May 29, 2022.

33 Author interview of Eugene Meyer, July 12, 2023; Author interview of John Meyer, July 11, 2023.

34 Guy Davenport to Hugh Kenner, January 11, 1963, in Burns, ed., *Questioning Minds*, 246.

35 Jerzy Hauptmann to Frank Meyer, November 17, 1961, FSM Papers.

36 Frank S. Meyer to Jerzy Hauptmann, December 1, 1961, FSM Papers.

37 Jerzy Hauptmann to William Y. Elliott, December 16, 1960, FSM Papers; Frank S. Meyer to [Henry] Kissinger, August 23, 1960, FSM Papers; Frank S. Meyer to Henry A. Kissinger, November 25, 1961, FSM Papers.

38 Frank S. Meyer to William Y. Elliott, March 16, 1961, FSM Papers.

39 Jerzy Hauptmann, "The Goal of Society Is Free Individual," *Kansas City Times*, November 30, 1962, Box 19, Frank S. Meyer Collection, Hoover Institution Library & Archives; "Meyer Speaks on Education and Communism," *Park Stylus*, November 29, 1962, 1, Box 18, Folder 1, Frank S. Meyer Collection, Hoover Institution Library & Archives.

40 "By Way of Explanation," *The Exchange*, undated (circa spring 1962), FSM Papers, 1.

41 "By Way of Explanation," *The Exchange*, 1; FSM to Ivan W. Bierly, May 21, 1962, FSM Papers.

42 Milton Friedman, "Tentatives: Notes on Free Trade, Tariffs and the Common Market," *The Exchange*, undated (circa spring 1962), FSM Papers, 2.

43 James M. Buchanan to Frank Meyer, October 30, 1964, FSM Papers; Frank S. Meyer to James M. Buchanan, November 3,

1964, FSM Papers.

44 Richard A. Ware to Frank S. Meyer, October 1, 1962, FSM Papers.

45 Kenneth S. Templeton to Frank S. Meyer, February 6, 1963, FSM Papers; Frank S. Meyer to Kenneth S. Templeton, February 14, 1963, FSM Papers; Kenneth S. Templeton to Thomas A. Bolan, March 20, 1963, FSM Papers.

46 Kenneth S. Templeton to Thomas A. Bolan, March 20, 1963, FSM Papers; FSM to Ivan W. Bierly, May 21, 1962, FSM Papers; Russell Kirk to District Director of Internal Revenue, May 21, 1960, Box 111, Folder 11, William A. Rusher Papers, Library of Congress; William A. Rusher to Thomas Bolan, October 5, 1965, Box 111, Folder 11, William A. Rusher Papers, Library of Congress.

47 Frank S. Meyer to W. Clark Durant III, February 25, 1972, FSM Papers.

48 Frank S. Meyer to Merle E. Lamson, January 31, 1963, FSM Papers; Merle E. Lamson to Frank S. Meyer, February 7, 1963, FSM Papers.

49 Examples include Edwin F. Klotz to Frank S. Meyer, August 1, 1966, FSM Papers; R. Emmett Tyrrell Jr., to Frank S. Meyer, May 23, 1968, FSM Papers; John F. Crosby to Frank S. Meyer, February 11, 1970, FSM Papers.

50 William H. Roberts to Frank S. Meyer, May 5, 1967, FSM Papers; James E. Dornan Jr., to Frank Meyer, November 5, 1967, FSM Papers.

51 Paul Craig Roberts to Frank S. Meyer, April 30, 1969, FSM Papers; Ellis Sandoz to Frank S. Meyer, May 29, 1968, FSM Papers; Ralph Raico to Frank [Meyer], April 27, 1970, FSM Papers.

52 Margaret H. Behringer to Frank S. Meyer, March 31, 1967, FSM Papers.

53 Willmoore Kendall to Frank Meyer, undated (circa November, 1963), "Wednesday," FSM Papers. On University of Dallas letterhead.

54 Frank S. Meyer to Kenneth E. Howell, July 13, 1968, FSM Papers.

55 Author interview of Roger Phelps, May 29, 2022.

56 Wills, *Confessions of a Conservative*, 42. Therein, Wills re-
counts the visitor as a truant officer. When he told the story
in an unsigned editorial eighteen years earlier, he called the
visitor a census-taker. See "The Obsolescence of Parents,"
Richmond News Leader, June 10, 1961. Accompanying the note
was an unsigned, undated note to Elsie from a writer with
penmanship matching that of Garry Wills found elsewhere
in FSM Papers. John Meyer remembers the visitor as neither
truant officer nor census-taker but a social worker. See John
Meyer to author, email, January 29, 2024. Mackenzie helped
identify *Richmond News Leader* typeface in the clipping sent
by Wills. Author interview of Ross Mackenzie, February
3, 2024.

57 Frank S. Meyer to Reginald Bennett, September 21, 1953,
FSM Papers; Frank S. Meyer to Reginald Bennett, September
2, 1954, FSM Papers; Frank S. Meyer to Reginald Bennett,
September 2, 1955, FSM Papers; Frank S. Meyer to Reginald
Bennett, September 4, 1956, FSM Papers; Frank S. Meyer to
Reginald Bennett, September 14, 1957, FSM Papers; Frank S.
Meyer to Reginald Bennett, September 18, 1958, FSM Papers;
Frank S. Meyer to Reginald Bennett, September 30, 1959,
FSM Papers; Frank S. Meyer to Reginald Bennett, October
5, 1960, FSM Papers; Frank S. Meyer to Reginald Bennett,
October 6, 1961, FSM Papers; Frank S. Meyer to Reginald
Bennett, September 17, 1962, FSM Papers; Frank S. Meyer to
George R. Sullivan, September 21, 1963, FSM Papers; Frank
S. Meyer to George R. Sullivan, September 26, 1964, FSM Pa-
pers; Frank S. Meyer to George R. Sullivan, October 18, 1965,
FSM Papers; Frank S. Meyer to George R. Sullivan, October
4, 1966, FSM Papers; Frank S. Meyer to George R. Sullivan,
August 6, 1967, FSM Papers; Frank S. Meyer to Harold R.
Snyder, September 30, 1968, FSM Papers; Frank S. Meyer to
Harold R. Snyder October 14, 1969, FSM Papers.

58 E. Alden Dunham to Frank Meyer, September 21, 1962, FSM
Papers.

59   Frank S. Meyer to E. Alden Dunham, October 26, 1962, FSM Papers.

60   Frank Meyer to Robert F. Goheen, February 8, 1963, FSM Papers; Frank Meyer to E. Alden Dunham, March 23, 1963, FSM Papers.

61   Frank Meyer to Allan Hoey, March 7, 1955, FSM Papers.

62   Guy Davenport to Hugh Kenner, March 17, 1963, in Burns, ed., *Questioning Minds*, 292.

63   Author interview of Ross Mackenzie, November 8, 2023.

64   *The Report of the President's Committee on the Freshman Year*, April 13, 1962, accessed December 4, 2023, https://www.yale.edu/sites/default/files/files/freshman_year.pdf.

65   H. B. Whiteman Jr., "Dean's Honor List," Yale University, January 1964, FSM Papers; "Groups for Lindsay to 'Cooperate,'" *Yale Daily News*, September 20, 1965, 1, 6; "Mate from the Right," *Yale Daily News*, September 23, 1964, 4.

66   Allie Wenner, "Lives: E. Alden Dunham, '53," *Princeton Alumni Weekly*, February 3, 2016, accessed March 22, 2023, https://paw.princeton.edu/article/lives-e-alden-dunham-53.

67   Karl Marx, *The Eighteenth Brumaire of Louis Bonaparte* (Peking, China: Foreign Languages Press, 1978), 9, accessed March 22, 2023, http://www.marx2mao.com/M&E/EBLB52.html.

CHAPTER 26

1   L. Brent Bozell to Elsie and Frank [Meyer], October 20, 1956, FSM Papers.

2   [Frank Meyer] to Brent Bozell, February 8, 1961, FSM Papers.

3   Author interview of John Meyer, March 10, 2021.

4   Buckley, *Living It Up at* National Review, 188.

5   L. Brent Bozell and Frank S. Meyer, contract, September 16, 1959, FSM Papers.

6   "Tuition and Mandated Fees, Room and Board, and Other Educational Costs at Penn, 1950–1959," accessed September 6, 2023, https://archives.upenn.edu/exhibits/penn-history/

tuition/tuition-1950-1959/.

7   Form 1040 U.S. Individual Income Tax Return: Frank S. and Elsie Meyer, 1959, Memorandum B to Line 21, Schedule C, "Telephone and Telegraph," FSM Papers.

8   Form W-2: Frank S. Meyer National Review, Inc., "Withholding Tax Statement, 1960," Copy C—for Employee's Records, FSM Papers; Form 1040 U.S. Individual Income Tax Return: Frank S. and Elsie B. Meyer, 1960, Memorandum B to Line 21, Schedule C, "Telephone and Telegraph," FSM Papers.

9   Author interview of Arlene Croce, July 28, 2021.

10   Author interview of Neal Freeman, May 19, 2020.

11   [Frank Meyer] to Brent [Bozell], November 21, 1961, FSM Papers; Brent [Bozell] to Frank [Meyer], undated (circa 1961), "Thursday night," FSM Papers.

12   Frank S. Meyer, "The Twisted Tree of Liberty," *National Review*, January 16, 1962, 25.

13   [Frank Meyer] to Brent [Bozell], February 6, 1962, FSM Papers.

14   Brent [Bozell] to Frank and Elsie [Meyer], January 23, [1962], FSM Papers.

15   Brent [Bozell] to Frank [Meyer], February 16, [1962], FSM Papers.

16   The exchange starts the book George W. Carey, ed., *Freedom and Virtue: The Conservative/Libertarian Debate* (Wilmington, DE: ISI Books, 1984, 1998), 1–12.

17   Brent [Bozell] to Frank and Elsie [Meyer], January 23 [1962], FSM Papers; [Frank Meyer] to Brent [Bozell], July 27, 1962, FSM Papers; Brent [Bozell] to Will, undated (circa 1962), "Tuesday," FSM Papers; [Frank Meyer] to Brent [Bozell], August 12, 1962, FSM Papers.

18   [Frank Meyer] to Brent [Bozell], May 14, 1961, FSM Papers; FSM to Willi [Schlamm], June 11, 1961, FSM Papers; [Frank Meyer] to Brent [Bozell], July 19, 1961, FSM Papers; FSM to Sam [Bown], September 25, 1964, FSM Papers.

19   Brent [Bozell] to Frank and Elsie [Meyer], April 6, 1962, FSM

Papers.

20 [Frank Meyer] to Brent [Bozell], February 6, 1962, FSM
Papers.

21 Brent [Bozell] to Frank and Elsie [Meyer], April 6, 1962, FSM
Papers; [Frank Meyer] to Brent [Bozell], April 16, 1962, FSM
Papers.

22 [Frank Meyer] to Brent [Bozell], April 16, 1962, FSM Papers;
Brent [Bozell] to Frank [Meyer], April 26, 1962, FSM Papers.

23 [Frank Meyer] to Brent [Bozell], July 27, 1962, FSM Papers.

24 Daniel Kelly, *Living on Fire: The Life of L. Brent Bozell Jr.*
(Wilmington, DE: ISI Books, 2014), 3, 11.

25 Brent Bozell, "Freedom or Virtue?," *National Review*, September 11, 1962, 187.

26 Bozell, "Freedom or Virtue?," *National Review*, 185, 183.

27 Bozell, "Freedom or Virtue?," *National Review*, 181.

28 Bozell, "Freedom or Virtue?," *National Review*, 181–186.

29 Frank S. Meyer, "Why Freedom," *National Review*, September 25, 1962, 223.

30 Meyer, "Why Freedom," *National Review*, 223.

31 Meyer, "Why Freedom," *National Review*, 225.

CHAPTER 27

1 Frank S. Meyer to H. W. Luhnow, July 29, 1957, FSM Papers.

2 Henry Regnery to Frank Hanighen, July 13, 1955, Box 27,
Folder 16, Henry Regnery Papers, Hoover Institution Library & Archives.

3 Russell [Kirk] to Henry [Regnery], June 25 [1955], Box 39,
Folder 10, Henry Regnery Papers, Hoover Institution Library & Archives.

4 Henry Regnery Company, Frank Meyer, contract, "In Defense of Freedom," February 12, 1960, FSM Papers.

5 Frank Meyer to Willmoore Kendall, December 12, 1959, FSM
Papers.

6 "Regnery: fall list PREVIEW for 1961," advertisement, Henry
Regnery Company, FSM Papers; Henry Regnery to Frank S.

Meyer, June 5, 1961, FSM Papers.

7   H. W. Luhnow to blank, March 15, 1962, FSM Papers.

8   Frank S. Meyer to Henry Regnery, April 12, 1960, FSM Papers.

9   Jameson G. Campaigne Jr. to Mr. Meyer, July 14, 1962, Private Papers of Jameson Campaigne Jr.; Author interview of Jameson Campaigne Jr., May 7, 2020.

10   Frank S. Meyer to Jameson G. Campaigne Jr., July 22, 1962, Private Papers of Jameson G. Campaigne Jr.

11   Henry Regnery to Frank S. Meyer, March 27, 1961, FSM Papers.

12   [Frank Meyer], to Jim [Cameron], December 5, 1960, FSM Papers.

13   Frank Meyer to Willmoore Kendall, October 30, 1962, FSM Papers; Willmoore Kendall to Frank Meyer, undated (circa fall 1962), "Tuesday," FSM Papers.

14   Henry Regnery to Frank S. Meyer, May 26, 1961, FSM Papers.

15   Frank Meyer to Henry Regnery, July 22, 1962, FSM Papers.

16   Frank S. Meyer, *In Defense of Freedom: A Conservative Credo* (Chicago: Henry Regnery Company, 1962), 1.

17   Meyer, *In Defense of Freedom*, 2.

18   Meyer, *In Defense of Freedom*, 3.

19   Meyer, *In Defense of Freedom*, 14.

20   Meyer, *In Defense of Freedom*, 15–19.

21   Meyer, *In Defense of Freedom*, 74–75.

22   Meyer, *In Defense of Freedom*, 40–48.

23   Meyer, *In Defense of Freedom*, 27.

24   Meyer, *In Defense of Freedom*, 35.

25   Meyer, *In Defense of Freedom*, 56.

26   Meyer, *In Defense of Freedom*, 53.

27   Meyer, *In Defense of Freedom*, 82.

28   Meyer, *In Defense of Freedom*, 89–92.

29   Meyer, *In Defense of Freedom*, 126.

30   Meyer, *In Defense of Freedom*, 91–92.

31   Meyer, *In Defense of Freedom*, 122–123.

32   Meyer, *In Defense of Freedom*, 128.

33   Meyer, *In Defense of Freedom*, 127–129.

34   Meyer, *In Defense of Freedom*, 94.

35   Meyer, *In Defense of Freedom*, 97.

36   Meyer, *In Defense of Freedom*, 168–169.

37   Meyer, *In Defense of Freedom*, 170.

38   M. Stanton Evans, "Individualism and the Moral Order," *The Individualist*, September 1963, 10, Box 19, Frank S. Meyer Collection, Hoover Institution Library & Archives.

39   John Chamberlain, "Defending Individualism in the Collective Age," *Wall Street Journal*, December 27, 1962, 10, Box 19, Frank S. Meyer Collection, Hoover Institution Library & Archives.

40   Senator Barry Goldwater, "The Meaning of Freedom," *Congressional Record-Senate*, January 21, 1963, 616, Box 19, Frank S. Meyer Collection, Hoover Institution Library & Archives.

41   Russell Kirk, "An Ideologue of Liberty," *Sewanee Review*, Spring 1964, 349, Box 19, Frank S. Meyer Collection, Hoover Institution Library & Archives.

42   Royalty Statement for *In Defense of Freedom*, November 12, 1962 to December 31, 1962, Henry Regnery Company, FSM Papers; Royalty Statement for *In Defense of Freedom*, November 12, 1962 to June 30, 1963, Henry Regnery Company, FSM Papers; Royalties Statement for *In Defense of Freedom*, 1962 through June 1970, Henry Regnery Company, FSM Papers.

43   Jeannette E. Hopkins to Frank S. Meyer, July 20, 1960, FSM Papers.

44   Henry Regnery to Mrs. Frank S. Meyer, March 29, 1973, FSM Papers; Henry Regnery to Mrs. Frank S. Meyer, October 4, 1973, FSM Papers.

45   Lois McDonald to Daniel J. Flynn, email, May 6, 2024, 4:25 p.m. Eastern. McDonald, the associate curator of Monte Cristo Cottage, confirmed the desk the Meyers donated to the New London museum came from O'Neill's dune shack on Cape Cod by way of his son.

46   Paul Gottfried, "Frank Meyer's Fusionism and the Search for

Consensus Among Conservatives," *Chronicles*, September 20, 2022, accessed November 24, 2023, https://chronicles-magazine.org/web/frank-meyers-fusionism-and-the-search-for-consensus-among-conservatives/.

47   Murray Rothbard, "Frank S. Meyer: The Fusionist as Libertarian Manqué," *Modern Age*, Fall 1981, 352–363.

48   Michael Warren Davis, "The Fatally-Flawed Fusionism of Frank Meyer," January 19, 2018, accessed November 24, 2023, https://theimaginativeconservative.org/2018/01/frank-s-meyer-fusionism-michael-davis.html.

49   John P. East, *The American Conservative Movement: The Philosophical Founders* (Chicago: Regnery Books, 1986), 102.

CHAPTER 28

1   Dedication page in Frank S. Meyer, *In Defense of Freedom*.

2   William Rickenbacker to William F. Buckley, memo, September 12, 1962, FSM Papers.

3   Frank Meyer to Willmoore Kendall, July 27, 1962, FSM Papers.

4   William Rickenbacker to William F. Buckley, memo, September 12, 1962, FSM Papers.

5   William F. Rickenbacker to Frank Meyer, July 3, 1962, FSM Papers.

6   William F. Rickenbacker to Frank Meyer, September 12, 1962, FSM Papers.

7   William F. Buckley, Jr. to Frank [Meyer], undated (circa early 1963), "Monday," FSM Papers.

8   Willmoore Kendall to Frank Meyer, undated (circa April 1961), FSM Papers.

9   Willmoore Kendall to Frank Meyer, undated (circa spring 1961), "Thursday," FSM Papers.

10   Frank Meyer to Willmoore Kendall, May 1, 1961, FSM Papers.

11   Willmoore Kendall to Frank Meyer, undated (circa April 1961), FSM Papers.

12 [Frank Meyer] to Brent [Bozell], June 9, 1961, FSM Papers.

13 Brent [Bozell] to Frank and Elsie [Meyer], undated (circa Spring 1961), "Monday night," FSM Papers.

14 Brent [Bozell] to Frank [Meyer], May 16, [1961], FSM Papers.

15 Brent [Bozell] to Frank [Meyer], May 16, [1961], FSM Papers.

16 Brent [Bozell] to Frank [Meyer], May 16, [1961], FSM Papers.

17 Owen, *Heaven Can Indeed Fall*, 152.

18 Willmoore Kendall to Frank Meyer, undated, "Sunday," FSM Papers. "Tel. 12/11/62."

19 Willmoore Kendall to Frank Meyer, undated, "Sunday," FSM Papers. "Tel. 12/11/62."

20 Willmoore Kendall to Frank Meyer, undated, "Sunday," FSM Papers. "Tel. 12/11/62."

21 Willmoore Kendall to Frank Meyer, undated, "Sunday," FSM Papers. "Tel. 12/11/62."

22 Willmoore Kendall to Frank Meyer, undated, "Sunday," FSM Papers. "Tel. 12/11/62."

23 Willmoore Kendall to Frank Meyer, undated, "Sunday," FSM Papers. "Tel. 12/11/62."

24 Willmoore Kendall to Frank Meyer, undated, "Sunday," FSM Papers. "Tel. 12/11/62."

25 Owen, *Heaven Can Indeed Fall*, 158.

26 Willmoore Kendall to Frank Meyer, undated, "Sunday," FSM Papers. "Tel. 12/11/62."

27 *National Review*'s contents remain available in either microfilm or bound form at most major libraries.

28 Owen, *Heaven Can Indeed Fall*, 176; Judis, *William F. Buckley*, 211.

29 Judis, *William F. Buckley*, 211–212.

30 William F. Buckley to Willmoore [Kendall], February 13, 1964, FSM Papers.

31 Willmoore Kendall to Frank Meyer, undated (circa November, 1963), FSM Papers. Letter written under University of Dallas letterhead.

32 Frank Meyer to Willmoore Kendall, November 10, 1963, FSM Papers.

33   Willmoore Kendall to Frank Meyer, undated (circa November 1963), "Wednesday," FSM Papers; Willmoore Kendall to Frank Meyer, undated, "Tuesday," FSM Papers. The "Wednesday" letter is under University of Dallas letterhead; the "Tuesday" letter is under Los Angeles State College letterhead, written in red ink that switches to the characteristic green in the second line of backside.

34   Willmoore Kendall to Frank Meyer, undated (circa November 1963), FSM Papers; Willmoore Kendall to Frank Meyer, undated (circa November, 1963), "Wednesday," FSM Papers. Both letters are written under University of Dallas letterhead.

35   Willmoore Kendall to Frank Meyer, undated (circa November 1963), FSM Papers. Written under University of Dallas letterhead.

36   Willmoore Kendall to Frank Meyer, undated (circa November 1963), "Wednesday," FSM Papers. Written under University of Dallas letterhead. Examples of the type of talks that Kendall criticized include Frank S. Meyer, "The Education of Communists," Vanderbilt University, June 30, 1964, Institute on Communism and Democracy Tapes, Heard Library, Vanderbilt University; Frank S. Meyer, "The Appeals of Communists," Vanderbilt University, June 30, 1964, Institute on Communism and Democracy Tapes, Heard Library, Vanderbilt University.

37   Willmoore Kendall to Frank Meyer, October 10, 1963, FSM Papers.

38   [Frank Meyer] to Willmoore [Kendall], April 12, 1965, FSM Papers; [Frank and Elsie Meyer] to Brent [Bozell], September 29, 1962, FSM Papers. In the September letter, Meyer references an advance on royalties.

39   Willmoore Kendall to Elsie [Meyer], undated (circa late 1963, early 1964), FSM Papers.

40   Willmoore Kendall to Elsie [Meyer], undated (circa late 1963, early 1964), FSM Papers.

41   Willmoore Kendall to Elsie [Meyer], undated (circa late 1963,

early 1964), FSM Papers.

42 Willmoore Kendall to Frank [Meyer], undated (circa November/December 1964), FSM Papers.

43 Owen, *Heaven Can Indeed Fall*, 177.

44 Kelly, *Living on Fire*, 90.

45 Kelly, *Living on Fire*, 82–85, 93–101, 142; L. Brent Bozell to Bobbs Merrill Company, Inc., March 16, 1970, FSM Papers.

46 Nellie [Kendall] to Elsie [Meyer], January 11, 1968, FSM Papers.

47 Frank S. Meyer to Yvona Kendall Mason, October 18, 1967, FSM Papers.

48 William S. Schlamm to Elsie [Meyer], July 18, 1967, FSM Papers.

49 Kelly, *Living on Fire*, 213–217.

50 William S. Schlamm to Elsie [Meyer], July 18, 1967, FSM Papers.

51 Author interview of Neal Freeman, May 19, 2020.

CHAPTER 29

1 FSM to WFB Jr., memo, "Re: Proposals for Agenda of Editorial Conference, 1-28-63," January 25, 1963, FSM Papers.

2 [Frank S. Meyer] to Bill [Buckley], February 27, 1963, FSM Papers.

3 [William F. Buckley Jr.] to Frank [Meyer], undated (circa February 1963), FSM Papers. Begins, "Thanks so much for your letter . . ."

4 [Frank S. Meyer] to Bill [Buckley], February 27, 1963, FSM Papers.

5 "Random Notes from All Over: Goldwater Aides Counter Right," *New York Times*, September 16, 1963, 30.

6 Goldwater and Jack Casserly, *Goldwater*, 147–148.

7 Frank S. Meyer to Dwight Macdonald, William F. Buckley, Jr., James Burnham, and John Gregory Dunne, memo, December 10, 1963, FSM Papers.

8 Owen, *Heaven Can Indeed Fall*, 175.

9   Jeff [Hart] to Frank [Meyer], November 29, 1963, FSM Papers.

10   Special Agent in Charge New York City to FBI Director, memo, "Irving Potash," December 23, 1963, accessed September 13, 2023, https://www.archives.gov/files/research/jfk/releases/docid-32175685.pdf; SAC Chicago to FBI Director, memo, "Communist Party, USA (CPUSA), Domestic Administration Issues, IS-C," accessed September 25, 2023, https://www.archives.gov/files/research/jfk/releases/docid-32164535.pdf; SAC New York to Director, SAC Baltimore, Dallas, and New Orleans, memo, "Communist Party, USA IS-C, Assassination of President John F. Kennedy," November 26, 1963, accessed September 25, 2023, https://www.archives.gov/files/research/jfk/releases/docid-32166389.pdf; Mr. W. C. Sullivan to Mr. F. J. Baumgardner, memo, "Communist Party, USA Internal Security-C, Assassination of President Kennedy," November 25, 1963, accessed September 25, 2023, https://www.archives.gov/files/research/jfk/releases/docid-32161721.pdf.

11   FSM to Jeffrey Hart, December 4, 1963, FSM Papers.

12   Goldwater and Casserly, *Goldwater*, 149–150; Theodore H. White, *The Making of the President, 1964* (New York: Atheneum Publishers, 1965), 94–96.

13   Kelly, *James Burnham and the Struggle for the World*, 194.

14   Quoted in Frisk, *If Not Us, Who?*, 177.

15   Author interview of Arlene Croce, July 28, 2021.

16   Author interview of Neal Freeman, May 19, 2020.

17   JB to WFB, WAR, WFR, FM, PB, memo, "Re: N.H. Primary," February 23, 1964, FSM Papers.

18   Bill Buckley to the Editors, C.C. WAR and PLB, memo, March 5, 1964, FSM Papers.

19   FSM to JB, WFR, WAR, PLB, WFB, memo, undated (circa late winter 1964), FSM Papers.

20   WFR to WFB, JB, FSM, WAR, PLB, memo, March 2, 1964, FSM Papers.

21   "NR and Goldwater," *National Review*, January 14, 1964, 9.

22   FSM to WFB Jr., JB, WFR, WAR, PLB, memo, "Re: WAR's

Memorandum of June 30," July 6, 1964, FSM Papers; Bill
Rusher to the Editors, memo, June 30, 1964, FSM Papers.

23 Frank S. Meyer to J. Gordon Hall, September 10, 1963, FSM
Papers; Frank S. Meyer to J. Gordon Hall, November 19,
1963, FSM Papers.

24 "Conservative Sees GOP Death," *Syracuse Post-Standard*, April
4, 1963, 6; "Barry G. to Win Over JFK," *Siskiyou News*, April
4, 1963, Box 18, Folder 1, Frank S. Meyer Collection, Hoover
Institution Library & Archives.

25 M. Catherine Babcock, Inc., Frank S. Meyer, Neil House
Hotel Grand Ballroom, Columbus, Ohio, November 2, 1963,
FSM Papers; M. Catherine Babcock, Inc., Frank S, Meyer,
Hampshire House, Lima Ohio, February 18, 1964, FSM Pa-
pers; M. Catherine Babcock, "Details of Engagement," Frank
S. Meyer, Alumnae Memorial Building, Emory University,
September 25, 1963, FSM Papers; "Meyer Sees Victory for
Goldwater in '64," *Daily Northwestern*, April 19, 1963, 1. Box
18, Folder 1, Frank S. Meyer Collection, Hoover Institution
Library & Archives; "YAF Banquet Speaker Lauds Sen. Gold-
water," October 14, 1963, Box 18, Folder 1, Frank S. Meyer
Collection, Hoover Institution Library & Archives.

26 [Frank Meyer] to Jay [Gordon Hall], December 28, 1963, FSM
Papers.

27 William Loeb to Frank Meyer, March 5, 1964, FSM Papers;
William Loeb to Frank Meyer, March 13, 1964, FSM Papers.

28 Frank S. Meyer to [Jay Gordon Hall], February 3, 1964, FSM
Papers; [Frank S. Meyer] to J. [Gordon Hall], March 8, 1964,
FSM Papers; J. [Gordon Hall] to Frank [Meyer], March 16,
1964, FSM Papers.

29 Judis, *William F. Buckley* (New York: Simon and Schuster,
1988), 229.

30 Barry Goldwater to Frank S. Meyer, May 21, 1964, FSM
Papers.

31 Nelson Rockefeller, Speech Before the Republican National Convention, San Francisco, California, July 14,
1964, accessed May 30, 2023, https://www.c-span.org/

video/?c4583565/user-clip-rockefeller-64-convention.

32   Perlstein, *Before the Storm*, 391–392.

33   Perlstein, *Before the Storm*, 390–392.

34   Buckley, *Living It Up at* National Review, 127–131; Judis, *William F. Buckley*, 148, 229.

35   Daisy Ad, accessed September 25, 2023, https://www.youtube.com/watch?v=riDypP1KfOU; White, *The Making of the President, 1964*, 322.

36   Nash, *The Conservative Intellectual Movement*, 274.

37   "Dr. King Foresees Social Disruption If Goldwater Wins," *New York Times*, September 13, 1964, 66.

38   Warren Boroson, "What Psychiatrists Say About Goldwater," *Fact*, September–October, 1964, 24–64.

39   Stephen [Tonsor] to Frank [Meyer], December 12, 1963, FSM Papers.

40   Frank S. Meyer, "A New Political Map of America," *National Review*, August 11, 1964, 687; Frank S. Meyer, "Where Is Eisenhower Going?," *The American Mercury*, 126.

41   Frank Meyer, "Freedom, Tradition, Conservatism," in *What Is Conservatism?*, ed. Frank Meyer (New York: Holt, Rinehart, and Winston, 1964), 10.

42   Frank Meyer, "A New Political Map of America," *National Review*, 687.

CHAPTER 30

1   Frank S. Meyer to Sir Shane Leslie, December 10, 1964, FSM Papers.

2   Frank S. Meyer to Sir Shane Leslie, January 2, 1963, FSM Papers; F[rank] S. M[eyer] to Erik von Kuehnelt-Leddihn, April 13, 1965, FSM Papers.

3   William A. Rusher, N. R. Newsletter (Confidential), December 1964, 1, FSM Papers.

4   Frank S. Meyer, "What's Next for Conservatism?," *National Review*, December 1, 1964, 1057.

5   Frank S. Meyer, "Conservative Strategy Now," *National*

Review, December 29, 1964, 1145.

6   Author interview of Lee Edwards, September 15, 2020.

7   FSM to WFB, JB, WAR, ML, PB, WFR, LBB, memo, "Confidential," January 17, 1962, FSM Papers.

8   Henry Regnery to Frank C. Hanighen, December 8, 1953, Box 27, Folder 16, Henry Regnery Papers, Hoover Institution Library & Archives.

9   "Organization of Americans for Conservative Action," memo, Marvin Liebman and Associates, circa late 1960–early 1961, FSM Papers.

10   William Loeb to Frank S. Meyer, December 4, 1964, FSM Papers; Frank S. Meyer to William Loeb, December 24, 1964, FSM Papers.

11   Author interview of Lee Edwards, September 15, 2020.

12   Author interview of Bob Bauman, April 23, 2020.

13   Board of Directors of the American Conservative Union, minutes, December 18-19, 1964, Box 134, William A. Rusher Papers, Library of Congress, William A. Rusher Papers, Box 134.

14   "Minutes of the Meeting of the Board of Directors of the American Conservative Union," December 19, 1964, Box 134, William A. Rusher Papers, Library of Congress.

15   William F. Buckley, Jr., "The Conscience of George Lincoln Rockwell," *National Review*, September 19, 1967, 1011.

16   Steve Allen to Barry Goldwater, William F. Buckley, Russell Kirk, Frank Meyer, William Rusher, Edwin McDowell, Morrie Ryskind, Priscilla Buckley, memo, December 1, 1964, FSM Papers.

17   Frank Meyer, "The Birch Malady," *National Review*, October 19, 1965, 919–920.

18   Stuart Samuels to Frank Meyer, August 18, 1969, Box 63, Folder 25, William F. Buckley Jr. Papers, Sterling Memorial Library, Yale University; Pyke Johnson Jr. to Frank Meyer, August 22, 1969, Box 63, Folder 25, William F. Buckley Jr. Papers, Sterling Memorial Library, Yale University.

19   Frank S. Meyer to Steve Allen, August 25, 1965, FSM Papers.

20 Frank S. Meyer to Sir Shane Leslie, May 26, 1965, FSM Papers.

21 Minutes of the Meeting of the Board of Directors of the American Conservative Union, March 20, 1965, Box 134, William A. Rusher Papers, Library of Congress.

22 Stefan T. Possony, David N. Rowe, Frank S. Meyer, *Vietnam: ACU Task Force Study* (Washington, DC: American Conservative Union, 1965), 11, 14.

23 John Dos Passos to Frank [Meyer], June 14, 1965, FSM Papers.

24 Sylvester Petro, *Taft-Hartley Act Section 14 (b): The Choice: Responsible or Corrupt Unionism* (Washington, DC: American Conservative Union, 1968), Box 136, William A. Rusher Papers, Library of Congress; John A. Howard, *Financing American Education: To Safeguard Its Integrity, to Maintain Its Independence* (Washington, DC: American Conservative Union, 1965), Box 136, William A. Rusher Papers, Library of Congress; Martin Anderson, *Urban Renewal: The Claims, The Facts* (Washington, DC: American Conservative Union, 1965), Box 136, William A. Rusher Papers, Library of Congress.

25 "Organization Meeting in Philadelphia," April 25, 1964, accessed September 3, 2023, https://phillysoc.org/tps_meetings/organizing-meeting-in-philadelphia/; "The Philadelphia Society—Western Meeting," San Francisco, California April 25, 1964, accessed October 6, 2024, https://phillysoc.org/wp-content/uploads/2024/03/1964-April-25-Western-Meeting.pdf; Stephen [Tonsor] to Frank [Meyer], April 19, 1964, FSM Papers.

26 Stephen [Tonsor] to Frank [Meyer], April 19, 1964, FSM Papers.

27 Author interview of Ed Feulner, May 8, 2020; Linda Bridges, "Philadelphia Society at 50," July 2, 2014, accessed September 25, 2023, https://www.nationalreview.com/2014/07/philadelphia-society-50-linda-bridges/.

28 Author interview of Ed Feulner, May 8, 2020.

29 Henry Hazlitt to Frank S. Meyer, October 19, 1961, FSM

Papers.

30 Author interview of William Campbell, May 11, 2020.

31 "Past Meetings of the Philadelphia Society," accessed September 3, 2023, https://phillysoc.org/meetings/past-meetings/.

32 Author interview of Ken Grubbs, July 21, 2023.

33 Author interview of Don Devine, January 29, 2020.

34 Author interview of David Keene, April 14, 2020; Author interview of Ed Feulner, May 8, 2020.

35 Author interview of Morton Blackwell, May 16, 2022.

36 Author interview of Howard Segermark, May 23, 2022; Author interview of Morton Blackwell, May 16, 2022; Author interview, Ken Grubbs, July 21, 2023.

37 Author interview of Howard Segermark, May 23, 2022.

38 Harry Jaffa, "Reconstruction, Old and New," *National Review*, April 20, 1965, 330–331.

39 F. S. Meyer, "Books in Brief," *National Review*, June 15, 1965, 520.

40 Lawrence Sork Jr., "Letters to the Editor: Meyer on Lincoln," *National Review*, July 27, 1965, 621, 661.

41 William F. Buckley, "Letters to the Editor: Meyer on Lincoln," *National Review*, July 27, 1965, 661.

42 Harry [Jaffa] to Frank [Meyer], August 17, 1965, FSM Papers.

43 Frank Meyer to Harry Jaffa, August 24, 1965, FSM Papers.

44 "In This Issue," *National Review*, August 24, 1965, 705.

45 Frank S. Meyer, "Lincoln Without Rhetoric," *National Review*, August 24, 1965, 725.

46 Harry V. Jaffa, "Lincoln and the Cause of Freedom," *National Review*, September 21, 1965, 827.

47 Meyer, "Again on Lincoln," *National Review*, 71.

48 Harry [Jaffa] to Frank [Meyer], October 3, 1965, FSM Papers.

49 Public Affairs Conference on Liberalism and Conservatism, photograph, April 29–May 2, 1965, FSM Papers.

50 Leo Strauss to Frank S. Meyer, March 11, 1965 FSM Papers; Leo Strauss to Frank S. Meyer, October 18, 1957, FSM Papers.

51 Frank S. Meyer, "Conservatism," in *Left, Right, and Center: Essays on Liberalism and Conservatism in the United States*,

ed., Robert A. Goldwin (Chicago: Rand McNally, 1966). For a condensed version, see Frank S. Meyer, "Conservatism and Republican Candidates," *National Review*, December 12, 1967, 1385.

CHAPTER 31

1   Author interview of Jameson Campaigne Jr., August 9, 2021.

2   Stephen [Tonsor] to Frank [Meyer], February 8, 1963, FSM Papers.

3   Wills, *Confessions of a Conservative*, 38–39.

4   Frank Meyer to Bill [Buckley], October 1, 1957, FSM Papers; Wills, *Confessions of a Conservative*, 38–39.

5   G. Wills, "Books in Brief," *National Review*, March 21, 1967, 317.

6   Garry Wills, "Madness in Their Method," *National Review*, February 13, 1962, 98.

7   Garry Wills, "Heap Big Waters," *National Review*, April 23, 1968, 407.

8   Buckley, *Living It Up at* National Review, 187–188.

9   Author interview of Noel Parmentel, February 12, 2023.

10 Joan Didion, "Finally (Fashionably) Serious," *National Review*, November 18, 1961, 341.

11 Joan Didion, "Seventeen Interns, One Golk," *National Review*, May 7, 1960, 305–306.

12 Joan Didion, "Smellie on Seventh Avenue," *National Review*, January 30, 1960, 83–84; Joan Didion, "Two Up for America," *National Review*, April 9, 1960, 241; Joan Didion, "Marriage a la Mode," *National Review*, August 11, 1960, 90–91.

13 Joan Didion, "Inadequate Mirrors," *National Review*, July 2, 1960, 430–431.

14 Author interview of Noel Parmentel, February 12, 2023.

15 Author interview of Noel Parmentel, February 12, 2023.

16 Frank Meyer to Hugh Kenner, March 20, 1962, FSM Papers.

17 Noel Parmentel, "The Acne and the Ecstasy," *Esquire*, August 1962, 44–46, 112–114; Noel E. Parmentel Jr., "Gnostics at the

Garden," *Commonweal*, March 30, 1962, 13–15; Noel Parmentel, "Walpurgis Night at Carnegie Hall," *The Nation*, October 3, 1959, 188–189.

18   William F. Buckley to the Editors, memo, "Confidential: Memo to the Editors . . . Re 1962 Editors Meeting," August 21, 1962, FSM Papers.

19   Author interview of Noel Parmentel, July 25, 2023; Author interview of Noel Parmentel, September 2, 2023; Noel X and His Unbleached Muslims, *Folk Songs for Conservatives*, Toad Recordings, LP Record. Though a ninety-seven-year-old Parmentel could still sing verses of "Frank S. Meyer, Please," the song evidently did not make the 1964 album's final cut.

20   John Gregory Dunne to *National Review* Editor, November 15, 1963, FSM Papers; Greg [Dunne] to Frank [Meyer], undated (circa November 1963), FSM Papers.

21   Greg [Dunne] to Frank [Meyer], November 11, 1963, FSM Papers.

22   Gregory Dunne to Bill [Buckley], November 11, 1963, FSM Papers; Dan Wakefield, *New York in the 50s* (New York: Houghton Mifflin, 1993), 332.

23   John Gregory Dunne to Frank [Meyer], March 16, 1964, FSM Papers.

24   Greg [Dunne] to Frank [Meyer], February 22, 1964, FSM Papers.

25   FSM to John Gregory Dunne, February 25, 1964, FSM Papers.

26   John Gregory Dunne to Frank [Meyer], March 16, 1964, FSM Papers.

27   Parmentel, "The Acne and the Ecstasy," *Esquire*, 114.

28   Author interview of Noel Parmentel, September 9, 2023.

29   FSM to William F. Buckley, Jr., February 27, 1964, FSM Papers.

30   John Gregory Dunne, "Fictitious Novel," *National Review*, March 8, 1966, 226–228.

31   Parmentel, "The Acne and the Ecstasy," *Esquire*, 114.

32   Joan, John, and Quintana Dunne to [the Meyers], cards,

undated (circa December of 1966, 1967, 1968, and likely 1972), FSM Papers.

33 Theodore Sturgeon to Frank Meyer, undated (circa early June 1963), FSM Papers. Note explains, "Tel. 6/8/63."

34 Marcia [Burnham] to Frank [Meyer], February 6, 1962, FSM Papers.

35 Theodore Sturgeon, "The Scientist Fictionist," *National Review*, November 20, 1962, 403.

36 Theodore Sturgeon, "Titanic Tome from the Tik-Tok Man," *National Review*, May 7, 1968, 457–458.

37 Theodore Sturgeon, "Beginning with the 19th Century," *National Review*, April 5, 1966, 322.

38 Sturgeon, "The Scientist Fictionist," *National Review*, 403.

39 [Theodore Sturgeon] to Robert Heinlein, March 21, 1962, Robert A. and Virginia Heinlein Archives, Correspondence, 1961–1962.

40 [Theodore Sturgeon] to Poul Anderson, November 3, 1966, FSM Papers.

41 T. H. Sturgeon to Frank Meyer, August 8, 1966, FSM Papers.

42 Theodore Sturgeon to Wm. F. Buckley, November 1, [1966], FSM Papers.

43 Wm. F. Buckley, Jr. to Theodore Sturgeon, November 17, 1966, FSM Papers.

44 T. H. Sturgeon to Frank [Meyer], November 3, [1966], FSM Papers.

45 Author interview of John Meyer, July 11, 2023.

46 Author interview of Eugene Meyer, February 3, 2020.

47 Greg [Dunne] to Frank [Meyer], February 22, 1964, FSM Papers.

CHAPTER 32

1 FSM to All Concerned, memo, "Memorandum NR Editorial Conference," May 23, 1966, FSM Papers.

2 Author interview of Tad Crawford, October 2, 2023.

3 Frank Meyer, "The LSD Syndrome," *National Review*, March

21, 1967, 301.

4   Author interview of Ken Grubbs, July 21, 2023.

5   Author interview of David Zincavage, October 6, 2021; Author interview of Paul Gottfried, July 21, 2023; Party of the Right to Frank S. Meyer, invitation, undated (for January 30, [1968] event), FSM Papers. Gottfried attended the event, remembered Zincavage's exchanges regarding marijuana, and labeled the entire discussion as "very animated."

6   Frank S. Meyer, "The Council for a Volunteer Military," *National Review*, July 11, 1967, 749; James Burnham, "The Antidraft Movement," *National Review*, June 13, 1967, 629.

7   Frank S. Meyer, *In Defense of Freedom*, 166.

8   James D. Griffin to Frank S. Meyer, September 13, 1967, FSM Papers.

9   [Frank S. Meyer] to J. Daniel Mahoney, December 15, 1969, FSM Papers.

10   Frank S. Meyer, "The Constitutional Crisis," *National Review*, October 26, 1957, 378.

11   Frank S. Meyer, "The Negro Revolution," *National Review*, June 18, 1963, 496.

12   Frank S. Meyer, "The Violence of Nonviolence," *National Review*, April 20, 1965, 327.

13   Meyer, "The Violence of Nonviolence," *National Review*, 327; Frank S. Meyer, "Showdown with Insurrection," *National Review*, January 16, 1968, 36; Frank S. Meyer, *National Review*, "Liberalism Run Riot," March 26, 1968, 283.

14   Frank S. Meyer, "The Negro Revolution—A New Phase," *National Review*, October 4, 1966, 998.

15   Meyer, "The Negro Revolution," *National Review*, 496.

16   American-African Affairs Association, report, "1969 Program: Report, September 1965-December 1968," 1–13, Box 127, Folder 4, William A. Rusher Papers, Library of Congress.

17   Frank S. Meyer, *The African Nettle: Dilemmas of an Emerging Continent* (New York: John Day, 1965), 11–16.

18   Author interview of Carol Dawson, April 30, 2020.

19   Author interview of Bob Bauman, April 23, 2020.

20   Author interview of Serphin Maltese, May 14, 2021.

21   Author interview of Herb Stupp, November 3, 2021.

22   1040 U.S. Individual Tax Return: Frank S. and Elsie B. Meyer, 1965, January 31, 1966, FSM Papers. See attachment: Schedule C; Wage and Tax Statement Copy C: Frank S. Meyer, 1965, *National Review*, FSM Papers.

23   1040 U.S. Individual Tax Return: F. S. and E. B. M., 1966, FSM Papers. See attachment: Frank S. Meyer, Wage and Tax Statement, 1966, *National Review*, Copy C, undated.

24   Author interview of Ron Robinson, April 15, 2021.

25   Bill Rusher to the Editors, memo, December 8, 1966, FSM Papers.

CHAPTER 33

1   [Frank Meyer] to Willi [Schlamm], March 14, 1968, FSM Papers.

2   Frank S. Meyer, "Ten Days in April," *National Review*, May 7, 1968, 453.

3   Frank S. Meyer, "The Right of the People to Bear Arms," *National Review*, July 2, 1968, 647; Meyer, "The Council for a Volunteer Military," *National Review*, 749.

4   Author interview of Mark Rhoads, May 4, 2024.

5   Luke A. Nichter, *The Year That Broke Politics: Collusion and Chaos in the Presidential Election of 1968* (New Haven, CT: Yale University Press, 2023), 64.

6   Frank S. Meyer, "A Conservative Convention," *National Review*, August 27, 1968, 859.

7   Meyer, "Liberalism Run Riot," *National Review*, 283.

8   William F. Buckley, "Ronald Reagan: A Relaxing View," *National Review*, November 28, 1967, 1319–1325.

9   Hugh Kenner to Guy Davenport, January 16, 1968, in Burns, ed., *Questioning Minds*, 1017

10 Hugh Kenner to Guy Davenport, February 14, 1968, in Burns, ed., *Questioning Minds*, 1027.

11 WFB to Those Concerned, memo, "Notes on Editorial Conference January 29, 1968," undated (circa winter 1968), FSM Papers.

12 Bill Rusher to Frank Meyer, February 28, 1968, FSM Papers. Enclosures.

13 Guy Davenport to Hugh Kenner, February 24, 1965, in Burns, ed., *Questioning Minds*, 700–701.

14 Hugh Kenner, "A Nervous View of Ronald Reagan," *National Review*, May 7, 1968, 444–446; Jeffrey Hart, "Wading in the Serbonian Bog," *National Review*, May 7, 1968, 446–447.

15 Guy Davenport to Hugh Kenner, May 11, 1968, in Burns, ed., *Questioning Minds*, 1069.

16 Hugh Kenner to Guy Davenport, May 15, 1968, in Burns, ed., *Questioning Minds*, 1072.

17 Hugh [Kenner] to Frank [Meyer], July 8, 1965, FSM Papers; Hugh [Kenner] to Bill [Buckley], December 18, 1964, Box 31, Hugh Kenner Folder, William F. Buckley Jr. Papers, Sterling Memorial Library, Yale University; Wm. F. Buckley, Jr. to Hugh Kenner, December 22, 1964, Box 31, Hugh Kenner Folder, William F. Buckley Jr. Papers, Sterling Memorial Library, Yale University; William F. Buckley, Jr., "Hugh Kenner, RIP," April 4, 2008, accessed August 29, 2023, https://www.nationalreview.com/2008/04/hugh-kenner-rip-william-f-buckley-jr/.

18 Guy Davenport to Hugh Kenner, May 11, 1968, in Burns, ed., *Questioning Minds*, 1069.

19 Guy Davenport to Hugh Kenner, May 11, 1968, in Burns, ed., *Questioning Minds*, 1069.

20 "National Review," *National Review*, May 21, 1968, 474; "National Review," *National Review*, June 4, 1968, 528.

21 Frank S. Meyer, "Why I Am for Reagan," *The New Republic*, May 11, 1968, 17–18.

22 Ronald Reagan, "A Time for Choosing," October 27, 1964, accessed July 18, 2023, https://www.youtube.com/watch?v=qXBswFfh6AY.

23 Frank S. Meyer, "The Importance of Reagan," *National*

Review, December 27, 1966, 1315.

24   FSM to WFB, JR., JB, WFR, AC, WAR, PLB, memo, May 25, 1968, FSM Papers.

25   Nichter, *The Year That Broke Politics*, 21; FSM to Bill [Buckley], March 9, 1968, FSM Papers.

26   FSM to Bill [Buckley], March 9, 1968, FSM Papers.

27   [Frank S. Meyer] to Bill [Buckley], March 21, 1968, FSM Papers.

28   "Nixon for Prez," *National Review*, November 5, 1968, 1097, 1098.

29   Author interview of Noel Parmentel, July 25, 2023.

30   Joan Didion, "Pretty Nancy," *Saturday Evening Post*, June 1, 1968, 20.

31   The last issue that Joan Didion appeared on the masthead was "Contributors," *National Review*, July 13, 1971, 732. See also WFB to All Concerned, memo "Editors' Conference—June 14, 1971," undated (circa late spring of 1971), FSM Papers.

32   Garry Wills, "The Second Civil War," *Esquire*, March 1968, 71–81, 136–151.

33   Garry Wills, "Convention in the Streets," *National Review*, September 24, 1968, 952–959.

34   Frank S. Meyer, "Richard Daley and the Will to Govern," *National Review*, October 8, 1968, 1015.

35   David Brudnoy, "Letters: Frank S. Meyer, RIP," *National Review*, May 12, 1972.

36   [Frank Meyer] to Willi [Schlamm], March 14, 1968, FSM Papers.

37   Frank S. Meyer, "The Mandate of 1968," *National Review*, November 19, 1968, 1170.

CHAPTER 34

1   Henry A. Kissinger to Frank S. Meyer, July 30, 1962, FSM Papers.

2   Frank S. Meyer to Henry A. Kissinger, December 15, 1968, FSM Papers.

3   [Frank S. Meyer] to Bill [Buckley], March 10, 1963, FSM Papers.

4   [Frank S. Meyer] to David [Futch], August 13, 1970, FSM Papers.

5   Frank S. Meyer, "Attack on Middle America," *National Review*, October 20, 1970, 1112.

6   [William F. Buckley, Jr.] to Garry [Wills], Box 279, Garry Wills Folder, William F. Buckley Jr. Papers, Sterling Memorial Library, Yale University.

7   Bill [Buckley] to Garry [Wills], undated ("6/8/70" written on letter), Box 279, Garry Wills Folder, William F. Buckley Jr. Papers, Sterling Memorial Library, Yale University.

8   Frank S. Meyer, "The Course of Garry Wills," *National Review*, July 28, 1970, 791.

9   Wills, *Confessions of a Conservative*, 44.

10   Author interview of Jameson Campaigne Jr., November 5, 2023.

11   Frank S. Meyer, "The Future of the Republican Party," *National Review*, December 1, 1970, 1273.

12   Meyer, "Attack on Middle America," *National Review*, 1113.

13   David Brudnoy to Frank Meyer, October 14, 1969, FSM Papers.

14   Author interview of Eugene Meyer, July 10, 2023.

15   Phil [Ardery] to Frank [Meyer], January 19, 1970, FSM Papers.

16   Elsie Meyer to William F. Buckley, April 3, 1970, Box 202, Folder 1556, William F. Buckley Jr. Papers.

17   Author interview of John Meyer, March 10, 2021.

18   Barney Hoskyns, *Small Town Talk: Bob Dylan, The Band, Van Morrison, Janis Joplin, Jimi Hendrix & Friends in the Wild*

Years of Woodstock (Boston: Da Capo, 2016), 2, 8–9, 29, 97, 170–176, 182–183.

19   Author interview of Eugene Meyer, July 10, 2023.

20   Howard Sounes, *Down the Highway: The Life of Bob Dylan* (New York: Grove Press, 2001, 2021), 246; Hoskyns, *Small Town Talk*, 116–117.

21   Bob Dylan, *Chronicles: Volume One* (New York: Simon and Schuster, 2005), 116–117; Author interview of Eugene Meyer, February 3, 2020.

22   Author interview of John Meyer, March 10, 2021.

23   Dylan, *Chronicles*, 116–117.

24   Author interview of John Meyer, March 10, 2021.

25   Antoni E. Gollan, "The Evolution of Bob Dylan," *National Review*, June 28, 1966, 638–639; Peter J. McCann, "Bob Dylan: A Pre-Obituary," *National Review*, February 9, 1971, 156.

26   Meyer, *The Moulding of Communists*, 96.

27   Author interview of David Franke, April 8, 2020.

28   Author interview of Ed Feulner, May 8, 2020.

29   Author interview of David Franke, April 8, 2020.

30   Author interview of Jerry Smith, November 29, 2023.

31   Author interview of Danny Boggs, November 29, 2023; Author interview of William Dennis, March 31, 2023.

32   C. H. Simonds, "At Home," *National Review*, April 28, 1972, 469.

33   Author interview of Ross Mackenzie, November 8, 2023.

34   David [Brudnoy] to Mr. and Mrs. Meyer, June 22, 1970, FSM Papers.

35   Author interview of William Kristol, November 2, 2023.

36   Author interview of R. Emmett Tyrrell, December 31, 2019.

37   Author interview of David Keene, April 14, 2020.

38   Author interview of Jameson Campaigne Jr., May 7, 2020.

39   Jerome Tuccille, *It Usually Begins with Ayn Rand* (New York: Stein and Day, 1971, 1973), 54.

40   Author interview of Arnold Steinberg, December 11, 2023.

41   Thorburn, *A Generation Awakes*, 255.

42   Author interview of Arnold Steinberg, December 11, 2023;

Tuccille, *It Usually Begins with Ayn Rand*, 84–91; Thorburn, *A Generation Awakes*, 255–256.

43   Thorburn, *A Generation Awakes*, 269–270.

44   Thorburn, *A Generation Awakes*, 249–279.

45   "In This Issue," *National Review*, December 16, 1969, 1247.

46   Donald Atwell Zoll, "Shall We Let America Die?," *National Review*, December 16, 1969, 1263.

47   Frank S. Meyer, "What Kind of Order?," *National Review*, December 29, 1969, 1327.

48   Donald Atwell Zoll, "Order and Repression," *National Review*, March 10, 1970, 259–260.

49   John Attarian, "Zoll, Donald Atwell (1927–)," in *American Conservatism: An Encyclopedia*, ed. Bruce Frohnen, Jeffrey Nelson, and Jeremy Beer (Wilmington, DE: Intercollegiate Studies Institute, 2006), 938.

50   Frank S. Meyer, "In Re Professor Zoll: I—Order and Freedom," *National Review*, March 24, 1970, 311; Frank S. Meyer, "In Re Professor Zoll: II—Defense of the Republic," *National Review*, April 7, 1970, 362, 373.

CHAPTER 35

1   Author interview of James Buckley, May 1, 2021.

2   "Agnew Won't Apologize for Jorgensen Remark," *New York Times*, October 13, 1970, 38.

3   Mahoney, *Actions Speak Louder*, 18.

4   Author interview of James Buckley, May 1, 2021.

5   Frank Meyer to Jim Buckley, Clif White, Dan Mahoney, and Dave Jones, memo, July 17, 1970, FSM Papers.

6   Author interview of James Buckley, May 1, 2021.

7   Frank S. Meyer to Tibor Szamuely, November 24, 1970, FSM Papers.

8   Frank Meyer, "New York Conservatives and the Two-Party System," *National Review*, 486.

9   Author interview of Phil Ardery, November 1, 2023.

10   Phil [Ardery] to Elsie and Frank, undated [June 30, 1969],

"Monday," FSM Papers.

11 Author interview of Phil Ardery, November 1, 2023.

12 Bill Rusher to Frank Meyer, memo, May 26, 1966, FSM Papers.

13 Author interview of Phil Ardery, November 1, 2023.

14 Frank S. Meyer, "Mr. Nixon's Course?," *National Review*, January 26, 1971, 86.

15 [Frank S. Meyer] to Dan [Mahoney], January 24, 1971, FSM Papers.

16 Frank S. Meyer to Serphin R. Maltese, July 15, 1971, FSM Papers.

17 "Minutes of the Meeting of the Board of Directors of the American Conservative Union," February 5, 1971, Box 134, William A. Rusher Papers, Library of Congress.

18 Smant, *Principles and Heresies*, 334.

19 "YAF Hears Nixon Berated," *Yale Daily News*, April 14, 1971, 1.

20 "Leading Conservatives Suspend Support of Nixon," *Human Events*, August 7, 1971, 1.

21 Judis, *William F. Buckley*, 330; Steven F. Hayward, *M. Stanton Evans: Conservative Wit, Apostle of Freedom* (New York: Encounter Books, 2022), 167–168.

22 Author interview of Randal Teague, June 1, 2020.

23 Author interview of Allan Ryskind, June 6, 2020.

24 "Leading Conservatives Suspend Support of Nixon," *Human Events*, 1.

25 Frank S. Meyer, Speech Before the Philadelphia Society, New York, October 9, 1971, accessed January 31, 2024, MP3, phillysoc.org/wp-content/uploads/2019/03/1971-10-Meyer-F.mp3.

CHAPTER 36

1 Author interview of Ron Docksai, December 16, 2020.

2 "Minutes of the Meeting of the Board of Directors of the American Conservative Union," December 5, 1971, Box 134, William A. Rusher Papers, Library of Congress.

3   Author interview of Randal Teague, June 1, 2020.

4   Author interview of John and Eugene Meyer, January 19, 2024.

5   Author interview of Jerry Smith, November 29, 2023; Smant, *Principles and Heresies*, 337.

6   Frank Meyer, "Isolationism?," *National Review*, December 3, 1971, 1356.

7   Meyer, "Isolationism?," *National Review*, 1356.

8   Linda Bridges and John R. Coyne Jr., *Strictly Right: William F. Buckley, Jr. and the American Conservative Movement* (Hoboken, NJ: John Wiley and Sons, 2007), 143.

9   William F. Buckley, Jr., "Frank S. Meyer," *National Review*, April 28, 1972, 466.

10   Ron Docksai to Frank S Meyer, telegram, March 8, 1972 (0658 EST), FSM Papers.

11   Ron Docksai to Young Americans for Freedom National Board, memo, "RE: Frank Meyer's Health," March 13, 1972, Private Papers of Jameson Campaigne Jr.

12   FSM to Ronald Docksai, March 11, 1972, FSM Papers.

13   Elsie [Meyer] to Jameson G. Campaigne, March 31, 1972, Private Papers of Jameson Campaigne Jr.

14   Buckley, "Frank S. Meyer," *National Review*, 466.

15   Author interview of John and Eugene Meyer, January 19, 2024.

16   Buckley, "Frank S. Meyer," *National Review*, 466–467.

17   Elsie Meyer to M. E. Bradford, March 29, 1972, FSM Papers.

18   Author interview of John and Eugene Meyer, January 19, 2024.

19   Author interview of David Keene, April 14, 2020.

20   Author interview of George Marlin, April 13, 2021.

21   Author interview of David Zincavage, October 6, 2021.

22   Buckley, "Frank S. Meyer," *National Review*, 466–467.

23   Author interview of Karen Myers, August 22, 2022.

24   Author interview of David Zincavage, October 6, 2021.

25   Buckley, "Frank S. Meyer," *National Review*, 466.

26   In 1965, through an intermediary, Meyer conveyed to

D'Arcy his influence upon him: "I attended a discussion he led on St. Thomas and learned enormously from him things which lay fallow for twenty-five years in my mind, but helped me immensely in the period of my transition." See Frank S. Meyer to Rev. Philip Conneally S. J. July 21, 1965, FSM Papers; Philip Conneally S. J. to Frank [Meyer], undated (circa mid-summer 1965), "Sunday," FSM Papers.

27   Author interview of John Meyer, February 4, 2020.

28   Buckley, "Frank S. Meyer," *National Review*, 466–467.

29   Father Gene Clark to Elsie Meyer, May 8, 1972, Box 202, Folder 1556, William F. Buckley Jr. Papers, Sterling Memorial Library, Yale University.

30   Buckley, "Frank S. Meyer," *National Review*, 467.

31   Garry Wills, "The Teacher," *National Review*, April 28, 1972, 473; William Rusher to Garry Wills, December 28, 1971, Box 98, William A. Rusher Papers, Library of Congress.

CONCLUSION

1   Ralph and Birgitta Peterson to Mrs. Meyer, undated (circa April 1972), FSM Papers; George McCadden to Mrs. Meyer, card, undated (circa April 1972), FSM Papers.

2   Joanne Lockhart to "Dear Sir," undated (circa spring 1972), FSM Papers.

3   Jack Dunman to Frank [Meyer], April 24, 1949, FSM Papers; Jack Dunman to Mrs. Meyer, July 3, 1972, FSM Papers.

4   Jack Dunman to Mrs. Meyer, July 3, 1972, FSM Papers.

5   Joanne Lockhart to "Dear Sir," undated (circa spring 1972), FSM Papers.

6   "In This Issue," *National Review*, May 26, 1972, 554.

7   Author interview of George Will, November 18, 2021.

8   Author interview of George Will, November 18, 2021.

9   M. Stanton Evans to William F. Buckley, Jr., April 4, 1973, Box 135, Folder 738, William F. Buckley Jr. Papers, Sterling Memorial Library, Yale University; Stanton Evans to Bill [Buckley], April 18, 1973, Box 135, Folder 738, William F.

Buckley Jr. Papers, Sterling Memorial Library, Yale University; M. Stanton Evans to William F. Buckley, Jr., April 26, 1972, Box 135, Folder 738, William F. Buckley Jr. Papers, Sterling Memorial Library, Yale University; Wm. F. Buckley, Jr. to M. Stanton Evans, May 2, 1972, Box 135, Folder 738, William F. Buckley Jr. Papers, Sterling Memorial Library, Yale University.

10 M. Stanton Evans to William F. Buckley, Jr., April 4, 1973, Box 135, Folder 738, William F. Buckley Jr. Papers, Sterling Memorial Library, Yale University.

11 Theodore Sturgeon, "Peaks and Beacons," *National Review*, January 19, 1973, 103.

12 Guy [Davenport] to Bill [Buckley], April 9, 1973, FSM Papers.

13 Kirk, *The Sword of the Imagination*, 188. After undiagnosed cancer sidelined Meyer in the fall of 1971, William F. Buckley Jr. calved off "arts and manners" from the book section to create, at least within the magazine, two separate fiefdoms nominally still overseen by Meyer. See W. F. B. to All Concerned, memo, "Editors' Conference—November 30th, 1971," undated (circa fall 1971), FSM Papers.

14 Author interview of George Will, November 18, 2021.

15 Author interview of Eugene Meyer, February 3, 2020.

16 Author interview of George Will, November 18, 2021.

17 [Elsie Meyer] to Richard de Mille, March 13, 1973, FSM Papers; Edie Downs to Elsie Meyer, March 14, 1972, FSM Papers; Frank S. Meyer to Gilbert Comte, July 9, 1966, FSM Papers.

18 Author interview of John and Eugene O'Neill, January 19, 2024.

19 Author interview of David Zincavage, January 24, 2024; Author interview of Tad Crawford, October 2, 2023; Author interview of Tad Crawford, January 26, 2024.

20 Author interview of Tad Crawford, October 2, 2023; Author interview of Tad Crawford, January 26, 2024.

21 Author interview of John and Eugene Meyer, 2024.

22 Mrs. Frank S. Meyer to Harvey B. Plotnick, December 15,

1972, FSM Papers.

23 Extant copies in the FSM Papers include *The Exchange*, May 1973, 1-4; *The Exchange*, August, 1974, 1-4; *The Exchange*, November, 1974, 1-4. The message "Dedicated to the memory of Frank S. Meyer" under the title and its editor listed as "Mrs. Frank S. Meyer" conveyed the degree to which Elsie advertised her efforts as continuing those of her late husband.

24 Frank S. Meyer, introduction to *Breathes There a Man: Heroic Ballads & Poems of the English-Speaking Peoples*, ed., Frank S. Meyer (Lasalle, IL: Open Court, 1973).

25 Neil McCaffrey to Frank S. Meyer, December 16, 1969, FSM Papers; Neil McCaffrey to Aaron, Al Rosenberg, Marvin, Randy, and Ted, memo, April 29, 1965, FSM Papers.

26 Flora Rheta Schreiber to Elsie [Meyer], November 23, 1951, FSM Papers.

27 "History-Europe 800–1789 notes," undated, Box 8, Folder 1, Frank Meyer Collection, Hoover Institution Library & Archives; Frank S. Meyer, "Western Civilization: The Problem of Political Freedom," *Modern Age*, Spring 1968, 120–128.

28 Mrs. Frank S. Meyer to John P. East, July 23, 1973, FSM Papers.

29 Wm. F. Buckley, Jr. to M. Stanton Evans, May 2, 1972, Box 135, Folder 738, William F. Buckley Jr. Papers, Sterling Memorial Library, Yale University; Gerhart [Niemeyer] to Bill [Buckley], September 22, 1969, Box 11, Gerhart Niemeyer 1960 folder, William F. Buckly Jr. Papers, Sterling Memorial Library, Yale University.

30 William F. Buckley, Jr., "Elsie Meyer, R.I.P.," *National Review*, May 23, 1975, 547.

31 Author interview of David Zincavage, October 6, 2021.

32 Author interview of Tad Crawford, October 2, 2023; Author interview of Tad Crawford, January 26, 2024.

33 Author interview of David Zincavage, January 24, 2024.

34 Laura Cohen, "Soph Takes on 19 at Once in Special Chess Exhibition," *Yale Daily News*, October 26, 1972, 1.

35   Author interview of Eugene Meyer, July 10, 2023.

36   Author interview of Tad Crawford, October 2, 2023.

37   Frank S. Meyer, "Where Is Eisenhower Going?," *The American Mercury*, 125.

38   Roger Ebert, "Meyer, Lefever Clash on Coexistence," *Daily Illini*, March 20, 1962, 1, Box 18, Folder 2, Frank S. Meyer Collection, Hoover Institution Library & Archives.

39   Frank S. Meyer, "Where Is Eisenhower Going?," *The American Mercury*, 125.

40   FSM to WFB Jr., LBB, JB, JC, WAR, and FLB, memo, "NR position on Presidential candidates," May 10, 1960, FSM Papers.

41   American Conservative Union Meeting, draft minutes, undated (circa fall 1965), FSM Papers.

42   Ronald Reagan, Remarks at the Conservative Political Action Conference, Washington, DC, March 20, 1981, accessed May 7, 2024, https://www.reaganlibrary.gov/ archives/speech/remarks-conservative-political-action-conference-dinner.

Index

Jerome, V. J., 88, 179
John Birch Society (JBS), 269–77, 348; explosive growth of, 271; founding father of, 270; media attempts to set up, 347; metastasis of, 286; *NR* issue devoted to, 349; *NR*'s taking on of, 275–76
Johnson, Arnold, 182
Johnson, Hewlett, 71
Johnson, Lyndon, 331, 379
Jones, John, 409
Jouhy, Ernest, 61
Joyce, James, 52
Judd, Walter, 260
Judis, John, 261

Keene, David, 353, 398, 417
Kell, Vernon, 76
Kelley, Charles, 332
Kelly, Daniel, 327
Kempton, Murray, 202
Kendall, Willmoore, 5, 57, 269, 293, 352; demotion of, 323; departure of (from *National Review*), 321, 329; *In Defense of Freedom* dedicated to, 317
Kennedy, John F. (JFK), 266, 273, 331, 334, 427
Kennedy, Robert, 379, 403
Kenner, Hugh, 4, 290, 381, 382
Kerr, Philip, 56
Khrushchev, Nikita, 221, 252, 429
Kilpatrick, James J., 392

King, Martin Luther, Jr., 341, 374, 379
Kipling, Rudyard, 280
Kirk, Claude, 288
Kirk, Russell, 190, 195, 275, 430; Buckley contrasted with, 202; rebutting of Auerbach by, 296; reflection on Meyer by, 423
Kissinger, Henry, 286, 389
Kitchel, Denison, 332
Kittredge, George Lyman, 94
Klehr, Harvey, 137
Knight, Frank, 352
Knox, Ronald, 419
Kristol, Bill, 397
Kristol, Irving, 5, 353
Ku Klux Klan, 144

La Follette, Suzanne, 187, 195, 229, 329, 369
Lander, Ruth, 160, 167
Lane, Rose Wilder, 192, 197, 206, 217; Meyer's disagreements with, 307; review of *The Moulding of Communists* by, 254
Lansbury, George, 43, 71
Laski, Harold, 47, 49, 64
Last of Mrs. Cheyney, The, 37
Latimer, Ira H., 183
Lattimore, Richmond, 361
Law, The, 195
Lawson, John Howard, 124
Lenin, Vladimir, 204
Leonard, John, 228

vision for, 330; conspiratorial right vs., 269; crackup of, 317–30; Davenport's resignation from, 423; departures marking the end of, 329; direction of, 229–47; discord at, 209–28; disputations of, 301; endorsement of candidate by (1964), 336; golden era of, 5; Hiroo Onoda of, 329; inaugural issue of, 201; Jaffa's dispute appearing in, 355; "Principles and Heresies" columns in, 265, 295, 401, 407, 415, 425; rebuilding of, 345–57; running joke at, 293; Rusher as publisher of, 213; taking on of John Birch Society by, 275–76
National Rifle Association, 398, 428
National Student League (NSL), 70
Nazi–Soviet Pact, 120
Needles, Robert J., 197
Nehemkis, Peter, 30, 36
Nehru, Jawaharlal, 54
New Class, The, 219
Newman, John Henry, 360
New Masses, 119, 127
New Republic, 54, 136
Newton, Isaac, 88
New York Post, 154, 157
New York Times, 202, 204, 255, 283, 284, 332, 407, 416
New York World-Telegram, 127

Nichols, Louis, 250
Niemeyer, Gerhart, 262, 425
Nineteen Eighty-Four, 203
Nixon, Richard, 7, 380, 389–402, 413, 427; approach to U.S. Senate race by, 403; defeat of (1960), 347; Meyer's distrust of, 392; as presidential nominee, 263; State of the Union address of (1971), 407
Nixon Agonistes, 391, 392
Nock, Albert Jay, 186, 310
North, Joseph, 182
NR. See *National Review*
NSL. *See* National Student League

Oban, Willie, 159
October Club, 41, 42, 112, 421; disruption of Armistice Day remembrance perpetrated by, 60; hosting of Wells by, 56; Meyer as foundation member of, 175
October Revolution, 41
Officer Candidate School, 109
Oliver, Revilo, 57, 270, 275, 322
One Day in the Life of Ivan Denisovich, 255
O'Neill, Eugene, Jr., 154, 159–65, 188, 397; church's condemnation of, 418; estate of, 167–73; as member of Communist Party, 139; Ph.D. diploma of, 170; substitute,

Scan this code

for exclusive photographs of

Frank S. Meyer

and his family and associates

Or visit

www.encounterbooks.com/frankmeyer